Irish Family and Local History Handbook

Robert Blatchford and Elizabeth Blatchford

contents

take a closer look inside...

Search for your Irish roots online using a database of the largest
collection of parish records and other sources on the island of Ireland.
Or commission one of our county genealogy centres to research your
Irish family history.

www.rootsireland.ie

editorial

The Family and Local History Handbook is firmly established as a leading publication in the family history arena. We recently published The Family and Local History Handbook 13 adding to our previous twelve issues. The print run for each issue sells out very quickly. We are frequently asked for copies of these previous issues. It is uneconomic for us to reprint them so we published The Family and Local History Handbook Omnibus Volumes 1 - 10, our Data Disk, which is now also 'out of print.' We are preparing an updated data disk which will have all of the 'out of print' issues on it in pdf format. Our publication Herbert Chapman on Football is still available.

We have been constantly asked to produce more specialised versions of The Family and Local History Handbook. After visiting the Back to Our Past event in Dublin and Who Do You Think You Are? LIVE in London we had many requests to produce a volume dedicated to Ireland.

The population of Ireland is nearly six and a half million people. Historical events in Ireland provided a legacy to the world with nearly 70 million people having Irish ancestry. Of these as many as 35 million Americans and one in five British people are of Irish descent.

The Irish Family and Local History Handbook has been created to help people research their Irish ancestry. Adopting the style and formula established over several years The Irish Family and Local History Handbook will provide essential guidance for the beginner as well as the experienced researcher. The Irish Family and Local History Handbook stands alone and contains original and unpublished material which is relevant to the whole of Ireland. We have tried to provide a wide and interesting range of topics from the articles submitted to us.

We hope The Irish Family and Local History Handbook becomes an indispensable tool for your Irish family history research. The listings in The Irish Genealogical Services Directory section have been checked, updated and extended especially for this issue.

This book is intended to be an essential companion to your research whether it is by using the extensive material in libraries, archives and museums or from the Internet. However with regards to the internet, which serves us well, we must raise a cautionary note. There is a vast array of information on the internet and care should be taken when using unverified data found there as it can easily lead us astray. The fact that if it is on the internet 'it must be gospel' leads many people to include wrong information in their histories. Always remember when dealing with any information that nothing should be taken for granted and where possible original documentation should be checked. It is important that our descendants are able to rely upon the accuracy of our researches and by following this advice you will create a family history which will become an heirloom.

The help from Elizabeth in producing this book increases with each issue and her input is invaluable. The design and layout of the Handbook is my responsibility.

We are again grateful to all our authors for their expertise and willingness to contribute to each issue.

We hope that you, our readers, enjoy this dedicated Ireland issue as much as our previous ones.

ROBERT AND ELIZABETH BLATCHFORD

Ulster Historical Foundation is an entirely self-funded educational non-profit organisation.

Our aim is to encourage an interest in the history of the province of Ulster, promote a positive image of Northern Ireland overseas, strengthen the links between Ireland and those of Ulster descent and to broaden access to historical documents and records for Irish and Scots-Irish genealogy.

If you need genealogical advice, would like to commission research or want more information on our other services, please contact us using the details below.

☎ (0)28 9066 1988

✉ enquiry@uhf.org.uk

f facebook.com/UlsterHistoricalFoundation

or visit **www.ancestryireland.com**

BOOK PUBLISHING

We are a leading publisher of quality historical, educational and genealogical books and have produced over 200 titles to date. You can find our bookstore online at **booksireland.org.uk**

FAMILY RECORDS

We have over 2 million records including Birth, Marriage & Death records, Gravestone Inscriptions, Street Directories and much more available on our website.

CLASSES & TOURS

Throughout the year we run a variety of classes, tours and activity holidays across Ulster, our most popular being our annual genealogy Summer School which runs in June.

BECOME A MEMBER

To access a range of specialist resources and services as well as discounts on all of our titles, visit **ancestryireland.com/index.php?guild**

an irish education

Researching Irish Ancestors
An Introduction to the Sources and Archives

William Roulston
Ulster Historical Foundation

Interest in researching Irish ancestors has never been greater. Given Ireland's history of emigration, it is hardly surprising to find that around the world tens of millions of people have family connections with the island. Much of this interest comes from the USA, Canada, Australia and New Zealand. Many people in Britain also have an Irish connection and I am no longer surprised at the extraordinary number of individuals who want to quiz me on how to trace Irish ancestors when I am giving talks in England and Scotland. This article provides a basic introduction to researching Irish ancestors. It highlights what the major sources are and where they can be found. For a fuller look at Irish genealogy the reader should refer to some of the books noted below. Prior to 1922 Ireland was under one jurisdiction and so where I refer to Ireland I mean the entire island. Where I am referring specifically to Northern Ireland or the Republic of Ireland I will try to make this clear.

Some Background Information
Exploding a myth

A popular misconception about researching Irish ancestors is that it is a fruitless exercise because so many records were destroyed. There is no denying that the loss of so many records in the destruction of the Public Record Office, Dublin, in 1922 was a catastrophe as far as historical and genealogical research is concerned. However, since 1922 the work of archivists to gather records of historical importance has resulted in a vast amount of material being available for the genealogical researcher to peruse. In addition there are other repositories in Ireland where the collections have survived virtually intact, as well as categories of records now available that were not in the Public Record Office in 1922 and so escaped destruction.

Three main categories of record were destroyed in 1922:
- Virtually all census returns, 1821-51
- The registers from over 1,000 Church of Ireland parishes
- Virtually all original wills probated before 1900

Many other records, including records relating to government and the courts, were also lost. However, not destroyed in 1922 were the registers from some 600 Church of Ireland parishes as well as church records for all the other denominations in Ireland. Neither were official records of births, deaths and marriages destroyed.

Getting Started

As is the case anywhere, the best way for someone to begin researching their ancestry is within their own family. In nearly every family there is at least one member with an encyclopaedic knowledge of who married who and how many children they had and where they lived etc., etc. Collect as much information as possible on names, dates and places relating to your family; write it down and begin to plot out the skeleton of a family tree. Occasionally wrong information may be given, yet it is surprising just how often an elderly person's reminiscences prove to be an accurate recollection of the facts. A family Bible is another possible source of information on your ancestors. Gathering this information before you visit the archives can save a great deal of time. Once you find out what you do know you will then be aware of the gaps and will have a clearer idea of what you should be looking for.

What's in a name?

In carrying out research in Ireland, or anywhere for that matter, it is important to take into consideration all possible variant spellings of a name. Frequently

Four Courts, Dublin

Bank of Ireland, Dublin

the O and Mc or Mac prefix will be dropped. For example, a Sarah McElhatton of County Tyrone became Sarah Hatton when she moved to the north of England in the late nineteenth century. Names can also change slightly. Two examples of changes between Ireland and Scotland that I have encountered are Mooney to Moodie and

McMahon to Maughan. Often names were changed slightly to remove some of the 'Irishness' about them and to allow newcomers to better assimilate into the host population.

The Internet

The internet has transformed genealogy around the world and Ireland is no exception. To list all the websites that deal with Irish genealogy would be impossible as they seem to be increasing almost by the day. A website providing a fairly comprehensive listing of internet sites relating to Irish genealogy is www.cyndislist.com/ireland.htm. Some websites focus on a particular county or district and contain extensive lists of digitised sources, while others concentrate on a particular family. It must be remembered that many Irish sources are not yet available online and it may be many years before basic sources such as births, deaths and marriages, church records and census returns are fully digitised and available over the internet. Most of the main archives in Ireland now have a website and these are listed below along with other contact details.

Sources for the History of Irish Civilisation

When initially starting out on Irish family history research, it is extremely advisable to consult the multi-volume guides to sources compiled under the editorship of Richard Hayes. *Manuscript Sources for the History of Irish Civilisation* (Boston: G. K. Hall, 1965) includes four volumes on persons, two each on subjects, places and dates, and a single volume containing a list of manuscripts. Places are arranged alphabetically within counties. Estate records and maps are also listed by county. Five years later there appeared *Sources for the History of Irish Civilisation: Articles in Irish Periodicals* (Boston: G. K. Hall, 1970). This included five volumes on persons, three on subjects and a single volume covering places and dates. After a further nine years there appeared the *First Supplement, 1965–75* (Boston: G. K. Hall, 1979) in three volumes. Copies of Hayes's guides are available in many libraries and repositories across Ireland and beyond. The information in these volumes is now available online as the 'Sources' database on the website of the National Library (http://sources.nli.ie). This comprises over 180,000 catalogue records for Irish manuscripts as well as articles in Irish periodicals.

Books

Numerous books on Irish genealogy have been written. Probably the best general guide is John Grenham's *Tracing your Irish Ancestors* (2006), now in its third edition. Grenham discusses the principal sources available for those wishing to find out more about their family history. Another useful guide is *Tracing Irish Ancestors* by Máire Mac Conghail and Paul Gorry (1997). A more recent volume is Anthony Adolph's Collins *Tracing Your Irish Family History* (2007). Other volumes deal

Grafton Street, Dublin

more closely with a specific area, period or theme. Ian Maxwell's *Tracing your ancestors in Northern Ireland* (1997) is primarily concerned with records in the Public Record Office of Northern Ireland. He is also the author of two county guides published by the Ulster Historical Foundation: *Researching Armagh Ancestors* (2000) and *Researching Down Ancestors* (2004). Genealogical guides for counties Cork, Donegal, Dublin, Kerry, Limerick and Mayo have been published by Flyleaf Press. William Roulston's *Researching Scots-Irish Ancestors: the essential genealogical guide to early modern Ulster, 1600-1800* (Belfast, 2005) provides a comprehensive overview of sources for studying family history in the seventeenth and eighteenth centuries, including a summary listing of sources for virtually every parish in Ulster.

Administrative divisions

The main units of administration in Ireland are:

Barony

A unit used in Ireland between the sixteenth and nineteenth centuries for administrative (census, taxation, and legal) purposes. Often drawn on pre-existing Gaelic divisions, baronies consisted of large groupings of townlands within a county. The 1891 census was the last to use the barony as an administrative unit.

County

There are 32 counties in Ireland, six of which are now in Northern Ireland. The county system as a form of territorial division was introduced into Ireland shortly after the Norman conquest in the late twelfth century. The creation of counties or shires was gradual, however, and the present arrangement of county boundaries was not finalised in Ulster until the early seventeenth century. In 1898 local councils based on county divisions were created. County councils remain the principal administrative body of local government in the Republic of Ireland but were abolished in Northern Ireland in 1973.

Parish

This territorial division refers to both civil and ecclesiastical units. Civil parishes largely follow the pattern that was established in medieval times. Ecclesiastical parishes do not always coincide with civil parish boundaries, however. Following the Reformation in the sixteenth century, the Church of Ireland more or less maintained the pre-Reformation arrangement. Church of Ireland parishes are, therefore, largely coterminous with civil parishes. When the Catholic Church began its institutional re-emergence in the late eighteenth and nineteenth centuries, it constructed a new network of parishes which did not necessarily follow the civil parish network.

Poor Law Union

Under the Irish Poor Law Act of 1838 commissioners were empowered to "unite so many townlands as they think fit to be a union for the relief of the destitute poor". A Union was a group of parishes usually centred on a market town, where a workhouse might be built, with parishes and townlands as subdivisions. Rates, land based taxes, were collected within these areas for maintenance to the poor. They were named after a large town. The same districts later became used as General Register Districts.

Province

Provinces are composed of groups of counties. There are four provinces in Ireland: Ulster in the north, Leinster in the east, Munster in the south, and Connacht or Connaught in the west.

Townland

This is the smallest administrative territorial unit in Ireland, varying in size from a single acre to over 7,000 acres. Originating in the older Gaelic dispensation, townlands were used as the basis of leases in the estate system, and subsequently to assess valuations and tithes in the eighteenth and nineteenth centuries. They survive as important markers of local identity.

The Archives

The most important archival repositories in the Republic of Ireland are the National Archives of Ireland, the National Library of Ireland and the General Register Office. An indispensable book is *Guide to Irish Libraries, Archives and Genealogical Centres* by Robert K. O'Neill (2nd edition, 2006) which provides contact details, as well as summary information on collections held by the main archives in Ireland.

The abbreviations used in this article for the main archives are:

- GROI – General Register Office of Ireland
- GRONI – General Register Office of Northern Ireland
- NAI – National Archives of Ireland
- NLI – National Library of Ireland
- PRONI – Public Record Office of Northern Ireland

Civil Registration

Civil registers of births, marriages and deaths provide basic family history information. However, their usefulness for the genealogist will depend on the period being researched. Civil or state registration of all births, deaths and marriages began in Ireland on 1 January 1864. Non-Catholic marriages, including those conducted in a government registry office, were required in

law to be registered from 1 April 1845. Civil registration followed the administrative divisions created by the Poor Law Act of 1838. Under this act the country had been divided into over 130 Poor Law Unions. The Poor Law Unions were subdivided into dispensary districts, each with its own medical officer. Under civil registration the area covered by a Poor Law Union was used as the basis of each superintendent registrar's district, while the dispensary districts corresponded to the registrar's districts. In some cases the medical officer also served as the registrar. In overall charge of registration was the Registrar General in Dublin. Certified copies of all registers compiled locally were sent to his office and, from these, master indexes covering the whole of Ireland were produced.

Birth Certificates

Birth certificates record the date and place of birth of the child. Normally the name of the child is also given, but in some cases only the sex is given, i.e. the child had not been given a name by the time the birth was registered. The name and residence of the father is given. Usually this will be the same as the place of birth of the child, but in some cases it will show that the father was working abroad or in another part of Ireland when the child was born. The father's occupation is also given. The mother's maiden name is provided as well as her first name. Finally, the name and address of the informant is given, together with his or her qualification to sign. This will usually be the father or mother or someone present at the birth, such as a midwife or even the child's grandmother.

Marriage Certificates

Civil records of marriage normally give fuller information than birth and death certificates, and are the most useful of civil records. Information on the individuals getting married includes their

O'CONNELL BRIDGE, DUBLIN. 1704 V

High Street, Belfast

name, age, status, and occupation. The names and occupations of their fathers are also given. The church, the officiating minister and the witnesses to the ceremony are named. In most cases the exact age of the parties is not given, and the entry will simply read *'full age'* (i.e. over 21) or *'minor'* (i.e. under 21). If the father of one of the parties was no longer living, this may be indicated in the marriage certificate by the word *'deceased'* or by leaving the space blank, but in many cases it is not.

Death Certificates

Civil records of death in Ireland are rather uninformative in comparison to other countries. The name of the deceased is given together with the date, place and cause of death, marital status, the age at death, and occupation. The name and address of the informant is also given. Usually this is the person present at the time of the death; this may be a close family member.

The Indexes

Indexes to civil marriages 1845–63 are hand-written, but thereafter all indexes are printed. From 1864 to 1877 indexes for births, marriages and deaths consist of a single yearly volume covering the whole of Ireland. From 1878 the annual indexes are arranged on a quarterly basis. In each index the surnames will be arranged alphabetically, followed by the first names. The name of the superintendent registrar's district is also given, followed by the volume number and page number of the master copies of the registers in Dublin. In the indexes to deaths the age of the deceased will be provided. When using the indexes it is important to bear in mind possible variations of the name being researched. In the birth indexes an unnamed child will appear as *'male'* or *'female'* after the surname.

The General Register Office of Ireland

The administrative headquarters of the General Register Office in the Republic of Ireland is now in Roscommon, but there is a research facility open to members of the public in the Irish Life Centre, Lower Abbey Street, Dublin. The GROI holds master copies of births, death and marriages for all of Ireland up to 1921 and thereafter for the Republic of Ireland only.

General Register Office of Northern Ireland

The General Register Office of Northern Ireland (GRONI) records of births, marriages and deaths for the six counties that now make up Northern Ireland. At GRONI it is possible for members of the public to book an index search (with verification of entries by staff) or an assisted search which allows for a general search of records for any period of years and any number of entries.

FamilySearch Record Search

In 2009 the website FamilySearch www.familysearch.org made available online civil registration indexes for Ireland 1845-1958. Rather than searching the indexes in Belfast or Dublin genealogists can now search a single name index of births, deaths and marriages for the period 1845-1921 with additional indexes for the Republic of Ireland after 1922.

The FamilySearch website also hosts the International Genealogical Index (IGI). The IGI contains information on family history drawn from a variety of sources and is always worth consulting for it may provide clues as to the place of origin of an ancestor. Very usefully it includes abstracts of civil births in Ireland from 1864 to 1880, giving the exact date of birth, child's and parents' names and a location which can vary from the townland to the county. It is also possible to search by parents' names which can be a good way of finding additional siblings.

Irish Family History Foundation

The Irish Family History Foundation is the co-ordinating body for a network of county genealogy centres on the island of Ireland. The databases on its website (www.rootsireland.ie) comprise the largest online collection of Irish civil records and church records. The records available cover most counties in Ireland, though the comprehensiveness of the coverage varies from county to county, with some being better for civil records and others stronger on church records. The indexes to the databases are free, but the records themselves can be purchased on a pay-per-view basis. The new Advanced Search facility allows many more options in searching for ancestors and in narrowing down the entries most likely to be of interest.

Church Records

Prior to the commencement of civil registration the main sources of family history information are church registers. PRONI has a vast collection of microfilms and photostat copies of church records, as well as some original material, relating to nearly all denominations in Ulster. Family historians should consult the *Guide to Church Records*. This lists, parish by parish, all the church records held by PRONI. Copies of the *Guide* are available in PRONI. The National Library of Ireland has microfilms of over 1,000 sets of Roman Catholic registers for the whole of Ireland. The Representative Church Body Library in Dublin has many Church of Ireland records both in original form and as microfilms. The Presbyterian Historical Society in Belfast has a few Presbyterian records that are not available elsewhere.

Denominations

The single largest denomination in Ireland is the Roman Catholic Church. Following the Reformation in Ireland the Catholic Church went through a lengthy period when its activities were severely curtailed. The Penal Laws were a series of enactments of the late seventeenth and early eighteenth centuries designed to remove the rights of Catholics to public office and to careers in certain professions. In spite of the Penal Laws, Catholic priests and bishops operated freely in most areas. During the eighteenth century the Catholic Church was able to set up diocesan and parochial structures. It is important for family historians to bear in mind that Roman Catholic parishes generally do not conform to civil parishes. Many Roman Catholic parishes have more than one church. Sometimes only one register was kept for the entire parish, but at other times each church had its own registers.

The Church of Ireland is the largest Protestant denomination on the island of Ireland. Until 1870 it was the established or state church and enjoyed various privileges in consequence of this. The Church of Ireland was required to keep proper records of baptisms, marriages and burials from 1634, but very few registers survive from the seventeenth century. In general, however, the records of the Church of Ireland start much earlier than those of other Protestant denominations and of the Roman Catholic Church. The Church of Ireland is organised into parishes which in general conform to civil parishes. In 1922 over 1,000 Church of Ireland registers were lost in Dublin in the destruction of the Public Record Office of Ireland.

Presbyterianism came to Ireland from Scotland in the early seventeenth century. It did not become an organised denomination until the second half of the seventeenth century, however. The distribution of Presbyterian churches in Ulster is generally a reflection of the pattern of Scottish settlement in the province. As well as the main Presbyterian Church in Ireland there are two smaller historic denominations, the Non-Subscribing Presbyterian Church and the Reformed Presbyterian Church.

Methodism emerged in Ireland in the eighteenth century as a result of John Wesley's many visits to the island. To begin with the majority of Methodists belonged to the Established Church and they remained members of their own local churches. Therefore they continued to go to the parish church for the administration of marriages, burials and baptisms. In 1816 a split developed between the Primitive Wesleyan Methodists, who retained their links with the Established Church, and the Wesleyan Methodists, who allowed their ministers to administer baptisms.

The information found in church records can be categorised as follows:

Baptismal Registers

The basic information provided in a baptismal register is the name of the child, the name of the father and the date of baptism. The mother's name will usually be given as will a specific location. The occupation of the father and the date of birth of the child may also be provided. Roman Catholic registers will normally give the names of the sponsors of the child.

Marriage Registers

Prior to the standardisation of marriage registers after 1845 for non-Catholics and 1864 for Catholics, these will give in their simplest form the date of the marriage and the names of the bride and groom. The residence and the

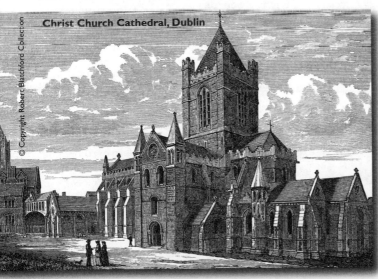

Christ Church Cathedral, Dublin

name of the father of each party are often provided. The names of the witnesses may also be given.

Burial Registers

Burial registers can be fairly uninformative, with the name of the deceased, the date of burial and occasionally the occupation and age at death given. The deaths of children will usually include the name of the father, while the burial of a wife may include her husband's name. Many Catholic 'burial' registers are actually registers recording payments made at the funeral of the deceased.

Vestry Minute Books

Vestry minute books record the deliberations of the parish vestry and will be found, where they survive, with the Church of Ireland records for a particular parish. The role of the vestry included the upkeep of the Church of Ireland church, the maintenance of roads in the parish and the care of the destitute and abandoned children. The money to pay for these things was raised through a cess or tax on the land in the parish. Vestry minute books are a rich source of information on life in a parish in bygone times. Occasionally they will include a list of the names of the parishioners drawn up for taxation purposes.

Online Access to Church Records

Mention has already been made of the online availability of Irish church records on the website of the Irish Family History Foundation (www.rootsireland.ie). As previously noted, the comprehensiveness of the coverage varies from county to county. The majority of Irish Catholic registers have been indexed, but many Protestant church records from the north of Ireland have yet to be digitised. The website Irish Genealogy (www.irishgenealogy.ie) hosts a free database of church records for selected areas, including Church of Ireland records for the city of Dublin and Roman Catholic records for the diocese of Kerry. Church records are available on many other websites, sometimes on a restricted basis and on other occasions free. See Bready Ancestry - www.breadyancestry.com - for what has been digitised for one corner of County Tyrone.

Gravestone Inscriptions

The value of gravestone inscriptions for ancestral research has long been recognised. The discovery of a single gravestone may provide more information on the history of a family than could otherwise be gleaned from hours of searching through documentary sources. A visit to the graveyard in which your ancestors are buried is, therefore, an essential part of compiling your family tree. Discovering the graveyard in which your ancestors are buried is not necessarily straightforward. They may be buried in the graveyard adjoining the church to which your family belongs. Alternatively they may be buried in a graveyard no longer in use or adjoining another church. Burial registers kept by a church are one way of finding the place of burial, but as was explained above, these have limitations and do not survive for every graveyard. In many of the older graveyards it is not unusual to find all denominations buried.

The information recorded on a gravestone varies considerably. Some gravestones will record the dates of death of several generations of one family. Others may simply record the family surname. In most graveyards there will be at least one gravestone that has an overseas connection, recording the name of a family member who had died abroad. Ages of death on gravestones should be treated with some caution as they are often guesses or have been rounded up. Nonetheless they provide a basis for working out the year of birth which can be useful when it comes to looking for a birth certificate or record of baptism.

The recordings from many graveyards have been published in local historical or genealogical journals or books. Many websites with also host gravestone inscriptions from burial grounds across Ireland. John Grenham's *Tracing your Irish ancestors* provides a good guide to what has appeared in print and also what is available online.

Census Records

The first census was held in Ireland in 1821 and thereafter every ten years until 1911. Unfortunately, the earliest census that survives in its entirety for the whole of Ireland is the 1901 census. Census returns 1821-51 were almost entirely lost in 1922 in the destruction of the Public Record Office in Dublin. Census returns 1861-91 were completely destroyed by government order, many pulped as scrap paper during the First World War.

Queenstown, Cork reverted to its Irish name Cobh in 1922

1901 Census

On 31st March 1901, a census was taken of the whole island of Ireland. The information in the census is listed under the following headings: name; relationship to the head of the household; religion; literacy; occupation; age; marital status; county of birth (or country if born outside Ireland); and ability to speak English or Irish.

1911 Census

The 1911 census was taken on 1st April of that year and contains additional information including the number of years a wife had been married, the number of children born alive and the number still living.

1901 and 1911 Census Online

Census returns from both 1901 and 1911 are now available online thanks to a joint initiative between the National Archives of Ireland and Library and Archives Canada (**www.census.nationalarchives.ie**).

1821 - 51 Census Survivals

Portions of census returns 1821-51 do survive for certain areas. For example, returns for over a dozen parishes survive for County Cavan for 1821. For County Londonderry an abstract of the 1831 census is available which provides the name of every head of household as well as numerical information on the composition of the household. All or parts of a number of parishes in County Antrim survive from 1851.

Old Age Pension Claims

It is worth checking the old age pension search forms, as they contain extracts from the 1841 and 1851 censuses, the originals of which were almost completely destroyed. The old age pension was introduced on 1 January 1909 for those over seventy years of age. For many born before 1864, when the state registration of births began in Ireland, it was necessary to pay for a search to be made of the 1841 and 1851 censuses in order to prove their entitlement to the pension. The forms submitted by the claimants include such information as the names of parents, location at the time of the 1841 or 1851 census, and age at the time of the claim and during the relevant census year.

Individual application forms completed by or on behalf of the applicant are known as 'green forms'. The green forms are held at the National Archives, Dublin, under reference CEN/S/8. Another form of evidence related to the old age pension returns are 'form 37s', which were submitted by local pensions offices. These include the applicant's name, stated age, parents' names and address at the time of the census. Two volumes, one covering Northern Ireland and the other the Republic of Ireland, based mainly on surviving old age pension claims were compiled by Josephine Masterson of Indianapolis, USA, and published as *Ireland: 1841/1851 Census Abstracts*.

Records Relating to the Occupation of Land

The Primary or Griffith's Valuation, 1848–64

The 1848–64 valuation gives a complete list of occupiers of land, tenements and houses. This Primary Valuation of Ireland, better known as Griffith's Valuation after the Commissioner of Valuation, Sir Richard Griffith, is arranged by county, within counties by Poor Law Union division, and within Unions by parish. It includes the following information: the name of the townland; the name of the householder or leaseholder; the name of the person from whom the property was leased; a description of the property; its acreage; and finally the valuation of the land and buildings. Griffith's Valuation is of particular interest to anyone wishing to trace their family tree, due to the fact that so little of the nineteenth century census returns has survived.

A set of the bound and printed version is available at PRONI and NLI while partial or complete sets can also be found in libraries across Ireland. These volumes are arranged by Poor Law Union within counties, and then into parishes and townlands. There is an index at the front of each volume which enables searchers to identify the page or pages in which a specific townland may be found. The valuer's annotated set of Ordnance Survey maps showing the location of every property is available at PRONI for Northern Ireland and at the Valuation Office in Dublin. These enable a researcher to identify the exact location of the house in which an ancestor may have lived.

In the recent years a number of free indexes to the information contained in Griffith's Valuation have been made available online. The most useful of these websites is www.askaboutireland.ie which provides a free search facility. You can search by surname and/or first name or limit your search by county or parish. Not only does the website include scanned images of the original printed version of Griffith's Valuation, it also includes the annotated valuation maps which allow you to pinpoint the precise location of every property in Ireland at that time.

Valuation Revision Books, from 1864

The manuscript valuation books were updated on a regular basis. The so-called *cancelled books* consist of manuscript notebooks kept by the valuation office and updated to take account of changes in tenure. When a change of occupancy

15

Irish Village

occurred, the name of the lessee or householder was crossed off and the new owner's name written above it, while the year was noted on the right-hand side of the page. Different-coloured ink was often used to differentiate between years with a key at the start of each book to indicate which colour went with each year.

The years in which changes in occupancy took place help to establish significant dates in family history, such as dates of death, sale or emigration. On rare occasions there can even be a comment to the effect that a family had emigrated or that an individual had died. Changes in the valuation of buildings can indicate when a new house was built or when the existing one was abandoned. By the early years of the twentieth century most of the occupiers of land had become landowners, thanks to a series of land purchase acts. This explains the initials L.A.P. (Land Act Purchase) that may be found stamped on an entry in the revision lists. In Northern Ireland valuation revision books are available in PRONI and for the Republic of Ireland they may be consulted in the Valuation Office in Dublin.

Tithe Valuation

In 1823 the Composition Act was passed which stipulated that henceforth all tithes due to the Established Church, the Church of Ireland, were to be paid in money rather than in kind as they previously could have been. This necessitated a complete valuation of all tithable land in Ireland, the results of which are contained in manuscript form in the tithe applotment books arranged by parish. The tithe applotment books contain the name of the tithe-payer, the size of his farm and the amount of tithe he paid. Copies of the tithe applotment books for Northern Ireland are available in the PRONI and for the Republic of Ireland in the National Archives of Ireland.

Landed Estate Records

Until the early part of the twentieth century, most of the land in Ireland was possessed by landowners whose estates ranged in size from 1,000 acres or less to, in some cases, over 100,000. Nearly all of the farmers in Ireland were tenants on such estates. The records generated by the management of landed estates are a major source of genealogical information. The best collection of Irish estate papers is housed in the Public Record Office of Northern Ireland. A two-volume *Guide to Landed Estate Papers*, covering the six counties of Northern Ireland, is available for consultation in the Public Search Room. It is arranged by county with the estate collections listed alphabetically according to the name of the landowning family. PRONI also holds estate collections from other counties in Ireland, notably Donegal and Monaghan. For several of the larger estates there are excellent records. In the Republic of Ireland the best collection of estate papers is in the National Library.

Some categories of estate papers are more useful to genealogists than others. Title deeds are concerned with the legal ownership of an estate, and are generally of limited value to genealogists. The same can be said of mortgages. Wills and marriage settlements usually refer only to the members of the landowner's family. However, rentals, leases, lease books, maps and correspondence can all be extremely useful to those searching for their ancestors within landed estate records.

Wills and Testamentary Papers

Prior to 1858 the Church of Ireland was responsible for administering all testamentary affairs. Ecclesiastical or Consistorial Courts in each diocese were responsible for granting probate and conferring on the executors the power to administer the estate. Each court was responsible for wills and administrations in its own diocese. However, when the estate included property worth more than £5 in another diocese, responsibility for the will or administration passed to the Prerogative Court under the authority of the Archbishop of Armagh.

Unfortunately, nearly all original wills probated before 1858 were destroyed in Dublin in 1922. However, indexes to these destroyed wills do exist. In the absence of a will letters of administration were sometimes granted. These were usually issued to close family members. The original administration bonds were also destroyed in Dublin in 1922, but index volumes for dioceses are available. On the PRONI website (www.proni.gov.uk) it is possible to search many of the diocesan will and administration bond indexes for the north of Ireland under its Name Search facility.

From 1858 - 1899 transcripts of original wills are available at the Public Record Office of Northern Ireland for the district registries of Armagh, Belfast and Londonderry. From 1900 onwards original wills for Northern Ireland can be read at the Public Record Office of Northern Ireland and for the Republic of Ireland at the National Archives.

The PRONI website now includes a database of entries from the printed will calendars relating to the three district probate registries of Armagh, Belfast and Londonderry covering the period 1858 - 1943. Over 90,000 digitised images of entries from the transcript will books covering the period 1858-1900 are now available online, making it possible to read the actual contents of wills from that period.

Early Sources

The further one goes back in time the more difficult it becomes to discover precise details about family history. Sources specific to the seventeenth and eighteenth centuries are rarely more than lists of names, sometimes arranged by townland and parish. They will usually not provide information on family relationships, and because they almost always give the name of the head of the household nearly all of the names will be those of men. Occasionally two men with the same name will be found in the one townland and may be distinguished with the words, 'senior' and 'junior,' in which case it is reasonable to infer that they are father and son. At the same time, despite their limitations sources from the seventeenth and eighteenth centuries are useful if they can be used to demonstrate that a particular name occurred in a parish or townland at a certain date.

The principal sources from this period are listed below. In several cases the originals were destroyed in 1922, but transcripts survive. For more information on early sources for the province of Ulster and where they can be accessed refer to William Roulston, *Researching Scots-Irish Ancestors* (Belfast, 2005). Some of them are searchable online at www.ancestryireland.com/scotsinulster.

Fiants of the Tudor Sovereigns, 1521 - 1603

Fiants were a documentary series unique to Ireland. These documents preceded the issue of royal grants. When Irish chiefs were granted pardons under the *'surrender and regrant'* policy they often listed scores of members of their extended families as well as gallowglasses (mercenary soldiers), horsemen and yeomen, husbandmen, tenants and even, on occasion, cottiers. Individuals were identified with their full names, often with specific locations. Originally published as appendices in the steady stream of annual reports published by the Public Record Office of Ireland in the years 1875 - 1890 (Reports nos 11-13, 15-18 of the Deputy Keeper of the Public Records of Ireland), they were reprinted in in 1994 as four volumes, including a comprehensive index, for the years 1521-1603 by Edmund Burke.

Hearth Money Rolls 1660s

In the 1660s the government introduced a tax on hearths as a means of raising revenue. The returns, arranged by parish and usually with townland locations, list the names of all householders paying this tax survive for half the counties in Ireland with coverage most complete in Ulster (in full or in part for all counties except Down).

'Census of Protestant Householders' 1740

What has generally been termed a *'census of Protestant householders'* was compiled in 1740. The returns were made by the collectors of the hearth money and it has, therefore, been suggested that this 'census' is actually a hearth money roll and for some areas includes Catholics as well. It is no more than a list of names arranged by county, barony and parish and, reflecting its supervision by the inspector responsible for collecting hearth money, it is occasionally divided into 'walks'. Some parishes are also divided into townlands.

The Religious Census of 1766

In March and April 1766, Church of Ireland rectors were instructed by the government to compile complete returns of all householders in their respective parishes, showing their religion, as between Church of Ireland (Episcopalian), Roman Catholic (termed *'Papists'* in the returns) and Presbyterians (or *Dissenters*), and giving an account of any Roman Catholic clergy active in their area. Some of the more diligent rectors listed every townland and every household, but many drew up only numerical totals of the population.

Patrick Street, Cork

Petition of Protestant Dissenters 1775

The Petition of Protestant Dissenters is a list of names of Dissenters on either a parish or a congregational basis which were submitted to the government in October and November 1775. Most of them relate to the province of Ulster.

The Flaxgrowers' List 1796

In 1796 as part of a government initiative to encourage the linen industry in Ireland, free spinning wheels or looms were granted to farmers who planted a certain acreage of their holdings with flax. The names of over 56,000 recipients of these awards have survived in printed form arranged by county and parish. A photocopy of the original volume is available in PRONI.

Other sources

School records

A state-run system of education was established in Ireland in 1831. Prior to this (and for some time after it) there were several different organisations and institutions providing education in Ireland. These included the Capel Street Association for Discountenancing Vice, the Kildare Street Society, the London Hibernian Society as well as the different churches. From 1831 National Schools were built with the aid of the Commissioners of National Education and local trustees. Between 1832 and 1870 about 2,500 national schools were established in Ulster. The records of over 1,500 schools in Northern Ireland are held at PRONI. A relatively small number of school records are in NAI. Of particular interest are the enrolment registers.

These record the full name of the pupil, his or her date of birth (or age at entry), religion, father's address and occupation (but unfortunately not his name), details of attendance and academic progress and the name of the school previously attended. A space is also provided in the registers for general comments, which might tell where the children went to work after leaving school or if they emigrated. Some registers have an index at the front that can greatly ease searching. As they include the age of pupils, school registers can be cross-referenced to other records such as baptismal records or birth certificates.

Election records

Election records come in various forms. Registers of freeholders list the names and addresses of individuals entitled to vote at parliamentary elections. Poll books (often in printed form before the Ballot Act of 1872) list the names of voters and the candidates they voted for. Until the late nineteenth century the qualification for voting was generally linked to the tenure of land, and only a small minority of men had the right to vote. In Ireland, from 1727 to 1793, only Protestant men with a 40-shilling freehold had the right to vote. Between 1793 and 1829 both Protestants and Roman Catholics with 40-shilling freeholds had votes, although a Catholic still could not become a member of parliament. The 40-shilling freehold was property worth 40 shillings a year above the rent, and either owned outright or leased during the lives of named individuals. Many important and indeed prominent people had no vote because they leased their property on the wrong terms. Surviving electoral records are available at PRONI, NLI, NAI and elsewhere. Most of those of PRONI have been digitised and are available as a database on its website.

Board of Guardians Records

The new English system of Poor Law administration was applied to Ireland in 1838. Destitute poor who were previously granted relief at parish level were to be accommodated in new workhouses, where conditions were to be as unpleasant as was consistent with health. Ireland was divided into 137 Poor Law Unions. These ignored traditional divisions, such as the county, barony and parish, and were centred on a market town where a workhouse was built. The management of the workhouses was the responsibility of the Boards of Guardians. In the minute books kept by the Guardians are details of the day-to-day running of the workhouse, including information on many of the inmates and those employed in the workhouse as teachers, nurses, chaplains, etc. Indoor registers provides the names of those who were admitted to the workhouses. The information recorded also includes the townland, age, spouse's name and religion of each inmate. Outdoor relief registers include similar information to the indoor registers, but concern those who received assistance without going into the workhouse. Vaccination registers are another useful source among the Board of Guardians records. Surviving Board of Guardians records for Northern Ireland are deposited at PRONI under reference BG. Access to some of these records can be a problem, as there is a 100-year closure rule on all documents in the Boards of Guardians papers. Many Board of Guardians records in the Republic of Ireland remain in local custody and some are more accessible than others.

Street directories

Street directories contain a great deal of information on the gentry, the professional classes, merchants, etc. They include information on even the smallest of market towns and ports in Ireland. Beginning with a description of the town and surrounding countryside, the names and addresses of the local butchers, pawnbrokers, blacksmiths and coach-builders are given, as well as the various places of worship, with the names of the local ministers etc. and the location of local schools. Street directories can therefore be useful if you wish to find out which church or school your ancestor attended. The names and addresses of the local members of parliament, magistrates, Poor Law Guardians and town commissioners are also included in many street directories. In fact the only classes that are generally excluded from directories are the small tenant farmers, landless labourers and servants. There are good collections of street directories in Belfast Central Library, the Public Record Office of Northern Ireland, and the Linen Hall Library, and the National Library of Ireland as well as numerous other libraries

Newspapers

Newspapers are an important source of family history information. The major drawback with using them is usually the lack of an index of names. Of particular interest to genealogists are birth, death and marriage notices. In many cases a newspaper notice may be the only record of one of these events if it took place prior to civil registration and if a church record has not survived. The Newspaper Library of Belfast Central Library, the Linen Hall Library, PRONI and the National Library all have good newspaper collections.

Archives and Libraries

The following is a list of the most important archives and libraries in Ireland. **Note:** it is vitally important that you make contact prior to your visit to ensure that the institution in question is open. Some of the archives and libraries listed here are only open at certain times or have restrictions on who can access them.

GENERAL REGISTER OFFICE OF NORTHERN IRELAND, Oxford House, 49/55 Chichester Street, Belfast, BT1 4HL T: + 44 (0)28 9025 2000 E: gro.nisra@dfpni.gov.uk (Birth, Death and Marriage Certificate Enquiries) W: www.groni.gov.uk

GENERAL REGISTER OFFICE OF IRELAND (Administrative Headquarters) , Convent Road, , Roscommon, Ireland T: +353 (0)90 6632900 W: www.groireland.ie

GENERAL REGISTER OFFICE OF IRELAND (Public Research Room), Irish Life Centre, Lower Abbey Street, Dublin 1, Ireland

LINEN HALL LIBRARY , 17 Donegall Square North, Belfast, BT1 5GD T: +44 (0) 28 9032 1707 E: info@linenhall.com W: www.linenhall.com/Home/home.html

PUBLIC RECORD OFFICE OF NORTHERN IRELAND, 2 Titanic Boulevard, Belfast, BT3 9HQ E: proni@gov.uk W: www.proni.gov.uk

NATIONAL ARCHIVES OF IRELAND, Bishop Street Dublin 8 T: (01) 407 2300 E: mail@nationalarchives.ie W: www.nationalarchives.ie

NATIONAL LIBRARY OF IRELAND, Kildare Street, Dublin 2 T: +353 (1) 603 0200 E: info@nli.ie W: www.nli.ie

William Roulston is Research Director of the Ulster Historical Foundation.
He is the author of a number of publications including *Researching Scots - Irish Ancestors: the essential genealogical guide to early modern Ulster, 1600-1800* (2005).
He holds a PhD in Archaeology from Queen's University, Belfast, and has worked on several radio and television projects including research for *Who Do You Think You Are?*

Using Local Genealogists

Aiden Feerick MAPGI - Ancestor Network Ltd

With so many resources online or about to go online, why should you hire a local genealogist? What does an intimate knowledge of Ireland's highways and byways bring to the table? Well, the professional Irish genealogist brings what could be called knowledge of the territory, its history and geography, its administrative structure, its language and the location of its main records. All this requires a word of explanation.

Background

Ireland is a small but complicated country on many levels. Parts of the western seaboard, like Sligo and Mayo, have been inhabited by farming and fishing communities for over 5,000 years and other parts on the eastern seaboard, like the *Newgrange Burial Site* in Co Meath, are older than the Pyramids of Egypt. Settlements like Armagh (*Eamhain Macha*) in the province of Ulster and Dublin (*Eblana*) on the east coast are named in *Ptolemy's Map of Ireland* made about 150 AD. When Christianity came to Ireland with Saint Patrick in about 430 AD, writing also came and from that time there are historical records mainly in Latin but also in Old Irish.

As befits a country with a long history, its administrative organisation is also complex. Again, like most European countries at that time, the organisation was tribal. This tribal structure was the basis of some of our most important surnames which came at a later date. The *O'Neills*, for example, have always been associated with Ulster and it was probably one of that sect who invaded Wales and brought back a young Roman slave to Ireland. That young slave stated in one of his writings that, in a dream, he was called back to this country to bring Christianity to his former captors. Today, he is our patron saint, St Patrick.

Superimposed on the tribal organisation, was the monastic structure of the early Irish church. However, the ecclesiastical organisation of the country as we know it today goes back to the 12th century with its basic division of parish, diocese and archdiocese. Knowledge of the church structure of the country is very important to visitors who come to seek their ancestors in the Church records. When people of Irish origin from overseas come to *The National Library*, they are disheartened to find that the Roman Catholic Parish Registers have not been transcribed and must be searched using microfilm copies of the originals. Despair sometimes sets in.

One type of civil organisation of Ireland was overlaid on the ecclesiastical one with the Anglo-Norman baronies, themselves largely but not completely based on the tribal division of land called the *Tuatha*. Each barony comprised a number of townlands. There were 273 baronies in Ireland and they were subdivisions of the Irish counties and widely used for administrative purposes from the sixteenth to the nineteenth centuries. The first great land survey in Ireland, the *Down Survey* (1654-59), was carried out along baronial lines.

Then came the division of Ireland into counties. This additional administrative level was superimposed on Ireland between the thirteenth and sixteenth centuries as part of the process of shiring, that is, the process by which common law and centralised government control was extended to embrace the whole of the country. In Ireland today, counties have distinct personalities and identities and many have nicknames like the States in America; Armagh, for example, is called *The Orchard County* because of its outstanding apple production.

And finally, for the most consulted civil records like the Births Marriages and Deaths at *The General Register Office* and the Census returns, there was yet another division of the country into *Poor Law Unions*. These were administrative areas introduced into Ireland in 1838 as an extension of the English *Poor Law Act 1834*. Previously established county and baronial borders were ignored and each Union was determined by taking a market town and including land within a ten mile radius of it. The townlands within its boundaries were then grouped together into electoral divisions. This is what we find when we seek Vital certificates and when we examine Census returns.

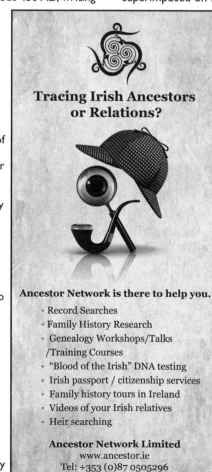

Chris Horan with John Hamrock and Aiden Feerick of Ancestor Network

river). There well are over 50,000 such place names in Ireland.

Knowledge of the language also helps when surnames have been distorted by immigration officials; for example, *Feehily* became *Feely* and the modern *O'Rourke* can be written *Rorke, O'Rorke* and *Rourke*. It is often difficult for people seeking their roots to grasp the concept that dates were unimportant to most of their ancestors; that accuracy of spelling was not crucial in a pre-literacy age before social security numbers, PIN numbers, bank accounts and tax returns. Added to this is the contribution to our surname pool of the various people who have settled here, *Normans, English, Scots, Welsh, Huguenots, Palatines, Jews* and other smaller groups. An awareness of these nuances can turn out to be crucial when tracing families beyond the nineteenth century.

Spelling of both place names and surnames can cause great concern among immigrants seeking their roots. Irish people are quite used to seeing different spellings of the same name. And many people have lived through modernisations of place names. The descendants of emigrants do not always remember that not many of their ancestors who left Ireland could read or write and what they said about their homeland was written by their descendants who were unaware of their background. And many immigrants, especially those who came from poorer backgrounds, were unwilling to go beyond generalities when speaking of the land and family they had been forced to leave. And for many, a new life meant a new beginning without harking back to what had been left behind.

Searching Repositories

Because the Internet offers so much, many people looking for Birth, Marriage or Death records of their ancestors are unaware that what is available on websites like Family Search or in the research room of the General Register Office are only indices. All civil certificates, even copy certificates, have to be obtained through the General Register Office on the payment of a fee. These, of course, can be ordered online but with common surnames and without knowledge of the Registration Districts, people spend a lot of money ordering certificates which are not of their ancestors. This is the scattergun approach. The professional Irish genealogist can generally narrow down the certificates ordered because of his/her knowledge of the territory. This could be called a targeted approach.

Many visitors to the *National Library of Ireland* in Dublin are unaware of online indices of the Baptism and Marriage records of some Church Parish Registers are often frustrated by what they find, or rather what they cannot find. The Roman Catholic registers were microfilmed in the 1950s and 1880 is the general cut off point because by then Civil Registration of Births, Marriages and Deaths had become the norm. The early registers frequently

Therefore, when our records are examined, these layers of history and administrative organisation can, to say the least, be daunting.

Compared to those countries where Irish people migrated, such as the *United States of America, Australia* or *New Zealand* Ireland embodies a very old organisation with its records correspondingly complex. The emigrants went to these countries where the administration had already evolved from complexity towards relative simplicity.

Local knowledge

The first reason to retain a professional Irish genealogist is because of his or her familiarity with place names which is a particular obstacle to visitors. Place names have been in existence for a very long time and many of them have been anglicised and have changed their spelling over the years. When one compares modern townland names with, for example, the names of townlands and parishes from *Sir William Petty's* maps of the 1650s, or the townlands in the *1838 Ordnance Survey*, there can often be significant discrepancies. In addition, place names have evolved throughout centuries and the ones remembered by immigrants may well have been reproduced phonetically or names of towns, baronies and parishes may be confused with one another. Place names are of fundamental importance in searching for ancestors as all available records are based on place. Identifying the exact place opens the door not only to civil and church records but to land records as well.

This leads to another reason for retaining a professional Irish genealogists, namely, knowledge of the Irish language. This is a key to the understanding of place names where the original Irish lies just behind the anglicised version. The place name, *'Owenbeg'* is a short step away from a feature of the landscape of the area, namely *'Abhainn beg'* (small contain many Latin abbreviations; the handwriting is often hard to read as if it were written in a hurry. In addition, the quality of paper used was often poor as was the ink with the result that entire sections have faded. Some Church registers are online - www.irishgenealogy.ie - and accompanied by images free of charge; others are available for most counties - www.rootsireland.ie - on a pay-per-view basis.

In addition, the records are located at disparate places. This is true about Dublin not to mention the rest of the country. *The National Library of Ireland* (www.nli.ie) containing the Roman Catholic Parish records is in Kildare Street beside the national parliament - the *Oireachtas*. *The National Archives* - www.nationalarchives.ie, containing wills, court records and some Church of Ireland records is located in Bishop Street near St Patrick's Cathedral. Should you wish to consult land records, *The Valuation Office* www.valoff.ie is located in the *Irish Life Building* on Abbey Street while our oldest repository, *The Registry of Deeds* www.landregistry.ie is in the area of Kings Inns. *The Registry of Deeds* was established in the early 1700s and continues to hold registered land transactions, wills and property transactions to this day. Most visitors want to go to the research room of *The General Register Office* - ww.groireland.ie- which is also located in the Irish Life Building not far from *The Valuation Office*. The professional Irish genealogist knows the area and the opening times and the shortcuts to get from one to the other.

For visitors whose ancestors came from Dublin city, there is *Dublin City Library and Archive* specialised in everything about the city. It is located on Pearse Street and its contents can be viewed on the web - www.dublincity.ie

Access to lesser known

Advice from a local farmer in Meelick, Co. Galway

Ancestor Network
the
Irish Genealogy Experts

Ancestor Network Limited
www.ancestor.ie
Tel: +353 (0)87 0505296
info@ancestor.ie

records or indeed records that have not yet been microfilmed requires the services of a professional on the spot. Wills, schedules of assets and court records, maritime records are some of the areas where traces of ancestors can be found. If traces are found, copies of the documents can be obtained more easily by the genealogist on the spot.

So, it is easier, and in the long run cheaper, to employ a local professional genealogist rather than make the long journey and go back home with very little to show for such an expense of time and money.

Initial assessment

The value of an initial assessment of a client's needs cannot be underestimated. A professional Irish genealogist will be able to say almost immediately whether a search is feasible. If the client says that all they know about their ancestor was that he or she immigrated from County Clare in the 1840s and was called McNamara, an honest assessment would be that without

Family Reunion in Cloonmacart, Parish of Drumlish, Co. Longford

both surprised and delighted to find out that she had relatives in the States and that they were coming to see her. She confirmed that the farm was exactly the same as indicated in both the 1901 Census and in *Griffith's Valuation*. She also clarified which headstone in the graveyard belonged to her family as there were several families of that name in the parish.

When the day of meeting came, she welcomed her American cousins to the house, introduced them to her son, daughter-in-law and grandchildren and offered the traditional whiskey, tea and cakes. Her relatives really wanted to go out and walk the fields their ancestors had tilled. Then the whole troupe went to visit her daughter who was the keeper of the family history and photographs were taken. Promises were made to keep in touch using Skype and Facebook.

What happened on that day could not have been accomplished at a distance. The genealogist became a facilitator of a family re-union in the real sense. It was a moving and emotional experience for all.

The Future

Over the last ten or fifteen years the Internet has revolutionised genealogy in that it has made family research accessible to all. It is, as it were, the democratisation of genealogy. Family history research is no longer the preserve of trained scholars who know their way around the repositories. Traditionally, genealogy has been a science that searched the past and tried to construct family trees which lead up to the present make up of that family.

Today the social networks like Facebook are reaching forward searching around in the vast archive of the present. And success stories abound. The local professional genealogist has perhaps a new role; not only must the past be researched but clients are anxious to know whether or not they have any living relatives. And this is precisely how the local professional can be of great assistance in bringing families together.

Conclusion

From what has been said, it is clear that the professional Irish genealogist has an edge both in the traditional searching of the libraries and archives and in the modern developments where he or she can be a facilitator of family reunions. The local professional is a unique resource which should not be overlooked.

more precise knowledge it would be impossible to find relatives in County Clare. Of course, there is a lot to be said about the McNamaras in Clare in general without indicating any particular place or family. Coupled with the generic nature of the information is the fact that so much time has elapsed and that the memory of the families who had been there has faded.

New Developments

The reduction in the cost of air travel has made it possible for the sons and daughters of emigrants to visit the places where their ancestors once lived and, if they are lucky, find their relatives still living in the same place and maybe farming the same land. This development has brought the local professional genealogists out of the archives and libraries and into the countryside to search locally.

As an example, we were recently engaged to search for living relatives of the Horan family from California and New York. They had a lot of information about their ancestors, some of whom were from Drumlish, County Longford and some from Meelick in East Galway. While the search in Meelick did not uncover known living relatives, it was exciting for the family to visit the local church where their ancestors worshipped and to view the graveyard where they were buried even though no family specific tombstone could be found. What intrigued the family most on that visit was a conversation with a farmer in the townland where their grandfather had been born; they were impressed by his openness and friendliness and enthralled by the way he spoke. They filmed and recorded the scene as a souvenir of how their grandfather might have spoken.

It took a significant amount of preliminary on the ground research to identify the living relative in Drumlish because she had been married and had adopted her husband's surname. Once identified, a visit was arranged and the 85 year old woman was

The Irish Family History Foundation

karel kiely m.a.

The Irish Family History Foundation (IFHF) is a network of thirty three local **County Genealogy Centres** covering the island of Ireland that offer professional family history research services and an online research service at www.rootsireland.ie

The centres, many of which have been in operation for over 25 years, were formed in the 1970s and early 1980s when there was an upsurge in interest in roots and ancestor tracing. Following a model created at the centres in Corofin, County Clare and County Limerick, local groups around Ireland began to index their county's records. In 1984 many of these groups, in association with individuals interested in genealogy, came together to form the Irish Family History Society whose role was to develop standard procedures for indexing records and facilitate the development of links between the various groups. Gradually the indexing centres came to recognize that they shared a range of concerns and interests that could best be furthered by an umbrella organization dedicated to catering for the needs of local genealogy centres which became the Irish Family History Foundation.

The demand for genealogical research services from the Irish Diaspora required an all-island network of centres that led to the involvement of the centres from Northern Ireland. The initial work done on the indexation of the sources was manual; records were transcribed on to index cards, sorted and filed alphabetically. In the early 1990s a standard computer system and bespoke software were introduced in the majority of centres. The IFHF identified the various church records of baptisms, marriages and deaths as a priority for computerization. Other primary sources such as Griffith's Valuation, Tithe Applotment Books, 1901 and 1911 census and gravestone inscriptions were also included in the databases. Many centres have computerized civil records of births, deaths and marriages.

Substantial progress has been made in providing visitor facilities throughout the country with many centres operating full heritage/visitor centres and tourist offices. Some of our centres are based in some of the finest visitor facilities on the island, including Bru Boru in Cashel, Rothe House, Kilkenny and the Harbour Museum, Derry.

Sources used for family history research were originally recorded for other reasons such as taxation or as sacramental records. Family history research is a secondary use of this material. However, it is the original reason for this data being recorded that determines the structures, access and guardianship of these historical records. As many of those with Irish ancestry do not know where their ancestry may have originated in Ireland it makes sense to bring together all the counties available databases on one site to assist research. The All Ireland database offers the most efficient means of locating ancestors where no place of origin is known and of working out the complex relationships that family history research entails.

Parish Registers

Parish Registers of all denominations are the the primary source that we hold. These are an excellent source of genealogical research and the best starting point as they include baptisms, marriages and sometimes deaths for all classes of the population. They also pre-date civil registration which did not begin in Ireland until 1864 (Church of Ireland (Anglican) marriages were recorded from 1845).

Roman Catholic Registers are kept in individual parishes and, in most cases, were not deposited in national

COTTAGERS AT KILDARE.

CHURCH and TOWER at CASTLEDERMOT, Co: KILDARE.

repositories. This ensured their survival from the Public Record Office fire in 1922 and makes them one of the most comprehensive records available. The **Church of Ireland**, as the Established Church, had a more regular system of recording entries, using formatted books long before its Catholic counterpart, making their registers easier to research. These registers may be held locally by the rector or, more usually, will be in the **RCB (Representative Church Body) Library**. The IFHF centres have compiled computerized indexes from the original registers of all the major churches in Ireland. Please consult the information in **SOURCES** on the www.rootsireland.ie website for the individual county centres to find out which parishes are computerized. As work in the centres is ongoing further parishes will be available on an ongoing basis.

Civil Registration

Civil registration of births, marriages and deaths began in Ireland in 1864. These records are an important source of genealogical information; the registration of non-Catholic marriages began in 1845. The information available is concise and accurate, though there may be some omissions, particularly in the immediate aftermath of the introduction of civil registration.

Census Returns

For the purpose of genealogical research in Ireland the two complete census returns are those of 1901 and 1911. Some counties hold partial surviving census returns for other years. Please check the SOURCES list for each county to see what is available. From 1821 a census was carried out every ten years. Unfortunately, a large amount of this material was either destroyed by British government order, in the civil war in 1922 or pulped for paper during World War I. The returns give detailed information relating to all persons, including householders and their dependents, residents of army and R.I.C. barracks, convents, hospitals, and other institutions, similar to present day censuses. The barony, civil parish and townland were the territorial divisions used.

Gravestone Inscriptions

These can be very useful, particularly the Church of Ireland ones. However, many people did not erect gravestones. The recording of inscriptions varies from county to county and is also work that is ongoing in many places.

The Primary Valuation of Tenements,

The Primary Valuation of Tenements also known as **Griffith's Valu**ation, was undertaken in order to establish the value of land and buildings in Ireland as a basis for levying a local system of fair taxation under the **Irish Poor Law Act of 1838** and was carried out between 1848 and 1864. It listed every property holder in the country, with details of their houses, outbuildings, fields and gardens. The purpose of the vast survey was financial; to estimate the net annual value of every property in Ireland and determine the local taxation rate payable by each householder. It can be a useful indicator of the possible location of a particular family in an area, especially if the surname is an uncommon one.

The Tithe Applotment books

The Tithe Applotment books provide a record of

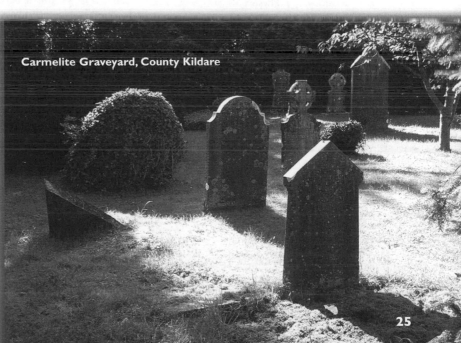

Carmelite Graveyard, County Kildare

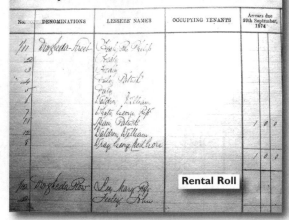

Rental Roll

the tithable land in each parish and were compiled in accordance with the Irish Tithe Composition Acts passed between 1823 and 1838. The purpose was to make an assessment of land values for the payment of tithes which was a tax levied on land for the support of the church. A tithe was a tax paid to Established Church (Church of Ireland), calculated as one-tenth of the rateable value of one's agricultural produce. Although an excellent genealogical source, it was only concerned with persons occupying upwards of 5 acres of land, thus excluding other classes such as cottiers, landless people and those living in urban settlements.

How should one start?

Trying to locate a particular person in the millions of Irish records can be daunting. A name or surname is not enough. You need to compile as much information as possible before you can start searching records in order to have the best possible chance of locating your ancestors. It is easier to focus on one or two individuals initially as you gain experience in your research. You should start your research where you know the ancestor spent the last years of their lives. Where did they live and where did they die? Do they appear in census records in their adopted country? Where were they married? Where were their children baptized? Are there other Irish families in the same area? Was there an obituary in a local paper? Did they name their farm after a place in Ireland?

If you start in your ancestor's home county or country and go back from location to location retracing the ancestor's footsteps you may be able to pinpoint locations where you need to search for records. If your ancestor emigrated from Ireland do not start your research in Ireland. It is also important not to skip generations.

What makes up a picture of your ancestors?

Name, name variations, Age, Physical description, Occupation, Religion, Spouse's name, Parents' names, Age of parents, Friends and associates, Other family members, Social/economic status

It is important to try to establish when they left Ireland as this may help to establish their age when they emigrated. If they were very young they may have been with their parents or other siblings. If older they may have already been married and travelling with a spouse and perhaps even children born in Ireland. The year of emigration can be checked with particular events in Irish history as different groups migrated at different times from particular locations. If you can learn when your ancestor left Ireland it may point to a particular location in Ireland. If you can establish the ship, date and port of arrival you can look for the passenger list for a particular voyage. This can provide information about whether they traveled with family members, neighbours or friends. Check the names of fellow passengers against land, church or census records.

If your ancestors did not emigrate from Ireland you will still need to follow the same steps by working back from the present, generation by generation. Use gravestones, memorial cards, and family memories to assist you. You will need to know a first name, surname and approximate year of birth, marriage or death. Remember there may be many variations of the surname. It is important to know the religious denomination. There are many people who do not have a county or parish of origin for their Irish ancestor. This means that a search can be impossible in some cases where the surname is very common; however, it can still be possible for some people to locate their Irish ancestor because of an unusual first name or because a combination of a husband's name and a wife's name reduces the likely possibilities. The IFHF's Online Research System offers you the ability to search across all the participating counties' records or to select one or more counties to limit/extend your searches.

Problems you may encounter

If your ancestor was born or married before 1820 it can be difficult to locate records of baptism and marriage. Many Catholic parishes did not keep records until around this date. The start dates of parishes vary from county to county. Church of Ireland (Anglican) parishes can be available from a much earlier date; sadly, however, a lot of these records were lost during the Irish Civil War. A county genealogy centre may assist in such cases by pinpointing the occurrence of a surname in a particular parish or location within a parish. The original parish registers can vary in content; there are omissions, gaps, mixing up of names, incorrect dates, torn or damaged pages and so on.

Some Searching Tips - www.rootsireland.ie

The recording of **first names** (or Christian names) varies from record to record, e.g. Elizabeth or Lizzie, Patrick or Pat. Please consult our First Names listing for guidance. Remember the wild card search facility can used, e.g. PAT% or %LIZ% On some records one or more of the parents' first names may not have been recorded in the original source, may have been illegible or been recorded incorrectly by the priest.

Because of the variant spelling of Irish **surnames** it is useful for a genealogist to be able to search for a range of spellings of a surname by the input of one surname only. Thus a search for the surname *Smith* can find all the records for *Smith, Smyth, Smythe,* and possibly another half a dozen variants. The main problem with this facility is not in its implementation in software, but in the choice of surnames that belong to each standard surname. The list may be too long: for example if *Smyth* includes surnames such as *Smitters, Smithies, Sixsmith, McSmyth* and *Smithson, Smithdale, Smithwick,* and many others, then the recall (meaning the coverage of possible options) will be very full. But the list of hits may then be so large that you cannot find what you need, i.e. the precision of your search may be too low to be useful.

When performing a **Standard Surname** search on www.rootsireland.ie, the search results includes the "surname (plus variants)". Clicking on this will allow you to view all surname variations that are being matched for your search. We recommend that you first try the Standard Surname Index to find what you are looking for and if that returns too many records select the Wild Card or Exact Match methods to reduce the number of results. Note that there are no standard first names used in the searches. First names searches are always done as a wild card search, e.g. the first name of Mar% will return matches for Mary, Maria, etc. but if you enter Mary, variants such as Maria will not be returned. Often the mother's surname was not recorded on baptismal records or it may be recorded on one child's baptism but not on that of a subsequent child.

You can search by year and increase or decrease the span of years according to your knowledge of possible dates of events. If a lot of records are returned for your search criteria (> 10) and no year was entered you will need to enter a year +/- 10 or 5 years to narrow your search results. You can choose to search all counties or one county or any combination of counties.

Please check the current **SOURCES** list for the county's whose records you wish to search to see what is available online. You may be searching for records too early or too late for the available sources. Computerization is still ongoing and the parish you wish to search may not be available.

Which record is that of my ancestor?

A search of the data may uncover many possibilities, e.g. a search for John Hughes in 1870 located 5 matches. You can either pay to view the details of each record or you can narrow the search results by entering more information in the search fields. For example, when searching for a baptismal or birth record enter the father's name, if known, to reduce the number of results returned. In the Advanced Search option you can enter the mother's names if known. However, there is no guarantee that the names are recorded exactly as you have entered it in the search fields or they may not be recorded in the original record.

On the All Ireland search you can search across all available (or any combination of) counties. If you know the county you can click to go that county and search its data only. On each county's own site you can narrow your search further by selecting the parish. The list of parishes also shows the denomination code after the parish name. In the census search you can alternatively select the DED (District Electoral Division). Changing the **Surname Match** method will also affect the number of matching records returned.

Why did I not find the record(s) I am looking for on this website?

There are few records in the database pre 1700 or after circa 1920. Please check that the year, parish or district that you are interested in is available on the site in our SOURCES list. Some parish registers have gaps in their records. Some civil births, deaths and marriages were not registered, especially in the earlier years of state registration which began in 1864 in Ireland. Church of Ireland (Anglican) marriages only were registered civilly from 1845. If you are unable to find the records that you are looking for please bear in mind the following:

Have you checked all the alternative or variant spellings of surnames and first names? As the parish registers were usually completed by the officiating minister, priest or registrar, it is not uncommon to find variations in the spellings used. Parish registers can be difficult to decipher; names and addresses were not standardized, and it may not be possible to find a complete family in one parish as families did move between neighbouring parishes and bordering counties.

The relevant set of church/civil records which contain your ancestors' records may not yet be computerized and available online. If you cannot find what you are looking for please note that not all records are online yet but may be held in the local genealogy centre and can be searched by the centre's staff on request. Please contact the relevant centre directly for more information. Please note that fees apply for commissioned research.

For further information on tracing your Irish roots and using our website please see www.rootsireland.ie or email enquiries@rootsireland.ie

The National Library of Ireland

The National Library of Ireland derives its origins from the Library of the Royal Dublin Society, founded in 1731. In 1877 a substantial portion of the Royal Dublin Society library was purchased by the State and the new National Library of Ireland was established.

The National Library of Ireland was established by the Dublin Science and Art Museum Act, 1877, which provided that the bulk of the collections in the possession of the Royal Dublin Society, should be vested in the then Department of Science and Art for the benefit of the public and of the Society, and for the purposes of the Act.

An Agreement of 1881 provided that the Library should operate under the superintendence of a Council of twelve Trustees, eight of whom were appointed by the Society and four by the Government; this Agreement also conferred on the Trustees the duty of appointing the officers of the Library. This historic arrangement ended with the establishment of the National Library of Ireland as an autonomous cultural institution on 3rd May 2005 under the National Cultural Institutions Act, 1997.

Situated in Kildare Street, Dublin, the Library aims to collect, preserve, promote and make accessible materials on or relating to Ireland, whether published in Ireland or abroad, together with a supporting reference collection. The Library's current collection of some six million items constitutes probably the most outstanding collection of Irish documentary material in the world, an invaluable representation of Irish history and heritage. Books, serial publications, newspapers, manuscripts, maps, photographs, official publications, prints, drawings and ephemera make up the bulk of the collections.

The National Library is open, free of charge, to all those who wish to consult the collections for material not otherwise available through the public library service or an academic library. A Reader's Ticket is necessary in order to consult most categories of material.

The Library does not lend books and reading is done in the various reading rooms. There is also a copying service and it is possible to get photocopies, photographs, slides, or microfilm of most items in the collections. The Library has an ongoing programme of exhibitions.

The Genealogical Office, the Office of the Chief Herald in Kildare Street, and the National Photographic Archive in Temple Bar are all part of the National Library.

Every year thousands of people visit the National Library to carry out family history research. Library material used by family history researchers includes the microfilms of Catholic parish registers, copies of the important nineteenth century land valuations (the Tithe Applotment Books and Griffith's Valuation), trade and social directories, estate records and newspapers.

The National Library has long been one of the key centres for family history research in Ireland. In recognition of this the Library's Genealogy Service - an expert service staffed by a panel of professional genealogists, together with experienced Library staff - is designed with the specific needs of family history researchers in mind. The Service, which is freely available to all visitors to the Library, offers the opportunity to consult with expert researchers who will advise on specific records and research procedure. Visitors to the Genealogy Service are offered expert advice on their research together with access to reference material and finding aids. Information leaflets, including a series on family history research in the Library, are readily available.

While the Genealogy Service is of particular value to first-time researchers, the Library also encourages more experienced family history researchers to continue to use the facilities for next-step advice from the genealogists and Library staff there.

The records most used by family history researchers in the National Library fall under the following headings:

Parish Records

For most family history researchers parish registers are the earliest direct source of family information, providing clear evidence of links between one generation and another (via baptismal registers) and one family and another (via marriage registers). They are particularly important for any information they provide for the period before the commencement of civil or State registration of all births, marriages and deaths in 1864.

The National Library holds microfilm copies of almost all Roman Catholic parish registers up to circa 1880. Most of the registers begin in the period 1810-1830 but some - particularly in counties along the western seaboard - begin somewhat later. In a number of counties in the province of Leinster registers begin in the 1780-1790s, while in the cities the start dates may be as early as 1760. In the case of three dioceses - Kerry, Limerick and Cashel and Emly - formal written permission to consult registers must be obtained in advance from the relevant diocese. Contact addresses and telephone numbers for these dioceses are listed in National Library Family History leaflet no. 2 (Parish registers), a copy of which may be obtained from the Library.

The Library's parish register microfilming programme is ongoing, with gaps in the collection being steadily reduced. A comprehensive listing, by diocese, of the Library's holdings may be consulted in the Genealogy Service and in the main Reading Room.

Land Valuation Records

The *Tithe Applotment Books* and *Griffith's Valuation* are nineteenth-century property valuation records which are much used by family history researchers providing, if only in part, a substitute for the loss of almost all nineteenth-century census records for Ireland .

The Tithe Applotment Books

The *Tithe Applotment Books* were compiled between 1823 and 1838 as a survey of titheable land in each parish. (They do not cover cities or towns). In general, the information contained in the *Tithe Books* is as follows: name of occupier; name of townland; acreage; classification of land; amount of tithe due.

The *Tithe Applotment Books* are available on **microfilm** in the National Library of Ireland. A guide to the Tithe Applotment Books on film is available in the Reading Room and in the Genealogy Room. The originals of the *Tithe Applotment Books* are held at the National Archives, Bishop Street, Dublin 8.

The Primary Valuation of Ireland (Griffith's Valuation)

The *Primary Valuation of Ireland* or *Griffith's Valuation* - carried out between 1848 and 1864 - is an important Census Substitute. It provides the only detailed guide to where people lived in mid-nineteenth century Ireland and to the property they possessed.

It is arranged by county and, within each county, by Poor Law Union. Each Poor Law Union is divided into electoral divisions, parishes (Civil Parishes) and townlands.

The *Valuation* contains the following information in respect of each townland or street: map reference number (location of the holding on the first edition six-inch Ordnance Survey maps); names of occupiers of holdings; names of immediate lessors (the person from whom the holding was leased); descriptions of tenements (holding) eg, "House, offices and land" ; area (in Acres, Roods and Perches) of each holding; valuation of buildings, land, etc. with Total Annual Valuation of each holding

Griffith's Valuation is available online at www.irishorigins.com

The Library makes this subscription service available free of charge to Library users in the Genealogy Advisory Room.

The county by county Index of Surnames, a listing of the surnames recorded in Griffith's Valuation and the Tithe Books, continues to be a much-used source. The Index of Surnames acts as a valuable aid to pinpointing relevant parishes and parish records, and to understanding the distribution of particular surnames in parishes throughout the country.

Trade and Social Directories

The National Library has extensive holdings of Dublin, provincial and countrywide trade and social directories. The first of the Dublin directories dates from 1751. Dublin directories, which steadily expanded in scope over the years, continue in publication up to the present time. While the earliest of the provincial directories - *Ferrar's Directory of Limerick* - dates from 1769, the nineteenth century saw the widespread publication of such directories. The nineteenth-century also saw the publication of countrywide directories such as *Pigot's Commercial Directory of Ireland* (1820 and 1824) and *Slater's Directories* (1846, 1856, 1870, 1881 and 1894), all of which may be consulted in the Library. To find out if the Library holds a printed directory for the area relevant to your research, check the Online Catalogue.

Newspapers

The National Library has the largest newspaper collection in Ireland, with complete files of many local as well as national newspapers. In newspapers, the bulk of information relevant to

Image © Courtesy of the National Library of Ireland

(Co. Sligo), Ormond (Cos. Tipperary and Kilkenny), Powerscourt (Co. Wicklow), Prior-Wandesforde (Co. Kilkenny), Sarsfield (Co. Cork) and Wicklow (Co. Wicklow). Estate archives contain the records of the administration of estates by landlords and their agents, and generally include leases, rentals, accounts, correspondence and maps, mostly dating from the eighteenth and nineteenth centuries.

The Department of Manuscripts in the National Library holds archives of many former landed estates. Estate archives contain the records of the administration of estates by landlords and their agents, and generally include leases, rentals, accounts, correspondence and maps. Please consult the Manuscripts Collections section on the website for more information.

Also of interest to family history researchers in the Department of Manuscripts are a number of collections of wills and will abstracts.

Information on Department of Manuscripts catalogues and guides is readily available from the National Library. For those intent on searching for relevant estate material, the expert advice from the Library's Genealogy Service will be of assistance in pinpointing who the relevant landowner might have been.

Maps

The Library's map collections comprise some 150,000 maps and include cartographic materials ranging from a 12th century coloured sketch map of Europe to the most recent Ordnance Survey maps. Special collections include the Down Survey maps (18th century copies of 17th century originals), 18th century estate maps - including the collection of surveyors Brownrigg, Longfield and Murray, maps commissioned by the County Grand Juries (late 18th -19th century) and Ordnance Survey maps (1830s onwards).

Both printed and manuscript maps are listed in a card catalogue. Manuscripts maps are also listed in the various manuscripts catalogues.

Other Sources

Other sources regularly consulted by family history researchers in the National Library include many printed family histories, often compiled and published for private circulation by individuals who have researched their own family history. It should also be noted that publications of local history societies from around the country often contain valuable transcripts of local sources, including gravestone inscriptions, freeholders lists, etc. Other relevant material in the Library's collections include the annual printed *Army Lists, Navy Lists, Royal Irish Constabulary (RIC)* publications including the annual *RIC Directories*, the *1796 Spinning Wheel Premium Entitlement List* (microfiche) and various other records of trades and professions, as well as a comprehensive series of *Registers of Electors*. Also, as research progresses, the appendices to nineteenth-century *Parliamentary Reports* may prove useful.

You will, most likely, reach a stage in your

genealogical research occurs in the form of advertisements and biographical notices (of birth, death or marriage). As there are few indexes available, relevant family information can be difficult to locate. As with the trade and social directories, newspaper information tends to be exclusive of the majority of the population: most births, marriages and deaths went unannounced and daily life continued without advertisement or report. Nonetheless, while direct family information may not be available, newspapers are rich in context and provide a sense of the community and times in which particular ancestors lived.

The NEWSPLAN database and Newspaper Index may be consulted on the National Library of Ireland website.

Manuscripts Records

The main components of the Library's manuscripts collections are Gaelic manuscripts, landed estates archives, maps, political material and literary papers. Of these, it is the archives of the former landed estates that are of particular interest to family history researchers. Among the more notable of these archives held by the Library are Castletown (Co. Laois), Clements (Cos. Leitrim and Donegal), Clonbrock (Co. Galway), Coolattin (Co. Wicklow), De Vesci (Co. Laois), Doneraile (Co. Cork), Headford (Co. Meath), Inchiquin (Co. Clare), Lismore (Co. Waterford), Monteagle (Co. Limerick), O'Hara

research when it will be impossible to find direct family information from the available records. While this may be disheartening remember that your ancestors lived as part of a community and that to understand something more of their lives and circumstances it is always rewarding to research the history of their locality. There are a multitude of sources for local history research in the National Library.

The Library's photographic collections - held at the National Photographic Archive in Meeting House Square, Dublin 2 - may also be of interest. Collections acquired from various commercial photographic studios such as Poole (Waterford and surrounding counties) and Wynne (Castlebar) include studio portraits and an unparalleled collection of topographical images of Ireland.

There are comprehensive finding aids to Library collections available in the Library Reading Rooms. Regularly updated information leaflets - with information on various Library collections and services - are readily available.

Exhibitions and publications: Exhibitions are held in both the main Library building and in the National Photographic Archive. The Library publishes a wide range of materials including books and guides, reports, booklets, document facsimile folders, CD-ROMS, calendars and postcards. These are available in the Library shop.

Admission to the National Library of Ireland: For Genealogy (microfilms) and Newspaper research, passes - which may be obtained in the main Library building - are required. Other readers must apply for a Readers Ticket (for which proof of identity and two passport photos are necessary). To view manuscripts, a supplementary Manuscripts Readers Ticket, issued by the Duty Librarian, is required.

Genealogy Advisory Service

The Genealogy Advisory Service is available free of charge to all personal callers to the Library who wish to research their family history in Ireland. No appointment is necessary. For first time researchers this Service is an ideal starting point, allowing them the opportunity to discuss their research with experienced Library staff, and ready access to important finding aids. More experienced family historians are also welcome to avail of the Service if they need assistance with on-going research. See Opening Hours.

The National Library does not offer a research service. If you wish to commission someone to carry out research on your behalf a list of researchers - private individuals and organisations - who have indicated a willingness to undertake family history research on a professional, fee-paying basis, can be downloaded from the Library website.

The National Library of Ireland does not sponsor or endorse the individuals or organisations named and will not be responsible for research arrangements, payments or results.

Library Opening Hours:
The Readers Ticket Office: Mon - Wed: 9.30am - 7.45pm; Thurs & Fri: 9.30am - 4.45pm; Sat: 9.30am - 12.45pm
Main Reading Room, Main Building, Kildare Street, Dublin Mon - Wed: 9.30am - 7.45pm; Thurs & Fri: 9.30am - 4.45pm; Saturday: 9.30am - 12.45pm
Genealogy Advisory Service Mon - Fri: 9.30am - 4.45pm
Manuscripts Reading Room 2/3 Kildare Street, Dublin Mon - Wed: 9.30am - 7.45pm; Thurs & Fri: 9.30am - 4.45pm; Saturday: 9.30am - 12.45pm
National Photographic Archive Reading Room, Meeting House Square, Temple Bar, Dublin 2 Mon - Sat: 10am - 4.45pm; Sunday: 12pm - 4.45pm
The photographic collections of the National Library of Ireland are in the process of being relocated to a new storage facility in the Library's Kildare Street Complex. The Photographic reference service will be available in the main Reading Room where a number of Photographic indexes and surrogate copies will be available. Staff in the Photographic Department may be contacted by email npaoffice@nli.ie

Contact details:
National Library of Ireland, Kildare Street, Dublin 2 T: +353 1 603 02 00 F: +353 1 661 25 23 E: info@nli.ie W: www.nli.ie

We are grateful for the help and assistance from Sandra McDermott and Ciara Kerrigan of The National Library of Ireland for their help and assistance with this article. All images that are the Copyright © of The National Library of Ireland are reproduced by Courtesy of The National Library of Ireland.

Robert & Elizabeth Blatchford

THE NATIONAL LIBRARY, DUBLIN.

AskaboutIreland.ie
A Key Resource for Family History Research
anne marie o'dwyer

The website, www.askaboutireland.ie provides a
wide range of valuable, free...

Valuation available to all, free of charge. It includes
a detailed map of Ireland, linked to every family
name and place name from the Valuation. In
...offers both modern and 19th
...ld and modern maps overlaid
...omparisons can be easily

...nd site also provides direct
...rdnance Survey Ireland
...vhich includes the 6 inch
...1837-1842 and the 25 inch
...1888-1913. The Ordnance
...osi.ie/) historic maps can
...odern maps, which are
...e access. Another mapping
...land.ie is the new map-based
...des users with a location-
...nd map-based access to
...dreds of articles on the site
...eography in every county.
...me Books and Letters is a
...boutIreland.ie. The townlands
...oks and letters are linked to
...Griffith's valuation, and to
...ompilation of place names,
...establish the origin of the
...s around the country. The
...e Irish version of place
...t forms of the name
...land. A range of interesting
...uded, such as details of
...d geographical features,
...f land in each townland.
...ovide a unique glimpse
...ferent parts of Ireland in

The Irish Family and Local History Handbook

Robert & Elizabeth Blatchford

www.genealogical.ie

...in excess of 1.5 million
valuation records, accompanied by full
map coverage of the country, with
each smallholding marked and
identified. This is the first time that a
major historical database for Ireland
has been linked to a powerful and
flexible map system. The *Ask about
Ireland* Griffith's Valuation project
makes a digitised copy of Griffith's

...oler civil parishes, namely St. John's
itself (most of), Dunmore, Rathcoole
(most of), Kilderry and Kilkieran.

The origin of the parish lies with the
original civil parish of the same name. A
parish of similar size seems to have
existed prior to the Norman occupation
of Kilkenny City. Its parish church
seems to have been in the vicinity of
Maudlin Street. The original name of
this parish has not survived.

John Street, Kilkenny
*Kilkenny County Library Postcard
Collection*
Enlarge image

After the Norman occupation, there was
an association with St. Stephen. Up to
1211, three separate parishes existed in this area, Fennell, Kilmologga and St. John's proper that corresponded to the
present city area of the parish. These three parishes along with a fourth, Loughmerans, were granted to the Augustinian
order in St. John's Priory by William Marshall in 1211.

John Street Flood 1947
*Photographic Collection of Kilkenny
County Library*
Enlarge image

After the Norman occupation, there was an association with St. Stephen. Up to
1211, three separate parishes existed in this area, Fennell, Kilmologga and St.
John's proper that corresponded to the present city area of the parish. These
three parishes along with a fourth, Loughmerans, were granted to the
Augustinian order in St. John's Priory by William Marshall in 1211.

The Reformation saw the amalgamation of these four small medieval parishes
into the civil parish of St. John's. All the Roman Catholic churches except St.
John's closed after the Reformation.

Search

· About Us · Lin
Libraries   EN

...lkenny City

Upload to this pag

Upload

Add your photos, text, vi
page.

Map Search

Find infor
videos by

Related Libraries

Kilkei
Cont

33 ontent

History & Heritage
Architecture
Big Houses of Ireland

the mid 1800s; an excellent resource for local history research.

Learn more about your local area from the digitised, historical collections of Irish public libraries, archives and museums

The virtual *Reading Room* on *AskaboutIreland.ie* includes extensive materials on historical, geographical, scientific and environmental topics of relevance to Ireland. Digitised photographs, maps, documents and illustrations on all aspects of Irish culture and history, past and present, can be located from among hundreds of articles. Sections from all public library authorities are provided on a wide range of Irish cultural topics for each county. The *History of Ireland* section includes a wide range of film clips on renowned events and famous figures in Irish history from the 1900s onwards. Sections also include Traditional Irish Crafts, Traditional Irish Cooking, Irish Traditions and Customs, Big Houses of Ireland, and Folktales of Ireland.

Specific information on the history and heritage of your local area can be easily located on *AskaboutIreland.ie* using the website's search facility, with links to hundreds of articles written by local studies librarians, academics and genealogists around the country.

View complete publications of digital books from the 1700s onwards

The *eBooks* section on *Ask about Ireland* allows you to enter a virtual library by providing online access to over five hundred ebooks from the 1700s onwards. Books can be searched by county or by subject. Additional eBooks are added to the collection on an ongoing basis.

The new *Talking eBooks* section offers a range of traditional Irish stories which are provided in both English and Irish languages. *Ask about Ireland's* unique collection of talking eBooks include *The Salmon of Knowledge, St. Brigid's Cloak, Oisín in Tír na nÓg*, along with many others.

Enjoy free access to the Irish Times and Jstor archives

Exact reproductions of all Irish Times articles published from 1859 to the present can be accessed through the Irish Times Digital Archive.

Numerous Irish journals in arts, humanities and science from the 1700s onwards can be accessed through the Jstor archives.

Access to both archives is available as a free service through www.askaboutireland.ie at your

local public library.

Explore the most comprehensive learning resource for children on the historical and cultural heritage of each county in the *Learning Zone* section

The Looking at Places section in the *Learning Zone* of *AskaboutIreland.ie* offers children a selection of educational activities, games and information on each county to learn about local Irish culture and heritage. Photographs, maps, drawings, pictures, audios, videos and eBooks can be located from among thousands of items on the site.

Discover more about Ireland's natural heritage on the new ENFO online service

The *ENFO* section provides practical, local and up-to-date information on environmental issues and step-by-step guides for greener living, many using traditional methods from the past.

Share your own information, photographs or video clips on all aspects of Irish culture and heritage

The upload facility on the *Ask about Ireland* website provides you with the opportunity to share your own research findings with others and contribute to the creation of the most comprehensive local and family history resource in Ireland.

www.askaboutireland.ie is managed by The Library Council and the Public Library Authorities. *E:* askaboutireland@librarycouncil.ie

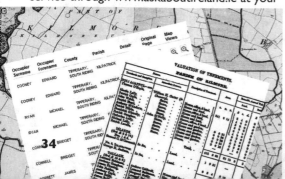

Irish Family Photography
1840-1940
Jayne Shrimpton MA

The history of Irish photography follows a similar path to photography elsewhere but its importance to the island's artistic and cultural life has only gradually been recognised. The study of Irish photographic history was re-awakened relatively recently by the work of specialists like Edward Chandler (see Sources) and some important books and useful online accounts have now been published, although further research would still be welcome, to advance our knowledge of the subject. This article aims to bring together some of the material currently available and to cast a specialist's eye over selected photographs, to show the main trends in portrait photography throughout Eire and Northern Ireland in the 19th and early 20th centuries. Hopefully it will provide a helpful historical context and some tips for family historians wishing to discover more about their Irish family photographs.

Beginnings of Irish Photography

The first Irish photographs were said to have been taken by Belfast engraver Francis Stewart Beatty in 1839 – the year in which the new invention of photography was officially announced to the world. In 1840 Beatty produced one of the earliest photographs of Belfast, his view of the city's Long Bridge (now Queen's Bridge) then

being described as a 'photogenic drawing'. For centuries men of science had been seeking more accurate methods of representing life than through drawing and painting and eventually, during the 1830s, ways of combining chemistry and optics to mechanically reproduce and fix images were successfully developed. In France Louis-Jacques-Mandé Daguerre was creating *daguerreotype* photographic images, while in England William Henry Fox Talbot was using a different process to produce *calotypes,* both men publicising their discoveries early in 1839. Groups of Irish amateurs – mainly members of the prosperous, leisured classes - experimented with photography during the 1840s using the atmospheric, shadowy calotype process, but entrepreneurs seduced by the commercial possibilities of the new medium followed the daguerreotype technique. The daguerreotype photograph - a unique, highly-detailed, mirror-like image on a silvered copper plate - was regarded as best-suited to portrait photography, for which there was a rising demand amongst the expanding middle classes.

Daguerreotype portrait studios

The UK's first professional photography studio was established by businessman Richard Beard, in London, in March 1841, swiftly followed by the opening of several more studios, mostly under license from Beard. However Ireland was exempt from the expensive license arrangements and its first *'Daguerreotype Portrait Studio'* opened in October 1841 on the roof of the Rotunda building in Dublin. Further studios soon appeared, including Leone Glukman's Dublin studio, which became well known during the 1840s from his popular lithographs after daguerreotype photographs of the Young Irelanders, including William Smith O'Brien, leader of the 1848 Rebellion. Daguerreotype studios were also established in other cities and large towns although industrial Belfast in

Fig.1 Carte de visite 1860s, by Nelson & Graham Photographers, Sligo
This undated photograph is an early carte de visite, the full-length view of the subject in a drawing-room interior typical of the 1860s. The gentleman supports himself, in usual fashion, with hand resting on a strategically-placed seat, the painted window also a common feature of studio settings of this decade. He is dressed formally in a stately, knee-length frock coat, genteel accessories including his top hat and furled umbrella. The reverse view of the mount, showing a neat design and advertising duplicates (photographic copies) suggests that a mid-1860s date is most likely.
Collection: www.cartedevisite.co.uk

Northern Ireland and Dublin in the south, with its well-heeled local clientele, were both in the forefront of commercial photography. Elegant daguerreotype photographs, protected under glass in velvet-padded folding cases, were essentially luxury portraits – the preserve of the successful middle and upper classes - so few examples survive in today's family collections. Their heyday in the 1840s and early 1850s was brief, for they were rapidly superseded by new photographic formats, but importantly daguerreotypes established the fashion for portrait photography and, in time, this would extend to a wider population.

Mid-century developments

In the post-famine years Irish country house photography flourished - amateur photography as practised by members of the landed elite, including Edward King Tenison and his wife Louisa, Mary, Countess of Rosse and Lady Augusta Dillon (nee Crofton), who achieved reputations for excellence on the photography exhibition circuit both at home and in England. Some of their albums and other surviving photographs are now held in public collections such as the National Photographic Archive, Dublin. www.nli.ie/en/photographs-introduction.aspx

Landscape photography was also very significant in 19th century Ireland – picturesque views of the island's dramatic scenery; many professional photographers specialised in scenic photography following the introduction of the new *wet collodion* process in 1851, which used more portable apparatus, facilitating work away from the studio. The rising status of photography at this time was reflected in the establishment of the Dublin Photographic Society in 1854, renamed the Photographic Society of Ireland (1858).

Our main interest here, however, is with portrait photography, which also advanced during the 1850s. Echoing trends in other areas, the number of commercial studios throughout Ireland rose throughout the decade, encouraged by the simpler and cheaper wet-plate photographic technique. Most professional portrait photographers followed the method developed in 1852 of blacking one side of the glass plate negatives with lacquer (*shellac*), to turn them into positive images. These *collodion positives* - popularly known as *ambrotypes* – were vulnerable, one-off glass photographs and, like daguerreotypes, were cased, or framed for hanging on the wall. Most popular between the mid 1850s and early 1860s, ambrotypes were affordable for some working-class ancestors and occasionally crop up in today's family collections, although surviving Irish ambrotypes are comparatively rare – no doubt partly due to the dwindling population associated with the Great Famine and mass-emigration.

Fig.4. Carte de visite c.1877-83, by J Mack Photo Artist, Belfast

This undated photograph is hard to date very precisely from the gentleman's appearance, although his full beard suggests at least the late 1860s or 1870s. The contrived 'outdoor' setting with painted backdrop and wooden fence indicates a likely year in the late 1870s or 1880s, which is confirmed by the Belfast trade data for J Mack listed on Flickr. Combined photographer dates and visual evidence offers a date rang of c.1877-83, while the design on the reverse, with its ribbon banner and filigree decoration, also accords well with this time frame. Collection: www.cartedevisite.co.uk

launched, following their introduction into Britain from France c.1858/9. The small *carte de visite* photograph mounted onto a card measuring about 10 x 6.5 cms first gained appeal in 1860 and, within a few years, cartes were available to many ordinary working people. They could be conveniently produced in multiples and were collected, given away and exchanged on a massive scale, leading to the production of the first purpose-designed photograph albums. As popular demand for photographic portraits soared, studios multiplied in Irish cities and towns, from Ballymena and Londonderry in the north, to Cork and Waterford in the south, to name but a few. Customers visited the photographer's studio mainly to mark special occasions in their lives, such as engagements, weddings, christenings, birthdays, *'breechings,'* coming of age, new job or retirement – or simply for the novelty of acquiring a picture of themselves posing in their *'Sunday best'* clothes. By the 1880s the larger cabinet print (measuring around 16.5 x 11.5 cms) was also becoming popular: together the carte de visite and cabinet print dominated 19th century photography and today many examples of both types of

photograph are to be found in
family collections.

Cartes de visite and cabinet
photographs continued to be
produced in the early-1900s but
they became increasingly
outmoded and were obsolete by
the First World War, while the
humble postcard became the most
common early 20th century format.
Scenic picture postcards were
already being created for the tourist
industry, but the new divided back
arrangement (with a line running
down the centre), introduced in 1902,
permitted a written message on one
half of the reverse of the card, leaving
the image on the
front untouched: thus
the postcard
became suitable
for portrait
photography.

The photographic images themselves looked
similar to earlier photographs, with their
contrived studio settings, and they remained
fashionable until the 1940s. People from all walks
of life were pictured on photographic postcards
mounts and many Irish examples survive today.

Amateur snapshots

Amateur photography, once the domain of the
upper classes, had been gaining ground since the
1880s, following the development of convenient
dry photographic plates and wider availability of
cheaper equipment, although it remained
essentially a middle class hobby until the early
20th century. In 1900 Kodak introduced
the user-friendly *Box Brownie*, which
came ready loaded with film, and this
popular camera was followed in the
1910s by new folding and pocket
models. By the 1920s many families and
individuals owned a camera and took
their own informal photographs or
'snapshots' of both special occasions
and everyday events. Usually snapshots
were taken outdoors, where there was
a natural source of light, and portrayed
their subjects relaxing in the garden at
home, spending leisure time with
friends and relatives, out and about on
day trips and enjoying their annual
holidays. Located in genuine settings,
these realistic images provide a
wonderful documentary record of the
not so distant past.

Fig.6 Cabinet print c.1895-6,
by Thomas Erwin, Ballymena
Cabinet prints were more
common than smaller carte de
visite photographs by the late
19th century and this distinctive
head and this shoulders oval
vignette composition was very
popular in the 1890s. Although
our view of the young lady is
limited, the style of her elaborate
bodice and full sleeves,
accentuated by broad lace
shoulder panels, demonstrate the
extreme fashions of mid-decade.
Collection: www.cartedevisite.co.uk

Dating and identifying Irish family photographs

As with many old family photographs surviving throughout the world, those originating in Ireland are often something of a mystery, bearing no helpful dates and names to help today's family history researchers. Successfully identifying pictures of past family members and placing them within the context of the family's history requires firstly accurately dating the photographs to within as close a time frame as possible. A combination of various techniques can be used for effectively dating photographs: identifying the photographic format (explained in the above sections); dating the physical characteristics of the card mount, including the design on the back; dating the visual image from the composition, studio setting and dress clues. Some of these methods are too involved to cover in a short article but they are discussed in detail in photograph dating books, while expert help is also available (see Sources).

Photographer information

One method used by many photograph researchers is investigating the photographer or studio named on the card mount. Most cartes de visite, cabinet prints and some postcards are printed with the name and address of the photographer or studio that took the photograph: by including these details, photographers aimed to identify their work and promote their business, but for us they offer helpful historical clues. In particular it may be possible to discover when a named photographer was operating at the given address: if approximate operational dates can be determined, these offer

useful time frame for the photograph, although this method produces variable results. If a particular studio only existed for only a few years, then obviously these offer a close date range, whereas if a business operated from the same address for many years, then the date range for the photographs that they produced will be correspondingly broader.

The main sources of information about photographers' activities are business advertisements in local trade directories and the census returns, which can supply a span of addresses and dates for a particular photographer/studio: however, it is important to be aware that they may not give complete operational dates as censuses will only show an address every ten years, while trade data is by nature inconsistent, since photographers did not always advertise their business every year. In some cases it may be necessary to consult the original census returns and local trade publications covering the area in question, although there may be a welcome short cut if the data being sought has already been compiled. For example, local Irish record offices and libraries may hold information about past photographers who operated in their respective city or geographical area. Some of the books covering photography in Northern Ireland and Eire listed in Sources below also include photographer listings.

Internet research

As with any aspect of genealogical research, the internet is also a very useful tool for investigating early photographers. Because Irish photography has not yet been fully researched and recorded, unfortunately there are not yet helpful online Irish regional photographer databases and listings comparable to those available for many parts of England, Scotland and Wales. However, a general internet search for the photographer or studio named on a family photograph may well produce some helpful links to public photograph collections or to local historical websites, individual blogs or a popular photo sharing site. For example, an internet search for J Mack of 84 York Street, Belfast (Fig.4) led to an unexpected A-Z Belfast photographer listing on Flickr (see Sources), the names and dates uploaded there

being based on advertisements in trade directories for certain years between 1863 and 1901. The useful professional website Photographers of Great Britain & Ireland 1840-1940 (www.cartedevisite.co.uk) provides biographies of selected photographers, including Irishman Robert William Simmons, who operated from c.1885 and became Galway's most fashionable photographer: this website is continually being updated and may well include more Irish photographers' profiles in the future. Some photographers were especially active and well known in their day: if any family photographs originated in such studios, it is possible to find out much about them on the internet and in books. The most famous example is the Lauder/Lafayette Studio, which began in Dublin in 1853 and expanded to become the premier Irish portrait studio with branches in Dublin and Belfast, finally closing in 1952 after almost a century.

An enduring legacy

Card-mounted studio photographs and family snapshots are all portable items: many were carefully packed alongside other treasured personal possessions and carried with Irish families who emigrated overseas in the 19th and early 20th centuries. As a result, large numbers of photographs originating in Ireland may now be found as far afield as the United States, Canada, Australia and New Zealand, either in public museum and archive collections or still in private hands, having been passed down through their families. Old Irish photographic portraits of earlier generations, whether they have travelled across the world or have stayed closer to home, provide a fascinating visual record of faces from the past: valued especially by the families to whom they connect, they also form an important part of Ireland's rich cultural heritage.

Sources
Public Photograph Collections
Here are just a few of the main collections but check for others.
National Photographic Archive (National Library of Ireland, Dublin)
www.nli.ie/en/photographs-introduction.aspx
The NLI historical photographs collection includes studio portraits and family albums
National Museums Northern Ireland, Belfast
www.nmni.com/um/Collections/History/Historic-Photographs
Historic photographs in the History Department collection includes portraits
Public Record Office of Northern Ireland, Belfast
www.proni.gov.uk
This collection includes many family group and wedding photographs from the Allison Studios, Armagh, which have recently been uploaded onto Flickr:
http://www.flickr.com/photos/proni
Blogs and photo sharing sites
Below are two examples of the kinds of random online sources that may provide information about Irish photographers and surviving examples of Irish photographs
jacolette.wordpress.com
This interesting blog is run by a photo-historian and librarian from Dublin, who. describes it as 'a gallery of Irish snapshot and vernacular photography.'
Flickr
http://www.flickr.com/photos/37053660@N02/4353121489This link to photographs on the popular picture sharing site provides a helpful A-Z listing of past Belfast photographers
Professional Services
Photographers of Great Britain and Ireland
www.cartedevisite.co.uk
The website's operator can supply operational data for Irish photographers for a fee
www.jayneshrimpton.co.uk
Portrait specialist, dress historian and photo detective dates and interprets family pictures
Books
Through the brass-lidded eye: Photography in Ireland 1839-1900, E Chandler & P Walsh (Guinness Museum, 1989)
A Century in Focus: Photography & Photographers in the North of Ireland, 1839-1939, W A Maguire (Blackstaff Press, 2000)
Photographs and Photography in Irish Local History, Liam Kelly (Four Courts Press, 2008)
The Irish: A Photohistory, 1840-1940 by Sean Sexton & Christine Kinealey (Thames & Hudson, 2002)
Family Photographs and how to Date Them, Jayne Shrimpton (Countryside Books, 2008)
How to Get the Most from Family Pictures, Jayne Shrimpton (Society of Genealogists, 2011)

John W Dulanty 1881-1955
from child labourer to irish ambassador
Claire Barlow

My grandfather, John Whelan Dulanty, was the last Irish High Commissioner and the first Ambassador to Britain (1930-1950). He was a friend of WB Yeats, Jack Butler Yeats, James Joyce, George Bernard Shaw and Count John McCormack, and knew all the Irish notables of the time and most of the influential British as well. He had a good relationship with Winston Churchill and was often received by King and Queen. In the 1960s in Dublin, I was told that *'were it not for your grandfather, Britain and Ireland would not be on speaking terms today.'*

His origins, however, were far more humble. I had always known that he had been born in Manchester of Irish parents and had worked in the cotton mills, but little else about his early life. I began research about four years ago and it has not been easy to find out much about his family and early life, though his later career is well documented.

In this article, I would like to pay tribute to a remarkable man and to his family who faced the horrors of industrial England in the nineteenth century. Many of you with Irish ancestry will have the same sort of stories and face the same difficulties in tracking them down.

Dulanty?

My first hurdle was finding his family in the censuses and BMD records. I soon discovered the bane of all family historians – spelling. Until the 1901 census, there are only two occasions where the family name is written as *'Dulanty'*: Delanty, Dellanty, Dulinty, Dulandy, Delahunty, Dolahunty, Doulanty and Dillanty all are used.

Now my searching is much easier. The variations in all the spellings involves mainly the vowels, so by using *'wildcards,'* most possibilities will come up by using *'D*I*nty'* or even *'D*I*y.'* I have found this works for most names, though occasionally there is an error in the initial letter – once I was looking for the name *'Catty,'* which I eventually found under *'Eleatty!'*

John William Delanty was born on 11th May 1881 at 9, Great Newton Street, Newton, Manchester to John Delanty, a builder's labourer and Ellen Delanty, formerly Cowley. Ellen had registered his birth on May 21 and *'made her mark.'* This was the first clue I had to her illiteracy, which explains so much. When she registered her children's births and deaths, the clerk made up his own spelling of the surname, which accounts for the variations. My grandfather had an amazing memory by all accounts, nurtured no doubt by his mother, who probably had developed hers to compensate for her illiteracy. I think that she probably encouraged her children's education in order that they should have better lives than hers.

Leeds

John Dulinty and Ellen Crowley had been married on 30th August 1874 at St Anne's Roman Catholic Church, Park Lane, Leeds, Yorkshire. They both lived in Wharf Street, Leeds. He was a bachelor, aged 30, a bricklayer's labourer and his father, Daniel, was a farmer. Ellen Crowley was a spinster, aged 27 and her late father, Francis, had been a weaver.

John Dulanty senior.

My father, Brian, said that John had come from Templemore, Co Tipperary. I have found a John Delahunty, baptised on 17th August 1849 in Clonakenny, whose parents were Daniel Delahunty & Anne Cormick, but I am not sure it's him, though it is near Templemore.

John left Ellen and their children sometime in the 1880s. I cannot find him in the 1891 census, but there is a census entry for 1901, that may possibly be him. At Leeds Model Lodging House, a common lodging house for men only, Dyer Street, North Leeds, there was a John Dulanty, aged 62, married, labourer, *'Gen'l'* (general), born in Ireland. This house had a Superintendent, his wife and two sons, four deputies and 360 lodgers. In the 1911 census, the only possible entry is for *'John Delahunty, 71, formerly General labourer, born Glenmore Co Tipperar,'* an inmate at Manchester Workhouse, Prestwich. A *'John Delahunty'* died in 1915 at Prestwich, which would fit with evidence from Ellen – in 1911, she was married, but on her death certificate in 1926, she was a widow.

John Dulanty with Eamonn de Valera
President of Ireland 1959 & 1966

John Dulanty remains a very shadowy figure. My father said he was a 'bad lot and a drunk.' Dad had heard a story that John got out of Ireland quickly as his uncle had shot Lord Lansdowne's agent, but he didn't believe it. There are 'Dullantys,' 'Dullentys' and even a 'Daniel' in Tipperary in Griffiths Valuations. 'Daniel Dulanty' lived in the Parish and Union of Templemore on 23rd November 1786 according to the Freeman's Journal – possibly John's grandfather. But John has left another problem – when he was actually born. According to the age he gave at various times in his life, he was born sometime between 1839 to 1847, or as late as 1849.

Ellen Crowley and her family

Unravelling Ellen's background has been very difficult, but I am left with a profound admiration for this remarkable woman.

Ellen was born about 1844 in Leeds. There is no record of her birth in either the Free BMD or Yorkshire BMD. The parish records of St Patrick's Chapel, Leeds, where her parents married in 1840, were destroyed in a fire and she was not baptised at St Anne, where she later married.

After much searching through strange spellings and transcription errors, I have worked out that her parents were Francis Crowley and Alice Dorah Pilsworth, both born in Ireland. He was a 'stuff weaver' (stuff is the course part of flax) as were his father, Patrick, and his probable brothers, Patrick and James.

Aged 26, Alice was left a widow with two young children. They were living in 'Kendalls Buildings,' which I suspect was a slum tenement and pulled down before the 1891 census. I suspect the apartments were one room per family – if that. Nearly all its adult occupants in 1841 and 1851 were born in Ireland and most worked in the mills - weavers, winders, dressers, carders,

John Dulanty with George Bernard Shaw

spinners, reelers, dyers and dressers. It seems that most people got out of it as soon as they could, but poor Alice lived there from before her marriage in 1840 until at least 1853. By 1851, she was a 'carder in flax mill,' earning half a man's wages. Alice died in 1889, living with her son in Bradford - a remarkable woman who survived unbelievable losses and hardships.

Ellen had probably begun work in 1853, aged 9, possibly working a 10 hour day, and by 1861, she and James were living at home, working in the flax mill

Ellen, the single mother

In the 1891 census, Ellen Delanty, aged 46, was a charwoman (they were employed to do 'chores' in other peoples' houses and came in on a daily basis, unlike 'housekeepers' or 'maids,' who 'lived in'). Mary Ann, aged 15, was a 'cotton reeler' and Daniel, 14, was a 'mechanic's labourer.' John W, aged 9, was a 'scholar.' Ellen had managed to keep living in the same house with 4 rooms, despite the main wage earner's departure, but life could not have been easy for her.

Jack Willie

My grandfather only became known as John much later in life - as a child and young man, he was always known as 'Jack Willie.' Unfortunately very few of his papers survived at home – after his death, his housekeeper who 'drank,' burnt nearly everything, 'on Mr Dulanty's instructions' – my

Ellen and Family 1905

The Dulanty Family
Manchester 1913

from drowning. But when David was fished out he was dead.'

I did send for David's death certificate and he did indeed die of drowning on 6th December 1894 in the Rochdale Canal.

O'Leary continues,

'The half-timer passed to the mill of G. and W. Brown, and one of his most wistful possessions is a leaving certificate from there, at the age of thirteen, declaring that he was then fully qualified to be a full-timer.

A full-timer he became - no more schooling - at the cotton mill of Tootal, Broadhurst at Newton Heath, near Manchester.'

But that was not the end of his education. He enrolled at night school – the Manchester Municipal Evening School of Commerce - the cartoon comes from their 1908 student magazine. He took law lectures as they were held in late afternoons. He started a boy's club which became the United Irish League and where he first began speaking in public. Apparently he was a brilliant public speaker.

His education meant he could move up the social scale from manual labourer to become a railway clerk, then Secretary and Registrar of the Technical School. In

Our Cartoon, No. 1.—Mr. J. W. Dulanty.

"THE CELT."

historian mother was incandescent with rage. But I have found a few gems. An article by Con O'Leary gives a few stories of his early life. When John was eleven, his full time education ended and in 1892 he began work.

'From the age of eleven he worked half-time in a cotton mill. One week he would clock on in the mill at six in the morning and after early dinner would go to afternoon school. During the following week he would go to early morning school, and after the dinner-break clock on in the mill.

He says that nobody who has not been through that child-slavery can realise or describe the terrible physical and mental fatigue of it.

'Most of us half-timers died young,' Mr Dulanty says. 'But those of us who have survived count the hardest day's work a luxury cushion after that juvenile sweat and toil and terror.'

This next story took place in 1894.

He was a 'nervous kid.' In the winter fogs at half-past five in the morning he was in terror crossing the Rochdale canal over the lock gates. David Eyre, a young Englishman and a Protestant, used to guide him across by the hand.

David was the man in charge of him in the mill. David saved him from the 'new chum' jokes passed on all half-timers when they first went to work.

When a load of yarn arrived at the mill, young John would throw the bundles up to David, who would fling them through an open roof, where they were caught again. David, when he saw the boy growing tired, would come down to the lorry and fling each load up through the roof from the ground.

John would have given his life for David. Indeed he tried to die for him.

One foggy November morning they were crossing the canal. David missed his footing and fell in. Young John, who could not swim, dived to his rescue.

An Irish labourer, following on the top of the lock, cried: 'Is that young Dulanty that is gone?' hereupon he plunged in and saved the future High Commissioner

addition, he was appointed educational advisor to Indian students in the northern universities.

In 1908, he supported Winston Churchill's unsuccessful election campaign for the North-West Manchester seat. This connection with Churchill proved valuable for Britain and Ireland later on.

In 1909, he married my grandmother, Annie Hutton. They had been 'keeping company' for some years – I have a letter from him, written in 1907. He had upset her and this was his apology, but he showed his diplomatic skill, even then. What the row was actually about, I have no idea – in three pages, he gives not a clue!

The British Civil Servant

My Dad, Brian Hutton, was born in 1910 near Manchester, and his brother, Sean in 1912, but in 1913 the family moved to London. John had been appointed an examiner to the board of education. Their first daughter, Clodagh, was born in 1914 at the family's home in Ealing. At some time during the next few years he adopted the Irish version of his middle name – he became John Whelan instead of John William – possibly after the Easter Rising of 1916.

In 1916, he was appointed Chief Establishment Officer at the newly formed Ministry of Munitions, and in 1918, when Churchill was the Minister, Principal Assistant Secretary. At the end of WWI, he moved to the Treasury as Assistant Secretary. His wartime work earned him two honours – CBE in 1918 and CB in 1920, both of which he always wore with pride, despite being Eire's representative. Had he remained a British civil servant, he probably would have been given a knighthood. A contemporary wrote of him, *'CBs as young as he was are almost always made K.C.B. in another ten years or so.'* (J Spendan Lewis)

The Businessman

In 1920, he left the civil service and became Deputy Chairman and Managing Director of Peter Jones in Sloane Square, a branch of John Lewis. He was on a huge salary for the time - £3,000 a year. I had always wondered how they had afforded Dad's education at Westminster School. With his lack of formal education, he gave his children the best he could afford. But he was *'a man who put service to his country before personal reward.'* He left this well paid post for one far less lucrative.

Trade Commissioner

The Irish Free State appointed him Trade Commissioner in September 1926. He had worked behind the scenes in the 1922 Anglo-Irish Treaty negotiations, so was well known in British and Irish circles. His business experience and contacts proved invaluable and he explored many aspects of the trade,

'He travelled with a cargo of pigs from Waterford to Smithfield Market, London, watching closely every stage from farm to train and steamer, and then the long train journey to London and the street journey to market.' O'Leary.

What a wonderful picture – a herd of pigs walking through the City of London!

High Commissioner

His appointment to the post in December 1930 came shortly after another unexpected bonus – the birth of their daughter, Aislinn. John was 49, Anne was 46 and my father was 20 – when his mother, rather embarrassed, was telling him of her pregnancy, at first he thought that his 17 year old sister was *'in trouble!'*

His role during the 1930s was of tremendous importance – his entry in the Dictionary of Irish Biography by Michael Kennedy covers the main aspects and the several volumes of the Documents of Irish Foreign Policy include much of his correspondence. But as yet there is no full biography of him – perhaps one day.

A Proud Grandpa
Author's christening 16th September 1946

Wartime

During the early part of the war, Ireland and England's relationship was far from perfect and stretched to near breaking point. Issues such as Ireland's neutrality, conscription in Northern Ireland and execution of IRA bombers all contributed to this. John's role at this time was crucial – he was in close contact with many powerful figures and he was personally known, liked and trusted by much of the establishment.

Winston Churchill, who became Prime Minister in May 1940, considered that Ireland was *'at war, but skulking.'* His past connections with the Irish High Commissioner were to prove valuable – Churchill said that *'he acts as a general smoother, representing everything Irish in the most favourable light.'* (Gilbert). I was told that Grandpa would be summoned to Downing Street, usually late at night and by the back door. As he talked (and probably raged), Churchill would pace up and down. Rather than sitting helplessly watching and listening, Grandpa would pace with him and be able to get in the odd word. Since so many of Grandpa's meetings were unminuted, very little of these conversations will ever be known.

The Dulanty family suffered a severe blow on 13th April 1940. Clodagh, their eldest daughter, aged only 26, died of a heart condition. John had adored her and his wife, my *'Granny Nan,'* never recovered from it. He persuaded my Dad to join the Irish Army, telling him that Ireland would come into the War. Whether he actually believed it or just wanted to *'keep him safe,'* we will never know, but it profoundly affected my father. He felt extremely guilty that he was *not 'doing his bit,'* and eventually he left and joined the RAF.

John Dulanty Fishing 1954

Post War

I was born in 1946, their first grandchild. He arrived home one evening, carrying a huge cuddly toy, wearing his formal clothes. He told Granny that he had come on the Tube, but Granny suspected he had come by taxi to the end of the road – she thought they were a 'wicked waste of money'!

He carried on as High Commissioner, through yet another change of government in Ireland, until 1950. On 26th July 1950, he became Ireland's first Ambassador. George Bernard Shaw, on his 94th birthday said that *'My birthdays are an unmitigated curse to me,'* but this one had the consolation that,

'It has been chosen for giving John Dulanty official recognition of the position he really occupies, that of Ireland's Ambassador to England. His Excellency has been a fact so long that it is only diplomatic decency to make it a form as well.' (Manchester Guardian 25th July 1950)

The Last Years

For twenty years, he was the voice and ears of the Irish government in Britain, but as Kennedy says,

'He was more than simply an intermediary: he could build bridges across the widest and deepest chasms through friendship, diplomatic skill, his personal wit, and his innate cunning. His natural modesty played down these capacities.'

and

'His easy manner, genial ways, and quick mind were the components of an unruffled personality. He was always courteous but appropriately barbed, where needs be, without being insulting, and ensured that the Irish position was always swiftly and accurately delivered to the British political establishment from the monarchy through the government to Whitehall.'

After five months as Ambassador, Grandpa retired that September and the newspapers were full of tributes. A farewell lunch was given for him by Atlee at 10 Downing Street. He still kept busy, taking up various directorships, attending dinners and special events, even making a trip to America.

In 1952, Annie, his wife of 43 years, died, a loss he never got over. She was a wonderful woman, who I remember quite well. She gave up a promising career as a mathematician to marry him, but never regretted it, though she hated

official occasions. Never let it be said that *'political correctness'* is a new thing – every contemporary account of her said she was *'Manchester Irish.'* As far as I can discover, she did not have a drop of Irish blood – her mother was from Staffordshire and her father, headmaster of a big school in Manchester, came from a long line of ships' caulkers in the London docks. Grandpa's British birth was frowned upon at the time and, had it got out that his wife was an Englishwoman, it could have finished him. Equally his poverty stricken origins and lack of formal education were glossed over.

His last few years must have been a lonely time for him. I remember him coming to our house to fly fish in the river – I hated this as it meant we could not go swimming! He was not very good with small children, but a relative said he was wonderful with teenagers.

He died in Westminster Hospital on 11th February 1955. His requiem mass was held at Westminster Cathedral on the 17th with the Cardinal Archbishop of Westminster presiding. John's great niece attended his funeral and said it was a grand event, but, as was common at the time, no women went to the burial. So I have no idea where he was buried, though suspect he is buried with his dear wife, Anne, and his daughter, Clodagh, somewhere in London.

Conclusion

The John W Dulanty story is a real *'rags to riches'* one, but he was never motivated by love of money. His passion was for Ireland, its people and its Arts. From the young boy, attending night school after a hard day's work, to the Ambassador, welcomed by the highest in the land, this was his driving force.

I am immensely proud of my illustrious grandfather; my only regret is that I did not know him, except as an impediment to my paddling. Maybe researching his life is a way to compensate and discover the man I never knew. Mine is the cry of all family historians, *'Why didn't I listen to them when they were alive!'*

References
Mill Hand to High Commissioner Con O'Leary Sunday Graphic & Sunday News 28th October 1934
Cartoon from *The Student Magazine The Organ of the Manchester Municipal Evening School of Commerce* Vol. IV No. 3 - January 1908.
Copy of letter from **J Spender Lewis to his father, John Lewis** - January 3rd 1923 in the author's possession.
Documents of Irish Foreign Policy. Volumes I – VI. Dublin 1998 – 2011
Dulanty, John Whelan - Dictionary of Irish Biography Michael Kennedy - Cambridge 2009.
Churchill War Papers Volume II: Never Surrender Martin Gilbert May - December 1940 (1994)

Thousands are Sailing
joseph o'neill

Routed by hunger and plague, a million fled. They clung to life, their only possession. The spectre of death made it precious. Yet, had they known the horrors before them, surely many would have slumped in despair and died where they fell. If they had, the Catholic Church in America would have been immeasurably diminished. Today, there are people alive in America who can remember their grandparents' stories of crossing the Atlantic in the middle of the 19th century. That's how near we are to this great calamity of Irish history.

The horrors of the Atlantic crossing a hundred-and-sixty years ago are beyond our comprehension. Dr. Curtis, a Dublin surgeon, a man not easily shocked, made many Atlantic crossings and saw what was involved. The emigrants, he said, suffered the torments of hell.

The first destination for most of them was Liverpool. Some didn't survive even this stage of the ordeal, like those rammed aboard *The Londonderry* one winter's evening in 1847, when It set out from Sligo. A storm broke. The crew herded 174 passengers into a single cabin, ignoring their screams. When she docked in Liverpool the cabin was opened and seventy-two passengers were dead.

At the inquest the coroner said he was not surprised to hear that the shipping companies provided sheltered pens for the cattle, while there was no protection for the emigrants, because in every other respect the animals were far shown more consideration than the human cargo.

Yet the exodus continued. In the years between 1846 and 1851 three hundred desperate Irish emigrants landed in America every single day. Some days more than a thousand were washed up on a single tide. By 1850, one in four of the population of New York was Irish born. Many of these new arrivals had been dumped there.

They were the victims of absentee landlords, desperate to clear their lands of pauper tenants. It was cheaper for the likes of Lord Palmerston to ship them across the Atlantic than to pay for them in the poor houses that were filling up the length and breadth of Ireland. They were shipped out of every Irish port directly to Canada. Packed into the steerage of ships never intended to cross the ocean, many arrived no more than naked skeletons. One in six contracted typhus, the most infectious disease knows to man.

Many of the 1848 emigrants never forgot their first sight of the mouth of the St. Lawrence River. The corpses of fever victims lay so thick on the water it seemed possible to walk from ship to shore. So many had died in the Quebec area in 1851 there were six hundred orphans, the children of dead emigrants.

The fortunate emigrants sailed via Liverpool, in the bigger ships, the American packets of 1,000 tons. These carried over 400 passengers. It was common for ships intended to carry no more than three hundred passengers to have five hundred packed in. Many had been built to carry slaves and contemporary commentators remarked that conditions for Irish emigrants were worse than those endured by slaves.

Most emigrants travelled in sailing ships, with no power other than the wind. Many sailed in winter when the Ocean was bristling with icebergs and raging with gales. They set out on a three thousand-mile ordeal. If all went well, they could hope

Steerage Class 1860s

to travel at a walking pace.

The holds were fitted out with bunks four tiers high, each the size of a coffin. This was the only space they had for themselves and their belongings. They carried a few pots and pans and the tools of their trade. When the weather was fine, they were allowed on deck to wash and cook. But in bad weather they were locked below in complete darkness, the holds sealed against the demented waves. One emigrant wrote of how a man died and was laid outside his berth. When the ship ran into a storm, belongings, passengers and the corpse were flung about the hold.

It was impossible to predict the length of the journey. Four weeks was good, though two months was common. The longer the journey, the worse the suffering. The shipping company was required by law to provide water and food. Most of the passengers depended on this to keep them from starvation. Even if the captain was an exceptional man and gave them their dues, supplies of food and water ran out if the voyage was longer than expected. It was then that the emigrant went thirsty and suffered what one described as *'a good starving.'*

The *Industry* left Sligo on St. Stephen's Day 1846. Its passengers were poor tenants, many of them driven out by landlords. They ran into a barrage of storms and their progress was slow. Food and water ran low. Their meagre rations were cut and cut again. When they reached land on 11th April 1847, after one hundred and six days at sea, two seamen and fifteen passengers

had died of starvation. Only a hungry man would eat ship rations. Gerald Keegan, a Sligo schoolmaster, recorded in his diary that the passengers were given nothing to eat for the first four days of the voyage. As soon as their ration of rancid sea biscuits was produced, they devoured them.

The conditions aboard convict ships, bound for Australia, were far better than on emigrant ships. The law stated that felons were to have meat on three days a week as well as Sundays and on the other days meat broth. This was a sumptuous diet beyond the wildest dreams of steerage passengers. Convict ships did not carry cargo. Emigrant ships were often laden with dangerous loads such as iron, which shifted in mid ocean. It was only in 1876 that the Plimsoll line prevented the dangerous overloading of vessels. The medical provision for convicts enjoyed was unknown in steerage.

Before the famine era, winter sailing across the Atlantic was regarded as far too dangerous. But the starving emigrants didn't have the luxury of time. They had to brave the cold and dark and risk the prospect of two months at sea. During the merciless winter months, many ships were driven back into port. It was common for ships leaving Derry to be weeks at sea and still within sight of the Irish coast. Lightning struck the *Creole*, bound for Philadelphia out of Derry, and destroyed two of her masts and two thirds of her sails. After three weeks tossed on the winter seas, she reached Cork.

Not all the emigrants' suffering was at the hands of the weather. Vere Foster, a philanthropist appalled by conditions on board, wanted first hand experience of the journey. He kept a diary of his weeks aboard the *Washington* - one of the better ships plying the Atlantic. What he discovered was far worse than he could ever have imagined. Passengers were beaten with ropes. The crew refused them food and water for days on end. When he protested on their behalf, he was bludgeoned to the ground and threatened with death. And this was no empty bluster. For once at sea, emigrants were subject to the same discipline as the crew and whatever rules the captain chose to impose. Those who disobeyed could be charged with mutiny and hanged.

Even the welcome sight of the American coast beckoning through the mist was not the end of their suffering. Many reached their destination and settled. But they were often so weakened by their ordeal they died during that first harsh winter. But before the emigrant could settle, he had to negotiate the perils of the docks. Thieves, pickpockets, ticket sharks, boarding house runners, confidence tricksters and a thousand other fraudsters clad in bright green waistcoats lay in wait.

But there were also those who extended the hand of friendship. In 1850 the Emigration Industrial Savings Bank and *The Shamrock*

newspaper published details of jobs. The Irish Emigration Society, in Boston, boasted that it found 'a hundred jobs a day' for Irish girls. *'Although I am in a strange country, I am not among strange people,'* Samuel Laird of Philadelphia, wrote to his family back in Limavady on 4 May 1850. Most Irishmen worked and lived with their own. They built the great canals, railroads and roads that were linking up the continent. Others worked in the building trade as carpenters builders' mates or as boat-builders and dockers. Women often became house servants or worked in the great clothing industry as seamstresses. They were glad of any work as they faced many obstacles in obtaining employment.

Job advertisements were often accompanied by the legend *NINA - No Irish Need Apply*. The Irish were generally confined to the worst jobs and the lowest pay. Wages fluctuated: in bad times they were often less than 50 cents a day and rarely more than a dollar.

Despite everything, most prospered. By 1850, half of all foreign born Americans were Irish. And they remained Irish, indelibly marked by the journey that cast them up on a shore half a world from home. They made an indelible imprint on the quality of American Catholicism.

A Convict in the Family?
tracing ancestors transported from ireland
Joseph O'Neill

Most people's knowledge of transportation is confined to the lyrics of the *Fields of Athenry*, a song now popular with football fans throughout Ireland. The narrator, a transportee, is no ordinary criminal. He is driven to *'steal Trevelyan's corn'* as the only means of saving his children from starvation.

It is easy to dismiss this as Irish sentimentality. Yet the evidence suggests he is typical of many condemned to exile. An 18th century observer noted that the Irish were by far the best of the criminals in Van Diemen's Land because *'a man is vanished from Scotland for a great crime, from England for a small one, and from Ireland, for hardly no crime at all.'*

It is difficult to date the beginning of transportation as a penal policy. But it certainly predates the time when the first Europeans reached Australia. By then it was an established part of British colonial policy and the statutory punishment for a certain type of crime.

The Vagrancy Act 1547 was the first of many laws whereby beggars *'could be banished out of this realm to wherever the government thinks fit.'* The courts despatched the first victims of this policy to Virginia in 1607. After 1615 felons might be condemned to labour in the East Indies or the American plantations. In 1640 Cromwell exiled the first group of Irishmen to Virginia, Barbados and Jamaica. Their crime, like that of so many who were to follow them, was political – they had risen in rebellion against the alien *'planters'* who had displaced them from the land.

An Act of 1679 legalised what was already the common practice of pardoning criminals on condition they accepted transportation to the colonies. Henceforward, transportation became the government's response to a growing number of crimes and was prescribed for Quakers who refused to take oaths, dissenters and those who burnt hay ricks or barns by night.

But it was during the 18th century that transportation attained a central role in English criminal law. By the Transportation Act 1718 it became an alternative to execution and as the number of capital offences increased year by year so did the number of transportees. Most went to the American colonies, all of which, except New England, accepted some convicts at some time. Between 1719 and 1772 about 30,000 were transported from Britain, about two-thirds going to Virginia and Maryland.

Of these between 7,000 and 8,000 were Irish. As there was no Poor Law in Ireland an Act of 1736 decreed that *'vagabonds wandering about demanding victuals'* were liable to transportation for seven years.

But Britain's desire to be rid of troublesome subjects was seldom matched by the dependencies' enthusiasm to accept them. As early as the end of the 16th century the American colonists made clear their anger at being used as a dumping ground for Britain's undesirables. With the War of Independence in 1775 America was no longer available.

Before an alternative destination was found the government resorted to the hulks – rotting vessels moored on the Thames. As crime increased and conditions on the hulks deteriorated the impetus to resume transportation increased. Many of its advocates believed it was far more humane than incarceration.

It gave criminals the chance to reform and to make a valuable contribution to their host

**Success
The Last Convict Ship**

country. Once there they would have no choice but to develop habits of industry which would prevent them from relapsing to a life of crime. In the early years of transportation many opposed it not because they believed it was too harsh but because they feared it was not harsh enough and that it had little deterrent value.

The first convicts were shipped to Australia, Britain's newest colony, in 1787. It was not formally abolished until 1868 but in practice it was effectively stopped in 1857, and had become increasingly unusual well before then.

The first shipload of convicts left Ireland for New South Wales at the beginning of April 1791. Between 1787 until the termination of the system, Australia received over 160,000 convicts, approximately 26,500 of whom sailed from Ireland.

When a transportation sentence was handed down, the convict was usually returned to the local or county gaol until preparations were made for transmitting him or her to the port.

Transportees from the southern counties were lodged in the city gaol at Cork. Built over the old gate to the northern part of the city, it's rotted walls were crammed to bursting. Those brought to Dublin were housed, along with other offenders, mostly in Newgate and Kilmainham Gaols. Newgate, Dublin's city gaol, was under constant criticism from reformers because of its deplorable condition and the fact that all categories of offender were housed together. Kilmainham was Dublin's county gaol, with arrangements for convicts much the same as in Newgate, except that transportees were separated from debtors and petty offenders.

From 1817 a holding prison, known as a depot, was provided in Cork to house the large numbers of convicts accumulating there. From 1836 a depot was provided in Dublin for female convicts and between the Great Famine and the opening of Mountjoy convict prison in 1850, temporary depots and Smithfield in Dublin and Spike Island in Cork harbour were used for men.

What manner of Irish people suffered this sentence?

They made up a high percentage of those transported from Britain – about a quarter of the total were Irish. Thirty thousand were men, three time the number of women. As well as those transported directly from Ireland another 6,000 Irishmen were transported from England.

About one in five came from Dublin. Seventy-five per cent were first offenders, people never before in trouble. One reason for this is that many of the convicted, about twenty per cent, were, like the first transportees, political offenders.

Most of the Irish criminal and transportation records disappeared in the flames that engulfed the Four Courts in 1922. Yet remaining records show crime was less common in Ireland than elsewhere in Britain. Irish country people were remarkably honest.

The most celebrated political transportees were the men of 1798, the sixty Fenians sent to Western Australia in 1867 and the leaders of the 1848 rising – Smith O'Brien, John Mitchell, Thomas Meigher, Patrick O'Donohue, Terence McManus, Kevin O'Doherty and John Martin. Their writings in exile won much sympathy for the Irish people and their struggle for independence.

Many of those convicted towards the end of the 18th century received no trial, but were condemned because they were out after curfew or merely suspected of disloyalty. Akin to these were the 'social rebels,' whose crime was to resist the landlord system that subjected them to intolerable hardship. Among these were

The Old Prison Hulk

the members of the various agrarian societies –
the Whiteboys, the Peep-of-Day Boys, the
Thrashers, the Rockites and Ribbonmen.

Even the British authorities accepted that these
men were not ordinary criminals, acknowledging
that social conditions drove them to desperate
measures. A Select Committee of 1823 concluded
that *'a large portion of the Irish peasantry live in a
state of misery of which one can form no conception,
not imagining that any human beings could exist in
such wretchedness.'* Conditions got no better for
fifty years.

Many of the *'disturbances'* that led to
transportation resulted from evictions, when
tenants, unable to pay their rent, were turned out
onto the road and their homes demolished.
Especially in the early decades of the 19th century,
many of these unfortunates came from the
troubled counties of Limerick and Tipperary.

After 1830 the *'tithe war'* – opposition by poor
Catholic peasants to the payment of taxes to the
Protestant Church of Ireland – added to the rural
unrest. In certain years, such as 1838, about sixty
per cent of those transported were Ribbonmen.

The last large batch sent to Australia were
4,000 *'Famine criminals,'* despatched in September
1848. For most of these transportation meant a
reprieve from starvation. In 1868, sixty-three
Fenians, convicted in Ireland, but incarcerated in
England, were transported from London. They
arrived in Western Australia, on 9th January, 1868
on the *Hougoumont*, the last convict ship to sail
from England to Australia.

Reading John Boyle's description of conditions
on the *Hougoumont*, tells us why the twelve week
voyage into exile levied such a high death toll. *'The
smells were . . . among the notable feature of life on
board. The combination of animal and human
excrement, foul water . . . the remains of old cargoes
and the perpetually rotten wooden structure of the
vessel herself must between them have produced a
dreadful stench, unrelieved by any kind of ventilation
system in the ship.'*

Fortunately for the family historian a rich store
of those condemned to such conditions are held
at the Irish National Archives. Most of these
relate to New South Wales, the almost exclusive
destination of Irish deportees. In 1837 one-third
of the total population of the colony was
composed of Irish Catholics, nineteen-twentieths
of them convicts or emancipated convicts. The
present State of Queensland was then part of
New South Wales. To this day there is a
concentration of Irish Australians in New South
Wales and Queensland.

But before searching those archives it is wise to
consult some of the general accounts. *Bound for
Australia* and *Criminal Ancestors* are particularly
useful as they give transcripts and facsimiles of the
many different types of document that you may
wish to consult.

Unfortunately, there is no single name index of
those transported to Australia. To locate a convict
you will need to have a good idea of when he was

**Killard Village, County Clare
1850s**

Convict Workers

tried and/or the date and ship in which he sailed to Australia. There are several ways of doing this.

Begin with the published censuses or musters of the penal colonies which often give the place of conviction and the date and ship of arrival in Australia. The names of those who arrived on the First and Second Fleets have also been published and are available in The National Archives(UK).

The microfiche index to the New South Wales Convict Indents and Ships, compiled by the Genealogical Society of Victoria, records the names and aliases of the convicts who arrived in New South Wales and Van Dieman's Land between 1788 and 1842. It also indexes ships recorded on the same documents. A copy is also available in The National Archives (UK) Library.

If you look at The National Archives' transportation registers you will find that convicts are not listed by name but by ship and date of departure. Once you have uncovered this information the registers will tell you where and when your convict was tried. It's at this stage you may be tempted to consult the trial record.

This is invariably disappointing. Trial records don't normally contain transcripts of evidence or information about the age or family relationships of the accused. Information given about occupation and residence is rarely accurate.

An application for clemency is far more likely to provide valuable information about your convict. However, you should bear in mind that applicants for clemency or a pardon wanted to prove that they were worthy of mercy - so they often included a lot of information designed to establish how respectable they were. This is just the kind of information about personal circumstances and family background that family historians want to know. However, you should bear in mind that the application is likely to paint a glowing picture of the convict and unlikely to include anything that reflects badly on him.

Petitions for clemency are arranged in coded bundles so you will need to use the registers to identify the right one. The registers are arranged by the date of receipt of the petition. They date back to 1797 and include information about the response to the petition, so you can sometimes find out something useful about a convict even if the petition itself does not survive.

Reports and returns from the judges also make fascinating reading. They sometimes include an unofficial transcript of evidence (together with comments on the characters of both witnesses and juries) as well as memorials and petitions from friends and relatives of the accused. The judges' reports and their circuit letters are also indexed. Applications and reports are available at The National Archives.

The National Archives of Ireland (NIA) holds a wide range of records relating to transportation of convicts from Ireland to Australia for the whole period, 1788 to 1868. In some cases the researcher may strike gold and find records of members of his convict's family transported as *free settlers*. In 1988, the Taoiseach presented microfilms of the most important of these records to the Government and People of Australia as a gift from the Government and People of Ireland. A computerised index to the records was prepared with the help of IBM and is available for use at various locations in Australia.

This index to the transportation records of the NIA is available online. Unfortunately, the records from which the transportation database was compiled, transportation registers and petitions to government for pardon or commutation of sentence, are incomplete. The collection of convict petitions dates from the beginning of transportation from Ireland to Australia in 1791. But all the transportation registers compiled before 1836 were destroyed. Therefore, if the person you are researching was convicted before 1836, but was not the subject of a petition, he or she will not appear on this database.

It is impossible to underestimate the importance of Irish convicts to Australia's development. They and their children formed the majority of the population from the first settlement in 1788 to the 1820's. They formed the great labour force which laid the foundations of Australia prior to the Gold Rushes of the 1850's.

Many successful Australians number Irish convicts among their ancestors. Among these is the renowned author and Booker Prize-winner, Thomas Kenneally, on whose work *Schindler's List* is based. He is proud of his rebel ancestors and maintains that far from being the dregs of society they were the most principled and courageous of men, who resisted injustice. They brought their value to Australia and bequeathed to their adopted country an idealism that has served it well.

In return Australia gave them the chance of a better life far from the tyranny of landlords such as Trevelyan.

Further Reading
D T Hawkings, *Bound for Australia* (Chichester, 1987)
D T Hawkings, *Criminal Ancestors, a guide to historical criminal records in England and Wales* (Sutton, 1996)
R Hughes, *The Fatal Shore: A History of Transportation of Convicts to Australia, 1781-1868* (London, 1987)
C J Baxter, *Muster and lists of NSW and Norfolk Island, 1800-1802* (Sydney, 1988)
C J Baxter, *General Musters of NSW, Norfolk Island and Van Diemen's Land, 1811* (Sydney, 1987)
C J Baxter, *General muster and lands and stock muster of NSW, 1822*
N G Butlin, C W Cromwell and K L Suthern, *General Return of convicts in NSW 1837,* (Sydney, 1987)
P G Fidlon and R J Ryan ed, *The First Fleeters* (Sydney, 1981)
R J Ryan, *The Second Fleet Convicts* (Sydney, 1982)
M R Sainty and K A Johnson ed, *New South Wales: Census...November 1828* (Sydney, 1980)
For details of names of Irish ships, numbers embarked, numbers landed, dates, ports from which the vessels set out and their destinations, see Charles Bateson, *The Convict Ships* (Sydney, 1974).
The National Archives (UK)
For an overview of UK records relating to prisoners transported to Australia, see The National Archives' leaflet on 19th century criminals and transportation. ; Records of transportation to Australia see *Transportation to Australia 1787-1868* Records of transportation to America and the West Indies see *Transportation to America and the West Indies, 1615-1776.*
Published Censuses/Musters of Early Australian Settlers (Including Convicts) Available The National Archives (UK) Records relating to trials by Quarter Sessions court are now held by the relevant British County Record Office. Records of trials by an Assizes court are held by The National Archives, Kew, London which has a handy leaflet on the subject. Few records have survived relating to trials in Ireland of convicts transported to Australia.
Websites:
The National Archives of Ireland - www.nationalarchives.ie/searchO1.html
Irish Convicts Transported to Australia -n www.rootsweb.com/-fianna/oc/ozaz/pascontue.html
Claim a Convict - www.claimaconvict.net/
The International Centre for Convict Studies - http://iccs.arts.utas
The Society of Australian Genealogists - www.sag.org.au/assources/crime.htm
Convicts in the Family - www.homeaustarnet.com.au/wmr/convicts
The National Archives (Transportation) www.nationalarchives.gov.uk/records/research-guides/transportation-australia.htm

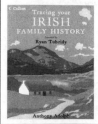
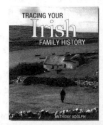

The Family and Local History Handbook 13

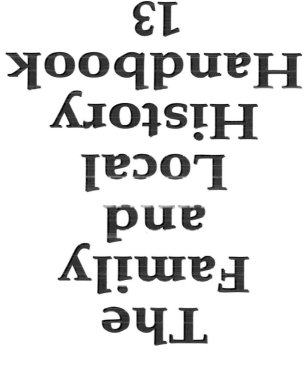

The Family and Local History Handbook 13

Irish Recorded Pedigrees

anthony adolph

Irish Surnames

Studying surname distribution is a useful and often reliable means of finding where your family came from in Ireland. Because families tended not to move about much, and had surnames that identified their kindred in terms of their common ancestry, there is every reason to believe that, right back into the Middle Ages at least, they are remarkably reliable indicators of ancestry.

The earliest Irish hereditary surnames were patronymics or papponymics, taking the name of the father of grandfather respectively. *Mac*, 'son [of],' is one of a handful of words common to languages worldwide that might have been part of the original tongue ('Proto-world') of our earliest human ancestors. It appears, for example, in native American tongues as *make* ('son'); in New Guinea as *mak* ('child'), Tamil as *maka* ('child') and Gaelic as *mac* 'son.' So when you address someone as 'Mac,' you're using a word that, in all probability, your 180,000 x great grandparents would have understood! M' and Mc are contractions of Mac, found in both Ireland and Scotland (it is a myth that Scots only used Mc and the Irish Mac: the spellings are completely interchangeable in both countries).

Papponymics, in which people took their grandfather's surname as their surname, are more common than people realise. Some *'Mac'* surnames, especially those that arose before the 11th century, often started as *mac meic*, meaning 'son of the son of.' MacLochlainn, for example, was

originally *Mac meic Lochlainn*. It arose with Domnall Mac meic Lochlainn and stuck, more because of Domnall's importance than anything his rather dull grandfather Lochlainn accomplished. The more usual papponymic, which became hereditary, thus including all male-line descendants of the ancestor so-named, was *Ua*, also spelled *Uí, O'* or *O*. In Irish society, the individual or his sons was not as formidable a social unit as a *fine* of interrelated first cousins: identifying yourself by who your grandfather was therefore made a lot of sense.

In the first millennia AD, before the Irish adopted hereditary surnames, people were defined both by their membership of a family group descended from a common ancestor, and also by non-hereditary surnames, that is, ones used for one person but which were not passed on to their children. Such surnames were chiefly nicknames and patronymics – Brian Boru's 'surname,' which was actually *Bóruma*, meant 'of the tributes,' whilst his patronymic was Brian *Mac Cennétig*, 'son of Cennétig,' for that was his father's name.

The first truly hereditary surnames emerged in the 8th and 9th centuries, amongst certain dynasties of abbots, such as the Uí Shuanaig in Rahen and Uí Búirecháin in Cloyne. The practise then spread into noble and royal families: Tigherneach Ua Cléirigh (O'Clery) Lord of Aidhne Co. Galway, appears in the Annals in 916 AD: his descendants claim to have the oldest surname still in existence. In royalty, High King Domnall of the Uí Néill called himself *Domnall Ua Néill*, not after his 5th century ancestor Niall of the Nine Hostages, but after his grandfather Niall Glúndub (d. 919), though the coincidence probably helped make it stick, for Domnall's son was called Áed Ua Néill and his great nephew Flaithbertach Ua Néill – the surname, later Anglicised as O'Neill, had become truly hereditary.

Tadhg Mac Dáire's 17th century poem *Contention of the Bards* maintains that Brian Boru (d. 1014) invented hereditary surnames, the better to preserve people's knowledge of their ancestry. This is clearly wrong, not least because the surname Ua Briain (O'Brien) only

Dun Ducathair, Inishmore, older than the oldest reliable Irish pedigree, yet full of atmosphere from the period covered by the legendary ones that go back to the sons of Milesius.

appears when his great grandsons Conchobar (d. 1078) and Cennétig (d. 1084) were exiled in the north, whilst the grandchildren of High King Muirchertach Ua Briain (d. 1119) called themselves not Ua Briain, as you'd expect, but MacMathgamna, after Muirchertach's son Mathgamain (d. 1129). It was from this time, however, that hereditary surnames started becoming widespread and clearly predated their general appearance in the British mainland and Europe.

As with Brian Boru's family, many Mac and O' surnames recorded not just any ancestor, but one who, as the progenitor of a clan or sept, was someone whose pedigree was likely to have been remembered. It was thus that, in his *Irish King and High Kings* (1973), Francis Byrne could write that *'many Irishmen boast descent from kings. The claim is not always justified, but it is not altogether preposterous, for Ireland had redundance* [ie, an excess] *of royal blood. In many parts of the country tribal sub-kings and provincial over-kings remained in power until the end of the sixteenth century, and by virtue of the Irish system of succession and of marriage laws, which approximated to polygamy, dynastic families proliferated at the expense of the commoner sort, so that Elizabethan officials complained that most Irishmen were bastards and claimed to be gentlemen.'*

North Gate, Athlone
Leinster

Sources for ancient genealogies

We know about ancient, orally-transmitted Irish genealogies because they were written down. The arrival in Ireland of literacy in the wake of Christianity in the 400s AD, and the extraordinary effect it had there, was described beautifully by Thomas Cahill in his *How The Irish Saved Civilisation* (1995). As he relates, the earliest written material probably took the form of historical annals and genealogies: these do not survive, but 7th or 8th century copies do.

Notable amongst the annals that contain much genealogical material are the *Annála Ríoghachta Éireann* – the *Annals of the Kingdom of Ireland*, now commonly known as the *Annals of the Four Masters*. Michael O'Clery and his companions, Peregrine O'Clery, Farfassa O'Mulconry, and my own possible relation Peregrine O'Duigenan, compiled these at the Convent of Donegal between 1632 and 1636, under the patronage of Fergal O'Gara, basing their work on *'the most authentic annals I [Michael] could find in my travels from AD 1616 to AD 1632 through the kingdom . . .'* Following these come two other compilations, *The Great Book of Genealogy* of Dubhaltach Óg Mac Firbhisigh (MacFirbis) (1666) and Roger O'Ferrall's *Linea Antiqua* (1709).

The Genealogical Office (GO) in Dublin is a treasure house of all forms of Irish pedigrees, for Gaels and incomers. Many of their records are also available, worldwide, on Mormon microfilm.

Sir William Betham, Ulster King of Arms, made substantial collections of Irish pedigree material. At the Genealogical Office (GO) in Dublin are his pedigrees of Milesian Families (GO 220-222) and Ancient Irish Families (GO 215-219). His transcript of O'Ferrall's *Linea Antiqua* (GO 145-7, indexed in GO 147) includes his own notes. His addition of coats of arms to this manuscript, though sadly without stated sources, are the basis for those in MacLysaght's *Irish Families*. Betham further collected genealogical extracts from plea and patent rolls from the reigns of Henry III to Edward VI (GO 189-193) and created two series of miscellaneous pedigrees (1st series, GO 261-276, 2nd series, GO 292-298). All his sketch pedigrees are indexed by McAnlis in GO 470. Betham's collections of received correspondence (GO 580-604 and NAI M.744-751) contain much useful material. Many of these records, of course, contain much on Cambro- Normans and later incoming families as well. In addition, the 16th and 17th centuries, Heraldic Visitations were made of the parts of Ireland where English families were most plentiful, to discover who was using coats of arms. If people could prove their right to do so, by male lineal descent from someone to whom arms had been granted by the heralds, their pedigrees were recorded. If not, they were forced publicly to 'disclaim' the arms, or quietly invited to pay for a new grant. The pedigrees (GO 47-9, indexed in GO 117) may go back a couple of generations or cover many centuries.

Also at the GO are records of Irish lords and baronets, largely but not always entirely duplicated by printed sources such as *Burke's Peerage*. Letter Books (GO 361-378) cover 1789-1853.

Genealogical research papers include those of Sir Edmund Bewley, T.U. Sadlier and Rev. H.B. Swanzy: material after 1943 includes much research on Gaelic family origins of migrant families as well as the more traditional subject of the Anglo-Irish. Many of the families and arms in all its papers are indexed in Hayes's *Manuscript Sources for the Study of Irish Civilisation* and a consolidated index to many of the GO's indexes was made by Virginia Wade McAnlis (NLI Ir.9291 C 11/1).

There are many genealogical details in the Topographical Poems and Annals, such as those of Innisfallen and Loch Cé, and much in the Irish Archaeological Society publications (especially John O'Donovan's notes) and the Journal of the Royal Society of Antiquaries Ireland. The Irish Manuscripts Commission's *Analecta I libernica* has published much useful material and criticism over the years, especially 'A Guide to Irish Genealogical Collections, 700-c. 1850' (no. 7, pp. 1-167); 'Treatise on the O'Donnells of Tirconnell . . .' (no. 8, pp. 375-418); 'Description and composition of Roger O'Ferrall's Linea Antiqua, 1709' (no. 10, pp. 289-299) and 'The O'Clery Book of Genealogies . . .' (no. 18, pp. 1-194).

Several modern attempts have been made to combine these older sources. John O'Hart, *Irish Pedigrees* (Dublin 1892: GPC, 1999) is a two volume work, the first cataloguing Milesian families, and second concerned with the Cambro-Normans and later incomers. O'Hart's laudable

Society of Genealogists Library

aim was to show that the 'mere Irishe' had a considerably more noble history and civilisation than their English oppressors and also, incidentally, to prove to the world that his own family were the rightful Princes of Tara. He drew heavily on *The Four Masters*, MacFirbis, O'Ferrall and other native sources, and also English-generated material such as the faints. 'The serious genealogist,' wrote MacLysaght, The Society of Genealogists in London has an interesting alternative collation of the main pedigrees, *Ancient Irish pedigrees, from Japhet Mac Noah to AD. 1265*, (anon Mss, 1908).

Much more reliable than O'Hart is M.A. O'Brien, *Corpus Genealogiarum Hiberniae* (Institute

for Advanced Studies, Dublin 1962). This names some 13,000 people alive before the 12th century. It is a secondary source, drawing heavily on MS Rawlinson B.502 (the earliest, dating from the 12th century); the *Book of Leinster Genealogies*; and the *Great Book of Lecan* and *Book of Ballymote*. Useful too is T. O'Raithbheartaig, *Genealogical Tracts 1: A. The Introduction to the Book of Genealogies; B. The Ancient Tract on the Distribution of the Aithechthuatha; C. The Lecan Miscellany* (Irish Manuscripts Commission, 1932).

M. Archdall (ed), *The Peerage of Ireland by John Lodge (1750)* 7 vols, Dublin, 1789) is important for ennobled Irish families to 1750. Since 1826, the family of John Burke (1786-1848) from Co. Tipperary, and later the Burkes' publishing house in its different incarnations have been publishing pedigrees of the peerage and gentry for the whole British Isles, including many Irish families, Gaelic and non-Gaelic alike. Because so many intermarriages have taken place over the centuries, very few Irish families – perhaps none – are really pure-bred Gaelic, Cambro-Norman or Anglo-Irish anyway. The latest *Burke's Peerage, Burke's Landed Gentry* and *Landed Gentry of Ireland* (supplement to 15th edition of the *Landed Gentry*) are on-line at www.burkes-peerage.net, but it is worth examining earlier volumes as well, using *Burke's Family Index* (Burke's Peerage, 1976) to discover all the families covered in different editions. Specifically Irish publications are B. Burke, *Burke's Irish Family Records* (Burke's Peerage, 5th edn, 1976), previously published as *Burke's Landed Gentry of Ireland* (1899, 1904, 1912 and 1958), and M. Bence-Jones, *Burke's Guide to Country Houses* vol. 1, 'Ireland' (Burke's Peerage, 1978). Notable too is a non-Burke's publication, J.J. Howard and F.A. Crisp, *Visitation of Ireland* (6 vols, London, 1897-1918).

The NLI, Trinity College Dublin, Society of Genealogists and the Mormons' Family History Library have huge collections of published family histories, of wildly varying quality and usefulness. Their catalogues, such as the Society of Genealogists at www.sog.org.uk/sogcat/access/ act as bibliographies. Many published sources are listed on the *Irish Ancestors* website www.irishtimes.com/ancestor/.

Older guides to published sources are:

The Irish section of the Society of Genealogists library in London, containing much material on early, recorded Irish pedigrees

B. de Breffny, *Bibliography of Irish Genealogy and Family History*, (Golden Eagle Books, 1964)

E. MacLysaght, *Bibliography of Irish Family History* (Irish Academic Press, 1982)

G.W. Marshall, *The Genealogists' Guide* (4th edn, 1903, repr GPC, 1973)

J.B. Whitmore, *A genealogical guide, an index to British pedigrees in continuation of Marshall's genealogist' guide* (repr J.B. Whitmore (1953)

116. Owen : son of Manus.
117. John : his son.

118. Andrew : his son.
119. John O'Crean : his son.

CROLY.*

Arms : Gyronny of ten ar. and sa.   *Crest :* A wolf pass. sa.

MAOLRUANAIDH, brother of Teige who is No. 108 on the "MacDermott" pedigree, was the ancestor of *O'Cruaidh-locha ;* anglicised *Crawley, Crolly, Croly, Crole, Crowley,† Campion, Hardy, Lake, Locke,* and *Poole.*

108. Maolruanaidh : son of Murtagh.
109. Teige : his son.
110. Dermod (Darby, Jeremy, or Jeremiah) : his son.
111. Sioda : his son.
112. Dermod : his son ; who was called *Cruaidh-locha* (" cruaidh ;" Irish, *hard ;* Gr. "kru-os ;" Lat. " cru-dus ;" and Irish " loch," gen. " locha," *a lake, a pool,* meaning " The Hardy Champion") ; a quo *O'Cruaidhlocha.*

113. Maccraith : his son.
114. Rory Mór : his son.
115. Hugh : his son.
116. Lochlann Mór : his son.
117. Lochlann Oge : his son.
118. Ranal : his son.
119. Connor : his son.
120. David : his son.
121. Donoch : his son.
122. Dermod (3) : his son.
123. Amhailgadh [awly] O'Croly : his son.

* *Croly :* Rev. George Croly, LL.D., poet, dramatic author, novelist, and divine, was born in Dublin in 1780. Having received his education in Trinity College, he went to London, and became distinguished in the world of letters. Throughout life he was a staunch Tory, in politics, and rendered material service to his party by contributions to *Blackwood* and other periodicals. He died suddenly on the 24th November, 1860, aged 80 years ; and was interred in the church of St. Stephen's, Walbrook, London, of which he had for many years been rector. His eloquence, his massive form, grave and inflexible countenance, and sonorous voice, rendered him a most attractive pulpit orator.

† *Crowley :* Peter O'Neill Crowley, a prominent Fenian, was born on the 23rd May, 1832, at Ballymacoda, county Cork, where his father was a respectable farmer. His uncle, Rev. Peter O'Neill, was flogged at Cork in 1798 for alleged complicity in the insurrection of that year. Peter inherited his farm, and cultivated it with great industry and thrift. He was a teetotaller from ten years of age ; he was studious in his habits, and was greatly beloved by relatives and friends. He early joined the Fenian movement, became one of its active propagandists, took the field in March, 1867, and formed one of a party under command of Captain M'Clure in the attack on the Knockadoon coastguard station. Afterwards he took refuge with a few comrades in Kilcloney Wood, county Cork, where, on Sunday, the 31st March, his small party was attacked and defeated by Military and Constabulary. He was mortally wounded in the fight, and died a few hours afterwards at Mitchelstown, whither he was conveyed—being treated with the greatest kindness and consideration by his captors. An immense concourse attended his funeral at Ballymacoda.

G.B. Barrow *The genealogists' guide, an index to printed British pedigrees and family histories 1950-75* (Research Publishing Co. (1977)

T.R. Thompson, *A catalogue of British family histories* (Research Publishing Co and SoG, 3rd ed 1980)

G.V. Flaming-Haigh, *Ireland: the Albert E. Casey Collection and other Irish materials in the Samford University Library: an Annotated Bibliography* (Birmingham, Alabama, 1976)

M.D. Falley, *Irish and Scotch-Irish Ancestral Research* (GPC, 1998). This includes several bibliographies.

The Croly (Crowley) pedigree from volume 1 of O'Hart's *Irish Pedigrees.* It shows the origin of the surname and a line coming down from it – no collateral branches are shown. To trace the line further back, O'Hart refers to the MacDermot pedigree, which in turn traces the line back to the O'Connor kings of Connacht, ultimately derived from the line of Heremon, son of Milesius. The numbering follows the system used in the 17th century genealogies, whereby Adam is 1, Noah 10 and their descendant Milesius 36.

The ancient pedigrees

Ultimately, Ireland owes its ancient pedigrees to its rich oral history. Gaelic Ireland had an *aos dána*

or 'mantic class' of professional bards, genealogists, poets, musicians and druids. Such a group is found in most tribal cultures that have not been crushed by invaders, for such were Homer and his contemporary poets in Greece, and the Jewish genealogists who remembered the ancient genealogies that were later recorded in the Bible. Under Brehon Law that persisted until the 17 century, ancestry underpinned the tribal system, which determined land holding, political allegiance and clan chieftainship: ancestors certainly counted, but it was not so much your ancestors as to whom you were related on account of your ancestry that really mattered. As John O'Donovan the great Ordnance Surveyor of Ireland wrote in 1849:

'those of the lowest rank among a great tribe traced and retained the whole line of their descent with the same care which in other nations was peculiar to the rich and great; for, it was from his own genealogy each man of the tribe, poor as well as rich, held the charter of his civil state.'

Maintaining this system were the *aos dána* were the *brithem* (law-giver, hence the term *'Brehon Law'*); the *filid* ('poet-seer'), to whom the *bard* was an attendant composer, usually of satires and panegyrics, and the *seanchaidhe* ('genealogist/storyteller/historian') particularly concerned with preserved oral genealogies. Their accuracy was astonishing: Yates once compared the *Tale of Dierdre* as recited by an illiterate storyteller with a *'very ancient manuscript'* at the Dublin Royal Society, and found the two compared 'almost word for word.'

The oral *seanchaidhe* or 'shanachie' (sometimes miscalled 'filid') traditions was severely disrupted by the English invasions of the 16th and 17th centuries, not least because the tie between genealogy and landholding, that had made their work so important, was broken. Some shanachies remained, however, though much reduced in prosperity. One of the last was Mrs Bridget Fitzgerald of Barrymore (1728-1808), called *Brighid na Senchas* or 'Bridget of the Histories.' She would go about the gentry's houses with her gold-handled walking stick, constantly updating her oral history, a practise perpetuated by at least two more generations of her family, probably with considerable accuracy. By her day, Bridget was a rarity, but by then many oral genealogies had been recorded.

How accurate are they?

Some pedigrees, such as the O'Neills,' are considered accurate back to the 5th century, but genealogies stretch much further back. 'Cuchulain, Fionn, Oisin, St Patrick, the whole ancient world of Erin,' as Yeats wrote rhetorically, *'may well have been sung out of the void by the harps of the great bardic order.'* They were more likely based in accurate oral traditions, but there is simply no way of proving this by cross checking them against any other sources – for there are none. Chadwick considered there was *'no adequate reason for doubting that the genuine native proportions [of the genealogies] may go back – I will not say without change,'* to the 1st century AD, *'or even one or two centuries earlier.'* Whilst some scholars are less generous, even the sceptical O'Rahilly accepted that Tuathal, who lived about 150-50 BC, was probably a real person.

It must be admitted that, if you look at ancient genealogies not so much as stores of ancient folk-memories than as charters to certain privileges and rights, subject to change according to the will of rulers and as political necessity demanded, it is easier to see why unhistorical features may have crept in. Ancient Irish genealogies tend to be divergent, tracing many lines back to common ancestors. This gives royal ancestry to many people with Irish roots. Whilst many pedigrees are undoubtedly accurate, some links may have been forged to flatter genealogists' patrons, to lend historical weight to contemporary alliances, or to legitimise usurpations or invasions. By showing ultimately that all Irish lords and princes were related, the ancient genealogists may also have been trying to impose a sense of unity on Ireland's disparate, warring tribes, in the hope of fostering a more peaceful society. Thus, Yeats wrote of the ancient bards *'riding hither and thither gathering up the dim feelings of the time, and making them conscious. In the history one sees Ireland ever struggling vainly to attain some kind of unity. In the bardic tales it is ever one, warring within itself, indeed, but always obedient, unless under some great provocation, to its high king.'*

The more prominent the king, the more lines were traced back to him. Often, early versions of royal pedigrees show far less offshoots than later ones, enabling us to see whose that may have been falsely added. The way to get the closest you can to the truth, therefore, is to work back to the earliest extant versions of the pedigree, and see what they have in common. Frustrating though the consequent lack of certainty can be, let's remember that very few countries have anything approaching Ireland's wealth of early genealogical material – at least the different pedigrees exist that can be argued over.

Going yet further back

Therefore, the average Irish genealogy will fall into several sections. First, the recent, 20th and 19th century family tree, alleged by oral history and supported by written records. It might stretch further back into the 1700s, perhaps only in the form of scattered references that can only be connected with dotted lines. In many cases, there will then be a gap, stretching back towards the start of the last millennium, to the character with whom the surname arose, the *'Dermot'* commemorated in the surname *'Mac'* [son of] Dermot, for example. In many cases, he will be found to have lived not far from where his surnamed descendants are still to be found, or, if not, there may be some tradition explaining the move of a sept or extended family from one area to another. The pedigree of the eponymous ancestor who is commemorated by the surname will then stretch back into the past. The more recent part of this is the likeliest to be accurate. Earlier on, especially before the 100s AD, one has to accept that a degree of wishful thinking may be involved, as the line connects back to ever greater Irish dynastic lines. Ultimately, almost all lines (especially those chronicled in O'Hart's work) go back to a central stem, coming down from Heremon, Heber and their brothers, the sons of Mil (or Milesius), who led the legendary Gaelic conquest of Ireland about 1,000 BC. He was in turn given an ancestry going right back to Noah, and thus to Adam and Eve.

The latter is a Christian conceit: all human had to be descended from Noah, the only man who survived the Great Flood. One of the purposes of the Milesian genealogies was to connect living Christians back to these Biblical patriarchs. To achieve this important link in the *'Genealogy of Salvation,'* the monks manipulated much older, traditional (and entirely non-Christian) material. Mil and his kin and their deeds are based in part on genuine memories of Iron Age invasions of southern Ireland from Celtic France and of Iron Age trade between southern Ireland and northern Spain (the traditional home of Mil). There was also a healthy input from the great Roman epic *The Aeneid*, written by Virgil at the end of the 1st century BC, and creatively retold and reinvented by sailors and merchants up and down the southern Irish landing towns in the first centuries of the Christian era. Mil's family, and the earliest genealogies coming down from them are not true, but that does not mean they are not worth exploring and appreciating. They serve to remind us all that there is a great deal more to Irish genealogy than lost parish registers and Griffith's Valuation. They connect us back, via the later, genuine Irish genealogies, to a rich world of mythology, whose lack of academic veracity is more than compensated by the glories of the tales themselves, and the many echoes they contain of our own ancestors' stories and beliefs: a fine, inspiring sustenance for us all.

This article is adapted from Anthony Adolph's book *Tracing Your Irish Family History*, which is published in the British Isles by Collins, and in north America by Firefly. For more information, see the author's website www.anthonyadolph.co.uk/bookspage.htm

Unearthing Your Mayo Roots
Karen Foy

Karen Foy looks back at the history of County Mayo and investigates the resources available to the family historian

Located in the West of Ireland, Mayo – in the Province of Connacht - is the third largest county in the country. Stretching from the Atlantic to the counties of Sligo and Roscommon and from Killala Bay in the north to Lough Corrib in the south, Mayo is packed with fascinating and picturesque areas to visit. The landscape is varied - rich in botanical, archaeological and historical places of interest. Clean sandy beaches are teamed with rugged cliffs whilst the lakes and flat terrain can boast a majestic backdrop of mountain ranges. The Irish spelling of Mayo is Maigh Eo meaning *'plain of yew-trees'* and with its dramatic vistas and heritage sites, the county has a great deal to attract those whose roots originate here.

Fight or Flight . . .

The 19th century saw Mayo's demographics change considerably. In 1800, the population of Ireland was estimated to be at four and half million people but within forty years this had doubled to just over eight million. The pressure on the economy was immense and inhabitants began to feel the strain as sections of land were divided into smaller and smaller plots. With barely enough land to keep families in food, for many, destitution followed and they became dependant on the humble potato as a staple food product to keep them from starvation. Just when it was thought things could not get any worse, disaster struck and in August 1845, the fungus *Phytophthora infestans* began to destroy the potato crops causing the green leaves to blight and rot, producing a terrible stench. With a third of the country's crop destroyed in that year alone and virtually all of the next year's crop unusable, Ireland suffered complete devastation as the Potato Famine took hold.

The workhouses were unable to cope or alleviate the poverty as they were already full to capacity and throughout the decade, with little in the way of relief or a change of fortune, many died of starvation related diseases.

County Mayo was struck particularly hard as nearly ninety percent of its population was dependent upon the potato. Families had very little choices and were left with the options of *'fight'* and try to get through this disastrous period, seeking food where they could – or *'flight'* and join the thousands of others who had decided to emigrate overseas to America, Canada or across the Irish Sea to England in an attempt to start a new life. In the ten years between 1841 and 1851 it is believed that the population of Mayo fell by over 100,000 as a result of deaths and emigration caused by the Potato Famine.

The county had nine workhouses at Belmullet, Castlebar, Swinford, Claremorris, Killala, Newport, Westport, Ballina and Ballinrobe. Swinford Union Workhouse was established under a Board of twenty eight guardians. Six acres of land on which to construct the building were acquired from landowner William Brabazon for an annual rent of £18.00. It had accommodation for 420 adults and 280 children with the first inmates admitted on the 14th April 1846. Remaining in use as a workhouse until 1926, it was initially inundated with people – often as many as 200 per day - desperate to seek relief and shelter at the height of the famine. But those 'lucky' enough to gain entry found little solace as conditions were harsh and undignified. Such was the high death toll from starvation and disease - even within the institution - that a grave was left open here to receive the continual stream of corpses. Today, the building is now the Swinford District Hospital but at the rear remains the site of one of the best preserved mass graves in the country which was restored to the memory of the 564 famine victims that are buried here. In 1960, a simple plaque was erected in respect for those who died without a coffin or even a simple sermon.

Perhaps your ancestors sought refuge in a Mayo workhouse or even used the services offered by the soup kitchens – a government scheme introduced in 1847 which started to phase out institutional relief and provided soup for the starving. The Quaker's (Society of Friends) were also instrumental in setting up soup kitchens in many areas when they not only provided sustenance but also distributed clothes (when people had pawned theirs for money

for food and wore nothing but rags) and seeds to help them to attempt to grow their own produce.

Where Next - Research Centres ...

Due to Mayo's mass emigration it has created a diaspora of people worldwide whose roots can be traced back to the county. Not all emigration was caused by the Great Famine – as far back as the 1700, Mayo emigrants settled in Monserrat and Jamaica whilst later, Australia, America and Canada drew those seeking new challenges and adventure. As a result, the Irish Genealogical Project has appointed two research facilities – The Mayo North Family Heritage Centre and the South Mayo Family Research Centre.

Mayo North Family Heritage Centre, Enniscoe, Castlehill, Ballina, Co Mayo, Ireland T: + 353 (0) 96 31809 E: normayo@iol.ie W: www.mayo.irish-roots.net
South Mayo Family Research Centre, Main Street, Ballinrobe, Co Mayo. Ireland T: + 353 (0) 94 954 1214 E: soumayo@iol.ie W: www.mayo.irish-roots.net

The resources available at the centres is staggering and a gold mine for anyone wanting to 'push back' further with their Irish roots. Alongside Civil Registration records and grave inscriptions there are Church of Ireland records from 1744, Roman Catholic records from 1794, Presbyterian records from 1819 and Methodist Records commencing ten years later. Dig deeper using Tithe Applotment books, Griffiths Valuation Tenements, Rent Rolls and lists of migrants. With over two million records housed between the two centres, the possibility of finding that next snippet of information which could open up a whole new avenue of your family research is vast.

Don't forget to search online at Ireland's largest family records database - www.rootsireland.ie/. The Irish Family History Foundation has ensured that there are over 18 million records online covering everything from Gravestone Inscriptions to Passenger Lists. Their system is easy to use and navigate your way to the Mayo records section. All you need to do is register to view the indexes but for further access into the record you will need to purchase credit vouchers from the site.

Perhaps you're trying to build a picture of the area in which your ancestors lived, then a great place to start is at www.genuki.org.uk/big/irl/MAY/ Genuki is a large genealogical information service for the UK and Ireland which lists a whole host of relevant resources specific to a particular town, village, city or area. The information gathered is like a huge tree in itself and provides links to other websites and possible avenues of research. Each page starts off with a description of the location along with details of its archives, libraries, church records, newspapers and periodicals – fantastic if you are not familiar with the area. We all hit a brick wall at some point during our genealogical quest so why not head over to Genuki and you may be inspired with another avenue of research that you'd previously not thought about.

It's often said that family history and local history research is closely related – in fact, they come hand in hand with the results of one often influencing the changes in another. Finding out more about the area in which your ancestor lived and worked is essential. Changes in industry may be the reason that they moved to or from the region, the demographics may explain the type of work your ancestor chose to carry out whilst built up areas and their poor housing conditions may explain a forebear's short life span or multiple deaths within their family. Historical Directories are fantastic for gauging this. Look out for Pigot's and Slater's Directories of Ireland at the local archives they will give details about your place of research during a particular year and list everything from the gentry, clergy, shopkeepers and traders to the names of its public houses and the times when the Post Office despatched its letters!

Perhaps you have a specific question about County Mayo or would like to find out more about a certain family name with known links to the area, then why not ask other likeminded researchers by joining the Rootsweb Mailing Lists at www.rootsweb.ancestry.com/ There are a number of pages that deal with queries on the county as well as 'offshoots' that concentrate on certain towns and villages within the region allowing you to target those with compatible knowledge. Also use the Rootsweb service to research a particular surname - you may find others with the same pursuit allowing you to share and expand your findings.

It's All in the Name ...

Whatever region you originate from there will always be a selection of surnames strongly connected to that area and Mayo is no different. Examples of the most common include: McNulty, Brennan, Foy, Kelly, Doyle, Walsh, Duffy, O'Conner, Murphy, Moran and O'Malley. Some of these will be more prevalent in the north of the county whilst others are more common in the south. The Ireland Genweb Project is a great online resource for finding out more about a specific Mayo surname by taking those of most historic importance or popularity within the county from the Matheson's birth index study of the 1890 census. The site allows you to click on certain names to find out more or post your own links and questions on the Mayo Mailing List. The Surname Registry is invaluable with huge lists of relevant names, their location in Mayo and the contact details of researchers whose descendants have emigrated to various parts of the world – indispensable if you're trying to track down a rogue ancestor. www.irelandgenweb.com/

Widening the Net ...

Don't worry if you're unable to get over to Mayo to carry out research in person – there *is* an alternative in the form of a professional genealogical research service which specialises in ancestry in this area at www.mayo.irish-roots.net/

Their findings will be presented in a family history report including copies of relevant genealogical documents and maps in an effort for you to learn more about the lifestyle your forebears led, the particular area they lived in and the occupations they were employed in. Well worth considering if you would like a thorough investigation of your Mayo roots – the costs involved of organised travel and accommodation

Westport monument to St Patrick of the Octagon

from afar to carry out your own enquiries may far out way the fees charged for this service.

Official birth, marriage and death certificates can be obtained from Castlebar Civil Registration Offices, New Antrim Street, Castlebar, Co. Mayo www.irish-certificates.co.uk/registry/comayo_castlebar.html whilst the Mayo County Library holds a substantial array of genealogical resources from census and parish information to descendant

Mainistir Chonga

Bunaíodh mainistir Chonga go luath sa 7ú haois agus scriosadh í go luath sa 12ú haois. D'athbhunaigh Toirdhealbach Ó Conchobhair, Árdrí na hÉireann, í timpeall 1135 agus rinne ardeaglais di. Chuir a mhac Ruaidhrí breis foirgneamh léi. Ghlac muintir na mainistreach le Riail Agaistín tamall ina dhiaidh sin, ach go gairid ina dhiaidh sin, sa bhliain 1203, rinne an ridire Normannach Uilliam de Burgo ionsaí ar bhaile Chonga agus b'éigin an mhainistir a thógáil dá bhara.

Ní sheasann anois ach fíodhrogán den mhainistir. Téann an séipéal atá anois ann agus b'fhéidir an cuibhreán iríse freisin, mar a mbíodh na manaigh tráth ag obair nó ag paidreoireacht, siar go dtí an 13ú aois bara. Tá sraith aon go bhfuil an doras thuaidh agus na doirse críochnála a oscláionn amach ar an gcláirseann ón taobh thois inne sínte sí dtia iontuaithe Uilliam de Burgo. Baineann an doras agus na fuinneoga breátha ar dhá thaobh de leis an Teach Caibidle, áit a mbíodh grú na mainistreach á thionantú agus caibidil as an Riail á léamh gach lá. Is anseo freisin a thagadh an mhuintir le chéile chun faoistin phoiblí a ghearú peacaí a dhéanamh. Tá na sníoláin sa mhainistir iar a bhfuil siar na cainamáille leis an Fhroinc(sí) ar chuid de na dealbha is fearr sa tír.

Fuíos – Na an scáth nóiríb a mainistir seo foir chairim í ionstamán as mBainacha Oibheacha Phoibíl.

Cong Abbey

The monastery of Cong, founded in the early 7th century, was destroyed by fire in the early 12th century. Turlough O'Conor, the high-king of Ireland, refounded the abbey around 1135, and his son Rory constructed new buildings. The community adopted the Augustinian rule several years later. Soon after, in 1203, the Norman knight William de Burgo attacked the town, and again the monastery had to be rebuilt.

Very little remains of the abbey. The present church, and possibly also the fragmentary cloister, where the monks once worked and prayed, belong to the rebuilding of the early 13th century. The north doorway of the church, and the elaborate doorways that open onto the cloister from the east range of the monastery, might pre-date the destruction by William de Burgo. The doorway with two fine windows on either side of it belongs to the chapter house, where the monastery's business was conducted and a chapter of the rule read every day. This was the also where the community gathered to confess their sins publicly. The sculpture in the abbey, which suggests links with western France, is some of the finest in Ireland.

Notice – This ancient monument is in the care of the Commissioners of Public Works for the state under the provisions of the National Monuments Act. The public are requested to aid the Commissioners in preserving it. Injury or defacement is severely punishable by law.

Cong—from Conga [the Narrow Neck of Land (between two lakes)]

Cong Abbey

Quiet Man Museum

every year. It is said that here, on the 21st of August 1879, an apparition of Our Lady, St. Joseph and St. John the Evangelist appeared at the south gable of Knock Parish Church and was witnessed by fifteen people. Perhaps follow in the footsteps of your forebears and enjoy the spiritual experience. Find out more at www.knock-shrine.ie/

Although Westport is probably the most popular tourist town, Castlebar and Ballina are the most highly populated. Castlebar was originally a garrison town and took its name from an early settlement which was built up around the de Barra Castle in the 11th century. Today, it

charts for local families – start your enquiry at www.mayolibrary.ie/en/LocalStudies/GenealogyResources/. Don't forget to widen your search using the National Archives of Ireland at www.nationalarchives.ie

Building the Bigger Picture ...

Situated in the south east corner of Clew Bay on the Atlantic ocean side is the town of Westport. Commissioned by Lord Sligo of nearby Westport House as a place for his workers to live, the town of Westport was designed by English architect, James Wyatt in 1780 – today, one of the hotels has been named in recognition of his contribution. The tree lined river Carrow Beg runs through the town and the famous mountain Croagh Patrick, one of Europe's best known places of Pilgrimage, provides a backdrop to the area. At the base of the Croagh Patrick and facing west to where many emigrants sailed across the Atlantic in search of a better life overseas, is the location of the Irish National Famine Memorial, commissioned by the Irish Government and unveiled by President Mary Robinson in 1997. Created by John Behan, the bronze sculpture is entitled *'Coffin Ship'* with its rigging depicted in skeletal figures – a stark reminder of desperate times.

If your ancestors lived in this part of the county, why not visit the Clew Bay Heritage Centre www.westportheritage.com/ here you will find more about the development of the town, its importance as a port and the influence of local families. The building is packed with artefacts from local ironmonger's ledgers and barber's chairs to windows from the Westport workhouse. They also run a successful family research service for the Westport and Clew Bay area providing a preliminary online questionnaire to help them to acquire the best information for you.

Nearby Knock (the Irish equivalent of Lourdes) attracts one and half million people to its Shrine

provides a central location for visiting the area. Ballina is situated on the banks of the River Moy and is home to Moyne Abbey, Rosserk Friary and St Muredach's Cathedral. Travel towards the border with Galway and you'll find the magnificent ruins of Cong Abbey confirming that wherever you venture in Mayo, the county has a rich and diverse history, taking you from medieval monasteries to its connection with 20th century film greats. (A small thatched cottage in the village of Cong houses a museum to the 1951 film *'The Quiet Man'* starring John Wayne and Maureen O'Hara and filmed on location here.) Whatever century your ancestors lived in Mayo, you're guaranteed to find something of interest to help you to build a bigger picture of their lives!

So, if you've discovered Mayo roots by birth or by marriage, it's time to research them further. There's no denying that there can be some hurdles to overcome with any Irish genealogical research but don't be put off. There are literally thousands of databases, records and resources out there waiting to be uncovered and provide that crucial information you need. From the professional archivist to the amateur family historian with specialist knowledge on the subject, you're guaranteed to find someone who is enthusiastic and willing to help you with your *'mission,'* answer your questions or point you in the right direction to find out more - enabling you to create a fascinating picture of the past and add to the Mayo branch of your tree!

Karen Foy has been a keen family historian for just over ten years. As a freelance writer her articles appear regularly in family history magazines such as Family History Monthly.

The National Archives of Ireland
aideen m. ireland
head-reader services division

The National Archives of Ireland was established by legislation on 1 June 1986 and was created out of the original State Paper Office (founded in 1702) and the Public Record Office of Ireland (founded in 1867). It is situated on the site of the original Jacob's Biscuit Factory in Bishop Street, Dublin 8.

The primary function of the National Archives is to collect, evaluate, preserve and make available the records for which it has responsibility.

The primary role of the National Archives is the preservation of departmental records and records transferred from other government agencies and making them available for public research under the terms of the National Archives Act, 1986 when they are thirty years old.

Apart from departmental records the National Archives holds testamentary and other court collections which are over twenty years old and business, charitable, estate, family, personal and trade union collections. The National Archives also holds some Church of Ireland parochial registers or abstracts or transcripts thereof.

Records of all Government departments which have existed since the foundation of the State (subject to legal restrictions) are now in the National Archives.

Reader's Tickets & Rules for Readers

The Reading Room may be used by any member of the public who holds a current Reader's Ticket. Members of the public may apply for a Reader's Ticket on the day of their first visit to the National Archives provided they have photographic identification. They must obey the Rules for Readers, which they must sign before a Reader's Ticket will be issued to them. Failure to observe the Rules for Readers may result in the cancellation of the individual's Reader's Ticket. An application for a Reader's Ticket may be downloaded in advance of visit - www.nationalarchives.ie/contactus/tickets.html - although the Reader's Ticket is only given on personal application.

Readers must have their Reader's Ticket with them at all times - both for entry to and exit from the building as well as for ordering documents or microforms. If a reader fails to bring along a Reader's Ticket, no records or microfilms will be issued for consultation.

Reading Room

The National Archives is open to the public for research. The Niall McCarthy Reading Room and Microfilm Room are fully equipped with finding aids to the various categories and forms of records held and staff at the public counters are available to give advice and assistance.

The Reading Room is open to the public from 10.00 a.m. to 5.00 p.m. Monday to Friday, excluding public holidays, the December media preview and a period over Christmas and the New Year. For further information on opening / closure dates please consult the National Archives website - www.nationalarchives.ie/contactus/closures.html

For information on ordering records and on record ordering times - www.nationalarchives.ie/contactus/opening.html

Readers should be aware that not all records are held on the Bishop Street site. For

College Green, Dublin

Burke's House, Arran Quay, Dublin

those holding a valid Reader's Ticket records may be ordered in advance of a visit - www.nationalarchives.ie/contactus/records.html

Genealogy Service

A Genealogical Service, staffed by professional genealogists, is also available on the same floor as the Reading Room. It operates the same hours as the Reading Room. The Genealogy Service is intended primarily for first - time researchers and visitors but more experienced researchers are also welcome to use it. No appointment is needed.

Responsibility for Records

The National Archives Act is primarily concerned with Departmental records (the records of Government Departments, the Courts, and the other state bodies listed in the Schedule to the Act). The National Archives Act enables the National Archives to give advice to state sponsored bodies, local authorities and other public service organisations on records under their control, and to acquire records from them.

The National Archives also has overall statutory responsibility for Church of Ireland parish registers of marriages which pre - date 1 April 1845 and baptisms and burials which pre - date 1 January 1871 since they were declared to be public records by Acts of 1875 and 1876. Until recently almost all the surviving registers were still held by the parish clergy, although most of them have now been transferred to the Representative Church Body

Library, Churchtown, Dublin 14 - http://ireland.anglican.org/index.php?do=about&id=42

The National Archives Act also permits the National Archives to acquire records from private sources.

Major Collections

Almost all of the records accessioned by the Public Record Office of Ireland before 1922 were destroyed by fire and explosion during the Civil War in June 1922. Included were some collections transferred from the State Paper Office, although most of these survived intact. All collections which are open to public research are held in the National Archives in Bishop Street or are available, on request, from off - site storage.

Records of Government and State Agencies:
Board of Health / Cholera, 1832 - 4
Board of Trade, 1840s - 1930s
Commissioners of National Education, 1831 - 1963
Commissioners of Intermediate Education, 1879 - 1918
Commissioners of Charitable Donations & Bequests, 1801 - 1961
Crime Branch Special, 1887 - 1920
Famine Relief Commission, 1845 - 7
Fenian Papers, 1857 - 83
Irish Crime Records, 1848 - 93
Irish Record Commission, 1810 - 30
National Archives (formerly P.R.O.I. & S.P.O.) 1867 -
Office of Public Works, 1831 - , and its precursors,
Directors General of
      Inland Navigation, (1730 -), 1800 - 31
Civil Buildings Commissioners, 1802 - 31
Ordnance Survey (part of), 1824 -
Penal Transportation, 1788 - 1868
Poor Law Commission
      & Local Government Board, 1822 - 1922
Prison administration records, including the
  • Government Prisons Office, 1836 - 80
  • General Prisons Board, 1077 - 1920
  • Prison registers, 19th - 20th centuries
Proclamations, 17th - 19th centuries
Quit Rent Office, 17th century - 1942
Registrar General of Shipping and Seamen and Mercantile Marine Office, 1863 -
Royal Hospital Kilmainham, 1684 - 1933
Shipping agreements and crew lists, 1863 - 1979
Tithe Applotment Books, 1828 - 37
Valuation Office, and Boundary Survey, 1827 - 1925

Chief Secretary's Office, 1790 - 1924; and its constituent departments / records including :
  • Chief Crown Solicitor's
      Department, (1815 -), 1859 - 90
  • Convict Department, 1778 - 1922
  • Official Papers, 1790 - 1880
  • Privy Council Office, 1800 - 1922
  • Rebellion Papers, 1790 - 1807
  • State of the Country Papers, 1790 - 1831

Official and non Official Sources
Census of Ireland, 1821 - 1911:
Enumerator's Returns / Heads of Household returns, 1901, 1911 are complete, survive for the whole country and are available on - line - www.census.nationalarchives.ie/

Partial survivals, 1821 - 51, which are incomplete or in transcript or abstract form, survive for:
Antrim 1851: Cavan 1821, 1841: Cork 1841: Fermanagh 1821, 1841, 1851: Galway 1821: King's County (Offaly) 1821: Londonderry (Derry) 1831 (supplemented 1834): Meath 1821: Waterford 1841
There are no census returns for the period 1861 - 91.

Church of Ireland Registers of baptisms, marriages and burials including:

- Original registers of some parishes; microfilms of surviving registers of some diocese, as well as abstracts and transcripts from other parishes.
- There are also thirteen volumes searches in parish registers against baptisms undertaken in the early part of the twentieth century as evidence of age.
- Some genealogical researchers, in the early decades of the twentieth century, have made specific surname searches in parochial registers.
- Parochial registers (including those for the Church of Ireland) are becoming available on-line at www.irishgenealogy.ie/.

Court Records

- Probate Office of the High Court (formerly the Principal Probate Registry) and the District Probate Registries, mostly 20th century.
- Incumbered / Encumbered Estates Court, Landed Estates Court, and Chancery and Land Judges, mostly 1850 - 20th century, Many of the Landed Estates Court Rentals now available at www.findmypast.ie/content/landed-estate-court-records

Diocesan Court Records / indexes

Records of the former Prerogative and Diocesan Registries, 16th century - 1858 :
Administration Bonds, 1612 - 1858
Administration grants, 1595 - 1804
Marriage licence bonds, 1623 - 1867
Wills, 1536 - 1858

Genealogical Abstracts

Abstracts compiled by Betham, 16th - 19th centuries
Genealogies etc. compiled mostly by Crosslé, Tennison Groves, Groves - White, Jennings, Thrift, 17th - 19th centuries
Parish registers, 17th - 19th centuries
Baptism, marriage, burial abstracts, 17th - 19th century
Wills and grants of probate, 16th - 19th century

Testamentary Records / calendars

Grants of administration, 1858 -
Grants of probate, 1858 -

Principal Registry Schedules of Assets,
(1873 - 90, with gaps) 1924 -
Wills, 1858 -

Transcripts / Calendars

Abstracts and indexes of archives which were destroyed in 1922, including:
- Calendars of court records, 13th - 19th centuries
- Fergusson, extracts from Exchequer records, 13th - 18th centuries
- Lodge, abstracts from Chancery patent rolls, mainly 17th century

Also:

Commissioners of Charitable Donations and Bequests, 1800 - 1961
Irish will registers and indexes, 1828 - 79
Irish administration registers and indexes, 1828 - 79
Marriage licences, 1629 - 1818
Marriage settlements, 18th -
Miscellaneous copies, transcripts and abstracts
Also older finding aids, 16th - 20th centuries
Searches in Census returns, 1841 & 1851 - largely for Old Age Pension purposes
Searches in parochial registers, 19th century - largely for Old Age Pension purposes

---

National Archives of Ireland
Bishop Street, Dublin 8
T: + 353 1 407 2300
F: + 353 1 407 2333
E: mail@nationalarchives.ie
W: www.nationalarchives.ie
All enquiries should be addressed to The Director

Opening Hours:
Monday to Friday 10.00 - 5.00

Facilities
Photocopying, photography:
Instant photocopying (small orders):
Self service microfilms: Genealogy Service

He left his heart in Ireland…

Follow your Irish family's journeys at Ancestry.co.uk

Our Irish records let you **visit your ancestors on their native soil.** You can then uncover the rest of their lives – wherever they ended up – with the world's largest online archive of family history information. Join Ancestry.co.uk and let us help you discover your family's stories – search today at **www.ancestry.co.uk/irish**

WHO WILL YOU DISCOVER AT ❀ ancestry.co.uk

The National Museum of Ireland
www.museum.ie

The Museum of Science and Art, Dublin was founded on 14th August 1877 after requests by the Royal Dublin Society for government funding for its expanding museum activities. The Science and Art Museums Act of 1877 transferred the buildings and collections of the Royal Dublin Society into state ownership. Other notable collections from the Royal Irish Academy and Trinity College Dublin were also incorporated. The Museum became the responsibility of the Department of Science and Art who were responsible for the South Kensington museums in London.

A purpose built new building on Kildare Street was opened to the public in 1890. The museum brought together significant Irish antiquities from the Royal Irish Academy including the Tara brooch and Ardagh chalice. Ethnographical collections and material from Captain Cooke's voyages were transferred from Trinity College Dublin together with material from the Geological Survey of Ireland. The old Royal Dublin Society museum on the Merrion Street side of Leinster House, which had opened in 1856, was devoted to natural history, zoology and had an geology annexe.

The building on Kildare Street was designed by Thomas Newenham Deane and was used to show contemporary Irish, British and Continental craftsmanship in its construction. Considerable benefit came from steady funding and a liaison with the state museums in London and Edinburgh. The collections grew over the years through purchase, donations and bequests. In 1900 control passed to the Department of Agriculture and Technical Instruction and in 1908 becoming the 'National Museum of Science and Art.' However in 1921 the museum's name was changed to the 'National Museum of Ireland.'

After the foundation of the Free State in 1922, the old Royal Dublin Society buildings of Leinster House were chosen to house the new parliament (Dáil). The Natural History building was given a new entrance directly onto Merrion Street and the architecture was altered to allow the present opening at the east end and the development of new staircases. Responsibility for the Museum went to the Department of Education in 1924 then to the Taoiseach's Department in 1984. In 1993 responsibility passed to several governement departments before becoming an autonomous state agency with its own Board in 2005.

Throughout the latter half of the 20th Century there was a great deal of pressure on available exhibition, storage and staff space for the Museum. In 1988 the Government decided to close Collins Barracks, Dublin. Established in 1702 'The Barracks,' changed its name in the early 19th Century to the 'Royal Barracks,' and when the Free State was established in 1922 was re-named Collins Barracks. The original buildings were designed by Colonel Thomas Burgh and the complex, which includes 18th and 19th Century buildings, housed troops for three centuries. It was assigned to Museum use in 1994 and opened in 1997 with the first exhibitions, and development continues on the site. In September 2001 the Museum's Country Life branch was opened at Turlough Park, County Mayo. Turlough Park House (a Venetian Gothic building designed

Bank of Ireland, Dublin

Images © Copyright Robert Blatchford Collection

by Thomas Newenham Deane) and its gardens house the Museum's National Folklife collections; these are devoted to traditional crafts and everyday life in rural Ireland in the century or so since the Great Famine.

The Collections

The Royal Dublin Society, founded in 1731, collected plaster casts, geological minerals, fine art and ethnographical material, in order to train artists and encourage industry. *The Royal Irish Academy*, founded in 1785, sought to advance the study of Irish antiquities, science and literature. *The Museum of Irish Industry*, established in 1847, sourced its material largely in the Great Exhibition of 1851 and the Dublin Exhibition of 1853.

The Science and Art Museum, established in 1877, brought all three collections together and expanded them through loans, purchases and donations, with the aim of developing the institution into *'a source of recreation and instruction.'* In 1900 it became the *National Museum of Science and Art*, placing much emphasis on the development of rural craft and contemporary design. The aim was that the Museum and its collections should be *'of commercial value to the country as well as of historical and scientific interest.'*

With the foundation of the Irish Free State, the institution was transferred to the Department of Education and became the National Museum of Ireland. Its concentration was now on collecting and exhibiting material of Irish interest and its stated aim was *'to increase and diffuse the knowledge of Irish civilisation, the natural history of Ireland and the relations of Ireland in these respects with other countries.'* The collections on view here reflect the various stages of the Museum's development, the political changes that altered its status, and the shaping of its collecting policy over the years.

The National Museum of Ireland has three locations in Dublin and one in County Mayo. Admission is free to all four museums.

Archaeology, Kildare Street, Dublin 2
The National Museum of Ireland - Archaeology is centrally located on Kildare Street, Dublin 2, next door to Leinster House (Government Buildings).

Decorative Arts & History, Collins Barracks, Dublin 7
Natural History, Merrion Street, Dublin 2
The National Museum of Ireland - Natural History is centrally located on Merrion Street, Dublin 2, next door to the National Gallery.

Country Life, Turlough Park, Castlebar, Co. Mayo
The National Museum of Ireland – Country Life has modern exhibition galleries in the spectacular grounds of Turlough Park House with its magnificent gardens and lake.

Opening Times: (All four museums)
Tuesday to Saturday 10.00.a.m – 5.00.p.m.; Sunday 2.00.p.m. – 5.00.p.m. Closed Mondays (including Bank Holidays), Christmas Day and Good Friday

Dublin City Archives

The City of Dublin has been governed by its own elected representatives since the 12th century. The Dublin City Assembly which flourished during the Middle Ages and survived until 1840, met at the great feasts of Christmas, Easter, Midsummer and Michaelmas for the transaction of business, but extra meetings could be held if necessary. The Mayor presided at meetings of the Assembly, whose members consisted of two sheriffs, 24 aldermen, 48 sheriffs' peers and 96 representatives of the Dublin trade guilds. The municipal franchise was not democratic in the modern sense, as it was largely confined to members of the trade guilds and to their descendants.

Dublin City Archives hold the historic records of the municipal government of Dublin from the 12th century to the present. The City Archives contain a significant number of medieval documents, including two important bound manuscripts written on vellum: the *White Book of Dublin*, also known as the *'Liber Albus,'* and the *Chain Book of Dublin*. This book contains transcripts of documents in abbreviated Latin, French and old English relating to the administration of Dublin illustrating civic transactions with lands, buildings, mills and water-supplies. It contains one hundred and eleven leaves written on vellum. The Archives also hold a series of Assembly Rolls, written on parchment, which record the minutes of the Dublin City Assembly (a forerunner of today's City Council) from 1447 to 1841. *The Assembly Rolls*, together with the *White Book* and *Chain Book*, were transcribed and translated by Sir John T and Lady Gilbert and published as Calendar of Ancient Records of Dublin (19 volumes, Dublin, 1889-1944).

Dublin City Charters 1171 - 1727

The magnificent series of 102 Charters granted to the city by successive English monarchs. The earliest charter was issued by Henry II in 1171-1172, giving the men of Bristol the right to live in the City of Dublin. Later charters contain grants to the city of rights, privileges and property, and taken together they form the basis of municipal law in Ireland.

In addition to these published materials, the Dublin City Archives contain a wealth of records which have not been published and are available for research. These records include City Council and committee minutes, account books, correspondence, reports, court records, charity

petitions, title deeds, maps and plans, photographs and drawings, all of which document the development of Dublin over eight centuries. The Archives hold the magnificent series of 102 charters granted to the city by successive English monarchs. The earliest was issued by King Henry II in 1171 giving the men of Bristol the right to live in the city of Dublin. Later charters contain grants to Dublin of rights, privileges and property, and taken together they form the basis of municipal law in Ireland.

Guild Records 1192 - 1841

Guilds were mutual benefit associations which flourished in western Europe from the 11th century. The Guild system in Dublin was licensed under a charter by Prince John in 1192 and dominated the commercial and political life of the city. There were four types of Guilds: Guild Merchant or Merchant Guild, Craft Guilds or Trade Guilds, Religious Guilds and Military Guilds. Guild membership could be acquired by three means:

Service – by completion of an apprenticeship with a guild member

Birth – obtained by sons of guild members

Freedom – honorary membership to be conferred on dignitaries

Freedom Records 1225 - 1922

The ancient Freedom of Dublin was instituted at the time of the Norman Invasion. The inhabitants of Dublin in the middle ages were either free or non-free. Holders of the freedom of the city were known as *'Free Citizens'* and were entitled to special trading privileges and the right to vote in parliamentary and municipal elections. In order to qualify for the freedom it was usually necessary to have been born within the city boundaries or *'franchises'* and to be a member of one of the trade guilds of Dublin. Members of 'the Irish nation' were excluded, but in practice many people with Irish surnames succeeded in obtaining the freedom. Under the Penal Laws, Roman Catholics were excluded from the Freedom of Dublin from 1691 until 1793. Under the Representation of the Peoples Act, 1918, the ancient Freedom of Dublin was abolished to make way for a more democratic franchise. Nowadays all inhabitants of the city of Dublin who have reached the age of 18 are entitled to vote in municipal elections. It is possible to trace several generations of old Dublin families through these lists which form a useful source of genealogical research.

There were six main categories of admission:

1. Admission by Service was granted to those who completed an apprenticeship in one of the Trade Guilds of Dublin.
2. Admission by Birth was granted to sons, and sometimes daughters, of Free Citizens. Several generations of one family could hold the Freedom of Dublin.
3. Admission by Marriage was granted to sons-in-law of Free Citizens.
4. Admission by Fine was confined to prosperous professional men who were required to pay a substantial sum of money into the city treasury. Sometimes the Fine consisted of the presentation of a pair of gloves to the Lady Mayoress.
5. Admission by Grace Especial also known as Special Grace was the equivalent of the modern Honorary Freedom, and was reserved for dignitaries and for craftsmen who were not in a trade guild.
6. Admission by an Act of Parliament to *'Encourage Protestant Strangers to Settle in Ireland'* was granted to French Huguenots and Quakers from England.

Lists of those admitted to the ancient Freedom of Dublin survive for the period 1225-1250, 1468-1512 and 1575-1918. These lists may be consulted at Dublin Corporation Archives, City Hall, Dublin
2. A computerised index to the lists is being prepared by the Dublin Heritage Group. The lists are of interest to students of social and economic history and are also important for genealogical research.

Honorary Freedom of the City of Dublin

The Honorary Freedom of Dublin was instituted under the Municipal Privileges Act, 1876 and is presently conferred under the provisions of the Local Government Act 1991. The founder of the Home Rule Party, Isaac Butt, was the first person to receive the Honorary Freedom of Dublin. Other illustrious recipients include Charles Stewart Parnell, George Bernard Shaw, John Count McCormack and John Fitzgerald Kennedy, President of the United States of America. In recent years, it has been conferred on Pope John Paul II; Mother Teresa of Calcutta; the

Entrance to St Stephen's Green, Dublin

world champion cyclist Stephen Roche; and the former President of Ireland, Dr. Patrick Hillery. Nelson Mandela received the Freedom in 1988, whilst still a political prisoner. It has also been conferred on Jack Charlton, manager of the Republic of Ireland football team; & Bill Clinton, President U.S.A.

Dublin City Surveyors – Book of Maps 1695 - 1827

Dublin City Assembly acted as one of a number of landlords with estates in the city following a policy of leasing its lands to improving tenants. The City Estate was leased to Dublin's merchant class who built houses, stables, warehouses and outbuildings on their holdings.

The post of the City Surveyor was established in the late 17th century when there was no overall planning authority for the city. The role of the City Surveyor was to record rather than to plan such development. His involvement in planning was confined to dividing ground in lots for setting. The collection is an example of urban cartography and documents the development of the ancient Dublin City Estate within the original walled city.

Wide Streets Commission

The Wide Streets Commission was established in 1757 to develop wide and convenient streets through the city of Dublin. Among its other achievements, the Commission built Parliament Street, Westmoreland Street and D'Olier St. as well as Carlisle Bridge (now O'Connell Bridge). The minute books, maps, title deeds and architectural drawings produced for the Commission before it was abolished in 1849 are all held in the Dublin City Archives. These important records tell the story of the layout and development of much of Georgian Dublin.

Dublin Mansion House Relief Fund 1880

Ireland was beset by harvest failure during the 1870's and in 1880 famine threatened the country. To prevent this, the Mansion House Fund was set up to collect money from Irish emigrants all over the world. The records of the Fund are held in the Dublin City Archives and are important for local history because they contain reports from 800 local committees who distributed relief in every county in Ireland. Records of other relief committees are also available for inspection.

Edmund Dwyer Gray, Lord Mayor of Dublin, set up the Dublin Mansion House Relief Fund on 2nd January 1880. Administered by a voluntary central committee moneys were raised in Europe, North America, India and Australia. It was an all-Ireland relief fund with over 800 local committees set up in the thirty-two counties, of which membership of clergy of all denominations and poor-law medical officers was a pre-requisite. The central committee provided funds to voluntary committees who distributed in kind, supplying Indian Meal, turf and clothes to the most needy. The *'Little Famine'* lasted a comparatively short time, autumn 1880 yielded a good harvest and the Mansion House Fund was no longer required for the relief of distress. It was wound up in December of that year.

Records of Urban District Councils

The areas of Rathmines and Rathgar and of Pembroke each had their own local government until 1930, and their records are preserved in the Dublin City Archives, describing the development of these suburbs from the mid 19th century. The records of the Howth Urban District Council are also available, from 1318 to 1940.

The Reading Room is open to all readers holding a current Research Card available on application to Dublin City Public Libraries. The City Archives are for reference and research and may not be borrowed; access to the storage area is not permitted. An advance appointment is essential. Some records, because of their antiquity or fragile condition, may be withdrawn for conservation treatment and may not always be available. The Archivist will be pleased to answer any queries relating to the records. Photocopying, photography and microfilm services are provided as appropriate. The Archivist can advise on costs and conditions of copyright.

Reading Room First Floor, 138 - 144 Pearse Street, Dublin 2 Tel: +353 1 674 4999 Fax: +353 1 674 4881 E: dublinstudies@dublincity.ie E: cityarchives@dublincity.ie

Opening Hours:
The Reading Room is open from 10am to 8pm Monday to Thursday and from 10am to 5pm on Friday and Saturday. We do not close for lunch.
Dublin City Library and Archive is closed on the Saturdays and Mondays of Bank Holiday Weekends.

The Dublin Castle Story
stephen wade

In 1885, Joseph Chamberlain said, '*I say the time has come to reform altogether the absurd and irritating anachronism which is known as Dublin Castle.*' The fact that he saw it as a problem indicates its power and status. In effect, that wish was not fulfilled until the Castle was handed over to the new Provisional Government in January, 1922.

As a recent edition of the guide to Dublin Castle proclaimed, '*the place is at the heart of Irish history.*' Tourists and commuters

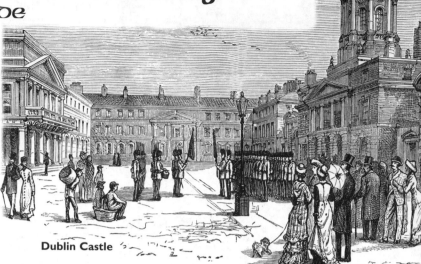

Dublin Castle

Images © Copyright Robert Blatchford Collection

walk past the gates every day, and the towers are on the skyline, but few know the profound material establishment inside those walls, with underground level foundations and the now subterranean river Poddle, which ran alongside the Liffey in the centuries when the Vikings controlled what was to become Dublin.

The Castle has been the scene of bold escapes and cruel detentions, sieges and important decisions; government and military strategy, and indeed, during the 1916 Easter Rising, one of the key sites held when the Republicans took on the British garrison. Whatever stance is taken to assess the stronghold within the city, the fact that is has been the centre of colonial rule is inescapable: people detained for political reasons were held and questioned there and military intelligence had its base inside the high walls.

The Castle has been there since 1204, when King John ordered its construction, and from that time it was, in many people's opinion, maintained as an establishment entirely on its own: an institution reminding everyone who stopped to reflect on it, that it existed as a court in miniature, with the Lord Lieutenant of Ireland existing in a vice-regal capacity.

In 1893 a magazine called *The Idler* had a feature on the Lord Lieutenant in a series called '*Lions in their Dens*' which had the attitude of indulging in celebrity worship. The author, Raymond Blathwayt, was conducted around the halls and towers by the Lord Lieutenant's sister, Mrs Arthur Henniker, and we may gain a picture of what life was like at the time with Blathwayt's account of walking in with her:

' *. . . we passed two sentries on guard at the entrance to the great hall, and proceeded up a*

staircase lined with rifles and through long, sunlit corridors, "*You must come with me to my own special sanctum . . .*" Here, in a lofty, white-panelled room, with windows looking down upon the private gardens of the castle in which His Excellency and one of the ADC's were walking up and down, Mrs Henniker and I sat talking about the past . . .'

The feature contains line drawings of guests arriving in carriages, elegant couples walking up the grand staircase to a ball, masses of guests waiting to be '*presented*' to His Excellency and a solemn photograph of ADC' in a group, some with bearskin hats, and others sporting kilts, plumes in hats and a multitude of braids, ribbons and medals. Outside, in the slums of the city, there were thousands living in tenements, hospitals full of paupers and disease rife among the poor, creating an alarmingly high infant mortality rate.

In its more recent history, the Castle has been the focus for one of the strangest mysteries in modern Irish history. On the morning of Saturday 6th July 1907, a cleaning lady called Mary Farrell was going about her duties and had reached the library when she noticed that the door was unlocked. She had found the same situation three days before that but no action had been taken by Sir Arthur Vicars when it was reported. Vicars was the Ulster King of Arms and he was responsible not merely for the security of the library and rooms around, but for something far more important – the Insignia of the Most Illustrious order of St Patrick, otherwise known as the Irish 'Crown Jewels.'

These were in a safe in the library because when the safe had been taken to the Castle from a bank vault, in order to be kept at the Office of Arms, it was found that the safe was too large to be taken in, so it was placed in the library of the

Bedford Tower. Not only was it a solid safe, it was also in a position where soldiers and police officers would always be in close proximity, so it must have seemed a safe place to store such valuables. How wrong could the men responsible have been – because later on after the cleaner made the second report on the sixth of the moth, William Stivey, who was an assistant to Vicars, went to the safe and found that it was unlocked and that the jewels had gone.

The jewels were the insignia of a group formed by George III in 1783, as an Irish form of the famous Scottish order of the Thistle. They had been made in London by a company called Rundell and Bridge and the glory of the collection comprised two items: a star and badge of the Order of St Patrick. The statutes and rules of the order had only recently been revised – just two years previously – and the Office of Arms had been moved to the Castle in that year. There was a whole panoply of officers and honorary members entrusted with the safety of the jewels, including the Dublin Herald Frank Shackleton, who was the brother of the famous explorer. He became a suspect, because clearly the valuables had been stolen by someone with access to a key, and he lodged with Vicars at his home in Clonskeagh Road.

Sir Arthur Vicars was born in Leamington in 1864, the son of Sir Arthur Edward Vicars, Colonel in the 61st Regiment. He had been educated at Magdalen College, Oxford, and then in 1893 he was appointed as Ulster King of Arms. *The Times* wrote of him on his death, '*He was thoroughly versed in the sciences of heraldry and genealogy… He was a Fellow of the Royal Society of Antiquaries and a trustee of the National Library of Ireland.*' Vicars had actually been the man who founded the Heraldic Museum at the Office of Arms. But all this counted for nothing after the disgrace and scandal of this daring and outrageous theft.

Vicars had in his possession the only two keys to the safe. One of the first lines of thought was that Shackleton had used or copied one of these. They had not actually been seen since 11 June, when Vicars had proudly shown them to a visitor, the librarian of the Duke of Northumberland. It was rare for anyone to open the safe but Vicars himself, and so for him to ask Stivey to open it, and to give him a key, on the day the theft was discovered, was a notable fact when the investigation began.

The police suspected Shackleton but on slender information, including the detail that a few days before the theft he had been heard to remark that one day the jewels might well be stolen. He was also in debt, and so had a motive.

It was a major scandal: the status of the Office of Arms was of the highest order; they had been established in 1552, and they administered the protocol and precedence at Dublin Castle. Vicars, as Ulster Kings of Arms was the Chief Herald of Ireland, Knight Attendant and registrar of the Order. In the records he was defined as '*the first and only permanent officer of the Lord Lieutenant's household.*' A painting of Sir Arthur Vicars in his ceremonial dress is at the Castle, showing him in Elizabethan court garb, with doublet and ruff, and with the harp of Ireland prominent on the lower left side of his garments.

The police went into action. They issued a poster offering one thousand pounds reward for information leading to the retrieval of the jewels. They are described there as having '*150 white, pure diamonds issuing from the centre*' and the badge was '*set in silver, with a shamrock of emeralds on a ruby cross surrounded by a sky blue enamelled circle* – with their motto, *Quis superabit* (who shall separate it). The whole was '*surrounded by a circle of large single Brazilian stones, surmounted by a crowned harp in diamonds.*'

There was to be a royal visit just four days after this discovery and that had, of course, been planned. There was to have been an investiture of a knight in St Patrick's Hall in the events of that visit, and of course that was something that caused a furore in London. The King, Edward VII,

Chapel Royal, Dublin Castle

demanded that Vicars be sacked. There was a smear campaign against him, including accounts of orgies he was supposedly involved in, and that allegation that he was homosexual, which was then a criminal activity of course, and Oscar Wilde's trial was fresh in the public memory.

When it came to the establishment of a Viceregal Commission of Enquiry, after a period when there had been no success in the hunt for the villains, Vicars kept out of it. The Commission met in January, 1908 and heard evidence from Shackleton. The due process of enquiry took place and in the end Vicars was totally at fault. It vindicated Shackleton and made it clear that Vicars was a disgrace to the office. The Commission was appointed by the Irish government and included Chester Jones, a London police magistrate and the Chief Commissioner of the Dublin Metropolitan Police. At the time, it was reported by the chairman that

'Sir Arthur Vicars had definitely declined to come forward to facilitate the Commission in any way. He recognised that the Commission had no power to control or to compel Sir Arthur Vicars to give evidence. The government considered that the enquiry should go forward ...'

Vicars was dismissed and went to live in County Kerry, where, on 14th April, 1921, a party of IRA men shot him dead. *The Times* reported on his death that he had faced a mob of gunmen before, a year earlier, and had stood firm when they demanded the key to his strongroom. On that occasion they had left, but the second attack was more desperate and determined. He was taken from his bed in his dressing gown and murdered outside his house. A label was placed around his neck with the words, *'Spy, Informers beware. I.R.A. never forgets.'* His house was then set on fire.

Irish Police Records
stephen wade

The Garda Siochana

The Garda Siochana, formerly known as the Civic Guard, was formed in 1922 by the Irish Provisional government, to be the police constabulary of the Irish Free State. Previously there had been the Royal Irish Constabulary together with the short-lived Irish Republican Police of 1919-1922. By the Garda Siochana Act of 1923 that name was formally adopted, but the Dublin Metropolitan Police still existed until 1925 when the two forces were combined. Since that time, the Garda has been the only national police force of the Republic of Ireland, and an officer is referred to as a *'Garda'* in much the same way as an English officer is called *'constable.'*

The force expanded in the early 1920s; in 1923 an advertisement announced 30 vacancies for cadetships, and these were open to officers of the national army who had at least two years of experience in the Volunteers in the pre-truce years. The usual police regulations on behaviour were then sorted out, as they had been by every constabulary since Peel's 1829 Act, as in Order number 14 for instance: *'No man of any rank who is addicted to drink will be permitted to remain a member of the Civic Guard. This is a penalty which will be rigidly enforced.'*

Proposals for the merger of the Garda and the Dublin Metropolitan Police were discussed in November 1924, and the amalgamation followed the next year. A few years later we have what may be read as the mission statement of the Garda, expressed in a speech by Kevin O'Higgins: *'The internal politics and political controversies of the country are not your concern. You will serve with the*

same imperturbable discipline and with increasing efficiency any government which has the support of the majority ...'

Today the Garda Museum is housed in Dublin Castle, containing a large collection of artefacts and memorabilia, going back to the earlier police forces, such as the one formed by Sir Robert Peel while he was Chief Secretary based in the Castle in the Regency years 1812-1818.

The Dublin Metropolitan Police

The force was formed in 1836 and existing until its amalgamation with the Garda Siochana in 1925; at the beginning, the creation of the new

Dublin 1880s

Some of these heroic officers took on extremely dangerous characters with courage and determination, such as Constable Joseph Daly, who was killed after an attack with a cleaver while arresting a man in 1881, and Inspector John Mills, who was beaten to death while escorting prisoners he had arrested at a political meeting.

In searching for ancestors in service records for this constabulary, the best place to begin is with Jim Herlihy's comprehensive reference work, *The Dublin Metropolitan Police: A Complete Alphabetical List of Officers and Men 1836-1925*, published by Four Courts Press, 2001. After that, consult the National Archives and Garda Archives, Phoenix Park, for service records, and details are at www.irishtimes.com Another useful place to go and ask specific questions for information on police ancestors in Ireland is at Ancestry.com message boards for '*Dublin Metropolitan Police service records*.'

constabulary sprang from Sir Robert Peel's Peace Preservation Force, which he established while he was Chief Secretary for Ireland, and of course, a little later, he was responsible for the 1829 Police Act which led to the Metropolitan Police. In fact, the London force provided a template for the organisation of the new Dublin force, not only in terms of the uniform design, but also their structure was similar, with a Commissioner at the head.

In the early twentieth century, the political division – G Division – were involved in the War of Independence, including involvement with the efficient intelligence corps formed by Michael Collins. One way to glean the more dramatic elements of their history is to look at the roll of honour -
www.policememorial.org.uk/Forces/IRELAND/DMP_Roll.htm

The Royal Irish Constabulary

The force began as the Irish Constabulary, and then in 1867 the name Royal Irish Constabulary was made official. Before that, the origins were in the Irish (Constabulary, Ireland) Act of 1836. Its men had a turbulent time and won great respect, as a certain '*Resident of County Clare*' wrote to *The Times* in 1878: '*I take it for granted that if the Irish people did not enlist as soldiers, they would not enlist in the Irish Constabulary, called by Her Majesty the "Royal" Irish Constabulary from the gallant stand which the members of that force made against the Fenians in 1867.*'

The Constabulary was very much in the headlines during the Land Wars of the 1880s and in letter to the press in 1881, one correspondent wrote of them: '*My object in writing is to draw the attention of the government and the country to the noble part played by a small but gallant band in Ireland ... the Royal Irish Constabulary ... Their bravery has been so conspicuous that on very many occasions a half-dozen men have kept in check enraged and desperate mobs of some hundreds ...*'

There were certainly some most remarkable men in their ranks, such as W V Harrel, who was born in 1866, then at the age of

Phoenix Park Riot, Dublin 1871

twenty he joined the RIC, and by 1898 he had risen to be an inspector of prisons in Ireland. Four years later he was appointed Assistant Commissioner of the Dublin Metropolitan Police, and was honoured with a Companion of the Bath award in 1912.

The first phase of its history related solely to peacekeeping, but later it assumed revenue duties, and the force was in existence until 1922. Service records later passed to the Home Office and then they were lodged at The National Archives.

The service records are found at HO 184 arranged by service number, and with an alphabetical index; other registers list indexes for officers and for auxiliary force members. These registers have a great deal of information, covering physical features, date of appointment, length of service, place where they served and date of retirement or death. There are also pension records here, covering registers and allowances for the years 1873-1922, at reference PMG48, arranged alphabetically mostly by name, or sometimes by award number. Deceased pensioners are also listed for the years 1877-1918.

After the disbandment of the force, those officers who were recommended for pensions are in lists by district, and in addition, separate lists were made for British and Irish officers. These are at HO 184/129-209. Not all records refer to the RIC directly, but are under the heading of Dublin Castle, and these are at CO 904/175-176. Particularly useful for digging into the earlier period, back in the Regency before the Irish Constabulary, are the superannuation lists given to Irish police: these are to be found in the House of Commons Sessional papers for 1831-1832, XXVI 465, and these provide name, period of service, the amount granted and the nature of the injury which led to the claim for superannuation.

As with all family history research, a fuller picture is needed, and all related social history is of immense value in understanding the nature of the work done by officers, and the administration process which controlled their working lives. Much of this material is available in the Dublin Castle records at CO 904 and the Irish office records at TNA, reference CO 906. This includes documentation of such aspects of police life as reports, civil disorder and force information such as circulars and instructions. This relates to major topics in Irish history, as the constabulary were known as the 'Irish gendarmerie' in some quarters, as they were involved in the Land Wars, the Fenian insurrections and later the 1916 rising and Civil War. At WO 35 there is material which provides excellent background information to these conflicts, and at HO 267 there are Home Office policy files with regard to Ireland. To back

The Peeler—See here, my man! your name's oblitherated!
The Jarvey—Bedad, an' ye're wrong--it's O'Brien.

this up, and to read first-hand accounts of actions taken by the RIC, a search of the Times Digital Archive is recommended, particularly for the years c.1880 - 1900. The Ireland Files at T192 cover the later years, 1920-1922 and there is also material in the Treasury archives, because the RIC worked with them also, on revenue, and they even did work as census enumerators. The Finance Files are at T160 and the Pensions and Superannuation Files are at T164, but as the research notes at TNA point out, there is no general index of names for these.

Any family history research for police in Ireland will inevitably present the reader with the challenge of understanding the complexity of modern Irish history, and although there is a massive library of booms available in this area, there are other sources of great value, and in particular, the National Library of Ireland produces files of original sources, reprinted with guides, to many of more complicated areas of history. For instance, their file of *Historical Documents: The Past From the Press* consists of a collection of newspaper and journal cuttings, including topics in political life, leisure and sport. This series of folders has been in print since 1976, and there is a collection of facsimiles on the Land Wars, which is of especial value to researchers with police ancestors. These are available from The National Library of Ireland, Kildare Street, Dublin 2 Eire.

The Landed Estate Court Rentals
ross weldon

Introduction

Microfilm record MFGS/39/1–66 at the National Archive of Ireland is listed as *'LEC Rentals (O'Brien),'* unassuming to those who have only started to skim the surface of their Irish family history. To those in the know, however, the Landed Estate Court Rentals represent one of the most valuable and under used sources for anyone engaged in Irish research. Up until now, the biggest problem with the Landed Estate Court rentals has been access which has meant they have stayed off the radar to a certain extent for most family historians. Although used by professional Irish genealogists the microfilm records stored at the National Archive of Ireland are disorganised and indexed by estate owner of which there are only 8,000 listed. This has made it difficult to find the 600,000 tenants also listed in the records, unless of course you know the name of the landowner that they rented from.

In early 2009 Brian Donovan and the Eneclann team made it their objective to digitise these records in order to open up this information to a whole new audience of amateur genealogists. They approached **brightsolid** online publishing, who have a vast amount of expertise in the digitisation of precious records for their family of sites including findmypast.co.uk. With the kind permission of the National Archives and an agreement to allow free access to the digitised images in five years' time, the 100,000 microfilm images were taken, digitised and indexed and are now available for the first time online at findmypast.ie

The Landed Estate Court rentals available on findmypast.ie

By the middle of the 19th century many of the large Irish estates were in serious financial difficulty. Land owners found themselves legally obliged to pay out annuities and charges on their land, mainly to pay mortgages or *'portions'* to family members contracted by marriage settlements and/or wills of previous generations. All of these payments had to be met, before the owner/occupier could take an income from their estate.

By the time of the Famine, as prices for sale or rental of land plummeted, the monies that had to be paid out from the individual estates remained the same, and many Irish estates became insolvent as debts exceeded earnings. However, the landowners could not sell their estates to discharge their debts, because the land was entailed. In 1848 and 1849, two Encumbered Estates Acts were passed to facilitate sale of these estates. Under the second act (12 & 13 Vict., c. 77), an Encumbered Estates Court was established, whereby the state took ownership of these properties and then sold them on with a parliamentary title, free from the threat of contested ownership. In fact, the LECs can be compared to the modern day National Asset Management Agency, the Irish governmental organisation charged with reclaiming property from those who have defaulted on payment and selling them on at the best possible price.

The LEC rentals available at findmypast.ie are known as the O'Brien rentals which include almost all records taken between 1849 and 1885. The other two sets of less complete records are the Quit Rent Office set of rentals, which includes rentals for the period after 1885 and which is available in the National Archives, and a smaller set of estate papers held in the National Library of Ireland. In Northern Ireland, another large set of the Rentals is held in the Public Record Office.

What were the Landed Estate Court Rentals?

The Encumbered Estates Court was established 1849. In 1852 it was replaced by the Landed Estates Courts, which was itself superseded in 1877 by the Land Judges Court, part of the Chancery Division of the High Court. Although there were some

Glendalough Lake Galway

© Copyright Robert Blatchford Collection

differences in the powers of these courts, their principal function remained the same, to sell off insolvent estates.

The Land Courts system was the first significant step towards the break-up of the old estates in Ireland. From the family historian's perspective, the rentals have an added value, because the estate records (rentals, maps, leases) that would have existed prior to these sales, no longer survive. This is because once the parliamentary grant to title was secured by purchase from the Land Courts, there was no need to retain any of the documentation regarding previous land title.

The Rentals were effectively printed sale catalogues, which were circulated to prospective purchasers in advance of the sale. They were compiled with the intention of attracting purchasers and of providing information on the estate in a clear and uniform manner. The Land Courts sold estates in every county in Ireland, and the rentals as a whole cover large parts of the country. The estates sold included urban as well as rural property and many of the Rentals relate to houses and other buildings in villages, towns and cities.

Level of detail

The title page in a Rental identifies the estate and gives the date and place of sale. This is usually followed by brief descriptive particulars of the estate and its situation, intended to attract prospective buyers. Anyone who has read the property section of a newspaper will know what to expect in this section.

To the family historian, the critical information contained in these catalogues are the rentals, especially the Lot descriptions. The details often include:

Map Reference: The rentals usually include a map to situate the estate or lot in relation to the surrounding countryside, and often also a detailed map of the lot itself. In the case of urban property you will find a village or town plan.

Names of tenants: the particulars will also name all lives contracted for (usually three) and any of those names still alive at the time of the sale.

Yearly rent in pounds, shillings and pence.

Day rent due: labelled as 'Gale days.'

Size of plot: in acres, roods and perches.

Length of tenure.

Observations: This column which lays out the terms by which the land is rented often includes interesting insights into the plots of land and those who rented them. It was typical for a lease to be given for 21 years or three lives (named). The date of the original lease is often given, and any circumstances of note regarding the tenant or plot.

The Case of Errislannan Estate

Image 1
Courtesy: findmypast.ie

Errislannan, or Flannan's peninsula, in the barony of Ballynahinch lies just south of the town of Clifden, Co.Galway. In the 1830s, the Reverend Richard Wall of Barmount Manor, county Wexford, rented from Colonel Lambert his quarter share of the Errislannan estate, 679 acres of which were held on lease from the Bishop of Tuam - **Image 2**. In April 1850, the estate was advertised for sale by Colonel Lambert. Reverend Wall purchased the land, renovated the shooting lodge and named it Errislannan Manor. The estate was eventually inherited by his daughter Henrietta, who married the Reverend George Heather in 1866. It remained in the ownership of the Walls and their descendants until 1958. The details of the rental record are described below.

The title page in a Rental identifies the estate and gives the date and place of the sale. So for example, *In the Court of the Commissioners for Sale of Incumbered Estates in Ireland, No. 14 Henrietta Street Dublin ... In the matter of the estate of the James S. Molloy, assignee of John Lambert, of Errislannan in the County of Galway, Owner ... Sale on Tuesday the 23rd Day of April 1850.*

In the Rental for sale of the estate of the Colonel Lambert, we can see from the information at the bottom of **Image 2** that on Lot 1 *'Mr.Lambert has erected a neat Residence and excellent offices; and the farm of 106 acres, which he had in his own hands, has been reclaimed, as well as other parts of the land.'*

If we turn to Lot 1, we get a full description of all tenants and can see how their rent is subject to variation according to the price of corn, under the provision of the Irish Church Temporalities Act.

Lot 1 comprises this and the three following denominations, which are held in fee under a conveyance from the Ecclesiastical Commissioners for Ireland, at the yearly rent of £18 8s 2d, payable to the Bishop of Tuam. The

In the Court of the Commissioners for Sale of
Incumbered Estates in Ireland.

RENTAL

OF THE

ERRISLANNAN ESTATE,

SITUATE IN THE BARONY OF BALLINAHINCH AND COUNTY OF GALWAY.

HELD IN FEE.

TO BE SOLD ON TUESDAY, THE 23RD DAY OF APRIL, 1850, AT 12 O'CLOCK, NOON.

Image 2 - Lot 1
Courtesy: findmypast.ie

NO. ON MAP.	DENOMINATIONS.	TENANTS' NAMES.	YEARLY RENTS. £ s. d.	GALE DAYS.	A. R. P.	TENURE.	OBSERVATIONS.
	LOT 1.						Lot 1 comprises this and the three following denominations, which are held in fee under a Conveyance from the Ecclesiastical Commissioners for Ireland, at the yearly rent of £18 8s. 2d., payable to the Bishop of Tuam. This rent is subject to variation according to the price of Corn, under the provisions of the Irish Church Temporalities Acts.
9	KILL, ...	Vacant, ...			78 1 0	. . . . .	
10	Ditto,	Simon Lydon and Edward Conneely,	9 15 0	1st May and 1st November.	11 0 0	Yearly Tenant.	
11	Ditto,	Michael Lydon, ...	6 0 0	Ditto.	19 2 10	Ditto.	
12	Ditto,	Michael Davin, ...	6 0 0	Ditto.	21 3 0	Ditto.	
13	Ditto,	Rev. William Kilbride, ...	16 0 0	Ditto.	12 0 0	Ditto.	
14	Ditto,	School, ...			0 3 0	Ditto.	
15	Ditto,	Mr. Lambert's demesne,	}		106 1 33		
16	Ditto,	Ditto,					
17	Ditto,	Thomas Lydon, ...	7 0 0	Ditto.	12 1 20	Ditto.	
18	Ditto,	Valentine Burke, ...	6 6 9	Ditto.	12 3 0	Ditto.	
	Ditto,	Profitable rocks, ...			5 3 0		
	Ditto,	Water, ...			14 3 32		
					295 2 15		
25	KEERAUN, NORTH,	Vacant, ...		Ditto.	12 3 0		
26	Ditto,	James Gorham, ...	11 13 1	Ditto.	17 2 34	Ditto.	
27	Ditto,	Vacant, ...		Ditto.	14 3 0		
28	Ditto,	Simon Conneely, ...	11 13 1	Ditto.	16 0 10	Ditto.	
29	Ditto,	John Conneely, ...	11 13 1	Ditto.	15 0 8	Ditto.	
30	Ditto,	Frank, David, and Pat. Manion,	11 13 1	Ditto.	21 3 0	Ditto.	
	Ditto,	Profitable rocks, ...			10 2 8		
					99 1 0		

2

NO.	DENOMINATIONS.	TENANTS' NAMES.	YEARLY RENTS. £ s. d.	GALE DAYS.	A. R. P.	TENURE.	OBSERVATIONS.
31	CURHOWNAGH, . .	Thomas Folan, ...	6 10 7	1st May & 1st Nov.	15 1 3	Yearly Tenant.	
32	Ditto,	Vacant, ...			17 2 24		
33	Ditto,	Vacant, ...			18 1 37		
34	Ditto,	Daniel Tanghan,	9 1 10	Ditto.	17 3 16	Ditto.	
35	Ditto,	Michael Folan, Sen.,	11 1 0	Ditto.	17 1 31	Ditto.	
	Ditto,	Profitable rocks, ...			32 2 0		
					119 0 26		
36	DERRYEIGHTER,	Patrick Conneely, ...	6 7 9	Ditto.	13 0 24	Ditto.	
	Ditto,	Waste, ...			2 0 32		
37	Ditto,	Vacant, ...			12 0 7		
38	Ditto,	Ditto, ...			12 3 36		
39	Ditto,	Ditto, ...			12 1 0		
40	Ditto,	Ditto, ...			12 2 28		
41	Ditto,	Ditto, ...			13 2 0		
42	Ditto,	Ditto, ...			13 0 8		
43	Ditto,	Michael Conneely, Martin,	7 14 6		14 1 25	Ditto.	
	Ditto,	Profitable rocks, ...			51 0 0		
	Ditto,	Water, ...			6 3 38		
					164 0 38		
	LOT 2.						These lands are called Drinagh on the Ordnance Map, from which the Map attached to this Rental is partly copied; but in the Deed of Conveyance to Mr. Lambert they are called Errislannan. This Lot is held in fee simple, and is not subject to Quit Rent. It comprises the subdenominations of Crumpawn, Lurgan, and Drinagh.
1	DRINAGH, ...	Vacant, ...			35 3 0		
2	Ditto,	Michael Kilmartin, ...	5 0 0	Ditto.	7 0 0	Ditto.	
3	Ditto,	Vacant, ...			8 1 30		
4	Ditto,	Vacant, ...			8 1 30		
5	Ditto,	Vacant, ...			3 2 35		
6	Ditto,	Vacant, ...			87 0 20		
7	Ditto,	Martin Conneely, ...	3 0 0	Ditto.	32 1 0	Ditto.	
8	Ditto,	Vacant, ...			135 0 0		
	Ditto,	Profitable rocks, ...			18 3 10		
	Ditto,	Water, ...			9 1 17		
					345 3 22		
		General Total, ...			1024 0 21		

Image 3 - Lot 2
Courtesy: findmypast.ie

THE above Lands are beautifully situated on the CONNEMARA Coast, on the small Peninsula called ERRISLANNAN, having ARDBEAR Bay on one side, and MANNIN Bay on the other. Clifden Castle, the Residence of H. DARCY, Esq., is on the opposite Coast of ARDBEAR Bay.

Both Lots adjoin each other, and are distant about five Miles by Land from the rising Town of CLIFDEN, but a much shorter distance by Water.

On Lot No. 1 Mr. LAMBERT has erected a neat Residence and excellent Offices; and the Farm of 106 Acres, which he had in his own hands, has been reclaimed, as well as other Parts of the Lands.

The Shores yield great quantities of Sea Weed, not only sufficient for the culture of the Lands, but also for Kelp. There is also a Fishing Weir and Oyster Bank attached.

There is a capital Road through the Property to the extreme end of the Peninsula.

A large School has also been erected on the Property.

It will be seen by the above Rental that three-fourths of the Lands are untenanted, and it may be fairly assumed that, if all were tenanted, they would produce an annual Rental of £400.

Both Lots will be sold subject to an Annuity of £120 per annum, payable during the lives of EDWARD HARTSON BURROUGHS, of Harcourt-street, Dublin, Esq., and HENRIETTA BURROUGHS, his wife, and the life of the survivor; but the purchaser of Lot No. 1 will be required to indemnify the purchaser of Lot No. 2 against the payment of said annuity. MR. BURROUGHS is now aged 46 years, and Mrs. BURROUGHS is 35.

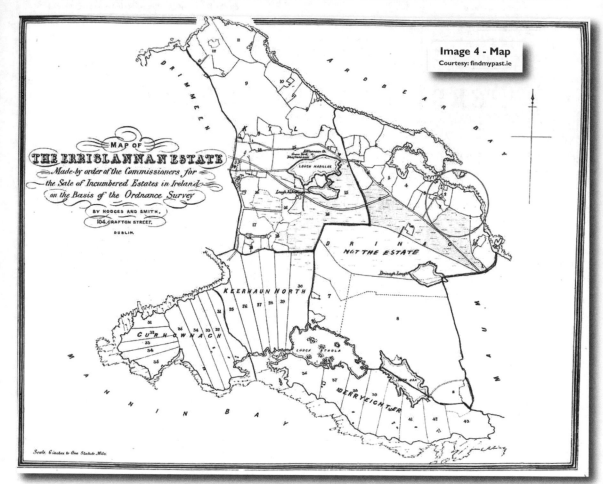

Image 4 - Map
Courtesy: findmypast.ie

rent is subject to variation according to the price of Corn, under the provisions of the Irish Church Temporalities Acts.

We can see the Rental for Lot 2 - **Image 3** which does not contain as much information and is a seemingly smaller plot. However, there is a wealth of information present at the foot of the image including:

'Mr.Lambert has erected a neat residence and excellent offices . . .' 'The shores yield great quantities of seaweed, not only sufficient for the culture of the lands, but also for kelp. There is also a fishing weir and oyster bank attached.'

This rental also includes a map to situate the estate or lot in relation to the surrounding countryside. Here we can see lots 1 and 2 marked - **Image 4.**

Why is it an important resource?

The information contained in this online edition of the Landed Estate Court rentals is a testament to the progress of family history research over the last decade. Previously, the amateur family historian would have been content to find out merely names and dates associated with their ancestors but the difficulties with even that in Ireland has led genealogists to think outside the box and look for more interesting windows into our past. The Landed Estate Court records are a perfect example of this as they provide not only names and dates but key facts about our ancestors' lives, such as where exactly they lived, who they lived with, what their lodgings were like and what the area in which they lived was like. By searching for your ancestors in the Landed Estates Court records you can find out not just what your ancestors' names were but what they did and how they lived.

Further Reading

Tracing your Irish Ancestors J Grenham Pub: Gill and Macmillan, 1992
Handy Book of Farm Tenure & Purchase under the Landlord and Tenant (Ireland) Act, Henry D Hutton Pub: R.D. Webb & Son, 1870
The Practice of the Landed Estates Court in Ireland Richard C MacNevin Pub: Hodges, Smith & Co., 1859
Landed Estates Database, Moore Institute www.landedestates.ie
Landed Estate Papers & the Search for Farming Families in Ireland W Roulston - The Irish Family & Local History Handbook 2012

Landed Estate Papers & the Search for Farming Families in Ireland
William Roulston

Until the beginning of the twentieth century the most important unit of land organisation across much of Ireland was the estate. Very few Irish farmers owned their farms outright, but rather leased them from a landlord or an intermediary known as a middleman. Landed estates in Ireland ranged in size from over 100,000 acres to under 1,000. For example, the Marquis of Conyngham owned more than 120,000 acres in County Donegal in the mid nineteenth century. In 1876 there were some 300 estates in Ireland of over 10,000 acres, while a further 3,400 were in the 1,000 to 10,000 acre range. There were thus considerable variations in the wealth and lifestyles of landowners, and to regard them as forming a homogeneous group would be wrong. The largest landowners were usually titled and often owned estates in several parts of Ireland and in Britain. Their homes were generally built on a grand scale and were set within extensive demesnes. They exerted considerable control over representative politics in their respective counties. The smaller landowners lived more modestly and in many cases were on the same level as many of the more substantial tenant farmers. One thing that most landowners shared was membership of the Church of Ireland. Only a small number of landowners were Presbyterians, and even fewer were Roman Catholics.

Because of Ireland's history of conquest and land seizure the landowning classes were often viewed as parasitical outsiders, oppressing the Irish peasantry while enriching themselves. By the early 1700s most land in Ireland was owned by landlords who were from, or whose roots lay, in England and Scotland. The early seventeenth-century Plantation of Ulster, the Cromwellian confiscations of the 1650s and the Restoration and Williamite settlements of the 1660s through to the beginning of the eighteenth century, as well as numerous other schemes, had all contributed to this situation. It was not until the passing of a series of acts of parliament in the late nineteenth and early twentieth century that an owner-occupier class of farmers was created. The removal of the landed class at this time was seen as

a triumph for the Irish farmer. Much of Irish historiography has followed this line. However, more recently historians, utilising a range of sources have come to different conclusions, finding, for example, that many estates were managed effectively by landlords and that evictions were neither as commonplace, nor as arbitrary as has been thought.

The documents generated by the management of landed estates in Ireland are among the most valuable records for the local and family historian. The first part of this article looks specifically at records generated by the management of landed estates. This is followed by a discussion of other sources that can be used to explore the workings of the estate system and illuminate the lives of farming families in Ireland.

Irish landed estate papers

The best collection of Irish estate papers is housed in the Public Record Office of Northern Ireland (PRONI). This comprises not only collections of estate papers for Northern Ireland, but also many for the Republic of Ireland, notably for County Monaghan. What makes the records in PRONI stand out is the fact that most of them have been expertly catalogued so that it is relatively easy to discover whether the records for a particular estate are available. A two-volume *Guide to Landed Estate Papers* is available for consultation in the Search Room. It is arranged by county, with the estate collections listed alphabetically according to the name of the landowning family. A brief synopsis of what is available is provided for each estate collection along with references. Because of the way in which the records have been calendared it is usually possible for the researcher to identify reasonably quickly the records of potential value. For many of the larger collections, detailed introductions have been prepared. Most of these introductions, which are now available to read on the PRONI website, were written by Dr A. P. W. Malcomson, its former director, and describe the history of the landowning family concerned as well as the way in which the collection has been organised (www.proni.gov.uk).

Donegal Castle

81

There are also collections of estate papers in the National Archives of Ireland and National Library of Ireland. The level of accessibility to these is generally not as good as in PRONI, but in recent times greater resources have been applied to cataloguing some of the more significant collections. For example, there is now a very good catalogue to the records in the National Library of the Conyngham estate in counties Clare, Donegal, Limerick, Meath and elsewhere, compiled by Sarah Ward-Perkins (Collection List No. 53, 2000). These catalogues can be downloaded as PDFs from the website of the National Library (www.nli.ie). There are also downloadable PDFs of catalogues of some of the estate collections in the National Archives of Ireland (www.nationalarchives.ie).

Before delving into estate papers, it is first of all necessary to establish which estate, if any, your ancestor lived in. If searching in the nineteenth century, the easiest way to identify the name of a landowner is to examine Griffith's Valuation of c.1850-60 (see below for more information on this source) for the relevant townland and note the name of the immediate lessor. For the researcher working in the eighteenth century there are clearly limitations in the usefulness of this. Although the landowning family in 1860 was often the same as in 1760, and occasionally in 1660, in many cases it will not be. Sometimes this will not be a problem, as the records of successive owners will be found in the one estate collection. One possible solution is to examine the Books of Survey and Distribution of the later seventeenth century. These chart the major changes in landownership at this time arising from the government confiscations of native Irish land for redistribution among British settlers. There are sets of the Books of Survey and Distribution in PRONI (ref. D/1854/1) and in the National Archives, Dublin.

Even after trying all these possibilities, it may be impossible to identify the appropriate estate collection. It must also be acknowledged that the records of many estates are not available for inspection in any archive. Some were destroyed in the disturbances of the early 1920s; others were lost in the more recent troubles, such as the papers relating to the Stronge Estate in County Armagh. Still others were burnt by their owners, who felt that they had no more use for them or wanted to clear some space. Some collections, a few of which are fairly extensive, remain in private custody. The records of the smaller estates, those in and around the 1,000–3,000 acre range, are especially poorly represented in the archives.

The range of records

Some categories of estate papers are more useful to genealogists than others. Title deeds are concerned with the legal ownership of an estate, and are generally of limited value to genealogists. The same can be said of mortgages. Wills and marriage settlements usually refer only to the members of the landowner's family. However, rentals, leases, lease books, maps and correspondence can all be extremely useful to those searching for their ancestors within landed estate records and a short discussion of each follows.

Rentals

Rentals, rent rolls or rent books record rent payments made by a tenant to his landlord. They are generally arranged by year (rents were usually paid half-yearly) or with several years covered by the same volume. The information provided will usually be limited to the name of the tenant, the extent and location of his holding and the rent payable by him. Occasionally rentals are annotated and may contain additional details such as a change in occupancy and the reason for it.

Leases

A lease was a contract between the landlord and the tenant under the terms of which the landlord gave the tenant the right to occupy his farm for a specific period of time. Two copies of the lease were usually prepared; the original lease was signed by the

Exclusive Dealing

Irish Landlord (boycotted)
"PAT, MY MAN, I'M IN NO END OF A HURRY. PUT THE PONY TO, AND DRIVE ME TO THE STATION AND I'LL GIVE YE HALF A SOVEREIGN!"

Pat (Nationalist, but needy).
"OCH SURE, IT'S MORE THANS ME LOIFE IS WORTH TO BE SEEN DROIVING YOU, YER HONOUR. BUT" - *slyly* - "BUT IF YER HONOUR WOULD JIST DROIVE ME, MAYBE IT'S MESELF THAT MOIGHT VENTURE IT!"

Images © Copyright Robert Blatchford Collection

landlord and kept by the tenant. The counterpart was signed by the tenant and kept by the landlord. The typical lease will include the following information:

the names of lessor(s) and lessee(s): the townland or location of the farm; the rent to be paid; the tenure of the lease; the conditions to be fulfilled by the lessee

The conditions to be fulfilled by the lessee could include a requirement to build a house of specific dimensions and materials, or to grind corn at the landlord's appointed mill, or to plant hedges and divide the farm into fields. In this way the landlord could regulate the appearance of the landscape. The planting of fruit trees was a frequent requirement, not only because they were a useful food supply, but also because they were regarded as having scenic value, adding beauty to the surrounding countryside.

A lease was usually for a term of years, 21 or 31 being quite common, but leases for three lives were in fairly widespread use. A three-life lease expired when all the three persons named in the lease died. Three-life leases are very useful for genealogists because a tenant often named members of his family as the lives. Frequently young relatives were named as the lives in the hope that at least one of them would survive for many years. Depending on the terms on which the lease was issued, a three-life lease could be renewed at the fall of each life by inserting a new name on payment of a renewal fine. The renewable three-life lease was therefore in reality a grant in perpetuity so long as the tenant wished to renew it. When new lives were inserted details of age and relationship were often included, and it is possible to work out when the old life died.

Tenants often sub-let the property, or part of it, to a third party; this was known as a sub-lease. The third party became an undertenant, paying rent to the tenant, who continued to pay rent to the landlord. Subletting was often frowned upon and many landlords tried with varying degrees of success to ban it. Undertenants are particularly hard to trace because often there was no paperwork in relation to the terms by which they held their plots of ground.

Lease books

Lease books can be among the most useful of estate papers as far as genealogy is concerned. They record in condensed form the same sort of information contained in the original leases, such as the name of the lessee, the location and extent of the holding and the rent payable on it. Generally covering an entire estate, they can be a much quicker way of finding information on a tenant farmer than searching through several bundles of leases. Lease books are particularly useful when they name the lives in a lease along with comments as to the status of each life. For example, for a farm in the townland of Aughadunvarran on the Downshire estate in County Down, one of the lives in the lease in the early nineteenth century was a James Sloane. The lease book reveals that he died in 1808 in the East Indies having previously spent some time in Botany Bay. The same lease book similarly reveals that one of the lives in a lease for a farm in the townland of Ballykeelartefinny was Michael Wilson who had '[en]listed as a soldier many years ago & supposed to be dead.' Information like this is priceless as it may be impossible to find it in any other source.

Maps and surveys

Maps form an important element in most estate collections. These show the property of the

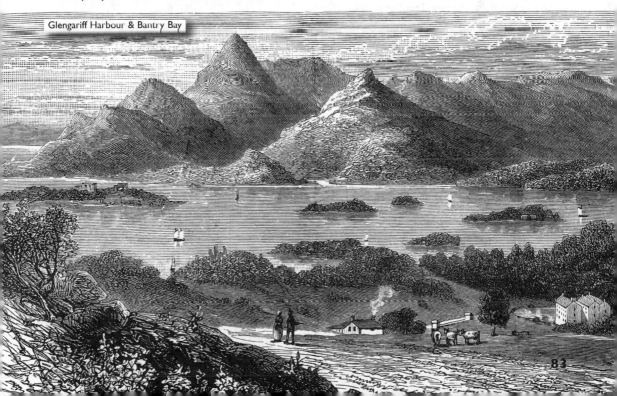

Glengariff Harbour & Bantry Bay

landlord, who employed a surveyor to illustrate the extent of his land and the more important features on his estate. Maps come in all shapes and sizes, and can be coloured or roughly etched in black and white. Early estate maps were often pictorial and included representations in relief of houses and other landscape features. Later, as surveying methods became more

King John's Castle, Limerick
Image © Copyright Robert Blatchford Collection

precise, such features usually disappeared from maps. For genealogical purposes, maps that name tenants and pinpoint the location of their farms are the most useful. The value of such maps lies in the fact that they enable a researcher to identify the location of the farm in which an ancestor lived perhaps 100 years before Griffith's Valuation. Occasionally estate maps have an accompanying 'terrier' that includes detailed information about each farm.

A landlord keen to improve his estate to maximise his income from it would periodically carry out a survey or a valuation of it. Often these surveys contain little of genealogical interest, as they concentrate on land quality and use. For example, William Starrat of Strabane worked extensively as a surveyor in west Ulster in the first half of the eighteenth century, but there is little in his surveys of value to the family historian. Nonetheless, while not containing the sort of information that will allow the family tree to be constructed, such surveys can provide a glimpse into the world of our forebears. Other surveys and valuations do, however, contain much of interest to the genealogist.

Correspondence

The correspondence between a landlord and his agent can be of immense genealogical value. Not only does it include details of the day-to-day running of the estate, but mention is often made of those who worked on the estate. The most serious drawback to using estate correspondence is the fact that it will almost certainly not be indexed. Furthermore, much of it lies unsorted in boxes. The best collection of eighteenth-century estate correspondence relates to the Abercorn estate in west Tyrone and east Donegal. Typescript copies of the great majority of the letters are available for inspection in calendar form in the Public Search Room of PRONI (ref. D/623/A). Most of the letters were written by the 8th Earl of Abercorn and his estate agents, John McClintock, Nathaniel Nisbett, John Colhoun, John Sinclair, John Hamilton and James Hamilton. The 8th Earl was an absentee landlord

who lived most of his life in London and only rarely visited his Irish estates. However, few absentee landlords can have known so much about their estates as the 8th earl knew about his. The letters cover a broad range of subjects and relate to all aspects of the estates' management. As an illustration of that can be gleaned from estate correspondence, the following extract from a letter of March 1786 from James Hamilton to Abercorn concerns particular problems associated with the 'new ferry' at Cloghboy in the manor of Dunnalong:

> The people going and coming from the new ferry and the people of the adjoining towns going to Derry, Strabane etc., trespass very much on David Ramsey and James Alexander of Gortmessan, who are both good farmers, who say if there was a road they would fence on each side of it. I am sure I saw more than half an acre of their ground that was ploughed that was so trod that they must plough it again, and they assure me that when their corn is growing they go through it an destroy it. . . . I think the road should be extended to Oliver Dunn's at Gortavea to let out a great many there to the great road; there would need an arch to be on the mearing between 'Tavnabree''' and Gortavea should the road go that far (ref. D/623/A/47/5).

Manor court records

Under the Plantation scheme of the early seventeenth century, the newly created estates were given the status of manors by royal patent. This converted a landowner into a landlord with power over his tenants. The manor provided the basic legal framework within which an estate could be managed, and was vital to its successful development. The lord of the manor was enabled to hold courts leet and baron to regulate the affairs of his estate. The courts also provided an arena where tenants could settle their disputes. The court leet, also known as a 'view of frank-pledge.' was originally a meeting of the freeholders of the manor called to exercise criminal jurisdiction. With the development of the criminal justice system and the rise of the magistracy, the importance of the court leet declined so that it became an administrative body. The court baron dealt with a range of civil actions including small debts, trespass and claims for damages. Usually a limit of 40 shillings was placed on the claims that the court could deal with. However, if a landlord wished to extend the power of his court he could have it made a 'court of record.' which could deal with larger claims. The courts were under the control of an official called a seneschal who was appointed by the lord of the manor. Only a relatively small number of manor court records have survived. The best collection is found in the Antrim estate papers in PRONI (D/2977). A good introduction to these records is Ian Montgomery, 'The manorial courts of the Earls of Antrim.' in *Familia* no. 16 (2000), pp. 1–23, which discusses the range of manor court records and the function of these courts.

Published information on estate papers

Most publications on Irish family history research now include a section on landed estate papers. In some instances these records are given merely passing mention, a paragraph or two highlighting the potential and limitations of using this category of record. John Grenham's, *Tracing Your Irish Ancestors* includes a summary of estate papers by county in Part III of his book. The depth of coverage varies between counties and generally only documents in the National Archives and National Library are listed. Nonetheless it provides the best readily accessible listing of estate papers on an island-wide basis. Appendix 2 of William Roulston's **Researching Scots-Irish Ancestors: the essential genealogical guide to early modern Ulster, 1600-1800** (Belfast, 2005) includes a detailed listing of some 250 estate collections relating to Ireland's northern province prior to the nineteenth century. This is arranged by county and provides precise references for most of the items listed. The great majority of these records are in PRONI, but others in private collections and repositories as far away as the Huntington Library in San Marino, California, are also listed. Published essays on particular estates are also included. Ian Maxwell's *Researching Down Ancestors* (Belfast, 2004) provides a summary listing of landed estate papers relating to County Down. His *Researching Armagh Ancestors* (Belfast, 2000) includes a brief listing of estate papers for that county.

Mention has already been made of the *Guide to Landed Estate Papers* produced by the Public Record Office of Northern Ireland and available in two ring bound volumes in the Search Room. PRONI has

also produced ring-bound volumes for counties Armagh, Fermanagh and Tyrone which includes lists of estate papers. It has also issued a ring-bound volume listing the papers of the London companies who possessed large estates in County Londonderry. These companies – the Clothworkers, Haberdashers, Goldsmiths, Fishmongers etc. – had been granted these lands in the early seventeenth century as part of the scheme for the Plantation of Ulster. Published in traditional format is *County Monaghan Sources in the Public Record Office of Northern Ireland* (Belfast, 1998) by Peter Collins (though with considerable assistance from Anthony Malcomson). Most of this book is given over to detailed introductions of eight '*big house*' collections of estate papers for Monaghan, while there is also a chapter providing shorter accounts of another dozen minor estates.

Local historical publications often include useful information relating to landed estates. This can include an account of the vicissitudes of the landed family most associated with a particular locality. Or it might be the names extracted from an estate rental. *Clogher Record*, the journal of the Clogher Historical Society is a veritable treasure trove of information on landed estates in, for the most part, counties Fermanagh and Monaghan. A few examples from the *Clogher Record* are set out below:

Lease abstracts for the Barrett Lennard Estate, Clones, over 200 items from the 17th and 18th centuries – *Clogher Record*, xviii (2003), 53-84
Rentals of the Kane Estate, Errigal Truagh, 1764 and 1801 – *Clogher Record*, xiii (1990), pp 72-91
Information on tenants on Ker estate, Newbliss, 1790-c.1830 – *Clogher Record*, xii (1985), pp 110-26
Survey of Ballybay Estate owned by Rev. Dr Henry Leslie, 1786 – *Clogher Record*, xi (1982), pp 71-6

Other local history journals across the length and breadth of Ireland include similar articles of interest.

The volume of published studies on Irish estates has increased considerably in the last two decades as greater interest has been shown in investigating them. At least part of the reason is due to the greater accessibility of some important collections of estate papers. Terence Dooley's volumes, *Sources for the history of landed estates in Ireland* (Ballsbridge: Irish Academic Press, 2000) and *The big houses and landed estates of Ireland: a research guide* (Dublin: Four Courts Press, 2007) provide an introduction to the value of estate collections and other records for studying

ENNISKERRY

landed estates. A short introduction to landed estates in the nineteenth century is W. E. Vaughan's *Landlords and tenants in Ireland, 1848-1904* (Studies in Irish Economic and Social History 2, 1984, revised 1994). For a longer read on more or less the same subject see Dr Vaughan's *Landlords and Tenants in Mid-Victorian Ireland* (Oxford, 1993). See also Olwen Purdue *The Big House in the North of Ireland: Land, Power and Social Elites, 1878–1960* (Dublin, 2009).

Case studies of individual estates and their owners are also becoming increasingly popular. W.H. (Bill) Crawford's *The management of a major Ulster estate in the late eighteenth century: the eighth earl of Abercorn and his Irish agents* (Dublin, 2001) is a short, but detailed account of estate management in north-west Ulster in the 1700s. Olwen Purdue's *The MacGeough Bonds of the Argory: an Ulster gentry family, 1880-1950* (Dublin, 2005) looks at the fate and fortunes of one landowning family during a period of considerable change. Jonathan Bell and Mervyn Watson have collaborated on several publications on aspects of Irish farming, the most recent being *A History of Irish Farming, 1750-1950* (Dublin, 2008). In addition Dr Bell has written *Ulster Farming Families, 1930-1960* (Belfast, 2005).

Other sources for studying landed estates

Most genealogical sources, with the exception of those exclusively relating to urban-dwellers, with contribute in some way to our understanding of the farming community. Church records will provide baptisms, marriages and burials, while civil registration will include births, marriages and deaths. The 1901 census will provide the names of everyone in a farming household on the night the census was taken. Many of the more substantial – and even some insubstantial – farmers made wills and erected headstones to deceased family members. The children of farmers will be found in school enrolment registers If researching a farming family, it is essential that sources such as these are utilised. However, it is not necessary here to go into such sources in detail. Those wishing to explore such records should consult any of the many Irish genealogical guides published in book form or online. There are a number of sources, however, that can be used alongside landed estate papers to gain a better understanding of the workings of rural life and the nature of land occupation and farming. Several of these are discussed in summary form below, though this list is not meant to be exhaustive.

Encumbered Estates Court

The Great Famine had a massive impact on the management and

economic viability of landed estates. Many estates were mortgaged and landowners unable to collect rents were forced to sell their estates. By an act of parliament in 1849 an Encumbered Estates Court was established with authority to sell estates on the application of the owner or encumbrancer (one who had a claim on the estate). After the sale the court distributed the money among the creditors and granted clear title to the new owners. The functions of the court were assumed by the Landed Estates Court in 1858. In advance of the sale of an estate a printed rental was prepared setting out what exactly was being put up for sale. These rentals contain very detailed information on tenants and holdings on each estate in order to attract potential buyers. The information in the rentals can be extremely detailed and can include the names of lives named in each lease as well as the status of each life. This can provide useful information on when someone died or where a particular individual was living at the time. Many of the rentals were beautifully illustrated with line drawings of country mansions as well as coloured maps showing the area being put up for sale. There are several sets of Encumbered Estates rentals which can be accessed at the National Library and National Archives, Dublin, and in PRONI (ref. D/1201).

Irish Land Commission

As noted in the introduction to this article, various acts of parliament transformed land ownership in Ireland in the late nineteenth and early twentieth centuries. The first of these acts was the 1870 Landlord and Tenant (Ireland) Act which sought to compensate tenants for improvements made by them to their holding or for any disturbance to their occupancy. Tenants wishing to purchase the title to their property could borrow up to two-thirds of the price, which they could repay at 5 per cent over 35 years. The 1881 Land Law (Ireland) Act established the Land Commission and the Land Court, while the 1885 Purchase of Land (Ireland) Act, known as the

Arigal Mountain, Donegal

Ashbourne Act, allowed tenants to borrow the full amount of the purchase price to be repaid over 49 years at 4 per cent. Between 1885 and 1888 more than 25,000 tenants purchased their holdings. The 1903 Land Act, known as the Wyndham Act, offered the landlords a 12 per cent bonus if they agreed to sell out their entire estate. This act, more than any other, brought about the transfer of estates from landlord to tenant.

The break-up of Irish landed estates generated a vast amount of material. From 1881 the Irish Land Commission oversaw this transfer of ownership. Title deeds, schedules, rentals, marriage settlements and wills can all be found among the papers for individual estates. The records of the Irish Land Commission concerning sales of estates in Northern Ireland to tenants were transferred from Dublin to Belfast in 1922 and were subsequently deposited in PRONI where they are classified as Land Registry papers. The *Guide to Landed Estate Records* in PRONI contains an index to the Land Registry papers by county. Of those records relating to the Irish Land Commission in the Republic of Ireland the main problem is one of accessibility. These records are now in the National Archives, Dublin, and it is best to consult staff there about availability. A catalogue compiled by Edward Keane for individual estates is available in the National Library, Dublin. This covers the period 1881-1909 and is primarily concerned with documents relating to title.

Parliamentary papers

From 1801 the papers generated by the Houses of Parliament, comprising printed reports of committees and royal commissions as well as accounts and other documents, provide an enormous amount of information on Irish society in the nineteenth century. Space does not permit a full discussion of these records, but researchers should be aware that many of the Irish parliamentary papers are available online as a text searchable database at www.eppi.ac.uk. See also William Roulston, *'British Parliamentary Papers and the Local Historian and Genealogist.' Familia,* no. 18 (2002), pp 63-82, which provides an overview of material of Irish interest in the early nineteenth century. Of particular interest for those wishing to find out more about the rural economy on the eve of the Great Famine is the *Report of Her Majesty's Commissioners of Inquiry into the state of the law and practice in respect of the occupation of land in Ireland* (1845). Popularly known as the Devon Commission, after the name of its chairman Lord Devon, this was a massive investigation covering the length and breath of Ireland. The commissioners visited nearly 100 places in Ireland in the course of their investigations and heard evidence from over 1,100 witnesses. The evidence given by the witnesses is included in the report and gives and amazing insight into Irish farming conditions at this time. Another parliamentary paper worth checking is the *Return of owners of land of one acre and upwards, in the several counties, counties of cities, and counties of towns in Ireland* (1876). A total of 32,614 owners are listed

along with their address and the acreage they possessed. Many British parliamentary papers relating to Ireland can now be viewed online at www.dippam.ac.uk.

Tithe Valuation

In 1823 the Composition Act was passed which stipulated that henceforth all tithes due to the Established Church, the Church of Ireland, were to be paid in money rather than in kind as they previously could have been. This necessitated a complete valuation of all tithable land in Ireland which was carried out between 1823 and 1838. The results of these investigations are contained in manuscript form in the tithe applotment books arranged by parish. Copies of these are available in PRONI and the National Archives, Dublin. The tithe applotment books contain the name of the tithe-payer, the size of his farm and the amount of tithe he paid. Though many people were excluded from the tithe valuation, it does act as a kind of census of Irish farmers in the early nineteenth century and can be a vital source for identifying where farming families were located at this time.

First Valuation

The First Valuation or Townland Valuation was compiled in the 1830s. It is of more limited value to the genealogist, especially for rural areas, as it is more concerned with land use and value. It does, however, record all houses valued at £3 or more (this was later raised to £5 or more) as well as the name of the head of each of these households. In many cases the actual dimensions of farmhouses and outbuildings are given as well as a coded lettering and numbering system which will provide an idea of how old the structures were and the materials from which they were built. The information is contained in fieldbooks arranged by parish. These are available in the Public Record Office of Northern Ireland and the National Archives, Dublin.

Griffith's Valuation

In the almost complete absence of nineteenth-century census returns, Griffith's Valuation is an essential genealogical source, being the first truly comprehensive survey of property in Ireland. A valuation of all properties in Ireland was started in County Dublin in 1847 and completed in counties Armagh and Down in 1864. A summary version of this valuation, known as the Primary Valuation or more popularly as Griffith's Valuation after Sir Richard Griffith, the man appointed Commissioner of Valuation, was published in some 200 volumes arranged by poor law union. In addition to the names of householders and landholders the valuation also provides the name of the person from whom the property was leased – the 'immediate lessor,' a description of the property, its acreage and the valuation of both the land and the buildings. A set of the printed volumes for the north of Ireland is available in PRONI, while the National Library, Dublin, has a set for the whole of Ireland. Local libraries will usually have the volumes for their area, while there are various online providers of information from Griffith's. The most useful of the websites hosting Griffith's Valuation is www.askaboutireland.ie which includes both the printed version and the annotated valuation maps.

The manuscript valuation books were updated on a regular basis. These so-called *'cancelled books'* or valuation revision books consist of manuscript notebooks updated to take account of changes in tenure. When a change of occupancy occurred, the name of the lessee or householder was crossed off and the new owner's name written above it, while the year was noted on the right-hand side of the page. Different-coloured ink was often used to differentiate between years with a key at the start of each book to indicate which colour went with each year. The years in which changes in occupancy took place help to establish significant dates in family history, such as dates of death, sale or emigration. On rare occasions there can even be a comment to the effect that a family had emigrated or that an individual had died. Changes in the valuation of buildings can indicate when a new house was built or when the existing one was abandoned. The valuation revision books for Northern Ireland are available in PRONI (ref. VAL/12B), while those for the Republic are available in the Valuation Office in Lower Abbey Street, Dublin.

The Agricultural Census of 1803

The threat of an invasion of Great Britain and Ireland by Napoleonic France recurred periodically during the late 1790s and the early years of the nineteenth century. The government in London made plans in 1797 and 1798 to abandon coastal areas and introduced new legislation for the defence of the realm. This legislation required the lord lieutenant for each county to make returns, especially from maritime parishes, enumerating

livestock (farm animals) and the wagons and horses available for transport, and giving the quantity of dead stock (crops stored). There are extant returns for some southern counties in England. During a scare in 1803 about an invasion of Ireland, resulting from the planned but abortive insurrection of that year, similar returns were made under the same legislation, which, after the Act of Union, applied to Ireland. The surviving returns relate to many parishes in County Down and the northern parishes of County Antrim.

The returns for County Down were made to the 1st Marquess of Londonderry. Presumably he received returns for each parish, although it is clear from those that have survived that there was considerable variation in their content. Most information is listed in various categories of livestock and dead stock, but in some returns the information also includes numbers of 'cars and carts.' of people 'able to drive cattle and load carts' or those 'willing to serve the Government gratuitously or for hire.' which underline the concern about a possible invasion. The returns for the agricultural census of 1803 are included in the Londonderry Papers of the 1st Marquess, held in PRONI. The PRONI reference for the census returns is D/654/A2/1-37A–C. A detailed analysis of the returns for County Down is provided by Duncan Scarlett in *Researching Down Ancestors* (Belfast, 2004).

The Flaxseed Premiums of 1796

In 1796, as part of a government initiative to encourage the linen industry in Ireland, free spinning wheels or looms were granted to farmers who planted a certain acreage

Connemara - Going to Market

of their holdings with flax. The names of over 56,000 recipients of these awards have survived in printed form, arranged by county and parish. Nearly two-thirds of the names relate to Ulster. The only copy of the book listing the names of these recipients known to exist until recently was held in the Linen Hall Library, Belfast. Another copy has now been acquired by the Irish Linen Centre in Lisburn Museum. The Ulster Historical Foundation has indexed this source and it is available as a searchable database at www.ancestryireland.com/scotsinulster

Registry of Deeds

The Registry of Deeds is an archive which is deserving of a more detailed study than can be given here. It was established by an act of parliament in 1708. The aim of the act was to provide one central office in Dublin 'for the public registering of all deeds, conveyances and wills, that shall be made of any honours, manors, lands, tenements or hereditaments.' To begin with registration was not compulsory, and the number of deeds registered varied from place to place. By 1832 over half a million deeds had been registered. The deeds registered include leases, mortgages, marriage settlements and wills. These can provide the researcher with names, addresses and occupations of the parties involved as well as the names of those who acted as witness. During registration, which often took place years after the original transaction, a copy of the deed called a memorial was made. The details of the memorial were then copied into a large bound volume. It is these transcript volumes that are available for public inspection.

Two indexes are available to the researcher: the Index of Grantors and a Lands Index. The format of the Index of Grantors has changed over the years. Before 1832 the Index gives the surname and the Christian name of the grantor, the surname of the grantee and the reference number. There is no indication of the location of the property concerned. After 1832 the Index is more detailed and includes the county in which the property is located.

The Lands Index is arranged by county, with one or more counties per volume. The entries are arranged alphabetically, but only with regard to initial letter. Each entry gives the surnames of the parties, the name of the denomination of land, and the reference number. After 1828 the Lands Index is subdivided by barony. The Index of Grantors and the Lands Index are available on microfilm at the National Library. PRONI has microfilms of both the indexes and the deeds (MIC/7 and MIC/311).

A popular misconception of the

Registry of Deeds is that it is of little value for those searching for eighteenth-century ancestors unless they were middle or upper class members of the Church of Ireland. This is far from the case and intensive research into the deeds has shown that, right from the beginnings of registration, a significant number do refer to Presbyterian tenant farmers and merchants. Nor is it true that ordinary Catholic tenant farmers are excluded altogether from the memorials in the Registry of Deeds. Furthermore, these deeds constitute a broad range of document types. The Registry of Deeds is located in a large Georgian building in Henrietta Street, Dublin. The main entrance for vehicles is off Constitution Hill. Although the layout of the building can be confusing, the arrangement of the records somewhat haphazard and the transcript volumes heavy and cumbersome, the Registry of Deeds is unlike any other archive in Ireland and is well worth a visit, if only for the experience of having used it.

Election records

Until the latter part of the nineteenth century, the right to vote was closely linked to land tenure. Throughout the seventeenth and eighteenth centuries only adult males in possession of a 40-shilling freehold were entitled to vote. A 40-shilling freehold was property worth 40 shillings a year above the rent, and either owned outright or leased during the lives of named individuals. The possession of a lease for years, no matter how many years, did not entitle one to vote. Many important and indeed prominent people had no vote because they leased their property on the wrong terms. The franchise was further restricted between 1727 and 1793, when Catholics were forbidden to vote. The franchise changed a number of times in the course of the nineteenth century and by the time of the general election of 1885 virtually all adult male householders were able to vote.

In the eighteenth and early nineteenth centuries election records are extremely useful for studying the farming community in that the electorate was mainly composed of tenant farmers. From 1728 onwards voters had to conform to an increasingly

Galway Market

tight system of registration, designed to prevent electoral fraud. Registers of freeholders list the names and addresses of individuals entitled to vote at parliamentary elections. Only by being registered to vote could a freeholder exercise his electoral rights. Poll books list the names of voters and the candidates they voted for. Until the eighteenth century, elections were held infrequently. Before 1768 there was no law limiting the duration of Irish parliaments and nothing to compel the government to hold a general election except the death of the reigning monarch. *The Octennial Act 1768* provided that a general election should be held at least every eight years. Nevertheless, until the nineteenth century very few elections were contested, and parliamentary representation remained firmly in the hands of a small number of powerful landed families.

In most of the freeholders registers and poll books the information provided is fairly basic – the name of the freeholder and his residence. The latter does not always include the name of the parish; further checking is required to discover this. Occasionally, however, some additional information of interest is provided. In the list of Armagh freeholders, c.1710–37 the names of the lives in the lease are often recorded. For example, the entry for William Lyndsay reveals that he held his freehold of Cargans from Oliver St John by virtue of a lease of 10 June 1726 for the lives of himself and his sons John and Thomas. By the early nineteenth century freeholders' registers tended to be printed and usually named the lives named in each registered lease. If a relevant entry is found in a freeholders' register it might be possible to use this information to search a landed estate collection or the Registry of Deeds to find a copy of the actual lease.

Newspapers

Newspapers are well-known as an excellent source of information on family history. From birth, death and marriage notices to items of local news, they can reveal a great deal about family networks in the past. Looking specifically at how newspapers can throw light on the management of landed estates and farming families, one particularly useful category of notice is the advertisement. The advertising of farms or even portions of estates for leasing was very common. Occasionally such advertisements will include information on the tenants of those townlands to be leased. For example, on 1 May 1770 an advertisement appeared in the Belfast Newsletter announcing that Lord Dungannon's estate in the parish of Island Magee in County Antrim was *'out of lease, and to be let for terms of years.'* In addition to announcing that the lands *'lie in a rich corn country'* with *'soil remarkable for producing all kinds of grain.'* the advertisement included the names of the sitting tenants by townland along with the size of their farms. The value of an advertisement like this is that it is the only known eighteenth-century document relating to Island Magee that names farmers by townland.

In the late nineteenth century newspapers can be useful in finding out the deliberations of the Land Courts of the Irish Land Commission. The sittings of the Land Courts were reported in considerable detail. These include the cases of individual tenants who placed their cases before the Commissioners. The Commissioners' decisions are often followed by a list of tenants with the old rent and the new judicial rent given. Lists such as these can provide evidence that an ancestor lived on a particular estate towards the end of the nineteenth century. A comprehensive index to the pre-1800 issues of the *Belfast Newsletter* is available online at www.ucs.louisiana.edu/bnl.

The Irish Trail
Janet Wilson

It all started with the letters. After my mother's death in 1988 I came across a number of letters between a distant Irish cousin Vida Chillingworth and my mother. I always knew we had Irish links but did not really know them. My Great Grandmother Charlotte Hamilton was Irish. Looking through the letters between my mother and Vida the names, Coote, Morphett, and (Morpeth) and Hamilton came up and the story went that three sisters married three army Officers. Eliza Coote born in Buttervant near Femoy, married Henry Hamilton who was in the 35th Regiment; Frances Coote married Captain William Adam Hay at St Finbar's Cathedral, Cork in 1838 who was in the 80th Regiment; Charlotte Coote married Sir Robert Charles Sinclair, 9th Bart of Caithness, in 1852 at Walton-on-the Hill, Liverpool. Robert was a Captain in the 38th Regiment.

So the big issue was where did I start to verify all the letters and hearsay regarding the family? Vida Chillingworth, the cousin seemed to think we were related to Sir Charles Henry Coote, the Coote's of Ballyfin, Mountrath, where the family home, which after eight years of restoration opened its doors as a hotel in May 2011. Some suites have been named after the Coote family. Also another relation was Lady Isabella, apparently the Earl of Carlisle's daughter. *Gosh this sounded so so good, but was it true!* Sadly after years of researching and although there is still an air of mystery regarding the Coote family, I am unable to prove this connection.

A name in one of the letters was Rev. Denis Hilliard. I wrote to him in Bray, Ireland only to discover he had died two years previously which was a little bit embarrassing, but his wife Florence replied and gave me details of someone who could help, and who was also researching the Coote Family. I got in touch with this lady - Christine McDonald, a nun from Nova Scotia, and a great great granddaughter of John Coote from his second marriage, and said if she ever had the opportunity to visit Ireland I would meet up with her. Much to my surprise a few months later I received news that Christine had arranged a sabbatical with her order and she had obtained permission to visit Ireland. Christine, at this point had previously done a considerable amount of research and was able to fill in various gaps.

So in 1996 we arranged to meet in Cork as this is near where our family came from. We met in a small Bed & Breakfast, having never known each other previously. I was a little apprehensive as I thought being with a nun would mean church every day, but Christine was very relaxed and Sunday was our church day; she even agreed to go into a pub with me, something she had never done in her life, she was casually dressed and was like a Nova Scotia nun on holiday.

After hiring a car, we planned a route to find out as much as we could and on our first day we went to the Cork City Library local history section where we were able to look at original newspapers. In *The Cork Examiner* we found a marriage announcement between John Coote

Charlotte Hamilton
Daughter of
Eliza Coote and
Henry Hamilton.

Charlotte married
Ariston Castelli

and Isabella Morphett, who had married at St Finbar's Cathedral in Cork - so this was our next visit. We were stunned by the beauty of this wonderful Cathedral and were amazed to think a relation of ours had actually married there.

We knew John Coote was our family link. (see tree) He had been stationed in Femoy and the family had lived in Kilworth, so off we went to visit there, and although we spoke to some lovely locals we did not find anything. John Coote, my great great great grandfather, was in the 71st Regt of Foot, he had served in The Peninsular War and received a medal with one clasp for the battle of Toulouse; he was also wounded at Waterloo and joined the 10th Veterans Battalion finally retiring on full pay, in 1821.

The next day we visited Cobh where some of the family had lived, and we went to St Mary's a local church. As mass was in progress, we waited till the end of the service and were invited to join the congregation for tea and coffee. We explained we were hoping to see some church records. It was our lucky day as we were introduced to Commander Crosbie who was Director of the Cobh Genealogical Project, and who held Cobh Protestant records. We gave him as much information as we could about our family, and he agreed to contact us the next day. He did so, saying he had found seven children of Vida Coote a sister to our link Eliza Coote.

Commander Crosbie found all this information on the Latter Day Saint site, (Family Search). In one of my mother's letters it stated that Vida Coote had died young but this turned out to be untrue which shows it is always better to verify any details passed down. Commander Crosbie arranged to have a wedding certificate sent to me showing the marriage between Vida and Issac Seymour, who was one of Eliza's other sisters. (see marriage certificate)

We had also found out that Isabella Coote had died in Whitegate in 1849 and was buried there so we paid a visit to look for her grave. Unfortunately we did not find it. It was probably there but because the inscriptions were so worn out it had disappeared. Following Isabella's death John travelled to Nova Scotia with two of the youngest children, Eyre and Mars where he was given 500 acres of land. John then remarried Mary McDowell in 1849 and had another daughter Ellen from whom Christine is directly descended.

We had established from the wedding announcement that Eliza Coote nee Morphett, had lived in Mallow, so this was our next call. We visited the Mallow Heritage Centre and the local Mallow Library where they had a family history section, both places were able to help us. They were able to provide us with the names of Eliza's parents and brothers and sisters, and we were able to visit the cemetery which was close by and actually find some very old grave stones of the Morphett family.

Christine and I had such fun on our trip, and I such had a giggle when she produced her gold credit card. Apparently the convent had saved all their Airmiles for Christine to come to Ireland and also she was entitled to use a gold card.

A few weeks later back in York, I received a message on my answer machine. It was from Commander Crosbie said that only a week or so after Christine and I had visited someone also researching the same family had met him and he left her phone number for me to contact her. I phoned Sally Benn (the name Commander Crosbie gave me) and she said she was coming to Harrogate the following week and could pop into York and see me.

Sally arrived with her four children, who went off to play with my two children, and we sat down and we put all our family history paper work on the

Page..............

CERTIFICATE OF REGISTRY OF MARRIAGE
TEASTAS CLARŪ PÓSADH

Pósadh do Ceiliúradh ag / Marriage Solemnized at Cove i / in the County de / of Cork i / in the Diocese of Cloyne

Uimh. No. (1)	Dáta an Phósta Date of Marriage (2)	Ainm agus Sloinneadh Name and Surname (3)	Dáta Breithe Date of Birth Age (4)	Staid Maidir le Pósadh Marital Condition (5)	Slí Bheatha (Sonrái Iomlána) Occupation (in full detail) (6)	Gnáth-áit Chónaithe roimh Pósadh Normal Residence before Marriage (7)	Ainm agus Sloinneadh an Athar, agus ainm na Máthar agus a Sloinneadh roimh Pósadh di Father's Name and Surname ~~and Mother's Name and Maiden Surname~~ (8)	An Ait a mBeartáitear Buan-Chónaí Ann ~~Intended Future Permanent Residence~~ Occupation of Father (9)
21	October 2nd 1845	Isaac Seymour	30	Bachelor	Ship agent	Cove	Henry Seymour	Ship agent
		Vida Coote	22	Spinster	—	Cove	John Coote	Lieutenant in the army

Arna bPósadh i / Married in the Church of Cove de réir Uird agus Deasgnátha Eaglaise na h-Éireann / according to the Rites and Ceremonies of the Church of Ireland, romham-sa, by licence by me – (not legible)

Céiliúradh an Pósadh so Eadrainn-ne / This Marriage was solemnized between us: Isaac Seymour, Vida Coote.

In ár Láthair-ne / In the Presence of us: John Coote, George Coote.

Dearbhaím leis seo gur fíor-chóip í seo as Chlár-leabhair na bPósadh an Pharóiste / I hereby certify the above to be a true Extract from the Marriage Register of the parish of Cove.

Ath-scríofa an / Extracted this 20th lá seo de / day of October i mBliain Ar dTiarna Míle Naoi gCéad agus / in the Year of our Lord One Thousand Nine Hundred and ninety six

Sínuí / Signed P J Anderson (Rector).

The Author outside St Finbar's Cathedral, Cork

has similar pictures to you, and especially if you are not aware of who they are, this opens up the possibility of identifying them and helping each other in the Family History trail.

Out of interest I did find out that our John Coote was probably a result of several Cootes from what was politely called *'A private marriage.'* Apparently the Coote fathers of the illegitimate offspring allowed them to use the family name and supported all their mothers!!! I had also contacted Sir Christopher Coote, the 15th Bart, who verified he knew about my John and that he was probably born *'on the wrong side of the blanket.'* Sir Christopher has over the years contributed a wealth of family history information and is a great researcher, and has been extremely helpful and informative.

During a visit to the Society of Genealogists in London following our trip to Ireland I was lucky to find on the top floor of the Society a book called *'Record of Coote Family'* by Rev A de Vlieger, and the book contained short biographies and notes on all the Cootes known to the author. It actually mentions Lieut. John Coote, our ancestor, although interestingly the author was unable to connect our John Coote with the rest of the Coote family.

I also paid a visit to the The National Archives in Kew and photocopied Army records showing that Lieut John Coote was an officer in the 71st (Highland) Regiment of Foot (Light Infantry) and on checking the Waterloo Roll shows that John was wounded in battle.

And as for 'Lady' Isabella she was plain Miss Isabella Morphett daughter of Richard Morphett Esq, of Cottage, Mallow. A visit to the Representative Church Body in Dublin, confirmed the marriage between Richard and Ann Andrews in 1782 at St Werbergs in Dublin.

Although we found quite a lot of family information some years ago, we still continue researching. The son of Vida Patrick Chillingworth and I also continue to try and find out information, as does Christine and I. We all know the researching never seems to end, seeking out another small detail that can make it all worthwhile. This takes us to places, when in a normal course one would not necessarily go to — meeting kind and helpful people along the way.

Yes, Frances Grace Coote married William Hay and then secondly was married to Dr William Montaque Smyth - there is no record of any children.

Charlotte Anne Coote married Sir Robert Sinclair in Liverpool. They lead an interesting life travelling to many places. From Sir Robert's Army Records I discovered that for many years they were stationed in Halifax Nova Scotia. They had no children.

floor. Now my husband who does not normally take much interest in family history came in and asked Sally if she had researched her husband's family history and she said, *'It is well documented.'* I still did not know who she meant, until my husband said, *'I have read his books'* so I knew then he meant the then Member of Parliament Tony Benn. Sally is married to his son Hilary Benn.

Since meeting Sally we have spent many an hour continuing with our research. Sally has been able to find out so much more about her side of the Coote family, even finding a picture of Vida Coote which she had copied after being supplied by a relation still living in Carrigaline. This family member also had a similar picture which I have of Charlotte Sinclair. I always find it a strange feeling when you discover someone you did not exist

St Finbar's Cathedral, Cork
Copyright Robert Blatchford Collection

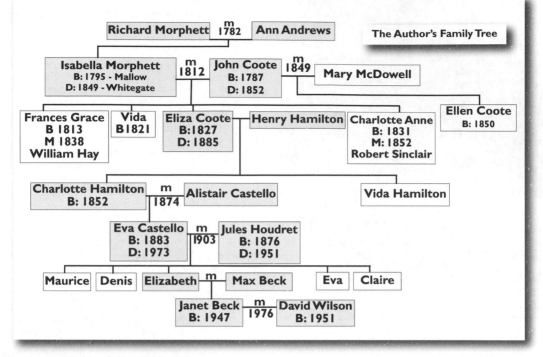

The Author's Family Tree

Richard Morphett — m 1782 — Ann Andrews

Isabella Morphett
B: 1795 - Mallow
D: 1849 - Whitegate
— m 1812 —
John Coote
B: 1787
D: 1852
— m 1849 —
Mary McDowell

Frances Grace
B 1813
M 1838
William Hay

Vida
B 1821

Eliza Coote
B: 1827
D: 1885

Henry Hamilton

Charlotte Anne
B: 1831
M: 1852
Robert Sinclair

Ellen Coote
B: 1850

Charlotte Hamilton
B: 1852
— m 1874 —
Alistair Castello

Vida Hamilton

Eva Castello
B: 1883
D: 1973
— m 1903 —
Jules Houdret
B: 1876
D: 1951

Maurice   Denis   Elizabeth — m — Max Beck   Eva   Claire

Janet Beck
B: 1947
— m 1976 —
David Wilson
B: 1951

Charlotte Castelli nee Hamilton

MAYALL,   224, Regent S[t]

However to date I can find no marriage record for Eliza Coote and Henry Hamilton, although we do have a birth certificate and death certificate for one of the children, with Henry Hamilton's name on it, which I found by chance at the Chester Family History Centre, in 2010. *We are still searching for the other evidence!! It's a mystery.*

We also do know that Eliza Hamilton (nee Coote) lived with husband Henry and children Charlotte, Henry and at 8 Codrington Terrace, Notting Hill in 1867. Amongst the letters my mother had, I found a Valentine's card sent to Charlotte at this address; we found out at the local studies section of Kensington Library the rent entry for this address and also that Codrington Terrace became 90 Ladbroke Grove. This building still stands today.

Altogether with the pieces of paper and letters left by my mother, it has certainly opened up an amazing interest, also amongst her belongings are pictures of various Army relations but there are no names, and although I have had an expert look at the pictures, the uniforms do not resemble any of the three Officers who married three sisters!

I still visit Ireland once a year and continue to try and verify the letters for our future families' interest.

The Coote Family Home, Ballyfin, Mountrath

The Irish Georgian Society
emmeline henderson
conservation manager & assistant director

On July 23rd 1957, *The Irish Times* published the following letter:
'Sir, As the Georgian Society seems to have lapsed, has anyone any objection to my restarting it? Our aims are to bring the photographic records up to date, publish further volumes of the Georgian Society's books, and fight for the preservation of what is left of Georgian architecture in Ireland. Yours, etc.
Desmond Guinness, Carton, Maynooth, Co Kildare.'

The original Georgian Society, which Desmond referred to in his letter to *The Irish Times* was founded in 1908 by Rev. John Pentland Mahaffy, Provost of Trinity College Dublin. The Georgian Society lasted for five years and published five volumes of photographs and drawings of Georgian architecture, one a year from 1909 to 1913. The first four volumes focused on Eighteenth-Century domestic architecture and decoration in Dublin, while the last volume published in 1913, was an examination of the Irish country house. The original Georgian Society was not founded as a preservation society but rather an architectural recording body. Whilst Mahaffy's preface to the Georgian Society Records does urge its readers *'to induce those who live in houses still containing good and interesting work both to take care of it, and to have sketches and*

photographs made,' the primary aim of the Society was to *'inspect and note the eighteenth-century (or Georgian) architectural and decorative work which remains in Dublin, and to record such work by means of sketches, measured drawings, and photographs.'* There was an air of fatalism about the Georgian Society, which viewed Ireland's architectural heritage to be doomed to *'decay and disappearance,'* with the Georgian Society being founded so as to record that heritage before it finally vanished.

Not so with the re-established Irish Georgian Society, which the Hon. Desmond Guinness and his late wife Mariga officially founded on the 21st February 1958, seven months after his letter to *The Irish Times* was published. Whilst the Irish Georgian Society recognised the need for recording Ireland's Georgian architecture, understanding that it is often the first step towards conservation, the Irish Georgian Society considered the conservation of Ireland's architectural heritage as fundamental and imperative.

It is difficult today to conceive of the conservation climate in which the Irish Georgian Society was founded. Widely perceived by both the government and the public to be the remnants of a colonial power, Ireland's attitude to its Georgian architecture was one of apathy and often antipathy.

The demolition by the government in July 1957 of two adjacent Georgian townhouses it owned on Kildare Place was symptomatic of this lack of regard for this aspect of Ireland's heritage, and it was their demolition, which provided the conservation cataclysm that spurred Desmond Guinness into founding the Society. No. 2 Kildare Place, which was built in 1751 by John Ensor to the designs of Richard Castle and its neighbouring building of a slightly later date, were both structurally sound. Today, bizarre as it may seem, the two buildings were demolished by the government because they had no perceived use for them and did not want to incur any expense in their maintenance. A plain brick wall, which today still remains, was erected in their place.

Further high profile demolitions, followed, which confirmed to Desmond and Mariga Guinness the dire need for an architectural preservation society. The most infamous of these demolitions was undoubtedly Fitzwilliam Street Lower. In 1961 the Electricity Supply Board announced their intention to demolish their Georgian offices along Fitzwilliam Street Lower and replace them with a new purpose built office block. In an endeavour to save the facades, the Irish Georgian Society, launched a vigorous conservation campaign, with the Society submitting a 10,000-signature petition to Dublin Corporation. Although the interiors of the ESB owned Fitzwilliam Street Lower houses were of

50 Mountjoy Square before restoration

negligible architectural significance on account of the extensive alterations already carried out when they were converted to office use, the buildings were of immense group and streetscape value, constituting with Merrion Square East, Fitzwilliam Street Upper and Fitzwilliam Place, the longest unbroken line of Georgian houses in Europe. Despite strenuous opposition, Dublin Corporation granted permission to the ESB to demolish these 16 Georgian houses on Fitzwilliam Street Lower and erect a new office complex in its place, resulting in the mutilation of the streetscape.

Another key early conservation battle occurred in 1964, when Desmond and Mariga purchased number 50 Mountjoy Square. Buying the house was a strategic move aimed at thwarting the plans of a developer, Matt Gallagher of Leinster Estates, who owned the adjoining buildings and wished to demolish the entire south side of Mountjoy Square and erect a large office development in its place. In retaliation the developer demolished the buildings flanking number 50 so as to remove all lateral support and exposing it to risk of collapse. Desmond and Mariga counter attacked by taking a successful high court action to have Leinster Estates, at their own expense, erect timber buttresses to stabilise number 50 Mountjoy Square.

The media closely followed the episode and the Irish Georgian Society's success in its legal challenge conveyed a clear message that property developers could not demolish Dublin's Georgian buildings with impunity. In addition, Desmond and Mariga's commitment to Mountjoy Square, resulted in many of the their friends and Society supporters purchasing and restoring houses in Mountjoy Square and the nearby streets located within Dublin's north inner city Georgian core.

So while the early days comprised successes and losses, even the losses, such as Fitzwilliam Street Lower can now be viewed as having some positive outcome, in that those conservation campaigns spearheaded by the Irish Georgian Society were central to shifting public opinion in favour of preservation. The Society must also be credited with encouraging an understanding that Ireland's Georgian buildings should not be viewed as relics of a colonial past but rather celebrated as being for the most part the work of Irish craftspeople.

Today the Irish Georgian Society can without immodesty claim to have saved many important buildings from destruction. Whilst the historic urban environment has always been high on the agenda, perhaps the most notable of the Irish Georgian Society's early preservation achievements was in the realm of the country house. Without the financial support and direct intervention of the Irish Georgian Society it is improbable that country houses such as: Ledwithstown House, County Longford; Roundwood House, Co. Laois; Damer House and Longfield, County Tipperary; and Riverstown and Doneraile Court, County Cork; would have survived into the 21st century.

Other notable achievements of the Irish Georgian

City Assembly House

Reproduced with kind permission of The Irish Georgian Society.

Society included the preservation of the Swiss Cottage in Cahir, Co. Tipperary and the Dromana Gateway in Cappoquin, Co. Waterford, as well as the Conolly Folly in Co. Kildare, which the Irish Georgian Society was to adopt as their symbol.

However, unquestionably the most celebrated conservation achievement of the Irish Georgian Society was the saving of Castletown House, County Kildare. Castletown, considered to be the largest and grandest Palladian country house in Ireland, was saved from threat of demolition when the Hon. Desmond Guinness purchased the house, some of the surrounding land, as well as the more important contents in 1967.

The next year the Society moved its headquarters from the Guinness's home, Leixlip Castle, to Castletown House. Members of the Society

Demolition of 2 Kildare Place

Reproduced with kind permission of The Irish Georgian Society.

Conolly Folly, County Kildare

participated in volunteer work parties, contributed financial assistance, and gifted and loaned furniture and paintings to Castletown. Since 1994 the house has been in the ownership of the Office of Public Works, while the collection is owned and managed by the Castletown Foundation.

Fifty years on the Irish Georgian Society, with President, Desmond FitzGerald, Knight of Glin and Director, Donough Cahill at the helm, is still to the fore in promoting and preserving Ireland's architectural heritage. The Society, a registered charity, is not in receipt of government core funding and depends on its members to underwrite its conservation work. The membership, comprising 2,600, is worldwide, with active chapters in Birr, Cork, Limerick, London, Chicago, New York and Palm Beach. Money raised through events and members' subscriptions allows the Society to deliver on its mission statement of promoting and preserving Ireland's architectural heritage, which is achieved through its four core programmes: Buildings at Risk; Scholarship and Publication; Conservation Education; and Conservation Grants.

The **Buildings at Risk Programme** involves the Society advocating for the protection of buildings of architectural and historical importance, which are threatened by neglect or inappropriate development. Vernon Mount, Co. Cork; Hazelwood, Co. Sligo; and Aldborough House, Dublin City; are the focus of major current advocacy work.

The Society's **Scholarship and Publication Programme** comprises several initiatives. Most notable is the Society's *Irish Architectural and Decorative Studies* journal. Now in its thirteenth year, the journal is the successor to the Society's quarterly bulletins, which were published from 1958 to 1997. Like the bulletin, the journal is rigorously academic and is distinguished by its publication of primary research. It is the only journal dedicated to publishing new research on Ireland's architects, craftsmen, artists, garden designers and patrons.

Another core initiative of the Society's Scholarship and Publication programme is the Annual Desmond Guinness Scholarship. Since 1996 the Desmond Guinness Scholarship has been awarded to scholars not yet established in research or publication who are conducting original documentary research on the visual arts in Ireland, including the work of Irish architects, artists, craftsmen, at home and abroad from 1600-1900. The scholarship is recognised for nurturing and fostering emerging Irish art historical talent.

The **Conservation Education Programme** is another cornerstone of the Society's work. Central to its delivery is the Society's annual *Traditional Building and Conservation Skills in Action Exhibitions*, which provides accurate and impartial conservation advice, free of charge, to owners of historic buildings. The exhibitions encompasses demonstrations by craftspeople skilled in such disciplines as: the use of lime based renders; dressing traditional slate roofs; restoration of timber sash windows; conservation of fanlights; restoration of historic ironwork; and cleaning and repair of decorative plasterwork.

During the last decade the Society has dispensed over €1 million through our **Conservation Grants Programme**. Recent major conservation grants include funding towards the reinstatement of the only intact Robert Adam designed decorative interior scheme in Ireland, namely the Eating Parlour at Headfort, Kells, County Meath and the reinstatement of a Georgian Garden at the RSAI, 63 Merrion Square, Dublin. The Society's next major project is the restoration of the City Assembly House on South William Street. Constructed between 1766-71 by the Society of Artists, who sought to provide a means to promote Irish art and artists, it was the first purpose built public art gallery in Ireland or Britain. Of particular interest is the great octagonal exhibition room. This has hosted the works of some of Ireland's greatest 18th century landscape artists. On completion of the restoration the Society will deploy the building as a centre for the promotion of Irish architectural culture and heritage.

In the delivery of these core programmes the Irish Georgian Society continues a campaign of more than half a century of promoting and preserving Ireland's historic architecture and allied arts. During this time the Society has played a pivotal role in altering attitudes and changing perceptions of the value of Ireland's built heritage.

Anyone wishing to support the Society's work is encouraged to become a member. If you are interested in reading more about the Society's history and conservation achievements see *The Irish Georgian Society: A Celebration* by Robert O'Byrne (Hardback €30 244 PP - numerous lavish illustrations) from the Irish Georgian Society, 74 Merrion Square, Dublin 2, Ireland. T: +353 (0)1 6767053 E: info@igs.ie W: www.igs.ie

New Premises for Old Documents
Dr Ann McVeigh

The Public Record Office of Northern Ireland (PRONI) is now open to the public in its new, state-of-the-art premises. Opening in March 2011, it was two months ahead of schedule, much to the delight of researchers both regular and new.

The new accommodation, which is fully compliant with DDA, comprises an expansive Public Search Room, with seating for 76; an integral microfilm area, accommodating 20 researchers and with two microfilm printers; internet and WiFi access and laptop-enabled tables. There are 35 computers giving access to the e-Catalogue and ordering system, while another 13 PCs will allow easy browsing of our databases, guides and website. The Reading Room, with seating for 80, provides greatly enhanced capacity and facilities for researchers, including access to the e-Catalogue and ordering system. A totally new feature is our self-service digital camera, where researchers can scan a document directly onto a USB pen.

The storage repositories have been greatly expanded and improved with bespoke 'rolling rack' shelving systems, fully compliant with the British Standard for the preservation of archival documents. The spacious ground floor area houses Reception; an exhibition area, which will feature 'A century of conflict, change and transformation', our opening interactive exhibition; a lecture and a conference room; three information/orientation points; a meeting area; public utilities, and a café with internet access. All public areas are Wi-Fi enabled.

We are happy to welcome both individuals and groups to our new premises (although groups of six or more should book in advance), and we look forward to being a vibrant part of the Titanic Quarter community.

PRONI Website

For those stating their research for the first time, the PRONI website (www.proni.gov.uk) is a great place to start your research as it contains information on the most useful archives to consult at PRONI, an updated set of PRONI's family and local history leaflets, and information on other sites that may be useful to your area of study. The 'Frequently Asked Questions' page covers a host of topics. One of the most useful and popular parts of the PRONI website is our extensive introductions to over 140 major private collections. These give users an excellent overview of each archive as well as detailed historical background information. Increasingly, however, we are putting more databases and guides online.

Records Available On-line

Several major databases are available on-line:

The Freeholders' Records relating to the six counties of Northern Ireland from the mid 18th to early 19th centuries, record the name and place of residence of those who were entitled to vote (or who actually voted) at elections. This online resource of over 5,000 high quality images of the registers is fully searchable and provides direct access to a unique resource for family and local history for a period that has a scarcity of documentary evidence.

The Ulster Covenant contains the names and addresses of those who opposed Home Rule in the early part of the twentieth century. Almost half a million people signed either the Covenant (men), or the Declaration (women). The database is searchable by surname and each surname is linked to an image of the actual document showing the handwritten signature. Next year (2012) sees the 100th anniversary of the signing of the Covenant.

The Wills Index is now searchable online. This application provides a fully searchable index to the will calendar entries for the three District Probate Registries of Armagh, Belfast and Londonderry. The database covers the period 1858-1919 and 1922-1943. Part of 1921 has been added, with remaining entries for 1920-1921 to follow in the near future. Digitised images of entries from the copy will books covering the period 1858-

and merchants. Some, for example, Matier's 1835-6 *Directory* and the 1831-2 *Directory* feature only Belfast, but will also generally include a list of the gentry in the neighbourhood. These 'village directories' include a list of the principal inhabitants living on the outskirts of Belfast, for example in Dunmurry, Jordanstown and Newtownbreda, as well as an alphabetical listing referred to as *'Country Residents.'* Occasionally the directory is only for some provincial towns, for example the 1840 *New Commercial Directory of Armagh, Newry, Londonderry*, etc. While there are problems with their accuracy, they are nevertheless, an invaluable resource for family and local historians.

Name Search, launched in 2009, currently includes the following sets of indexes:
• index to pre-1858 wills (which are to be found in various collections in PRONI) and a
selection of diocesan will and administration bond indexes
• surviving fragments of the 1740 and the 1766 religious census returns
• 1775 dissenters petitions
• pre-1920 coroners' inquest papers
The Public Record Office of Northern Ireland (PRONI) is committed to making its archives more widely available. While PRONI's eCatalogue has made access to PRONI's archives easier and speedier, in most instances it does not provide information on the actual content of the archives. PRONI has therefore embarked on a project to improve access to content by producing or reproducing indexes to some of the most popular records.

About the pre-1858 wills index: Although most originals were destroyed in the fire in the Public Record Office of Ireland (Dublin) in 1922, copies of testamentary records or extracts from them survive in a wide variety of PRONI sources. The pre-1858 wills index is an attempt to bring together pre-1858 wills and administrations found within the archives in PRONI. There are over 15,500 entries in this index. If a copy does survive, this will be noted.

About the 1740 and 1766 religious census: These returns are not only of value to the family and local historian but to those interested in Irish surnames and how they have been anglicised. The returns lists

1900 are now available online, allowing users to view the full content of a will. 93,388 will images are now available to view.

Although the original wills up to 1900 were destroyed and it is simply copies of these wills that have survived, they are the earliest complete set proved by the Supreme Court of Judicature in Ireland, who assumed responsibility for granting probate and letters of administration in 1858. The index is based on the entries in the will calendars that summarise every will proved and all letters of administration granted, amounting to over 148,000 entries. Although many wills relate to the professional classes and the landed gentry, most walks of life are covered, from farmers, labourers and grocers, to blacksmiths, innkeepers, watchmakers, and even a few people who died in the workhouse! The last testaments of well-known personalities are also represented, for example, Thomas Andrews, the director of Harland & Wolff who was aboard the Titanic when it sank in 1912, and Charles Lanyon, civil engineer and architect, who designed many of the finest buildings in Belfast, including Queen's University, the Custom House, and the Crumlin Road Court House.

Street Directories, previously on open access in the Search Room, were very heavily used and damage was becoming critical. Further handling would have endangered their long term preservation so it was decided to scan the directories to provide an on-line search. The online directories cover the years 1819 to 1900 but with some gaps in the series. PRONI does not hold copies of all street directories and even when the main run of the *Belfast and Ulster Street Directory* begins in 1852 there are gaps in the series up to 1900.

The directories were published for trade and business purposes largely as a result of the growth in trade at home and with the wider world, hence the emphasis on the listing of manufacturers, traders

created by the coroners, and indeed many older inquests have not survived. Consequently, if a record does not exist that does not necessarily mean that an inquest did not take place.

PRONI Photographs on Flickr

Images from the archives are now available on the photo-sharing website '*Flickr.*' A selection of images from the Allison photographic collection can now be viewed on PRONI's Flickr Photostream. You can view the images without a Flickr account but if you want to leave comments about the photographs, you will have to create a Flickr account. A basic Flickr account is free.

The first collection of PRONI images to be made available on Flickr are wedding and family group portraits taken by the Allison Photographic Studios, Armagh, between circa 1900 and 1955. The photos are arranged in sets alphabetically by family name, or you can use the search box to search for a particular name - just make sure you are searching the PRONI Photostream and not the entire Flickr site! Take a look to see if any of your ancestors appear in the shots and feel free to add a comment. Initially, 200 images were uploaded to Flickr, but now the entire collection of 1,530 wedding and family group portraits are available.

Guides

On-line Guide to Church Records: Church records are an invaluable source for the family historian, especially those that pre-date Civil Registration of births, deaths and marriages, introduced in Ireland in 1864. PRONI's *Guide to Church Records* is an easy way to identify what churches are in a parish, what records exist for each church, the covering dates for each series of records (for example, baptisms, marriages, vestry minutes etc.) and their PRONI reference number. Denominations included are: Church of Ireland, Roman Catholic, Presbyterian, Non-Subscribing Presbyterian, Reformed Presbyterian, Methodist, Moravian, Congregational, Baptist and Religious Society of Friends ('*Quakers*'). Normally, there will be more than one denomination of church in each parish. The denomination of a church can be identified in the Guide by the preceding code (for example, C.I. = Church of Ireland; P. = Presbyterian Church and R.C. = Roman Catholic Church). The majority of parishes covered in the Guide are located within the six counties of Northern Ireland; however, PRONI holds some records from parishes in the Republic of Ireland, particularly the border counties of Donegal, Cavan, Monaghan, Leitrim and Louth. You will still have to visit PRONI to see the actual records but at least by checking this guide, you can be confident that your journey will not be wasted.

the names of heads of households arranged largely by county, barony and parish and in at least half of the returns there is a breakdown by townland. No further information is given about the individuals. The returns show religion as either Roman Catholic (referred to as 'Papists') or Protestant. Protestants were sometimes distinguished as either Church of Ireland, or Dissenters, with Dissenters being mainly Presbyterians. The returns also give an account of any Roman Catholic priests operating in the parish and their names. There is often more than one person of the same name listed in a townland/parish but we have no way of knowing whether this was in fact the case or if names were duplicated in transcription.

About the Dissenters' Petition: The petitions are lists of names of Dissenters arranged either by parish, by congregation, by town and neighbourhood or in one instance by barony. Occasionally, members of the Established Church also signed the petitions. The lists usually indicate whether the signatories were Dissenters or Established Church members, although there are occasions when no such information is recorded.

About the pre-1910 coroners' inquest papers: Coroners in Northern Ireland are either barristers or solicitors and are appointed by the Lord Chancellor. They inquire into deaths that are unexpected or unexplained, a result of violence, negligence or accident, or any other unusual circumstances. Coroners' records held by PRONI date from 1872 to 1997 and are now referenced on the Name Search database. They contain details of the surname, forename, address, date of death and date of inquest.

A relatively small volume of inquests have survived for the former part of this period (1872-c.1960) in comparison to a much larger volume which has been retained in recent years (including the Troubles period). Name Search has indexed most inquest papers for the period 1872-1920 and the original documents are open to the public for this period. More recent inquest papers are closed to the public but requests for information can be made in writing to PRONI (see below for information on access).

PRONI does not take every inquest record

Electronic Catalogue: Perhaps the jewel in our website's crown, the Electronic Catalogue (E-Catalogue) enables researchers to browse the lists of practically all our collections from the comfort of their own computers. Providing web access to over one and a quarter million catalogue entries, the E-Catalogue contains approximately 70% of PRONI's total catalogue of which almost 92% is relevant to family history. The database can be searched by keyword, such as a name, townland or subject matter; by date; or by PRONI reference number. Some private documents have been transcribed, thus removing the need to see the original in a number of cases. This resource has made it so much easier to carry out research 24/7.

Coming Soon.

Work is currently underway to digitise the **Re-Valuation Books** (VAL/12B) to make these records available on-line in the future. The First General (Griffith's) Valuation was completed by 1864. However, this could be considered simply a snapshot in time as changes to land ownership and property developments are not recorded, hence the introduction in 1864 of the re-valuation books which noted any changes in land use. Thereafter, properties were valued annually until the early 1930s, with each volume of the re-valuation books covering approximately a ten-year period. Each year, assessors recorded any change in the quality or dimensions of the properties, or in the names of occupiers or immediate lessors, and any differences in the acreage and value. The changes were recorded in different colours of ink, one colour for each year, and the alterations are usually dated. This can help to establish significant dates in family history, such as dates of death, sale or migration.

Public Records

Many people are under the impression that, due to the fire in the Public Record Office of Ireland in the Four Courts in Dublin, there are no surviving public records before in 1922. In fact, there are many series of records that go back to the early 19th and even into the 18th century. For example, the Grand Jury Presentment Books that give the names of those who received money for the construction and repair of roads, bridges, gaols, and other public works, date back to the 1760s.

Other early sources include:
• Valuation records, dating from the 1830s to the present
• Tithe Applotment books, 1823-37,
• Copy wills, 1838-c.1900,
• Original wills, 1900 to 2004;
• Registers and inspectors' observation books of approximately 1,600 national/public elementary/primary schools, 1870s – c.1950s
• Grant-aid applications of the Commissioners of National Education, 1832 to 1889;
• Ordnance Survey maps (various scales) 1831 - present;
• Minutes, indoor and outdoor relief registers, and other papers of the Boards of Guardians who administered the workhouse system from 1838 to 1948;
• Records, including admission registers, of lunatic asylums, some dating back to the mid-19th century (but these are subject to extended closure for 100 years);

• Title deeds, leases and wills in the Irish Land Commission and the Land Purchase Commission archive, some of which date back into the 18th century.

Guides to using the more popular collections, such as the tithe applotment books, the large scale Ordnance Survey town plans, education records and probate records, are available in the PRONI search room.

Private Archives

Privately deposited records are also available at PRONI and can often be very adequate substitutes for those public records destroyed in the Four Courts Fire. The most important of those are:
• records of solicitors' firms, which include copies of wills, leases and title deeds;
• great landed estates (many of which go back into the 17th and 18th centuries);
• railway companies, who bought up a considerable amount of land;
• churches, where generations were baptised and married.

Equally useful are family and personal papers, and the working notes of antiquarians and genealogists who worked in the Public Record Office of Ireland prior to the fire of 1922. These scholars took copious notes from the early records and their notebooks contain information on documents dating back to the mid 17th centuries.

Almost all the major estate archives for Northern Ireland are held in PRONI and you can find descriptions of many of them on the PRONI website. Among the more notable estate archives are: Downshire (Cos Down and Antrim); Antrim (Co. Antrim); Abercorn (Co. Tyrone); Belmore (Co. Fermanagh); Gosford, Brownlow and Caledon (Co. Armagh); and Drapers' Company (Co. Londonderry). Other estate papers are also available.

Opening Times

PRONI is open to the public Mon - Wed and Fri 9.00 am – 4.45 pm; Thurs - 10.00 am – 8.45 pm. Latest time for ordering documents is 4.15 pm (Thursdays, 8.00 pm). There is no need to make an appointment unless you intend to bring a group. Group visits are very welcome but **must** be booked in advance.

Research is free for those pursuing personal and educational research, however, all visitors will need to obtain a Visitor Registration card at Reception which requires photographic proof of identity.

PRONI staff look forward to welcoming visitors to our new office.

The North of Ireland Family History Society

The North of Ireland Family History Society [NIFHS] is a voluntary, non-profit organisation with charitable status [XR 22524]. It began in 1979 as a group of people interested in family history and now has a dozen or so Branches around Ulster and a large Associate Membership scattered around the world – about a thousand Members in all.

The Society actively encourages the formation of new Branches, not just in the nine counties of Ulster but also anywhere that has a nucleus of people interested in researching their Ulster origins – many Ulster families moved to County Durham, England in the 1850s to work in or to support the mining industry and others moved to Liverpool or to Ayrshire and Lanarkshire and Renfrewshire as industry in those places developed – and many others built new lives in Canada, the U.S.A., New Zealand and Australia.

Website

Our website at www.nifhs.org is our public face and its continuing development is proving successful – the Society won 2nd place for the Best Website Award for Large Societies of the Federation of Family History Societies in 2010 and follows the same award in 2009 and commendations in the previous two years.

On the website are details of how to join the Society and how to purchase our publications, with the option to pay by PayPal; it has a catalogue of the material available in our Research Centre; there is information on each Branch – where it meets and when and its programme for the year; and there are a number of other resources. There are plans to develop the website further with a Members' area.

Journal and Newsletter

Our journal, *North Irish Roots*, began is published twice a year, in spring and autumn, and sent to all Associate and Branch Members. It contains articles, long and short, for example about families or about useful resources such as record offices, databases, books, CDs, events, maps or photographs; it contains correspondence, Branch programmes, transcriptions of records, news and profiles of leading Members; it contains lists of Members' interests and their queries and a register of reciprocal research. An index is available on the Society's website www.nifhs.org, where most back numbers are available for purchase together with binders; payment may be made via PayPal. Fully indexed back numbers of the journal are available as part of the Ireland Collection on the JSTOR website at www.jstor.org and access to the whole of this collection is free for Members. These were digitised in collaboration with the Queen's University of Belfast.

We are looking for our roots
Come and join us.

Our newsletter, *News 45* comes out twice a year, between issues of the journal, and is e-mailed to Members. Designed primarily to keep Associate Members in touch, it carries a variety of news, particularly about new websites that may be of use.

Research Centre

Our collection has now been fully indexed by Sandra Ardis and Edith Tuckey.

Projects and Publications

Various Branches have projects to transcribe and index such records as graveyard inscriptions and BMD announcements in newspapers and other material of general interest and these are published as books or CDs and can be purchased through our website www.nifhs.org using PayPal.

Also the Society is undertaking the publication of a series of booklets, called *Researching Your Ancestors in the North of Ireland*, to help Members and others in their research. The current titles are *A Beginners' Guide*, *A Research Guide*, *A List of Websites* and *Locating Church Records*; further titles are being prepared, including some county guides.

A useful database on our website is a collection of over 15,000 census strays – records of Irish-born people appearing in censuses elsewhere; contributed by many people, these records were coordinated by Jeanne Jordan and typed up by a team of Members. A current project, being undertaken by Anne Johnston, is to develop a database of all post-1600 churches in the north of Ireland and to make this available online using a map based system in collaboration with the Ordnance Survey of Northern Ireland. For each church it will have a photograph, a brief history and a list of extant records and where they may be found.

Branches

We also have branches in Bangor, Lisburn, Killyleagh), Belfast, Craigavon, Larne, Omagh, Ballymena, Fermanagh, Newtownabbey, Coleraine, Donegal, Portadown (now called North Armagh), Warrenpoint and Foyle.

Membership

We have two types of membership:

Our President, Randal Gill, accepting 2nd place *Best Website Award for Large Societies* of the Federation of Family History Societies from Lady Teviot, President of the Federation at the Federation's A.G.M. 2010.

Associate Membership for those unable to attend regular Branch meetings – an application form is downloadable from the website www.nifhs.org or you may join online, paying by PayPal.

Branch Membership for those able to attend regular Branch meetings – attend a meeting at your nearest Branch and, if you wish to join, ask the Branch Treasurer for an application form.

Either type of membership will entitle you to:

• *North Irish Roots*, our journal, which is published twice a year and contains a wide range of articles, correspondence, reviews, news and Members' interests and queries.

• *News 45*, our newsletter, which is produced twice a year and e-mailed to Members who have supplied an e-mail address.

• Submit profile forms with your surname interests, for publication in the journal or on the website or both.

• Request lookups from our collection of church registers and graveyard inscriptions if you are unable to visit the Research Centre.

• Free online access to JSTOR's Ireland Collection, which includes digitised and indexed back numbers of *North Irish Roots*.

Attendance at any of our Branch meetings, with the opportunity to meet like-minded family history researchers.

Outreach

The Society does not undertake genealogical research for anyone but Members of the Society often deliver talks to various organisations and organise or assist with courses on family history. These activities are helped by the good relationships that the Society and its Branches have built up with the public libraries and other organisations in the Province. The Society is also represented at an increasing number of family history fairs, both local and national – for example in recent years the Society has had a well-staffed stall at *Who Do You Think You Are? Live* at Olympia. Increasingly the Society is expanding these activities geographically, as with the London event at Olympia and similar events in Newcastle upon Tyne and Dublin, and these give opportunities for Associate Members in those areas to be involved.

Our publicity leaflet has been regularly updated since it was first produced in 1994 and is widely distributed in the north of Ireland each spring and summer and has brought an increase in membership.

Contacts

Our website is www.nifhs.org. The Society Office and Research Library are located in Park Avenue, off the Holywood Road, but our mailing address, to which all correspondence should be sent, is:

North of Ireland Family History Society, c/o School of Education, Queen's University, 69-71 University Street, Belfast, BT7 1HL. Email: nquire@nifhs.org

Delving into the Museum Treasure Trove
shirin murphy
acting curator mid-antrim museums service

Most people undertaking family history research will become familiar with the types of resources available to them. They will gather up birth, death and marriage certificates from the General Register Offices, they'll visit the Public Record Office and delve into their vast archives to search church records or landed estate records. They will go online to view census records as well as visit numerous other genealogy websites that have sprung up over the last number of years. Certainly there is no shortage to the number of avenues open to the avid genealogist keen to explore their past. But how many people will visit their local museum as a resource for exploring their family tree? Actually quite a number as it happens, as those of us who work within the *Mid-Antrim Museums Service* have discovered. We find ourselves dealing with an increasing number of family history enquiries. Some enquiries such as, 'Can I view the Clough burial records around 1880?' are straightforward. Other, more vague enquiries such as, 'My Great Grandfather lived in Ballymena in the late 19th century, can you send me a picture of his house?' were not so straightforward! The time had come for us to set out what your museum can do for you.

Mid-Antrim Museums

Mid-Antrim
Museums Service
Exploring the Past - Learning for the Future

Service operates through a partnership arrangement between four local authorities. Each operates its own museum service and manages its own sites: the *Mid-Antrim Museum* in Ballymena; *Sentry Hill House* and *The Museum at the Mill* in Newtownabbey; *Carrickfergus Museum* and the *Andrew Jackson and US Rangers Centre* in Carrickfergus and *The Museum and Arts Centre, Larne*. The Mid-Antrim Museums Service provides additional and complimentary resources for the four councils and brings our wide-ranging collections together for various exhibition and outreach projects.

Individually, each site has taken steps to provide resources for members of the public. At Larne Museum the public can access a multi-media community archive containing digital images, video and sound files. Carrickfergus Museum's community archive room contains a wealth of information relating to World War Two. Sentry Hill offers access to its rich archive, and a CD containing a variety of archival material available for purchase. Mid-Antrim Museum's website contains a searchable database of headstone inscriptions from 41 cemeteries in the Ballymena Borough, as well as a new online Picture Library containing images from the museum's photographic collection.

Although our museums have been dealing with genealogical enquiries for a number of years, it became clear that there is a strong public appetite for additional resources to facilitate family history research. With this in mind, it was decided to produce an exhibition highlighting the role that our museums can play in supporting family history research. The aim of this new exhibition is to offer a flavour of the rich and diverse collections held at each of our sites that can be of interest to the researcher.

Museums are not archives, yet they often contain records that can shed light on an ancestor's life. Rate books, burial records, municipal records such as council minute books, workhouse registers, petty sessions registers, and business ledgers are just a few examples of the kinds of records held within the collections of Mid-Antrim Museums Service, most of which can be viewed by prior appointment. You may discover a relative's name in a company's business ledger which shows when they were employed by that company. It can be exciting and useful to discover a name in such records. But what such records cannot tell you is what it was like to work in that factory or business. This is where museums can really help illuminate the world of our ancestors and offer an insight into the past. Through photographs, documents, maps, objects, and oral testimonies, we can understand more about past lives.

Much of our collections are made up of social history material, which means it comes out of homes like yours or your ancestors. You too can discover something about a relative through the items they left behind, perhaps stashed in a box in

Brooches belonging to
Margaret McKinney.
Sentry Hill Collection

the attic. Bring it out and what do you find? Medals, certificates, clothing, and personal mementoes?

What museums can do is put these treasured items in context, by explaining what they mean, or how they were used or worn. These can be little details that offer an insight into a relative's personality, in a way that archival records cannot always do. The *Exploring Your Roots* exhibition explores a number of themes relevant to our collections.

Examining the surroundings in which our ancestors lived can help us to discover the places and scenes that were familiar to them. Landscapes are in a constant state of change as old buildings are replaced and towns and villages expand into former fields. Prominent buildings, place names and street names can all tell a story about the past. Maps, drawings, paintings and photographs capture a scene in a moment of time.

Tracing ancestors who have emigrated is a key area of research for many family historians. Such was the impact of emigration in Ireland that there were few families unaffected by it. Emigrant correspondence not only provides valuable family information, it also shows how emigrants viewed new lands and cultures. *Sentry Hill House in Newtownabbey* has a wonderfully rich collection of family correspondence, providing a fascinating insight into the lives of the McKinney family. A search through Mid-Antrim Museum's collection may reveal that your ancestor was one of the hundreds who were offered *'assisted passage'* to emigrate abroad by the Ballymena travel agent, Cameron.

For those interested in exploring the working lives of their ancestors, our collections hold numerous records, documents and photographs of interest. Textile factories, foundries, shipyards and many other industrial places of work gave valuable employment to our ancestors. Objects and images relating to industry and commerce reveal elements that were a familiar part of everyday life to those who worked in those places. The world of those who made their living from the land can be explored through looking at farm machinery, agricultural tools and photographs of rural activities.

In tracing family history, school records can be an important source of information. In particular, school registers are valuable as they not only record the names of pupils but usually their dates of birth and sometimes details such as the occupation of the pupil's father, their address and religious denomination. School photographs provide a

Paul Rodgers' Shipyard, Carrickfergus.
Carrickfergus Museum

greeting cards and personal letters, the impact of war on local families can be explored in many of the museums in the Mid-Antrim Museums Service.

When researching family history it is amazing what can be found in our own homes. People often collect mementoes from important family occasions and these can be passed down from generation to generation. Look again at old photographs, letters, copies of wills, certificates, family Bibles and other documents found at home or perhaps in the possession of a relative. These can provide all sorts of clues about the history of a family. Exploring the home for clues about family history can be very rewarding and can yield all sorts of interesting information. Building on this knowledge, the researcher can then look to other sources, including museums where objects and information can help to understand the background to the lives of ancestors.

fascinating glimpse into the world of education and when the names are recorded these can reveal the faces of ancestors. Once familiar objects, copybooks, primers, inkwells and slates reveal how children learned in the past.

The two world wars of the twentieth century were enormously significant. Most communities in County Antrim were affected by these wars to some degree. Exploring the lives of those who were caught up in these conflicts can tell much about those periods in history and how war changed families, sometimes permanently. Through archival material, photographs, medals, memorial plaques,

There are many other institutions, which will be essential steps on the road to discovering your family tree, which is why we have produced a booklet to accompany the *Exploring Your Roots* exhibition. This not only provides a record of the exhibition and the resources held within our collections, but also offers the researcher guidance on where to go next. Mid-Antrim Museums Service worked in partnership with the Ulster Historical Foundation to produce this resource. It is hoped that this project will showcase our diverse collections as treasure troves for exploring the life and times of our ancestors and help us identify ways to further develop our genealogical resources.

The *Exploring Your Roots* Exhibition will be on tour across the Mid-Antrim Museums Service sites during 2012. Mid-Antrim Museums Service will also be offering a series of talks, workshops and site visits to complement the exhibition, including sessions with experts from Ulster Historical Foundation, Libraries NI, PRONI, Ballymena Family History Society, Queens NI Placenames Project and the NI Digital Film Archive. For further information Tel: +44 (0) 28 256 57161 or visit www.thebraid.com

Museums can be a real treasure trove for those seeking to discover more about their ancestors.

A group of families getting ready to sail to Canada, 1926
Mid-Antrim Museum

Tracing the Irish in Scotland
Chris Paton

The Irish have been settling in Scotland for centuries, from at least the times when Gaelic speaking raiders on Roman territories were known to them as the 'Scotti' or 'Scoti.' Throughout the sixth and seventh centuries AD the colony of Dál Riata (Dalriada) was founded by the Gaels in the western Scottish coastal territories of Argyll and Lochaber and in the modern Irish area now constituting Antrim, with its capital at Dunadd in Argyll. This new 'Scoti land' or 'Scotland' would spread across the north of Britain and in time unite with the Pictish tribes to the north and east, and with the Britons and Anglo-Saxons to the south. Throughout this colonisation and nation building much of the country would adopt the language of the Gaels, where it still survives today in its modern form of Scottish Gaelic (Gàidhlig).

From a modern family history point of view, migration from Ireland to Scotland extensively happened following the aftermath of the famine, but many Irishmen had poured into the country across previous centuries, either as economic migrants in times of prosperity or as virtual refugees in times of national crisis. Between 1801 and 1921 the entire island of Ireland was a constituent member of the United Kingdom, until the events of Partition led to the south breaking away to form an Irish Free State. The north, heavily settled by lowland Scots during the Plantations of Ulster, continued within the British state as the newly constituted country of Northern Ireland.

The biggest problem with those tracing ancestry back across the Irish Sea from Scotland usually lies in identifying the point of origin back in Ireland. Scotland is blessed with many continuous sets of runs of parish registers, census records, land records and more, but the treatment of the Irish within these can often be infuriatingly disappointing, and in most cases it may not be long before you have to leave the more obvious records to try to find help within more obscure and lesser used collections.

Unlike Ireland's early start in 1821, the Scottish census first began to record genealogically useful material from 1841, but the initial records are disappointingly vague at times. Those born in Ireland will simply be noted as coming from the country only, and details of ages will be rounded down to the nearest multiple of 5 for all adults over 15, so a 29 year old will be found in most cases as being '25,' for example. Relationships are not indicated, and in many cases occupations can also be absent. It is not until the 1851 census that such details are firmly recorded, and although the birthplace is more often than not noted as just 'Ireland,' in some cases a parish or county will be given. This can be rare, and so all census records from 1841-1911 should also be checked for prospective relatives. Both Protestant and Catholic Irish folk tended to be extremely clannish and often settled in the same neighbourhoods when they arrived in Scotland, so even if you do not know the first names of relatives it may pay to see who else shared the same surname in their area of residence.

Original images from the 1841-1911 Scottish censuses are available at the ScotlandsPeople pay-per-view website at www.scotlandspeople.gov.uk. This charges £7 for 30 credits – a basic search is free, but a detailed search return costs 1 credit and the image itself a further 5. Transcripts of 1841-1901 can be viewed at Ancestry - www.ancestry.co.uk - and will soon be on the British version of the FindmyPast site at www.findmypast.co.uk. Many parishes can also be accessed for free from 1841 and 1851 at www.freecen.org.

The ScotlandsPeople website also hosts indexes and images for statutory records from 1855 to the present day, though maintains closure periods for access to the original register images – 50 years for deaths, 75 for marriages and 100 for births. Civil registration commenced in 1855 in Scotland, nine years before being fully adopted in Ireland. If you have an Irish couple who married in Ireland prior to 1864 but had children in Scotland after 1855, you may be able to note a possible place of marriage for them from their children's birth records, as unlike Ireland, England and Wales, Scottish birth certificates usually state where and when a child's parents married.

Scotlands Peoples Centre

WELLINGTON

Image © Chris Pation

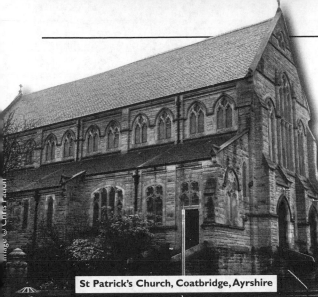

St Patrick's Church, Coatbridge, Ayrshire

Records for 1855 are considerably more detailed than subsequent years. A child's birth record from 1855 only will state the birthplace of each parent, whilst a marriage record from the same year will offer the birthplace of each spouse. All Scottish registered birth, marriage and death certificates also name both parents for the person or people concerned, so if your immigrant Irish ancestor died in Scotland in 1867 for example, you may find the names of both parents back in Ireland, which may provide a further clue when trying to use sites such as Roots Ireland - www.rootsireland.ie - to take your line back further. Uniquely for Scotland, all civil BMD records will include the mother's maiden surname as well as her married name.

One thing to remember when searching within the statutory records is that the registrars will have recorded names under the spelling deemed to be correct, and that many Irish Gaelic originated names will have been unfamiliar to their largely Protestant lowland ears. A good example lies with the death record of 34 year old John Brogan in Airdrie in 1861, where his father was recorded as 'Yohan Brogan.' In earlier records, this same father was also noted as 'Owen' and 'John.' In fact, his baptismal name was 'Eoin,' which one registrar heard as 'Yohan' and recorded accordingly, whilst others simply wrote down an equivalent anglicised version of the name.

Prior to 1855 the records of the churches have to be consulted for baptisms and marriages. ScotlandsPeople hosts the Church of Scotland records from 1553-1854, and Roman Catholic records, from 1703-1992 for baptisms, 1736-1934 for marriages and 1742-1955 for burials. Although the state based Church of Scotland was protestant it was Presbyterian by nature, and not Anglican as in Ireland. As banns for marriages had to be called in the Church of Scotland after 1829

for a marriage to be technically legal, you may actually find some Catholic couples noted in the Kirk's registers, but it is quite rare. This does not mean they married in the Kirk, simply that they had the banns called, and so you will likely find an equivalent marriage in the Roman Catholic register for the same parish. Some Catholic records go back to the early 18th century, but mainly for indigenous Scottish parishes untouched by the Reformation deep within the Highlands and Islands. The majority of the records, are from the 1840s onwards when famine migrants massively reintroduced Catholicism into Scotland. Most records do not state where Irish migrants hail from in their country of origin, with the sole exceptions being Greenock and Glasgow records from the early 1800s.

The famine was not the only reason for settlement in Scotland. Many who came to settle did so to work in mines, railways or domestic service, in places as diverse as Ayrshire, Glasgow and Lanarkshire, often settling in ghettoes established by earlier waves of their fellow countrymen. It always pays to do a simple Google search for records of the Irish in such areas as gems will often turn up, or to trace regional projects such as the impressive Lanarkshire based Coatbridge Irish Genealogy Project - contact Michael Reilly at michael.reilly@bms.com

Don't forget politics either. In 1912, Irish Protestants around the world signed the Ulster Covenant against Home Rule, and when signing this document, most Scottish based Irishmen listed their place of residence as their home parish in Ireland. The records are free at: http://applications.proni.gov.uk/UlsterCovenant/Search.aspx.

Another useful resource for trying to establish a parish of origin actually comes from the periods when people were destitute or out of work, via the poor relief records, which often contain a thorough investigation of an applicant's case. The best surviving Scottish collection is that consisting of over a million poor relief applications for Glasgow (1851-1948), Barony (1861-1898) and Govan (1876-1930), as held by Glasgow City Archives www.glasgow.gov.uk/en/Residents/Library_Services/The_Mitchell/Archives

A computerised index for the records up to 1901 is available within the search room (though sadly not online), and there are further records available for many other councils within Bute, Dunbartonshire, Lanarkshire and Renfrewshire. The Workhouses website at www.workhouses.org.uk will list where additional surviving Scottish poor relief records can be located, and online indexes exist for many areas, such as those for the Ayrshire parish of Ardrossan

at
www.threetowners.com/Ard%20folder/poor_application's.htm
A few Scottish family history societies have also
created CDs listing poor law records returns,
such as those for Jedburgh from 1852 - 1874, as
transcribed by Borders FHS - www.bordersfhs.org.uk

In some cases, Irish applicants were forcibly
returned to their parish of origin in Ireland. A
detailed article on the practice can be found
online at
http://movinghere.org.uk/galleries/histories/irish/se
ttling/removal_1.htm but the names of those who
were forcibly removed can also be found through
a separate database, the House of Common
Parliamentary Papers at
http://parlipapers.chadwyck.co.uk/marketing/index.jsp
This is unfortunately only accessible through
subscribing libraries and institutions, but if you can
gain access you can browse through entire lists of
people forcibly removed from poor law unions in
Scotland (as well as in England), and in some cases
view letters written about cases under dispute
between different poor law authorities in both
Ireland and Scotland. If you cannot gain access,
some records are freely available on Raymond's
County Down website at
www.raymondscountydownwebsite.com/html/index2.htm
covering the years from 1867 - 1869, and 1875 -
1878.

Image © Chris Pation

**Calum Paton at his Confirmation with his
Grandmother Pauline Giles of
County Kilkenny, Ireland**

the mystery of ireland's eye:
researching irish convicts on bermuda
stephen wade

Ireland's Eye is a small uninhabited island off the coast of County Dublin, Ireland and directly north of Howth Harbour. It was at one time part of the city of Dublin.

The Artist

William Kirwan had been married to Maria for twelve years in 1852, when they set foot on *Ireland's Eye* for the day. But he had also had his mistress, Mary Kenny, in the village of Sandymount, just a little way south of Dublin. It appears that the two women knew that they had to share their man almost from the marriage in 1840. By the end of that day, Maria was found dead, in suspicious circumstances, and Kirwan was destined to be charged and convicted of her murder.

William lived by his trade: when he was not earning from his art directly, he was an anatomical draughtsman, in Merrion Square, close to the centre of Dublin just a few streets from the Dail, the parliament house. He lived among medical men, and they were always in need of such skills. The example of George Stubbs, the famous painter of horses who studied anatomy in depth, shows this: his friend Dr Atkinson at York, found him work in drawing for anatomical studies. Artists had traditionally been assistants to surgeons, as was the case with the great surgeon, John Hunter, who had an artist called Bell as assistant; Hunter had issued a ten-year contract with Bell, for him to draw the contents of the surgeon's special collection of medical items. He even paid Bell to write a catalogue of specimens a

little later. An anatomical draughtsman was paradoxically a talented dogsbody in some places: though he had exceptional skill, he was not seen as a 'proper' painter.

It is not hard to imagine this Kirwan's complex life, a man trying to keep his business alive in one of the smarter areas of the city, while spending time with Mary as well as with Maria. What emerges is a double life – something common in the middle class Victorian world in which a mistress was often a family acquisition little different from a horse or a servant. Here was a man struggling to keep his head above water, an ironical metaphor, given his destiny. He was clearly increasingly desperate once his family with Mary grew apace: by 1852 he had seven children by her.

Money did not flow freely; aspirations were high. William had married into a little money and certainly had a status above the norm. But when Maria's body was brought in from the island, gossip was about insurance money. Yet the topic was never raised by the prosecution. For many it was a working class crime- insuring the lives of relatives who would die mysteriously. Just six years after Maria's death there was a case in Liverpool involving the systematic poisoning of a whole family for insurance profits.

We have a man living with a *'front'* of the respectability of Merrion Square yet with a family tucked away just down the road. In need of finance, he shows a false face to the world. His landlord in Sandymount was a Mr Bridgeford and he said in court: *'Mr Kirwan lived in one of the four houses in Spafield of which I am the landlord. He resided there for about four years. I saw a woman there whom I always supposed to be his wife. I saw children in the house. I have notes from the woman and I think she signed herself Theresa . . .'* This was Mary Kenny - her full name being Theresa Mary Frances Kelly.

The Kirwans were not so badly off, however, that they could not afford a servant: Catherine Byrne lived in the house as a maid and she told the court that there were seven children and that Kirwan was often there for long periods in the day, and often he stayed the night.

William Kirwan, then, was a man with one foot in respectable and bohemian Dublin, a man to find being sociable at parties or alone in the early hours being melancholic; the other foot was in the dangerous underworld of crime and fear along the bay by the South Wall. Was he a man who longed for the thrill, the challenge, the pump of adrenaline?

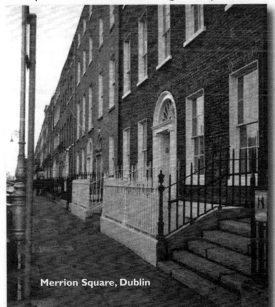

Merrion Square, Dublin

One writer in 1853 gave us a picture of William: '*Mr Kirwan is a little above forty, a native of Mayo . . . He is tall and well-looking, strongly built, and the expression of his countenance, firmness, corresponds with his strong limbs, broad chest and duly-proportioned body.*' The writer knew him and commented that he was admired as an anatomical artist '*from which he realised a handsome income.*' Yet he would have had to be vastly wealthy to support so many and two households' rent.

An artist who was reasonably well off then, but had an obstacle to further success which he had to remove? It makes no sense; he and Maria had taken a lodging for the summer at Howth and they often went out to Ireland's Eye. He had no reason to kill her. That was lost in the supposition and legal bungling.

Ireland's Eye

Ireland's Eye, *Inis Mac Neasáin,* is a large rock of 53 acres, jutting out of the bay opposite the fishing port of Howth. In Irish it is Inis Mac Neasain. No one lives there; it is a place to visit with a relaxed state of mind and a picnic basket. The little boats shuttle visitors across all day and there is evidence that in 1805 Howth was selected as the best place to have a storm-protection harbour, and also for a steam packet for the Dublin to Holyhead run. By 1822 that trip from Wales took just six hours and the future must have looked bright for the locals. But the harbour was always silted and there was no reliable docking for ships, so that by 1834, Dun Laoghaire took over the steam packet trade.

It is possible to live in Howth today and have a lifestyle of the modern artist, and indeed there is property for sale as I write this, on the Baily in Howth – '*a secret society of gated homes, all set high on the hill above Carrockbrack Road, hidden from view, yet boasting marvellous vistas.*' So says Alanna Gallagher of a €3.9 million (euro) home in *The Irish Times.*

Secret: the adjective is often applied to the Eye. It's a place with plenty of secrets. Some say that when the Vikings sailed down here from Orkney in 837 with 65 ships they saw a sheltered haven, protected by Howth Head, and with an island in the bay; they saw Howth Head as a cat mousing, and the Eye a spot waiting for the creature to pounce on. It has been a place of good fortune but also dark foreboding. Only a few years after the Kirwan story, a ship was wrecked there. The cat had put a hex on the place it was said – or was it the killer artist?

Images of Ireland's Eye from c1900 show the landmarks of Howth – the Church of the Assumption and a Martello Tower. There were still thatched cottages in Howth main street into the 1920s and it was a place held dear to Dubliners, comparing it to the sleepy seaside town of Bray to the south of the city. Yeats' sweetheart Maud Gonne lived there as a little girl after her mother had died of TB , and her memories of the village go to around 1870, not so long after the Kirwan affair. She recalls in her memoir, 'No place has ever seemed so lovely as Howth was then. Sometimes the sea was as blue as Mama's turquoises, more strikingly blue even than the Mediterranean because so often grey mists made it invisible and mysterious.' It may have been these were mists which, in fact, could have seeped into the rocks that day in 1852 when a day's leisure brought death on the Eye.

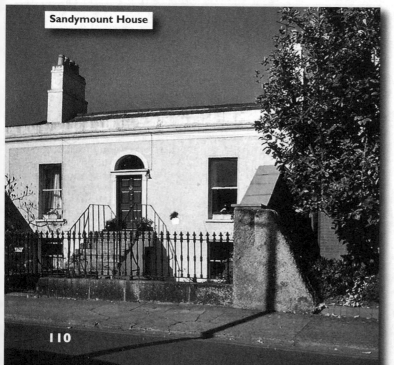

Sandymount House

A day out to Ireland's Eye back in the Victorian years was ideal for William and Maria Kirwan. He could sketch, or at least take in the perfectly framed picturesque vista while she let the breeze play on her lovely features and dream of the old days when ships came with rovers and chancers to make a new Ireland; maybe she heard the shrieks of the gulls, skrying danger, perhaps presaging a child's grief at her loss? She might have passed dreamily into sleep, the elements around her closing in, or the sea encroaching with its hidden terrors from beneath that benign seaside ease.

For the artist, it was perfect for taking his sketch book, for monitoring the changing moods and colours. He was doing what locals had seen him do many times before: take a picnic and his

BEN EIDER FROM THE NORTH BULL

HOWTH HARBOUR AND IRELANDS EYE

LANDING DUBLIN BAY HERRINGS

THE NOSE OF HOWTH

St MARYS ABBEY

Ireland's Eye

men in that habit; what he lacked was a reputation to match his lifestyle.

Maria was a very strong swimmer and loved to bathe in the sea. A witness later described her as ' a well-made and extremely good-looking woman.' She was confident to trust her skills in the sea, and she was very fit and well. At around four o'clock, she could have come back to Howth on her own, as a couple called Brue offered her a seat in their boat. She turned that down and stayed on.

But as the boat going to collect them set off, a man called Hugh Campbell heard a cry from the island. He was leaning against the harbour wall. Close to the area where ladies bathed at Howth, two women, Alice Abernethy and Catherine Flood, heard some cries as well. John Barrett was in a boat passing the island after a day's fishing; he heard cries coming from a place on the Eye called Long Hole.

sketch book out to a tranquil place, somewhere that city people were drawn to for their repose and their recreations. Maria and William took lodgings in Howth, at the home of Mrs Power. Maria went bathing and William sketched. On Monday, 6 September, they set off for the Eye at ten in the morning, taking Maria's clothes in a carpet bag, some food, two bottles of water and his art materials. When they landed, the boatman was told to pick them up at eight o'clock that evening. It was early September, so it would have been almost dusk at eight. He may have wanted that late, sinking residue of light, for the colours, following Turner, the artist who had taught all the Victorians about the colours in the skies above them.

Maria was 35 years old; the couple had been married for twelve years, and had been living at 11, Merrion Square, a very well-off Georgian area in central Dublin; in the mid-Victorian years, it was a residence of doctors. At number 60, Merrion Square, Daniel O'Connell, the great politician and lawyer, had lived a few decades before, and the square was in 1859, according to one Dubliner, 'closed off from the common mob.' The writer, Sheridan Le Fanu, also lived there, and is well documented, as Peter Somerville-Large has written, that 'A number of doctors were reputed to keep mistresses round Sandymount or Park Avenue, a pleasant gallop away from Merrion Square.' Kirwan was making enough money to join the medical

Four men were in the boat going out to bring home the artist and his wife: Patrick and Michael Nagle, Thomas Styles and Edward Campbell. William Kirwan was alone on a high rock above the landing-place, and stated that after a shower of rain, his wife had walked from him and he had not seen her since. Everyone started searching for her, and eventually one of the sailors saw a white shape below. Light was failing by then, but they climbed down to have a closer look, and there on a rock they found Maria's body, very dry and with the water well below her, but she was on her back and her bathing dress was pulled up. Her movement could have caused that, as nothing suggested an attack at the time.

William dashed to her in a frenzy and lunged over her body, shouting, 'Maria! Maria!' But her clothes, from the bag, were nowhere to be seen and William then asked the men to find them. Why did he want her clothes. Why was that his first thought? Those questions would haunt me later as I tried to piece together these events. He then went himself, and as he was gone, it was Patrick Nagle who found the clothes. The next step was very bold: in the dusk, the men rowed their boat around the island to the Long Hole, and there they took Maria's body, wrapped around in some sail-cloth. The party then returned to Howth.

For William, his own private hell was just

The tropical paradise of Bermuda received more than 9,000 convicts between 1823 and 1863; they were mostly detailed to build the Royal Dockyard. For many Irish relatives, however, the convict's story does not end with a return to Ireland, as with Kirwan, because a large proportion were held there until being sent on to penal colonies in Australia. Generally, Bermuda was seen as a much more unpleasant destination than Australia, and conditions were very harsh; in one memoir by an inmate, a tale is recalled of convicts swallowing ground-up glass or even blinding themselves, so they could be sent elsewhere. Illness was rife also, particularly yellow fever, and after an epidemic of that terrible and deadly infection in 1853, the end of Bermuda as a penal colony was close.

beginning. He had taken one short step to his ruin, and every word he uttered, every move he made, was then to be observed, and in that scrutiny, many could not forget his other woman, living nicely in Sandymount, while his wife lay stone-cold dead.

Questions were asked like rifle enfilades, but some obvious ones were left out, such as what was an artist doing wanting to sketch in the dusk? Was he looking for those Turneresque skies? Many thought he was looking, like Macbeth, for the 'cloak of darkest night' in which to kill his wife. The story was destined to be as two-faced as the accused and his life in the artistic colony around the clubs and dance parties.

Destination Bermuda

There is a very useful convict database available to search at the National Archives of Ireland, and although this only relates to Australia, many people would have gone to Bermuda en route, so a search is worthwhile, at: www.nationalarchives.ie/genealogy/transportation.html

As for Kirwan, who is not listed in the Irish archives, whatever really happened that day on the island, in 1852 the jury decided that Kirwan was guilty of murder, the death penalty was given and then a reprieve followed. His first stop in his life sentence was Bermuda. He would have been sent first to a London prison – usually Pentonville or Millbank – and then shortly after would be on board ship. The course of his sentence included several years in Bermuda, and then back to do some years on Spike Island, off Cork, before his release. Records for Millbank exist for the years 1816-1871, so Irish convicts awaiting transportation are listed on the prison register and records are at The National Archives at PCOM 2/139-140. Kirwan's time in Bermuda then lasted until 1863 when he was brought back to Spike Island.

Prisoners there petitioned for return, and Kirwan is listed at CO 37 at TNA for October, 1860, where the Colonial office was noted as still considering him, after rejecting some others. A list of nineteen convicts was sent to the Home Office by Freeman Murray, Governor of Bermuda, in August, 1860 and Kirwan was on the list. The deliberation was long, and fate stepped in, the Bermuda colony being closed in 1863. The Irish began to be returned to Spike Island: in 1860 for instance, Dr John Foggo claimed his passage back after travelling with 140 Irish convicts, who landed from the Markland at Spike Island. This prison closed in 1883, and oral tradition claims that Kirwan was the last to leave, but that is a myth, as he was released in 1879. Although his story had been a massive national sensation in 1852, his release was not news: the Zulu War was filling the front pages and crime stories were relegated to footnotes.

According to Dr O'Keife, a doctor on Spike Island, Kirwan went to Liverpool, and then on to America, where he was reunited with his Sandymount lover. His two daughters had gone to New York, but had returned to Dublin, where they became telegraphists. There is a record of a man looking like Kirwan standing on the beach at Howth, staring out to Ireland's eye, in 1880. If any of the boatmen from 1852 were still alive, they would not have approached him.

Seeking Irish Ancestors in South Africa
Rosemary Dixon-Smith

On 20th November 1857 the barque *Lady Kennaway* brought a cargo of 153 single Irish women to the port which would later be named East London, situated at the Buffalo River mouth in the Cape Frontier district known as British Kaffraria.

It's hard to imagine these women's first impressions when they saw the wild country which would be their future home. They had willingly agreed to undertake a risky sea voyage of nearly three months - in a forty-year old ship which had seen service as a convict transport. The passengers had been given scant detail about their destination. However, they had the promise of a fresh start, and husbands, and these factors must have been strong incentives for young women from Northern Ireland who had been living in poor conditions, many of them in workhouses.

The expedient of bringing in unmarried women to the colonies to correct the imbalance of the population (too many men and not enough women) was nothing new. It had been tried in North America in 1850 where, if the advertising of the time is to be believed, thousands of men *'having made their fortunes at the mines, are now anxious to throw themselves at the feet of the first passable specimens of womanhood whom fate and a happy wind may cast upon their shores.'* In the Cape Colony there were two attempts, in 1849 and 1851, to introduce small numbers of Irishwomen sent out under the auspices of British philanthropic societies.

So Cape High Commissioner Sir George Grey's suggestion that a group of Irish women should be shipped to British Kaffraria in the *Lady Kennaway* was not unprecedented. His intention was that the women should become wives for German military men, ex-legionaires who had been settled in the Eastern Cape as part of the frontier defence policy. It might have been anticipated – except, apparently, by Grey – that such a scheme was unlikely to succeed.

British Kaffraria was far from the civilized delights of Cape Town: the ship had not stopped there in case disappointing comparisons were made when the passengers reached the port on the Buffalo River. Here there was as yet no developed harbour and the *Lady Kennaway* had to anchor off shore with passengers being landed by boats in a protracted four-day disembarkation. Though accorded a warm welcome, particularly by the male segment of the population, it seems the attractions of the soldiery were not highly-rated and though a few women were married soon after arrival (not necessarily to Germans), many preferred to seek domestic or other employment in centres such as King William's Town and Grahamstown.

To add to the general air of disillusionment, the *Lady Kennaway* ran aground within the mouth of the Buffalo River in a gale on 25th November 1857, becoming a total wreck.

Thanks to Colonial Office record keeping, the names of the *Lady Kennaway* women, their ages and their counties of origin, have been preserved. A list can be viewed at www.eastlondon-labyrinth.com/cybertrails/kennaway-09.jsp#girls

Despite the fact that the venture wasn't a resounding success the *Lady Kennaway* story remains romantic, in the best sense: 153 Irish women chose to do something astounding and courageous, making history and changing their lives in the process.

Destination

South Africa is not a country that springs readily to the minds of family historians seeking Irish ancestors. Certainly, the flow of Irish immigrants to South Africa at no time resembled the huge tide which turned towards the shores of North America. An authority on Cape 19th century aided immigration, Esme Bull, says that government-assisted schemes brought approximately 14,000 Irish settlers to the Cape between 1823 and 1900. By comparison with American statistics, this is a drop in the ocean.

Nevertheless, for family historians this figure (which refers only to government-aided immigration schemes during the time-frame mentioned above) is sufficient to suggest South Africa as a possible destination for that elusive Irish forebear.

Cape Immigration Schemes

In the early 19th century there had been minor private schemes involving Irish immigrants. Henry Nourse, for example, a London merchant who had settled at the Cape, brought out a small group of Irish people as his employees in 1818, and advised that a government-sponsored immigration scheme

Lady Kennaway

would be beneficial to the Colony.

The authorities had already come to that conclusion. By 1819 the troubled eastern frontier of the Cape had become a permanent headache for the colonial government, while in Britain unemployment and discontent were rife. Sponsored emigration would reduce pressure at home, offering new prospects to many. At the same time, installing a buffer strip of farming colonists would be a way of defending the frontier. This thinking led to the arrival of what are today generally referred to as the 1820 Settlers. They were not one large unit, as this title seems to imply, but comprised a number of different parties each in the charge of a leader, making the journey out to the Cape in various ships.

Cape Town Harbour

Overshadowed by the mass of information available on the 1820 Settlers are the Irish immigrants who formed part of this 1820 initiative. Ireland, like England, was in the throes of economic difficulties including large-scale unemployment.

Several men of Irish origin formed their own settler parties, notably John Ingram who recruited would-be colonists, many of them Roman Catholics, from his own county, Cork. Ingram took them on as his employees, undertaking to pay them a wage and at the end of the three year period of service to give each man 10 acres of land, or ten pounds.

This group disembarked at Saldanha Bay in May 1820. Their names, including Ingram's, are listed at www.genealogyworld.net/nash/ingram.html

Ingram later continued his emigrant enterprise, recruiting more settlers from Cork. Under his auspices, 352 people came to the Cape in the ship Barossa, arriving on 12th December 1823. A list of the relevant surnames can be seen at www.genealogyworld.net/immigration/immigration.html

Another Cork merchant, William Parker, brought 75 men and their families to the Cape aboard the East Indian in February 1820. Their names are listed at www.genealogyworld.net/nash/parker.html

Captain Walter Synnot of County Armagh, arranged for a party of 10 labourers and their families of that county to sail from Cork on 12 February 1820. See www.genealogyworld.net/nash/synnot.html

Captain Thomas Butler of the Dublin Militia recruited labourers in Wicklow, his home county. Butler undertook to support them until they harvested their first crops, while the men promised Butler 200 days work each year for 4 years. This group sailed on the same vessel as Synnot's party, on 12th February 1820. See

www.genealogyworld.net/nash/butler.html

The source for information on these immigrant groups is M D Nash's The Settler Handbook. For more by Nash on this vast topic, including recent corrections and additions to the original volume see www.genealogyworld.net/nash/index.html

Regrettably the policy-makers had decided that Irish immigrants would be separated from the main body of 1820 settlers, placing the Irish in the Clanwilliam district on the Cape west coast – a remote and arid region. When the Irish became aware of conditions at Clanwilliam most of them successfully made representations to be moved to Albany, where the majority of the 1820 Settler groups were situated. Their problems did not end there, for the wheat crop failed due to disease in the first few years followed by floods in 1823. A few of the Clanwilliam settlers clung tenaciously to their allotments in that area.

Later Irish Settlers

Between 1846 and 1851 there were further arrivals based on a government-aided scheme. Of the 4 200 immigrants brought to the Cape about a third were Irish. Not all the passenger lists have survived. One of the ships, The Eclipse, brought 20 women from Irish workhouses.

Towards the end of the 1850s there was a shortage of labour at the Cape and the government hoped immigration might solve the dilemma. Esme Bull estimates that more than 11,000 British settlers were brought to the Cape between 1858 and 1862 in 32 ships. Of these immigrants nearly 5000 were Irish.

In Natal, the largest and most well known immigration scheme of the 19th century was the brain-child of a Dubliner, Joseph Byrne. Of the approximately 2200 British settlers who came out in 20 ships between 1849 and 1851, some were of Irish origin. Historian Shelagh Spencer suggests that most of the latter arrived on The Unicorn which sailed for Natal from Liverpool in June 1850. Names include Deane, Connelley, MacMinn, White, Scott and Williamson. All Byrne settlers and the ships on which they arrived are listed in John Clark's Natal Settler-Agent (see Further Reading).

There was a tendency, usually actively encouraged by government, for people already in residence in the South African colonies to send for other family members to join them.

Independent Arrivals

Not all Irish immigrants came to South Africa as part of a private or government-sponsored scheme. During the course of the 19th century families or solo travelers made the voyage in merchant ships at their own expense. Of these, my Waterford-born great grandfather is a typical example. In 1863 he paid his own passage out and chose to settle at Port Natal (Durban), where his descendants still live today.

It wasn't easy trying to find evidence of his arrival at Natal, though handwritten passenger registers have been preserved. Independent arrivals are more difficult to trace, especially if, as in my great grandfather's case, the surname is so curiously misspelled as to be almost unrecognizable. Checking the passengers' names against a list published in the press satisfactorily confirmed that it was the correct person. In this type of search the Natal European Immigration Index and Registers, held at Pietermaritzburg Archives Repository, are invaluable.

(Pietermaritzburg Archives Repository Post address: Private Bag X9012, PIETERMARITZBURG 3200 Street address: 231 Pietermaritz Street, PIETERMARITZBURG T: (033) 342 4712 Fax: (033) 394 4353 E: pmbarchives@kzndac.gov.za) For family historians at a distance, it is possible to delegate to a local researcher to check this source. Further details on the EI Index and Registers can be seen at www.genealogyworld.net/rose/euimmigr.html

Cape passenger records reflecting independent arrivals at Table Bay and other ports such as Algoa Bay (Port Elizabeth) exist for 1822-1917. These are limited to names of first class or 'cabin' passengers, ignoring those in second class or steerage - the latter being the people we generally want to know more about.

There are also Cape sources such as the so-called Permissions to Remain in - or to Leave - the Colony, Applications for and Letters of Naturalization, Correspondence received from settlers etc. These are useful alternatives to records of passenger arrivals.

One of the factors adding to the difficulty of identifying individual 19th century travelers is that people of British origin (including the Irish) were free to come and go at will throughout the Empire. There were no restrictions such as passport control.

Early Arrivals

From the earliest days of British government at the Cape, the Irish were among the civil servants and other officials involved in the day-to-day running of the Colony. They did not regard themselves as settlers. Most had no intention of remaining at the Cape and would eventually return home to Ireland.

Some were exotic personalities like Benjamin Green from Wexford who arrived in Table Bay on the *Lovely Maria* in December 1819. Not your average civil servant, he is said to have killed a leopard with his bare hands. After a brief but action-packed decade in South Africa, during which he became a pioneer trader in Natal and Zululand, Green succumbed to fever near Delagoa Bay in 1829.

There were Irish mariners at the Cape, too, mostly just passing through – or so they hoped. James Hooper, born in Ireland circa 1782, was accidentally left ashore at Cape Town in May 1808 when the East Indiaman on which he was employed as a Captain's servant sailed away without him. Perhaps being *'marooned'* in this way had an adverse psychological effect on Hooper, for he and Dubliner Michael Kelly later conspired together in the instigation of a slave revolt. There was no worse crime in the Colony. Both men were arrested and tried, Kelly being deported and Hooper hanged.

These individuals are among numerous Irishmen included in a fascinating list of 4 500 British residents occurring in a variety of Cape records between 1795 and 1819. (*British Residents at the Cape* by Peter Philip.)

Military

Family historians might not immediately perceive the military as a possible avenue for research into Irish ancestors in South Africa. Yet, wherever the British army served it included soldiers of Irish origin. These cannot be thought of as immigrants in the accepted sense of the term, but there's no doubt that many Irishmen having taken their discharge from the army while serving in South Africa, decided to stay in the country.

The Irish as members of the military were present from the time of the first British occupation of the Cape (1795 to 1803) and again from 1806 when British rule was re-established after a short hiatus. From then on there was no campaign in South Africa in which Irishmen did not serve, including the Cape Frontier Wars. Some had careers cut tragically short, such as Richard *Armstrong 'of Ireland,'* a Lieutenant in the 8th Light

Dragoons (King's Royal Irish Hussars) who died in June 1798 aged 18; his regiment was in South Africa from 1796. The more fortunate completed their period of service, married local girls of Dutch or other nationality and settled down after leaving the army.

Names of men, including some of Irish origin, who retired to pension between 1818 and 1826 and chose to remain at the Cape, are given at www.genealogyworld.net/immigration/SA%20pensioners.htm These names were transcribed from WO 23/147 at TNA, Kew; the list includes birthplace and regiment.

In the South African colonies fear of tribal incursions was endemic. British regiments garrisoned forts and towns throughout the 19th century. An example of an unusually long-serving garrison, the 45th Regiment was stationed in Natal for 16 years, from the early 1840s, and of the men finally discharged from the regiment a high proportion were Irish. Many elected to put down roots in Natal.

Later Conflicts

Irish troops saw service in various regiments during the Anglo-Zulu War and Irishmen were among the defenders of Rorke's Drift on 22nd January 1879. The popular belief that the 24th Foot, present at Rorke's Drift, was a Welsh

Irish Brigade - Anglo-Boer War 1899 -1902

regiment, is not accurate. The 24th Foot was originally the 2nd battalion of the Warwickshire Regiment. At the time of the famous Defence the 24th was an English Regiment, with over 20 Irishmen in its ranks. Their names include Horrigan, Turner, Lyons, Meehan, Gallagher, Hayes, Bushe, Caine, Connors, Minehan, Galgey, Connolly and others.

Not a member of the 24th Regiment but one of the defenders awarded the Victoria Cross for his valiant part in the action was Surgeon James Reynolds, born in Dublin. Gunner John Cantwell of the Royal Artillery was another Dubliner present at the Drift: he lived in Natal for many years and lies buried in Durban.

During the Anglo-Boer War 1899-1902, about 30,000 Irish troops fought for the British cause. Irish regiments included the famous Connaught

Rangers, the Inniskillings, the Royal Dublin Fusiliers, the 5th (Royal Irish) Lancers, the Royal Irish Rifles and others. Many saw action in the Natal theatre of the war, particularly during the Siege of Ladysmith.

It's well-known that a relatively small number of Irishmen fought on the Boer side, in two 'Irish Brigades.' The first and most effective of these was formed by John MacBride, born in County Mayo. The unit – about 700 strong - fought at Colenso, Spioenkop, Dundee, Tugela Heights and the Siege of Ladysmith. This meant that they found themselves fighting against their own countrymen, recognizing in the enemy ranks a cousin or a neighbour from 'back home.' A list of Irishmen who fought for the Boers, compiled by D P and C S McCracken, is given in *Southern African Irish Studies, vol. 2.*

After the Anglo-Boer War, some Irishmen who had fought in British regiments remained in South Africa, or returned with their families to settle in the country.

NAAIRS - South African National Archives and Record Service

It's always worth checking NAAIRS, the online index of the South African National Archives and Record Service, to see if there is any reference to the ancestor you are trying to find. Access the index at www.national.archives.gov.za/ Enter the relevant surname and forenames. Include a date parameter if possible.

If you have no clue as to which area of South Africa is appropriate, search on the database RSA which covers all provinces. There are some useful guidelines on the site for those new to navigating the index.

To cover the wide spectrum of people of Irish origin who left their imprint on South Africa is beyond the scope of this article: they included missionaries, clergymen, merchants, entrepreneurs, journalists, members of police forces, diamond diggers, gold miners and railway workers. Your ancestor could have been among them.

Sources and Further Reading

Bull, E: Aided Immigration from Britain to South Africa, 1857-67 (HSRC Pretoria 1991)
Dickason, G B: **Irish settlers to the Cape: History of the Clanwilliam 1820 Settlers from Cork Harbour**. (Balkema Cape Town 1973)
Philip, P: **British Residents at the Cape 1795-1819.** (David Philip 1981)
McCracken, D P (ed.): **The Irish in Southern Africa 1795-1910.** (Southern African Irish Studies vol. 2 1992)
Nash, M D: **The Settler Handbook**, A new list of the 1820 settlers. (Cape Town 1987)
Clark, Dr J: **Natal Settler-Agent; the Career of John Moreland, Agent for the Byrne emigration scheme of 1849-51.** (Balkema Cape Town 1972)
Spencer, S O'Byrne: **British Settlers in Natal 1824-1857**. 7 vols. (UNP, Pietermaritzburg)

Famine, Fear and Fraternity:
the irish in 19th century Liverpool and manchester
Joseph O'Neill

At least one in five of the population of Britain has Irish ancestry. Many of our Irish ancestors arrived in dire poverty in the middle of the nineteenth century and then faced a pestilence greater than any modern epidemic. Almost a million and half-desperate refugees swarmed through the port of Liverpool in search of salvation. Many took ship for America. But others stayed in Liverpool or walked to Manchester and it is with those who sought refuge from hunger and plague in the two most important Lancashire cities, one a great port, the other the centre of industry and commerce, that this piece is concerned.

By 1861 there were 806,000 people of Irish birth living in England. Almost half of these were living in Lancashire and Cheshire. The 1851 census shows that 13% of the population of Manchester and Salford was Irish born. Apart from Liverpool there was no city in England that was more Irish.

Those who arrived in the 1847 - 51 period, victims of the Great Hunger and its deadly fallout of disease and evictions, were largely rural in origin and totally destitute. Half a million of those coming through Liverpool during this period were paupers. They were met with fear and hostility.

To meet the needs of this influx an additional poor rate burden was imposed on householders, causing considerable resentment among the comfortable middle classes. Many indigenous workers saw the Irish as a threat to their wage rates. Popular mythology had it that the Irish were prepared to work for less than the going rate. Before the Irish arrived, typhus was already raging in the English cities. Nevertheless, it was known as the 'Irish Fever.' In 1847 an outbreak of cholera similarly decimated the slum population and fixed in the popular psyche the image of the Irish as the bearers of poverty and death.

What's more, these unwelcome newcomers had no right to stay there receiving the soup and bread that kept them from starvation. *The Liverpool Poor Law Union* could send them back to Ireland if they had not lived in the city for at least five years. Such was the fear of being sent back that many tried to support themselves by begging or lapsed into starvation rather than draw the attention of the authorities.

The local ratepayers financed the *Poor Law Union*. They resented the Irish landlords, who were shirking responsibility for their own paupers. They feared them as the carriers of typhus that was devastating the poorest parts of the city. To make matters worse, the number of Irish paupers flooding into Liverpool was so great that it threatened to overwhelm the system. As the law was in 1847, each pauper had to be summoned by a magistrate before he could be sent back to Ireland. This process was too slow and cumbersome for the liking of the authorities.

So the cities of Liverpool and Glasgow, supported by *The Times*, launched a campaign to make expulsion easier. In June 1847 the law was changed. *The Liverpool Poor Law Union* rented warehouses in the Clarence Dock area to house those who were to be expelled. The *Liverpool Poor Law Union* provided each pauper with a piece of bread and a shilling piece (5p.) and shipped from England to the port nearest his Irish home.

Between 1846 and 1853, sixty three thousand paupers were removed from Liverpool alone. As every one of these was destitute, weakened by hardship, hunger and sickness and abandoned at ports miles from their homes, it is certain that many of them soon died.

A section of the press blamed the steamship companies. They were criticised for charging the Unions four shillings for each pauper they returned. This is clearly one of the reasons why they were prepared to carry Irish paupers to England for nothing. Steamships out of Cardiff often carried returned paupers on coal ships. They took them some way up the coast and then landed them in another Welsh port, knowing that it was likely a Union would again pay them to return their reluctant cargo.

However, behind the statistics of those

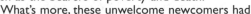

returned home there are numerous individual personal tragedies.

James Walsh, his wife, Catherine and their five children were taken into the Liverpool workhouse on 8th April 1847. He died four days later, soon to be followed by three of his children. On 15th July Catherine, Bridget, aged two and nine year old Catherine were removed to Ireland. Sadder still is the case of Bridget McGiveran.

Bridget and her four children were admitted to the workhouse hospital on 30th April 1847. She was suffering from the fever that had probably claimed her husband. Her son Patrick, aged seven, soon died and Bridget did not survive him long. The three remaining children, Michael, fifteen, Bridget, eleven and John, nine, were removed to Ireland on 12th July. There is no record of what became of them.

Sometimes the authorities used their power in a manner callous even for those harsh times. The case of Mary Ann King is notorious. She had lived in Manchester for eighteen years. In 1847 she left her child with neighbours while she travelled to Liverpool to collect a letter from her brother in America. While there she contracted typhus. As soon as she was strong enough, the Union forced her and forty others aboard a steamer bound for Ireland.

If the authorities disposed charity in a stingy, legalistic manner, there were numerous private charities that tried to make up for this deficiency. The most important effective was the Liverpool District Provident Society. In 1846 alone the Society fed nineteen thousand Irish families. The poor themselves gave generously to those even less fortunate than themselves. But the problem was far too great for private charity.

Most paupers had no choice but to throw themselves on the mercy of the parish officials whose duty it was to see that the poor did not die of starvation. Many went straight from the docks to the parish offices in Fenwick Street to beg for the precious tickets that entitled them to soup and bread. So many crowded in they were overwhelmed. In 1847 new relief offices were set up in each of the thirteen areas of the city where the Irish lived. The tickets they dispensed were all that stood between fifty thousand people and starvation.

Each ticket was exchanged for a quart of soup - enough to fill two modern milk bottles. It consisted of fish, pimento and treacle, made edible only by ravenous hunger. Those too frightened to risk coming to the attention of the authorities

resorted to begging. A few pence would buy bread and a roof for the night and a pauper who was lucky enough to be arrested for begging would get food and a bed in the cells. But few were so fortunate. Soon there were so many beggars the prisons could not accommodate them and the police refused to arrest destitute persons.

As the Liverpool magistrate Edward Rushton discovered, sending paupers to jail did not suit the authorities. When he sentenced an Irish woman to imprisonment for begging, the poor law official who was in court objected. If the woman were imprisoned, he said, the parish would have to feed her six children. The magistrate relented and sent all seven to the workhouse.

Mary Maganey was one of the many too frightened to attract attention by asking for public charity. She was found dead in a house in Vauxhall Road, one of the areas where the poor Irish sought shelter in night asylums, lodging houses and cellars. The coroner revealed that she had died of starvation and all she had in the previous four days was one cup of tea. Mary was by no means an isolated case.

Another coroner dealt with the case of an Irishman who died of starvation on the street. He said it was only one of many recent cases. But none stirred the public like the case of Luke Dillon.

Luke was eight years old. When the family arrived in Liverpool they were all ill. They found shelter in a cellar in Banastre Street. Hungry and cold they soon contracted typhus. With nothing to eat Luke, sick as he was, went begging. He collapsed and died of starvation.

But even such grim accounts of people dying of starvation were soon overshadowed by even greater horrors. In 1847 Liverpool was hit by 'Irish Fever.' This was nothing new as typhus was a frequent visitor to towns and cities in the mid nineteenth century. It struck Kilkenny and Cork and in 1847 reached Dublin and Derry. But when it arrived in Liverpool it swept in with terrifying ferocity claiming over six thousand victims in a year.

Liverpool's preparations were totally inadequate. The workhouse, which stood on the site of the modern Catholic Cathedral, had eighty beds for fever victims. Soon patients spilled into the chapel and the committee rooms and then filled the fever sheds that were built inside the workhouse walls to accommodate three hundred sufferers. These sheds were conveniently sited near the pauper cemetery.

As the spring turned to summer, the disease spread. There were so many victims that there was nowhere to treat them and most had to stay in their homes where they infected their families and neighbours. In four Irish streets alone there were five hundred people sick with fever.

The authorities opened new wards and even converted ships in the Mersey into hospitals. But the number of desperate people continued to outstrip the accommodation. Many who were taken in were beyond help. Like Roger Flynn, his wife Catherine and their six children. In the summer of 1847 all except seven year old Michael died of typhus. On 8th August he was sent to the orphanage.

In July the authorities decided that drastic action was needed. The cellars where most of the poor Irish lived were believed to be the main source of the disease. The authorities decided to clear them. Their occupants were turned out to die on the streets. Fifteen thousand people were forced back to Ireland. But the deaths still continued. So many were dying that the hearse used to take paupers to their unmarked graves, carried bodies piled six high.

Behind each cold statistic is the tragedy of a lonely death in a hostile land, far from home. Many couldn't face the shame of having their child buried in a pauper's grave and so kept the corpse in the house till they could afford a coffin. On one occasion police were called to an Irishwoman in Gloucester Street. She was carrying the corpse of her child from house to house, begging for money to bury him.

When it seemed that things could not get any worse, four hundred Irish children died of smallpox. The following month, March 1847, three hundred and seventy eight deaths from measles were reported. Most were Irish.

In all there were one hundred thousand people in Liverpool afflicted by fever and related illnesses in 1847. Of these, more than seventeen thousand died. Many others fled the city. Groups of ragged Irish, weak and sickly, were a common sight on the roads around the city.

It's little wonder that in his report for 1847 the Registrar General described Liverpool as 'the cemetery of Ireland.'

Some of those who fled ended up in Manchester, where there was already a considerable Irish community, viewed with universal hostility and fear.

The concentration of Irish immigrants in certain areas of the city was viewed as a sinister development. In the press the terms 'colony' and 'ghetto' were code for an Irish presence. Nothing did more to fix the notion of the teeming Irish ghetto in the popular mind than Little Ireland, Manchester. It had a population of 2,000 and was made famous by J. P. Kay's pamphlet, published in 1832, the year of the great cholera epidemic. '*A portion of low, swampy ground, liable to be frequently inundated, and to constant exhalation, is included between a high bank over which the Oxford Road passes, and a bend of the river Medlock, where its course is impeded by a weir. This unhealthy spot lies so low that the chimneys of its houses, some of them three storeys high, are a little above the level of the road. About two hundred of these habitations are crowded together in and extremely narrow space, and are chiefly inhabited by the lowest Irish.*'

He goes on to describe dwellings in which the ceilings were black with cockroaches. Cellars housed as many as could find space on the fetid straw covering the floor. Engels visited the area twelve years later, in 1844, when researching for ***The Condition of the Working Class in England***. He found it no better, '*about four thousand human beings, most of them Irish, live there. The cottages are old, dirty and of the meanest sort, the streets uneven, fallen into ruts and in parts without drains or pavements; masses of refuse, offal and sickening filth lie among the standing pools in all directions; the atmosphere is poisoned by the effluvia from these and laden and darkened by the smoke of a dozen tall factory chimneys. A horde of ragged women and children swarm about here, as filthy as the swine*

© Copyright Robert Blatchford Collection

that thrive upon the garbage heaps and in the puddles ... such a hateful and repulsive spectacle as can hardly be equalled.'

Kay's and Engels' accounts of Little Ireland so resonated with fear and revulsion that few social commentators could resist its power. It captured the quintessential dread evoked by the alien Irish hordes, who came to embody all the problems of the burgeoning industrial cities. Two of these problems were crime and the effects of drink.

An analysis of court records show that a disproportionate number of minor offences were committed by Irish immigrants, though this does not apply to more serious offences. In 1836 there was much evidence of the production and drinking of illicit alcohol, though the extent to which the Irish were more given to drink than the host community is hard to decide. Drinking on a Saturday night was common, but not on other nights.

There is a lot of evidence to suggest that the strong Irish sense of community posed a number of problems for the Manchester Constabulary. The police were seen as enemies and it was common for officers who found themselves in Little Ireland, to be attacked. The Irish had a reputation for resisting arrest, almost as a matter of principle, and would, in the words of one police witness, *'struggle until the shirt had been torn from their backs.'* By this time a crowd of locals had usually gathered to act in support of their countrymen.

Anti-Irish bigotry and its corollary, anti-Catholicism, were commonplace among all strata of English society. Around the mid-century these prejudices were frequently expressed in public disorder directed against the Irish community.

The first serious disorder in England associated with 12th July marches - when Orangemen traditionally celebrate King William's victory at the Battle of the Boyne - took place in Manchester in 1807 and recurred periodically

throughout the century. In 1888 a march through Ancoats, popularly known as *'Fenian Manchester,'* led to a riot as the nationalists sought to block the Orangemen's route.

It was at this time that anti-Catholicism developed as a popular rabble-rousing slogan. The restoration of the Catholic hierarchy in England and Wales led to an outpouring of anti-Catholic hysteria and the cry of *'No Popery'* was raised by unscrupulous politicians. Two Catholic churches in Stockport, a town outside Manchester with a substantial Irish population, were destroyed in anti-Catholic rioting.

The Fenian attack on Chester Castle, the events surrounding the execution of the Manchester Martyrs in 1867 and the Clekenwell explosion, in which civilians were killed, all served to inflame anti-Irish feeling. In 1867 the Irish community in Manchester was in the vanguard of the struggle for Irish independence. William Philip Allen, Michael Larkin, and Michael O'Brien – were members of the Irish Republican Brotherhood, an organisation dedicated to ending British rule in Ireland. The trio were members of a group of 30 – 40 Manchester Fenians who on 18th September 1867 attacked a horse drawn police van transporting two arrested leaders of the Brotherhood, Thomas Kelly and Timothy Deasy, to Belle Vue Gaol. Police Sergeant Charles Brett, travelling inside with the keys, was shot and killed as the attackers attempted to force the van open by blowing the lock. Kelly and Deasy were released after another prisoner in the van took the keys from Brett's body and passed them to the group outside through a grill; the pair were never recaptured, despite an extensive search.

Two others were also charged and found guilty of Brett's murder, Thomas Maguire and Edward O'Meagher Condon, but their death sentences were overturned. O'Meagher Condon was an American citizen and through the intercession of the United States government he had his death sentence overturned and Maguire's because the evidence given against him was considered unsatisfactory. Allen, Larkin, and O'Brien were publicly hanged on a temporary structure built on the wall of Salford Gaol, on 23rd November 1867, in front of a crowd of 8,000 - 10,000.

Brett was the first Manchester City Police officer to be killed on duty, and his memorial is in St Ann's Church, Manchester. Allen, Larkin, and O'Brien are also memorialised, There was widespread indignation both in Manchester and in Ireland where the Irish community made up more than 10% of the population. The three were regarded by many as inspirational heroes and the 'martyrs' were given a public funeral attended by over 60, 000 people.

The country was plunged into a fear of the Fenian. Hundreds of special constables were sworn in and the Irish areas were searched and hundreds of arrests made. The subsequent trial and public execution of Allen, O'Brien and Larkin, brought the struggle for Irish independence to England's industrial heart. The Irish in Manchester were seen as the most militantly nationalistic of their race.

The activities of William Murphy, the anti-Catholic demagogue, both exploited and stimulated these sentiments. Inspired by his invective, an Orange mob, enthusiastically backed by locals, attacked the Irish of Ashton-under-Lyme in October 1868, destroying homes in Cavendish Street and gleefully burning the possessions of those they had made homeless.

The English press depicted the Irish as ape like brutes, slaves to irrational anger and savage passions. Despite this large scale disturbances in Manchester disappeared after 1055. The Irish were winning a grudging acceptance. Yet there is no reason to believe that competition in the workplace diminished. Among unskilled workers, the Irish remained unwelcome rivals for employment.

This competition was nowhere more acute than in the building trade. It was the one key industry that remained almost untouched by mechanisation and mass production methods. Apart from the introduction of the machine-made brick, the building industry remained as labour intensive as ever. It employed almost three quarters of a million workers in 1871 and was the fourth biggest employer of labour in the country.

It was a magnet for Irish immigrants. It provided employment for the unskilled, offered the prospect of outdoor work to those used to farm labour, held out the hope of work with family and fellow countrymen and gave those with a background in the building trade back in Ireland the opportunity to exploit their experience. In 1851 there were about 20,000 building workers in Manchester and Salford and a very large percentage of these were of Irish origin.

The qualities which endeared Irish workers to their employers were precisely those which made them resented by local workers competing with them for employment. They had a reputation for hard work and it was said that they could toil at a pace which no Englishman could maintain. John Wallis, a master builder, told a Royal Commission that he preferred Irish workers because of their conscientious attitude and their courteous manner. His only complaint was that many of them went home to Ireland at harvest time.

Those who were in competition for work with the Irish accused them of working for lower rates of pay and thereby depressing wage levels. There is no evidence to support this and in fact much to indicate that it was not so in Manchester.

The findings of the 1836 Royal Commission suggests that the Irish were in the forefront of trade union activity and conspicuously active in all the major building disputes in Manchester from 1833 to 1870. The records of the *Manchester Bricklayers Labourers' Union* confirm this.

In 1856 it had 900 members, organised into nine lodges. All the officials were Irish, as were the great majority of members. The Union's activities seem to have been fully integrated into the life of the community, for its trustee and treasurer was Canon Toole, parish priest of St. Wilfred's, Hulme, an area to the south of the City centre with a sizeable Irish community.

The Irish in England brought with them a strong tradition of co-operation. Their suspicion of a government which regarded them as aliens in their own land gave rise to culture in which co-operative self reliance was a significant feature. Irish building workers in Ireland had a tradition of sound organisation.

The Irish in Manchester faced considerable hostility and hardship. The squalor of Little Ireland came to represent all the evils of modern industrial society. Despite this they gradually established themselves as a permanent feature of the developing city, while managing to retain their distinctive culture and identity. Many of the most damaging slurs made against them were groundless and despite official endorsement of popular prejudices, their potency diminished as the turn of the century approached.

The prominence of the Irish Question in British politics made it likely that events connected with the struggle for independence would affect attitudes to Manchester's Irish community. This was particularly the case in 1867, when the struggle for independence was fought out on the streets of Manchester and the Salford gallows.

Home From Home
Joseph O'Neill

Emigrant tales are part of Irish lore. Every townland has its own Ned Kelly or a Paddy Reilly, who pined in exile for Ireland. Yet when we talk of the Irish nation abroad we often forget the country once known as Ireland's home from home.

In the middle of the last century everyone in Ireland knew the glories of New Zealand. Government emigration literature and the newspapers were full of accounts of its vibrant young settlements and fertile soil. And no author extolled the wonders of its climate without telling his readers that it was like Ireland. New Zealand was promoted as a home from home. But the reality was different

The government of New Zealand needed Irish immigrants - but didn't want them. The authorities had no love of Catholics, especially Irish Catholics. But there was a desperate need for immigrants, especially women. Not only was Ireland a great source of the strong young men needed by the developing country but there were plenty of young Irishwomen prepared to make the long journey.

The New Zealand Company, which recruited immigrants, had three agencies: in Belfast, Dublin and one for the rest of the country. They concentrated on recruiting in the north. Later they set up a quota system to restrict the numbers of Catholics but had to abandon it because the country was so desperately short of women. Irish women and men went in droves.

Then, as now, emigration was for the young people. Most were under twenty-five and few were over thirty. Many were farm labourers with nothing to keep them in Ireland. As landless workers they would never be able to marry and support a family. But many of the better off also found the pull of New Zealand too strong to resist.

The gold rush in the 1860's was one reason for this. The prospect of instant wealth attracted many who had never lifted a shovel or swung a pick. But many skilled craftsmen and educated people, some with money to invest, saw New Zealand as the land of opportunity.

Most went via Scottish and English ports, as there were few ships sailing directly from Ireland. Some went to New Zealand after finding Australia was not to their liking. Though not as grim as the passage to America in the 1850's, the journey was long and hazardous. Minnie Williams emigrated from Ballymena, Co. Derry in 1881. Her account of the journey has survived.

Minnie left Ballymena with her parents, brother and three sisters. The first leg of the journey was delightful. They crossed from Larne to Stranraer and travelled down to London. Most of the ships bound for New Zealand sailed from ports in southern England. In London before boarding ship travelling from Euston station they went by bus to the home of the agent where they spent four days.

The family travelled third class and did all their own cooking. The Zealandia was not like the coffin ships that plied the Atlantic thirty years before. She was a great iron ship built especially for the long distance emigrant trade. While passing through the tropics they lived off rice because salt in the other food gave them

a raging thirst. Every week the captain gave each passenger a bottle of limejuice to protect them from scurvy. It worked because Minnie and her family remained in excellent.

Most weeks their rations ran out by Friday and the weekend was long and hungry. However this only heightened Minnie's pleasure when one of the second class passengers invited the Williams sisters to a birthday party. Five and a half weeks after leaving Ballymena they arrived safely in New Zealand. Minnie and her family's experience was not the norm.

Most of those who went from Ireland to New Zealand were single and a third of the married couples had no children. Children were a disadvantage because it meant that only one of the couple was available for full time work. The majority came from Ulster, Munster and Galway, the poorest of these from the south and west. When they arrived they had very mixed fortunes. Nothing shows this better than the story of the Quinn brothers.

Raised in Newry in the 1880's, Patrick and William Quinn moved to the Falls Road, Belfast with their parents. They later emigrated to New Zealand but gradually drifted apart. However, both continued to write to their family in Belfast.

William was steady and careful. He worked hard and prospered, becoming a solid citizen, a pillar of society. His brother's tale was very different.

Patrick was too fond of the drink. He drifted from job to job, town to town and barely made a living. In fact many of his letters home were begging letters, asking for a few shillings to keep him from hunger. Strangely enough, his mother, poor and ill as she was, was always able to oblige. Why? Because her other son, William, was a generous man who regularly sent money home. So, while one son sent money home to keep his mother in the old country, a mother sent money to her son to keep him in the New World.

Fortunately, Patrick's case was not typical. Most Irish people prospered in New Zealand and found their way into every walk of life. Today almost one person in five Kiwis is proud to claim Irish ancestry.

Glasnevin Trust
preserving the past for future generations

Glasnevin Trust is a voluntary, not-for-profit body (registered charity number 5849). The Trust is the largest provider of funeral services in Ireland. It operates five cemeteries (Dardistown, Glasnevin, Goldenbridge, Newlands Cross and Palmerstown) and two crematoria (Glasnevin and Newlands Cross).

- acts as guardian to those who have chosen us to care for their family, work with them, educate them, or offer practical services to them.
- is memorable, distinctive, functional, timeless and descriptive.
- reflects our credibility, reliability and confidence to fulfill our mission

Glasnevin Cemetery

It is the largest cemetery in Ireland and was first opened in 1832. Prior to the establishment of Glasnevin Cemetery, Irish Catholics had no cemeteries of their own in which to bury their dead and the repressive Penal Laws of the 18th century placed heavy restrictions on the public performance of Catholic services. It became common practice for Catholics to conduct a limited version of their own funeral services in Protestant cemeteries. This situation continued until an incident at a funeral held at St. Kevin's Cemetery in 1823, provoked public outcry when a Protestant sexton reprimanded a Catholic priest for proceeding to perform a limited version of a funeral mass.

The outcry prompted Daniel O'Connell, champion of Catholic rights, to launch a campaign and prepare a legal opinion proving that there was actually no law passed forbidding praying for a dead Catholic in a graveyard. O'Connell pushed for the opening of a burial ground in which both Irish Catholics and Protestants could give their dead dignified burial Glasnevin Cemetery was established as a place where all could bury their dead with dignity irrespective of their beliefs. The cemetery has since grown to become a national monument and a vital part of Irish Heritage.

Glasnevin Cemetery contains many historically interesting monuments. There are also the graves of many of Ireland's most prominent national figures — Brendan Behan, Kevin Barry, Christy Brown, Sir Roger Casement, Michael Collins, Daniel O'Connell, Pádraig Ó Domhnaill, Frank Duff, Charles Gavan Duffy, George Gavan Duffy Arthur Griffith, Maude Gonne, Seán MacBride, Constance Markiewicz,

Charles Stewart Parnell, Éamon de Valera, Jeremiah O'Donovan Rossa, as well as Luke Kelly of the Dubliners. The Boyzone singer Stephen Gately was cremated at Glasnevin Crematorium, which is located within the cemetery grounds, on October 17, 2009.

The cemetery also offers a view of the changing style of death monuments in Ireland over the last 200 years: from the austere, simple, high stone erections of the period up until the 1860s, to the elaborate Celtic crosses of the nationalistic revival from the 1860s to 1960s, to the plain Italian marble of the late twentieth century. Glasnevin Cemetery has grown from its original nine to over 120 acres.

The high wall with watch-towers surrounding the main part of the cemetery was built to deter bodysnatchers, who were active in Dublin in the 18th and early 19th century. The watchmen also had a pack of blood hounds who roamed the cemetery at night. Prime Minister, Robert Peel, when questioned in Parliament on the activities of the body snatchers, admitted that it was, indeed, a 'grave matter.'

Glasnevin Museum is a must see for anyone interested in Irish Heritage and Genealogy. The exhibitions over two floors, shows the social, historical, political and artistic development of modern Ireland through the lives of the generations buried in Ireland's necropolis. The tour includes a visit to the crypt of Daniel O Connell. Other Museum facilities include the Tower Cafe which offers a wide and varied menu and the Glasnevin Trust Shop which stocks exclusive gifts and souvenirs.

Genealogy at Glasnevin Trust

Due to the increase of shows such as *Who do you think you are?* Tracing your roots has never been as popular. Glasnevin Trust has captured the mood of the nation and provided access to our extensive records containing cemetery and crematoria records related to Glasnevin, Goldenbridge, Dardistown, Newlands Cross and Palmerstown as well as Glasnevin Crematorium and Newlands Cross Crematorium. The records date back to 1828, including unique records covering the famine, cholera, Spanish flu and small pox epidemics, records from union work houses and records of the children buried in the Angels Plots in Glasnevin Cemetery. There are over 1 million records available to view online, including actual extract images of the burial recorded in our registers.

Our specialised team is constantly updating the records available; Glasnevin Trust offers arguably the best resource to search the heritage and family history of those buried in Glasnevin Trust's cemeteries and crematoria. Find us online at www.glasnevintrust.ie/genealogy
Glasnevin Trust, Finglas Road Dublin 11 T: + 353 (0) 1 8826500, E: info@glasnevintrust.ie W: www.glasnevintrust.ie

Image © Glasnevin Trust

Irish Origins - www.origins.net
maggie Loughran

One of Ireland's greatest exports has been its people. People left Ireland for many reasons; voluntarily to travel the world, to explore, seek fame and fortune, as economic migrants, to trade, colonise, govern or forcibly transported, to fight or to garrison some far off settlement. With the close proximity to the British mainland – twelve miles at its nearest point, many of these 'travellers' went backwards and forwards seeking seasonal work or plying their trade.

It is estimated that there are over one million people of Irish birth in Britain today, plus numerous second, third or fourth generation Irish. In fact over 40 million people in the United States and 30% of Australian citizens as well as 15% of New Zealand residents can claim Irish ancestry. This does not take into account other countries worldwide that received Irish emigrants. The majority of the people undertaking Irish research are not resident in Ireland.

To undertake Irish research a little understanding of Ireland's history and the relationship with the rest of the British Isles is necessary. This can go a long way to understanding why the records were generated in the first place.

Irish History – A Brief Overview

In 1167, the King of Leinster was deposed and fled from Ireland to the English court of King Henry II to gain help in regaining his throne. He was allowed to recruit help from amongst the Norman knights in Wales. The price for this was acknowledgment that King Henry was his overlord. This set the scene for

the future path of Irish history.

Over the next three hundred and fifty years or so, English power and dominance in Ireland waxed and waned until the English gained full control of Ireland under Henry VIII, thereafter the English monarchs styled themselves Kings of Ireland. Substantial Protestant settlement of Ireland began in 1609, and Ireland was formally united with Great Britain by the Act of Union 1801. When the Irish parliament voted itself out of existence for Irish Home Rule in 1922 the six counties (part of the province of Ulster) of Northern Ireland remained part of the United Kingdom and the remaining twenty six counties formed the Irish Republic.

The history of Ireland has resulted in the fact that many records generated in England and Wales were never generated in Ireland. Additionally the records of the 'common man' do not generally start in Ireland until much later than they did on the British mainland. With the destruction of the Irish Public Records Office (Four Courts) in 1922 during the Irish civil war when many records were lost has made Irish research challenging. The result being that the researcher is consulting types of records, early into their research, that they would not usually do so if researching ancestors in other parts of the world.

Irish Origins has a whole range of material to help overcome these obstacles, including Griffith's Valuation, which lists all Irish householders, some surviving early census returns, and 19th century directories. For

those who can get back further, the site has indexes to over 200,000 Irish wills.

Established in 1997 Origins.net was the first British online data provider. Through its collection of Irish records access can be gained to the richest source of authentic Irish genealogy records from anywhere in the world via the internet.

Along with detailed indexes and transcriptions of many records, Irish Origins also has in depth research articles giving the full background and history of each dataset. What the actual coverage of each dataset is, the information that it contains plus tips and techniques on how to read, use and navigate your way though the data.

An Eviction
The landlords emergency men used a battering ram against the barricaded door of an Irish peasants cottage, assisted by Royal Irish Constabulary and English Hussars

Census and Census Substitutes
Griffith's Valuation 1847-1864

In order to produce the accurate information necessary for local taxation, the Tenement Act 1842 provided for a uniform valuation of all property in Ireland to be based on the productive capacity of the land and the potential rent of the buildings. Richard Griffiths was appointed Commissioner of Valuation, with the results of the valuers' work being published in a series of over 300 volumes between 1847 and 1864. These detailed the names of all the occupiers of property (not simply the owners) and the value of their house and land.

The edition of Griffith's Valuation found on Irish Origins is a compilation of all of these original publications, revisions and amended versions that were published over the 17 years it took to complete the valuation. No library in any country in the world, including Ireland, has a full set of Griffith's Valuation. Users can search the complete database of personal and place names, and then access scanned images of the original published pages.

Irish Origins subscribers can also access the original Ordnance Survey (OS) maps and town plans used by the team working on Griffith's Primary Valuation during 1847-1864 for the Republic of Ireland. The originals, now held by the National Archives of Ireland, are not accessible by the public.

The first full surviving census for Ireland is not until 1901 - the earlier census either being destroyed in the Four Courts or pulped by government order. This leaves Griffith's Valuation as a valuable 'census substitute' for mid-19th century Ireland, in the years between the Great Famine and the beginning of civil registration in 1864.

Dublin City Census 1851 Heads of Household Index

The 1851 Dublin City Census index was compiled by Dr D A Chart in the 19th century from the original census records which were later destroyed in the Four Courts fire in 1922. Covering central Dublin Chart's index gives names and addresses of 60,000 heads of household and includes absent family members.

Where the male head of household was absent, Chart recorded the wife or female head of household in his index. The index is not confined to householders, but includes persons working in various institutions on census night.

The index on Origins is accompanied by scanned images of the original 1847 Ordnance Survey Town Plans, to help users identify specific addresses.

Dublin City Census 1901: Rotunda Ward

This includes details of 13,556 individuals living in over 1,334 properties in the Rotunda Ward in Dublin City, and comprises a full extraction of the data in the relevant 1901 census records.
(Origins site contains a large amount of English and Welsh data, including Irishmen found in the 1841 and 1871 censuses)

William Smith O'Brien Petition 1848

William Smith O'Brien was an Irish Nationalist, Member of Parliament and leader of the Young Ireland movement. He was convicted of sedition for his part in the Young Irelander Rebellion of 1848 and sentenced to death.

There was a public outcry and between October 1848 and May 1849 over 70,000 people in Ireland and 10,000 people in England signed petitions clamoring for his reprieve. The sentences of O'Brien and other members of the Irish Confederation were commuted to transportation for life to Van Diemen's Land (Tasmania). O'Brien was released in 1854 and in May 1856, granted an unconditional pardon.

Fully searchable the William Smith O'Brien Petition records are essentially a census substitute: giving the names, addresses and oftimes occupations of the signatories.

The database of signatories to the William Smith O'Brien Petition can help researchers who have no other means of confirming whether people were present in an area during this period of the Famine.

1831 Tithe Defaulters

All occupants of land were required to pay an annual tithe (or religious tax) of 10% of the agricultural produce generated by that holding. This money was demanded by landholders, irrespective of their religion, and was paid directly to the official state church, the Anglican Church of Ireland.

However in 1830 and 1831, when increasing numbers refused to pay tithes, the Government set up the Clergy Relief Fund 1831 where Church of Ireland clergymen could claim for the arrears of 1831 tithes.

The 1,061 pages of Tithe Defaulters record 29,027 names, occupations plus other details across 232 Parishes June to August 1832. This unique record of names, addresses and occupations provides an important genealogical source for Ireland, especially given the near total destruction of the 1831 census.

Electoral Registers for Ireland 1832-38

This dataset details those eligible to vote in Ireland following the 1832 Reform Act. It contains over 52,600 names, details of occupations, addresses and entitlement criteria to vote. The information in this dataset comes from the Report of the Select Committee on Fictitious Votes, 1837-38.

The Select Committee was set up in the aftermath of Daniel O'Connell's election to Parliament in 1832, with its widespread accusations of corruption. The Commissioners of Police and Magistrates throughout Ireland were charged with creating what amounted to an electoral register for those entitled to vote in Ireland between 1832 and 1837 under the terms of the Reform Act.

Directories of Ireland

Only a handful of truly national Irish directories survive. The directories available on Origins.net are some of the most comprehensive Irish directories available covering the years 1824 to 1894.

Census of Elphin 1749

In 1749 at the behest of Edward Synge, The Church of Ireland Bishop of Elphin, a census of his diocese was taken. This covered most of Co Roscommon, part of Co Sligo and nine parishes in Co Galway.

The census containing records for nearly 20,000 people has been published by the Irish Manuscripts Commission, and it tells us about the occupation and religion of the heads of household, the size of their family, size of their household, who had servants and how many. The data is accompanied by digitised images of the full publication.

Irish Wills

The Irish Wills Index 1484 -1858 lists surviving probate material held at the National Archives Ireland (NAI). This consists of transcripts, original wills, copies, extracts and abstracts.

The index covers the years up to 1858, when the whole testamentary system was centralised. Prior to

Origins.net are offering **20% discount** on subscriptions. To claim your discount simply visit www.origins.net and enter **Irish2011** in the promotional box on the sign up page or the checkout page after a subscription has been chosen.

this the Church of Ireland had authority over all testamentary matters, including proving wills, grants of probate and administrations.

Each index entry contains the name of the person leaving a will etc, names of the executors, address, occupation, and the place where the document was proved.

Prior to 1922 the staff at the PROI (now NAI) compiled complete indexes of all the wills, administrations and marriage licences in their keeping. These indexes began to appear in printed form in 1895 with the publication of an index to the transactions at the Consistorial Court of the Archbishop of Dublin. This covered far more than just wills and administrations, and included marriage licences, commissions, decrees, letters of tutelage, and a host of other secular and ecclesiastical proceedings before the Consistorial Court.

This was followed by the publication of an Index to the Prerogative Wills of Ireland 1536 - 1810 by Sir Arthur Vicars. It contains an index to over 40,000 Irish wills, most of which were destroyed in 1922 with the destruction of the Four Courts. The Prerogative Court of Armagh was the highest court in Ireland for the proving of wills and grants of probate and administration.

Vicars based his work on the abstracts to the original wills compiled by Sir William Betham, and is the only index to his voluminous collections of abstracts and extracts in existence.

W.P.W. Phillimore & Gertrude Thrift began publishing their indexes to diocesan wills in 1909. This series, compiled from existing finding aids at the Public Record Office in Dublin, contains entries for over 30,000 wills for many of the Irish diocesan consistorial courts.

Deputy Keeper's Reports

On the establishment of the Irish Public Records Office (PRO) in 1867, records were progressively transferred to the new repository. Each year, between 1869 and 1920, the Office published an annual report, known as the Deputy Keeper's Report, which detailed records received, and work undertaken, during the previous twelve months. These reports can contain useful source material for researchers. Although usually brief, reports often contain copious appendices, which can be especially useful, due to the destruction of the PRO in 1922. Deputy Keeper's reports often represent the only record of lost primary source material.

Indexes to the Dublin Grant Books were published in two volumes of the Deputy Keeper's reports, the combined indexes containing more over 125,000 entries comprising of 83,600 marriages and 35,800 wills.

Irish people who owned property in England before 1858 may have had their wills proved in the Prerogative Court of Canterbury (PCC). The PCC Wills & Administrations 1383 - 1700

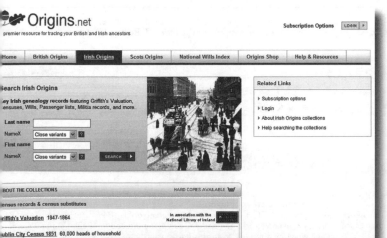

can be found in National Will Index on Origins.

Burial Records - Memorials of the Dead

Compiled by Ian Cantwell this dataset includes full transcripts of the surviving memorials (Gravestone Inscriptions) found in the 128 graveyards and churches of Counties Galway and Mayo. The dataset of over 3,000 pre 1901 memorials contains over 8000 names. Memorials have been often erected by American relatives whose details are also included in the dataset.

Between 1970 - 1990 Brian J. Cantwell transcribed and published eleven volumes of graveyard transcriptions primarily covering Counties Wicklow, Wexford and South Dublin. Other transcriptions were either published in journals (Galway and Kildare) or unpublished (Clare, Cork and Sligo) the latter deposited at the NAI. A Data CD of all published and unpublished memorial transcriptions was issued by Eneclann and the contents are now available on Irish Origins.

These transcriptions covered all pre 1880 memorials in graveyards and all surviving interior church memorials and contain the names of over 60,000 people.

Military, War and Rebellion Records

Militia Attestations Index 1872-1915

This is an index to Militia Attestation Papers, for the period 1872 to 1915, for over 12,500 militiamen in the Royal Garrison Artillery (present day Royal Artillery) in Ireland. The Royal Garrison Artillery had militia in the counties of Antrim, Clare, Cork, Donegal, Dublin, Limerick, Sligo, Tipperary, Waterford and Wicklow, plus Ulster.

These can be very fruitful sources of genealogical data being filled in at the time of recruitment and contain a great deal about these men plus their families.

The original documents are held at The National Archives, London - www.nationalarchives.gov.uk The index records includes all the information necessary to locate the original records in The National Archives or copies of original documents can be ordered via Origins.

Ireland's Memorial Records 1914 - 18

The objective of these eight volumes was to preserve the names of over 49,600 Irishmen who lost their lives fighting in the Great War. The collection, published in 1923, was compiled by The Committee of the Irish National War Memorial and was lavishly illustrated by the Irish artist Harry Clarke. It is the most complete record known and is unique in many ways.

Name, rank, regiment, regimental number, and in most cases, county/place of birth, and place and date of death are recorded. Subscribers to Origins can also view the original printed publication for every entry, which may contain more information. Not all of those listed gave their home addresses as Ireland, but all fought with Irish regiments or considered themselves to be Irish.

The 1798 Rebellion: Claimants & Surrenders

Taking place during a period of general unrest, following close on the heels of the American War of Independence and the French Revolution, the 1798 Rebellion was a watershed in Irish history. 30,000 people were killed during the uprising, with many more wounded. This dataset of over 8,000 names includes both individuals who made claims for compensation for loss of property during the rising, and also rebels who surrendered in Dublin City and Coolock Barony. The individuals named come from every social background, from poor Dublin city labourers to members of the aristocracy.

Passenger Lists

British & Irish Passenger Lists 1890 & 1891

This is probably the most complete and accurate transcriptions of the 1890 & 1891 passenger lists for sailings from British & Irish ports to the USA and Canada. It was compiled by Peter Coldham and the names of nearly 200,000 passengers are included.

The 1890 lists cover a total of 921 sailings, from ports scattered throughout the British Isles; the 1891 lists include 501 sailings from Irish ports. A breakdown by port (both departure and arrive) is available on Origins website.

Transatlantic Migration 1858-1870

With the threat of an imminent uprising by Fenians and their supporters in Ireland, the government in Dublin Castle required that the major ports in Britain and Ireland submit their incoming ships' passenger lists to them for scrutiny.

This Index taken from original records held at The National Archives (London) contains all the surviving details recorded on ships' passenger lists returning to Britain and Ireland from North America between 1858 and 1870 and runs to over 42,000 names most of whom were Irish, English or Scottish origin.

By 1870, following the failure of the Fenian insurrection in Ireland in 1867, the British authorities considered the Fenian threat over.

Places, Maps and Images

In addition to the maps etc already mentioned Irish Origins has a selection of interesting images that depict not only the great and the good but also national monuments symbolic icons of Ireland and everyday scenes that were part of our ancestor's lives.

Bibliography

Tracing Your Ancestors in Northern Ireland Ian Maxwell 1997
Researching Scots-Irish Ancestors William Roulston 2005
Tracing Your Irish Ancestors John Grenham 2006
Irish Genealogy - a Record Finder Donal F Begley 1987
Handbook on Irish Genealogy Donal F Begley 1984

Queenstown Harbour
First referred to as Cove in 1750, it was renamed Queenstown in 1849 to commemorate a visit by Queen Victoria. The name Cobh was restored in 1922. Many emigrant ships left from this harbour.

Irish Family History Research on the Web

Stuart A. Raymond

Who do you think you are? The question is much easier to answer today than it was even ten years ago, due to the invention of the internet. The internet revolution is founded on two previous revolutions – the invention of writing, and the invention of printing. So is genealogy. Without these two revolutions, the sources which we use would not exist. Writing enabled sources such as parish registers to be compiled; printing provided the printed forms which helped to improve their accuracy. It would have been difficult to establish civil registration without the use of printed forms. And the census could not have been taken without them. Transcripts and indexes to all of these sources were much more difficult to compile and disseminate before the advent of computers and the internet. The ability to compile databases from major sources, and to consult them instantly from anywhere in the world, has dramatically transformed the way we undertake research.

Nevertheless, there must always be a 'but.' The value of databases continues to depend on human agency - on the accuracy of the original scribe, of the transcriber, and of the indexer. All are open to error. An index which achieves accuracy greater than 95% is doing well. And sod's law states that the information you require will be amongst the 5% of entries which are not accurate!

The remedy for this problem is eternal vigilance, and a critical mind. That is particularly true given the penchant of database hosts to present you with a box which says 'search here for your ancestors.' It is very tempting to search without asking what lies behind the box. But the question must be answered if you want accurate information. Remember that what

comes out of a database can only be derived from what went in. Databases can only be as good as their sources, and sometimes not even as good as that. Indexes are only indexes – they are not the original documents, and do not necessarily record everything that could be found in those documents. It is important to find out what you are searching before you search, and to make no assumptions about the information in a database before you know who compiled a particular record, why it was compiled, and what the limitations of the data in it might be.

Most genealogical sources were not compiled in order to answer genealogists' questions. Scribes provided the information that they thought was relevant. Census enumerators asked very specific questions. They were not necessarily the questions that we want answered. And the enumerators may have made mistakes. The evidence we gather must be looked at critically. The internet makes that even more imperative. Databases are compiled by humans who can make mistakes. The fact that there is no entry in a database index for Cavan Walsh does not mean that he is not recorded in the document indexed. The indexer may have made a mistake.

There is also the difficulty that many documents have been lost. Ireland has been particularly prone to destruction caused by war, as well as the ravages of fire, flood, and mice.

Despite these caveats, the internet has made it much easier to trace family history in Ireland. There are now innumerable web guides to family history, and to specific sources, together with a substantial number of databases, and increasing numbers of digitised documents. A variety of gateways to these web pages are available. It is perhaps best to start with Genuki Ireland **www.genuki.org.uk/big/irl** Genuki is the major genealogical site for the British Isles. Its aim is to serve as a 'virtual reference library' of British and Irish genealogical information. Its links are a major feature of the site. But it also offers a great deal of general information and guidance. Its focus is on primary source material, rather than on particular families, and it does not link to commercial sites. The Irish section of the site has separate pages for each county, as well as much useful general information for the whole island.

Cyndis List: Ireland and Northern Ireland
www.cyndislist.com/ireland.htm is narrower in scope; its aim is to serve as a directory of Irish genealogical websites. It is part of a world-wide directory which is likely to link to 300,000 websites by the time you read this. It has an American bias, and its size is making it increasingly difficult to use. A more focused directory is provided by my book, *Irish Family History on The Web: A Directory* (3rd ed. Family History Partnership, 2007). This attempts to identify those sites which are likely to be most relevant to Irish researchers, and lists more than 2000 of them.

There are many introductory guides to Irish genealogy on the web, and it is impossible to list them all here. Many are provided on the websites of libraries and record offices. Perhaps the most useful site is that provided by:

Family Search: Ireland
https://wiki.familysearch.org/en/Ireland
This includes separate pages on a wide range of different topics, for example, cemeteries, civil registration, newspapers, poor houses. Like Genuki, it also has separate pages for each county.

There are a number of other extensive advice sites that are worth consulting:

Fianna Guide to Irish Genealogy
www.rootsireland.ie
From Ireland: Irish Genealogy and Family History www.from-ireland.net/genealogy
Irish Times.com: Irish Ancestors
www.irishtimes.com/ancestor
Irish Ancestors
http://freepages.genealogy.rootsweb.ancestry.com/~irishancestors

The websites of the major Irish record offices and

libraries offer much good advice, as well as extensive details of their holdings. See the National Archives of Ireland at www.nationalarchives.ie/genealogy and the National Library of Ireland www.nli.ie In Belfast, the Public Record Office of Northern Ireland www.proni.gov.uk holds many records.

Much useful advice can also be obtained from other researchers, through the numerous discussion groups and mailing lists listed at *'Ireland Mailing Lists'* **www.rootsweb.ancestry.com/~jfuller/gen_mail_country-unk-irl.html**

Some of these are specialist lists, dealing with topics such as cemeteries or emigrants. The majority however, cover particular counties or smaller areas. Curious Fox **www.curiousfox.com** has similarities with a mailing list, but also acts as a permanent noticeboard where you can record your interest in particular families and places.

Resources available in particular counties do vary, and it is always important to get advice on the peculiarities of the particular area your ancestors came from. County mailing lists provide one way of doing this. The county pages on advice sites such as some of those listed above also help. An alternative approach is to join a family history society. These have regular programmes of lectures, usually a quarterly journal, and sometimes useful source publications. They can provide you with much useful advice. In addition, their lists of members interests enable you to make contact with others researching the same families.

There are also a number of surname interest sites on the web. The major Irish listing is provided by the *'Online Irish Names Directory'* www.list.jaunay.com/irlnames

There are also many lists for particular counties, too many to list here. A full listing is given in my book. To search for the websites of particular families go to Surname Helper http://surhelp.rootsweb.ancestry.com

Most researchers are likely to begin their research by obtaining certificates of births, marriages and deaths from the General Register Offices in Dublin and Belfast. Sadly, neither the registers they hold, nor indexes to them, are online. Details of how to apply for certificates can be had from the General Register Office www.groireland.ie (for Eire), and from the General Register Office www.nidirect.gov.uk/gro (for Northern Ireland). For indexes held by the Latter Day Saints Family History Library, together with a good introduction to Irish civil registration records in Ireland see Family Search's Wiki page at https://wiki.familysearch.org/en/Ireland_Civil_Registration-_Vital_Records

The registers held by the two General Register Offices are copies of registers compiled by district registrars. Indexes to some of their registers compiled by District Registrars have been compiled by the county genealogy centres of the Irish Family History Foundation **www.rootsireland.ie** These centres have also compiled many indexes to parish registers and other sources.

Baptisms, marriages, and burials are also recorded

Ireland Civil Registration

(Redirected from Ireland Civil Registration - Vital Records)
Ireland

View the Ireland Civil Registration online tutorial from FamilySearch.

Contents (hide)

1 Introduction
2 Using Indexes
  2.1 Birth Indexes
  2.2 Marriage Indexes
  2.3 Death Indexes
3 Tips on Searching the Civil Registration Indexes
4 Additional Information about the Indexes
5 Tips If You Cannot Find an Individual in the Index
6 Locating the Actual Registration Information
7 Additional Information on Death Registrations
8 Additional Collections in Registrar's Office
9 Further Reading
10 External Links
11 Selected Bibliography

Introduction

Civil registration is the government recording and registering of births, marriages, and deaths. Registration began in Ireland in 1864. However, registration of Protestant marriages had begun earlier in 1845. Births, marriages and deaths were registered with district registrars. Registration districts were set up within the boundaries of the existing Poor Law Unions. Because Irish civil registration records are indexed and cover most of the population, they are an important source of genealogical data, particularly of names, dates, relationships, and places.

Below is a table showing the information that can be found in each record type in the civil records of Ireland.

Record Type	Start Date	Record Content
Birth	1864	Child's name; sex; birth date; birthplace; parents names (including mother's maiden name); father's occupation; informant's signature, residence and qualification (often the relationship to the child being registered.
Marriages	1845;Protestant; 1864;all	Marriage date, place and denomination (for church marriages); names of bride and groom, their ages (frequently given as "full age"); occupations, marital statuses, residences at the time of marriage; names and occupations of their fathers and whether their fathers were deceased; signatories of the bride, groom, and witnesses. Marriages were usually performed in the bride's parish and were registered by the performing minister, priest or registrar. In the Irish Republic, since 1956 both parties' states of birth and parents' full names have been recorded in addition to the future intended town or country in which the couple intend to reside.
Death	1864	Name, occupation, age at death, and marital status of deceased; duration of illness; date, place and cause of death;

Search Learning & How-To's

Subject, Place or Keyword

BROWSE
by country   A to Z by topic

New to the Research Wiki?

In the FamilySearch Research Wiki, you can learn about how to do genealogical research or share your knowledge with others.

Learn More

Views
Page
Edit
Discussion
History
Watch
View source

Toolbox

Community

Personal tools

---

in parish registers. Many registers have been transcribed or indexed for the internet – far too many to list here. A full list is given in my book. One of the difficulties of researching in Ireland is the fact that you need to check the registers of various different denominations. The Roman Catholics are dominant numerically, but the Church of Ireland was the established church, and the Presbyterians are strong in Ulster. There are also a variety of smaller denominations, eg Methodists, Quakers, Congregationalists. A useful *'Online Tutorial on Irish Church Records'* can be found at https://wiki.familysearch.org/en/Ireland_Church_Records. For an explanation of 'Irish Church Records' visit www.from-ireland.net/roman-catholic-parishes/Irish-Church-Records-Explanation. A detailed listing of Roman Catholic registers can be consulted at www.irishtimes.com/ancestor/browse/counties/rcmaps. Church of Ireland registers for Eire are deposited in the Representative Church Body Library, whose holdings are listed at http://ireland.anglican.org/index.php?do=about&id=109. Many registers for Northern Ireland have been microfilmed by the Public Record Office of Northern Ireland, and are listed in 'A Guide to Church Records' www.proni.gov.uk/guide_to_church_records.pdf. For Eire, many registers have been microfilmed by the National Library of Ireland; these are listed at www.nli.ie/en/parish-register.aspx. Many Irish baptism and marriage records have been indexed by the International Genealogical Index www.familysearch.org/eng/default.asp. For its coverage, visit www.pricegen.com/resources/globalbatchnumbers.htm (click 'Ireland'). It is, of course, possible to use this index to order microfilm of the documents indexed through your local Latter Day Saints' Family History Centre.

Few Irish parish registers survive from the eighteenth century and earlier. Likewise, few nineteenth century census records are available.

Family Search's Wiki on 'Ireland Census' https://wiki.familysearch.org/en/Ireland_Census provides the basic background. Broadly, only the 1901 and 1911 censuses are available for the whole island. Both can now be searched online on the website of the National Archives of Ireland www.census.nationalarchives.ie. Earlier fragments are available for some counties; most are available on microfilm through the Family History Library. Many are also available online; for a gateway to these, visit 'Ireland Census Records' www.censusfinder.com/ireland.htm.

In the absence of the census for most of the nineteenth century, it is necessary to have recourse to other sources. Some of these cover the whole of the island. Various 'Ireland Census Substitutes' are discussed at https://wiki.familysearch.org/en/Ireland_Census_Substitutes. Land valuations provide two of the major sources: the tithe applotment books, 1823-37, and Griffith's valuation, 1848-64. The tithe applotment books record the assessment of tithes, and list the names of tenants, townlands, area by acreage, valuation of the property and the amount of the tithe payable. Griffith's valuation was taken in order to assess liability to pay poor rates. It records occupiers of land and houses, with the names of landowners, descriptions of property, acreages of farms, and valuations of property. For detailed discussions of both these sources, see the PRONI *'Valuation Records'* page, www.proni.gov.uk/your_family_tree_series_-_04_-_valuation_records.pdf

The National Archives of Ireland website has separate pages for each valuation; these can be accessed from www.nationalarchives.ie/genealogy/beginning.html. National databases for both valuations can be found on a number of websites (see box). There are also many smaller websites providing details for particular places.

For an earlier source, it may be worth consulting the 1796 lists of Irish flax growers. Flax growing was encouraged by the government, who rewarded growers by giving them spinning wheels or looms. 60,000 names can be searched at www.failteromhat.com/flax1796.php A similar database is available on Ancestry.com (see box); a number of smaller websites offer lists from particular places.

Wills are another source which has suffered from the ravages of war and decay. Many were lost during the 1916 Easter Rising – although indexes do survive. For an overview of what is still available, consult Family Search's wiki page on 'Irish Probate Records' https://wiki.familysearch.org/en/Ireland_Probate_Records. The National Archives hold some probate records; details are given on its 'Wills and testamentary records' page www.nationalarchives.ie/genealogy/testamentary.html. The wills held are indexed in the 'Irish Wills Index 1484-1858' www.origins.net/help/aboutio-wills.aspx.

For more recent wills, see the page on 'Probate Records' www.nationalarchives.ie/research/probate.html. Many Irish wills were proved in the Prerogative Court of Canterbury, and have been digitised for the (UK) National Archives Documents Online database at www.nationalarchives.gov.uk/documentsonline/wills.asp. A variety of will indexes can be found at www.ajmorris.com/dig/toc/titlres.htm

A wide variety of other sources are available. Many sources covering the period 1600-1900 are discussed in the Public Record Office of Northern Ireland's 'Family History: More Sources' www.proni.gov.uk/index/family_history/family_history_more_sources.htm

The records of Poor Law Boards of Guardians for 1838-1948, for example, are extensive. In Northern Ireland, Workhouse indoor relief registers are almost continuous from the establishment of workhouses until 1948. They contain the names, addresses, religions, and occupations of those who entered the workhouse. A variety of other poor law records may be available, for example, registers of workhouse births and deaths, out-door relief registers. For a detailed listing of workhouses and their records throughout Ireland, visit *'The Workhouse'* www.workhouses.org.uk

Militia records are also extensive. Belfast holdings - mainly pre-1800 - are listed by 'Militia, Yeomanry Lists And Muster Rolls' www.proni.gov.uk/your_family_tree_series_-_12_-_militia__yeomanry_lists_and_muster_rolls.pdf. Militia records of a later date, covering the whole of Ireland (as well as the UK), are indexed at www.origins.net/help/aboutio-militia.aspx. This index covers militia attestations, 1872-1915.

Another useful source is provided by the records relating to convicts transported to Australia. Microfilms of records held by the National Archives of Ireland were microfilmed and presented to the Australian government to celebrate its bicentenary. For details, see the 'Ireland – Australia Transportation Database' at www.nationalarchives.ie/topics/transportation/search01.html

The microfilm is now held by the Australian National Library and a number of other Australian institutions.

Transportees, of course, were transported by the British government, who ruled the whole of Ireland up until 1922. Many Irish records are held with the archives of that government, at the (UK) National Archives. That includes, for example, records of Irish police, and of customs and excise officers. A wide variety of sources at Kew are described in the National Archives research guide to 'Irish genealogy' www.nationalarchives.gov.uk/records/research-guides/irish-genealogy.htm

Much more could be said about Irish genealogy on the web. Bear in mind that the internet is continually changing, and that, frustratingly, some of the sites listed here may disappear, or (perhaps more likely) change their URLs. On the positive side, new pages and more databases, are continually being added. In England, the number of sources that have been digitised is rapidly expanding. The same process is being repeated in Ireland. Research is therefore becoming much easier. That provides some compensation for the loss of records which Ireland has suffered in the past. Irish genealogy can be traced; the internet can provide a great deal of help in the process.

Some Database Hosts

Many Irish databases are hosted by commercial and other websites, who may charge a small subscription, or ask you to pay as you view results. The most important of these hosts, and some of their databases, are listed below. They also host numerous smaller databases relating to particular counties or places. Many of these databases are indexes rather than transcripts; a few contain digitised versions of original documents.

Ancestry.com www.ancestry.com
Griffith's Valuation 1848-64 : The Royal Irish Constabulary 1816-1921 : Tithe Applotment Books 1823-37 : Irish Flax Growers List 1796

Ancestry Ireland www.ancestryireland.com/database.php
Numerous small databases relating to Ulster

DIGdat www.ajmorris.com/dig/toc/titlres.htm
Various Will Indexes Land Owners in Ireland 1876 : Australian Transportee Records - National Library of Ireland 1791-1853

Find My Past www.findmypast.co.uk - Ireland's Memorial Records of the Great War

Irish Family Research www.irishfamilyresearch.co.uk
Memorials of the Dead c.1500s-1910 : Prerogative Wills Index 1536-1810 : Alumni of Trinity College Dublin, 1593-1846

Irish Origins www.irishorigins.com
Griffith's Valuation 1848-64 : Dublin City Census 1861 : Various Irish Will Indexes : Electoral Registers for Ireland 1832-8 : British & Irish Passenger Lists

Roots Ireland www.rootsireland.ie
Various Irish Birth Marriage & Death Records : Various Census Records : Various Gravestone Inscriptions : Griffiths Valuation : Tithe Applotment Books 1823-38

The Kearneys of Moneygall:
a nineteenth-century research case study
Rachel Murphy of eneclann

One of the most common misconceptions about Irish genealogy that we come across is that it's impossible to trace your Irish roots because all the records were burned. While it's true that some important historical records were destroyed, many other significant sources survive. In this article we will explain what happened to the records and, using Obama's Kearney ancestors as an example, show how it is possible to trace an Irish family in the nineteenth century using land and estate records.

Nineteenth Century Irish Research: What Happened to the Records?

The Public Record Office of Ireland was established in 1867. It was based in the Four Courts, which were seized by troops during the Irish Civil War in 1922. Tragically, ammunition they were storing in the building exploded and the building caught fire, along with most of the records in it. Records destroyed include the Irish census returns from 1821 to 1851; more than half of all parish registers of the Church of Ireland which were deposited there after 1869; and the majority of wills and testamentary records proved in Ireland to that date. The census returns for the later nineteenth century were either destroyed by government order, or mistakenly pulped during the First World War (when there was a demand for paper, and civil servants did not realise that there was only one copy of the Irish census rather than two as in Britain).

Despite those records mentioned above having been destroyed, there are still a number of very good sources that survive for the nineteenth century. These include the civil registration records (births, deaths and Roman Catholic marriages commencing at 1864 and non-Catholic marriages commencing in 1845), many parish records, and records relating to land, some of which may be used as census substitutes.

Tracing Obama's Roots to Ireland

American genealogist, Megan Smolenyak had traced President Obama's roots to Moneygall in Co. Offaly, Ireland. Fulmoth Kearney was Barack Obama's 3x great-grandfather. The pedigree chart shows Fulmoth's parents, Joseph and Phoebe Kearney and his siblings.

The family emigrated from Ireland in the mid-1850s. The Eneclann team worked to trace the family's history back from this point. Outlined below are some of the key sources our researchers consulted in order to do this.

Griffith's Valuation: locating the family holding

Megan Smolenyak had identified that the Kearney family were living in Moneygall prior to their

President Barack Obama at his Inauguration
January 2009

The Kearney Family Tree

Joseph Kearney Shoemaker b. ca. 1794 d. 3 Oct 1861 USA	=	Phoebe Donovan b. ca. 1800 m. 1825 (Marriage Licence Bond – Killaloe) d.

Timothy bap. 24 May 1829 Templeharry	Fulmoth b. ca. 1830 Emmgr. USA d. 21 Mar 1878	William b. 23 June 1831 bap. 17 July 1831 Templeharry	Mary Anne b. 24 Nov 1837 bap. 12 Dec 1837 Templeharry

Extract from Griffith's Valuation, Moneygall Townland, Parish of Cullenwaine, Co. Offaly, showing Phoebe Carney at No. 123. Accessed online via www.findmypast.ie

PRIMARY VALUATION OF TENEMENTS.
PARISH OF CULLENWAINE.

No. and Letters of Reference to Map.	Townlands and Occupiers.	Immediate Lessors.	Description of Tenement.	Area.	Net Annual Value — Land.	Buildings.	Total.
	MONEYGALL—con.			A. R. P.	£ s. d.	£ s. d.	£ s. d.
56	Roderick Ryan,	Rev. William Minchin,	House and garden,	0 0 14	0 4 0	2 1 0	2 5 0
57	James Tracey,	Rev. William Minchin,	Building ground & small garden,				0 5 0
58	William Burke,	Rev. William Minchin,	House and garden,	0 0 10	0 3 0	1 17 0	2 0 0
59	Rev. Robert Going,	Rev. William Minchin,	London Hibernian Society's School-house,			1 15 0	1 15 0
59 (pt of)	Mrs. Caroline Hunt,	Rev. William Minchin,	Teacher's apartments & garden,	0 0 13	0 4 0	0 16 0	1 0 0
60	Richard Hunt,	Rev. William Minchin,	Ho., offs., yard, & garden,	0 0 14	0 5 0	1 15 0	2 0 0
61	Vacant,	Richard Hunt,	House,			0 10 0	0 10 0
62	Maria Farrell,	William Hodgens,	House,			0 8 0	0 8 0
63	Mary Haskett,	William Hodgens,	Ruins,			0 1 0	0 1 0
64	Vacant,	William Hodgens,	Building ground,			0 1 0	0 1 0
65	Margaret Gleeson,	William Hodgens,	House, office, yard & gar.	0 0 26	0 5 0	1 15 0	2 0 0
66	Michael Harty,	William Hodgens,	House, office, yard & gar.	0 0 33	0 6 0	1 9 0	1 15 0
67	Daniel Guilfoyle,	Rev. William Minchin,	House, offices, and garden,	0 0 36	0 10 0	3 0 0	3 10 0
68	James Tracey,	Daniel Guilfoyle,	House, offices, and yard,			1 0 0	1 0 0
69	Patrick Connell,	Daniel Guilfoyle,	House,			1 5 0	1 5 0
70	Timothy Hassett,	Rev. William Minchin,	House, office, & garden,	0 1 22	0 10 0	2 15 0	3 5 0
71	Mary Corcoran,	Rev. William Minchin,	House, offices, & garden,	0 0 18	0 4 0	0 16 0	1 0 0
72	Vacant,	Rev. William Minchin,	Building ground & yard,			0 2 0	0 2 0
73	Guardians of the Poor of Roscrea Union,	Rev. William Minchin,	Auxiliary work-house, offices, yard and garden,	0 3 25	1 0 0	19 0 0	20 0 0
74	Vacant,	Rev. William Minchin,	Caretaker's house, offices, yard and garden,				
75	Constabulary Force,	Rev. William Minchin,	Ho., offs., yard & garden,	0 1 0	1 0 0	9 0 0	10 0 0
76	Patrick Flannery,	Rev. William Minchin,	Ho., offs., yard & garden,	0 0 20	0 5 0	6 10 0	6 15 0
77	Andrew Hickey,	Rev. William Minchin,	Ho., offs., yard, & garden,	0 0 17	0 4 0	3 16 0	4 0 0
78	Rep. Thomas Ryan,	Rev. William Minchin,	Ho., offs., yard, & garden,	0 0 15	0 5 0	3 15 0	4 0 0
79	George Ryan,	Rev. William Minchin,	Ho., offs., yard, & garden,	0 0 15	0 5 0	4 5 0	4 10 0
80	Pierce Ryan,	Rev. William Minchin,	House, office, and garden,	0 0 26	0 5 0	5 5 0	5 10 0
81	Vacant,	Rev. William Minchin,	House, office, and garden,	0 0 13	0 3 0	5 2 0	5 5 0
82	Catherine Hart,	Rev. William Minchin,	Ho., offs., yard, & garden,	0 0 13	0 5 0	4 10 0	4 15 0
83	John M'Donald,	Rev. William Minchin,	House and garden,	0 0 15	0 3 0	2 17 0	3 0 0
84	John Culbert,	Rev. William Minchin,	House and garden,	0 0 15	0 3 0	2 12 0	2 15 0
85	Michael Devenny,	Rev. William Minchin,	House and garden,	0 0 15	0 3 0	0 27 0	1 0 0
86	Michael Ryan,	Rev. William Minchin,	House and garden,	0 0 16	0 3 0	0 7 0	0 10 0
87	Daniel Carroll,	Rev. William Minchin,	House and yard,			0 5 0	0 5 0
88	Andrew Monahan,	Rev. William Minchin,	House and garden,	0 0 15	0 3 0	0 17 0	1 0 0
89	Lawrence Hassett,	Rev. William Minchin,	House, yard, and garden,	0 0 16	0 3 0	1 2 0	1 5 0
90	Catherine Hassett,	Lawrence Hassett,	House,			0 15 0	0 15 0
91	Vacant,	Rev. William Minchin,	House and garden,	0 0 15	0 3 0	0 12 0	0 15 0
92	Vacant,	Rev. William Minchin,	House and garden,	0 0 15	0 3 0	0 7 0	0 10 0
93	Denis Meara,	Rev. William Minchin,	House and yard,	0 0 38	0 13 0		0 13 0
94	Denis Meara,	Rev. William Minchin,	Garden,				0 10 0
95	Bridget Toby,	Rev. William Minchin,	Pound,			0 12 0	0 12 0
96	Michael Tobir,	Rev. William Minchin,	House and yard,			0 8 0	0 8 0
97	John Tobin,	Rev. William Minchin,	House and yard,			0 15 0	0 15 0
98	Timothy Quinlan,	Rev. William Minchin,	House and yard,			0 15 0	0 15 0
99	Bridget Hayes,	Rev. William Minchin,	House and yard,			0 5 0	0 5 0
100	John Hayes,	Bridget Hayes,	House and yard,			0 5 0	0 5 0
101	Denis Meara,	Rev. William Minchin,	Ruins and garden,	0 0 21	0 5 0		0 5 0
102	Denis Meara,	Rev. William Minchin,	House, offices, and yard,			3 0 0	3 0 0
103	Mary Murphy,	Thomas Tracey,	House,			0 5 0	0 5 0
104	Thomas Tracey,	Rev. William Minchin,	House and land,	0 1 35	0 4 0	0 5 0	0 9 0
105	Timothy Corbey,	Rev. William Minchin,	House and land,	0 0 36	0 3 0	0 7 0	0 10 0
106	Margaret Donohoe,	Rev. William Minchin,	House and garden,	0 0 31	0 5 0	0 13 0	0 18 0
107	James Jennings,	Rev. William Minchin,	House and garden,	0 0 27	0 5 0	0 15 0	1 0 0
108	Catherine Hearty,	Rev. William Minchin,	House and garden,	0 0 31	0 5 0	0 15 0	1 0 0
109	Vacant,	Rev. William Minchin,	House and garden,	0 3 0	1 0 0	0 15 0	1 15 0
110	Mary Meara,	Rev. William Minchin,	House and garden,	0 0 13	0 3 0	0 8 0	0 11 0
111	Daniel Carroll,	Winifred Kennedy,	House and garden,	0 0 11	0 3 0	0 9 0	0 12 0
112	Michael Hickey,	Winifred Kennedy,	House and garden,	0 0 11	0 3 0	0 12 0	0 15 0
113	Catherine Howe,	Winifred Kennedy,	House and garden,	0 0 11	0 3 0	0 13 0	0 16 0
114	Mary Gordon,	Winifred Kennedy,	House and garden,	0 0 11	0 3 0	0 12 0	0 15 0
115	Vacant,	Winifred Kennedy,	House and garden,	0 0 11	0 3 0		0 3 0
116	Ellen Harrisson,	Thomas Hunt,	House and yard,			0 5 0	0 5 0
117	Michael Dunn,	Thomas Hunt,	House and garden,	0 0 10	0 3 0		0 3 0
118	Daniel Carroll,	Thomas Hunt,	House and garden,			0 8 0	0 8 0
119	John Mahonphy,	Thomas Hunt,	House and small garden,			0 10 0	0 18 0
120	James Lewis,	Thomas Carry,	House and small garden,			0 18 0	0 18 0
121	Thomas Donohoe,	Thomas Carry,	House and small garden,			0 8 0	0 8 0
122	Michael Donohoe,	Rev. William Minchin,	House and garden,	0 0 10	0 3 0	0 17 0	1 0 0
123	Phoebe Carney,	Rev. William Minchin,	House and garden,	0 1 30	0 13 0	2 5 0	2 18 0
124	Eliza Byrne,	Rev. William Minchin,	House and offices,			3 0 0	3 0 0
125	Ann Goulding,	Rev. William Minchin,	House, office, and yard,			2 15 0	2 15 0
126	Daniel Slattery,	Rev. William Minchin,	House and garden,			0 5 0	0 5 0
127	Christopher Boolan,	Rev. William Minchin,	House and small garden,	0 0 13	0 3 0	0 10 0	0 13 0

available at www.findmypast.ie. Using Griffith's Valuation, our genealogists were able to identify the Kearney holding in Moneygall, Co. Offaly (then known as King's County). They found that in March 1851 Phoebe Kearney was leasing a house and outbuilding from the Rev. William Minchin.

The House Books: hinting at a greater prosperity?

The valuers who were working on the Primary Valuation had to do a huge amount of groundwork before arriving at the information that is found in Griffith's Valuation. They travelled the length and breadth of Ireland, gathering detailed information on each holding or 'tenement' in Ireland and organised this by townland into three types of notebook, referred to as house books, tenure books and field books. The books were often revised up until the publication of Griffith's Valuation, and as a result they can sometimes provide additional information, amendments being made when people died, moved away or acquired land. The house books include information relating to quality and dimensions of houses, amount of rent and tenure, and description and quality of land. Each plot can be easily identified as its reference number corresponds to the plot reference on the Ordnance Survey maps that accompany Griffith's Valuation.

Eneclann's researchers reviewed the house books for Moneygall (1844 and revised in 1851) and came upon an interesting piece of information. The image taken from the 1844 version of the house book for Moneygall shows that Joseph Carney (Obama's great-great-great grandfather) was the original occupier of the property, which was originally numbered 67 but is now number 123. However, his name has been scratched out and replaced with Phoebe Carney, his wife. Two properties are mentioned – a house which is 27 feet long, 18 feet wide and 13 foot high. Based on this, the valuation on the house is £2 3s and nine pence. It has been given a quality rating of B. The second property is an office, 20 feet 6 inches long, 12 feet 6 inches wide and 7 feet high. It has a quality rating of C. The valuation

emigration. Eneclann's researchers set out to identify where in Moneygall the family had been residing. Given the lack of census returns for the 1800s (other than fragments), other records have to be used in their place, acting as 'census substitutes'. Perhaps the most significant census substitute for Ireland is the Primary Valuation, more commonly known as Griffith's Valuation. This source provides a snapshot of who lived on the land in the mid nineteenth Century. The Valuation was compiled between 1847 and 1864 for taxation purposes. The valuers reviewed all property held in Ireland, assessing its annual rateable value. It includes information relating to 1.4 million distinct landholdings, and is useful as a census substitute as it also includes the names of over 400,000 householders.

The definitive version of Griffith's Valuation is

No. on Book	No. on Map of Towns	No. on Map of Premises	Denominations and Tenants' Names	Description of Holdings	Quantity of Land Statute Measure (A R P)	Quantity of Land Plantation Measure (A R P)	Yearly Rent and Rentcharge (£ S D)	Gale Days	Particulars of Tenure	Observations
			MONEYGALL, KILKEARAN otherwise RATHKEARAN & GURRANE							
33	36	...	James Jennings ...	House and Garden in Town	0 1 13	0 0 33	2 12 0	1st May and 1st Nov.	Yearly Tenant; tenancy determinable on 1st November in each year.	
34	37	...	Catherine Harty ...	ditto	0 1 9	0 0 30	2 15 0	ditto	ditto　　ditto	
35	38	...	John Kennedy ...	ditto	1 0 11	0 2 26	4 5 0	ditto	Lease; Rev. William Minchin to John Kennedy, dated 30th March 1848, for 21 years from 1st November 1847.	No. 35.—This Lease states this holding to contain but half an acre plantation measure, or thereabouts.
36	39	...	Bridget Hayes ...	ditto	0 0 16	0 0 10	0 15 0	ditto	Yearly Tenant; tenancy determinable on 1st November in each year.	
37	40	...	Timothy Quinlan ...	ditto	0 0 18	0 0 11	0 12 0	ditto	Yearly Tenant; tenancy determinable on 1st May in each year.	
38	41	...	Judith Tobin ...	ditto	0 0 19	0 0 12	0 10 0	ditto	ditto　　ditto	
39	42	...	Michael Lalor ...	ditto	0 0 35	0 0 22	1 0 0	ditto	ditto　　ditto	
40	43	...	Darby Tochy ...	ditto	0 0 25	0 0 15	1 10 0	ditto	ditto　　ditto	
41	44	46	Thady Guilfoyle ...	Three Houses and Gardens in Town / Part of Lands	0 0 25 / 2 2 0	0 0 15 / 1 2 8	} 6 0 0	ditto	Lease; Rev. William Minchin to Thadeus Guilfoyle, dated 27th October 1837, for the lives of said Thadeus Guilfoyle the lessee, and his wife Judith Guilfoyle, otherwise Ryan, both of whom are still living.	No. 41.—This Lease states the part of the Lands thereby demised to contain 1A. 2R. 30P. plantation measure, or thereabouts.
42	45	...	Winnifred Kennedy ...	Five Houses and Gardens in Town	0 1 9	0 0 30	1 3 0	ditto	Lease; Rev. William Minchin to Bartholomew Kennedy, dated 20th March 1834, for the lives of Bartholomew Kennedy the lessee, John Egan, eldest son of Michael Egan of Ballydonogh in the King's County, and William Egan, third son of said Michael Egan, with covenant for perpetual renewal on payment of a peppercorn renewal fine on the fall of each life.	No. 42.—This Lease describes the Premises thereby demised as being 78 feet in front, and containing 1 rood of 40 perches by Survey. This Holding was demised by William Minchin to James Kennedy by Lease dated 1st May 1797, for 3 lives renewable for ever, at the Yearly Rent of £1. 5s. 0d. late currency; the Lease of 20th March 1834 does not purport to be a renewal of this former Lease, but both Leases will be handed to the Purchaser. This Tenant also has liberty of Turbary on the said Bog of Green Hills for his own moderate consumption.
43	46 / 47	44	William Kearney and Thos. Carry, Reps. of Wm. & Jos. Kearney	Two Houses and Gardens in Town / ditto / Part of Lands	0 1 1 / 0 1 1 / 2 3 3	0 0 25 / 0 0 25 / 1 2 33	} 6 10 6	ditto	Lease; William Minchin to William Kearney and Joseph Kearney, dated 1st May 1800, of Two Dwelling-houses, together with Two Acres of Land "thereby," for the lives of the said William Kearney and Joseph Kearney (brother to the said William Kearney) and Joseph Kearney, son to the said William Kearney, of whom the said Joseph Kearney, the son of the said lessee William Kearney, is now the only surviving life, at the yearly rent of £7 late currency.	No. 43.—This Lease gives the Tenant liberty of Turbary on the said Bog of Green Hills for the use of the Houses thereby demised.

Extract from 1844 House Book, Moneygall, King's County National Archives of Ireland

on the office is 5 shillings and nine pence, bringing the total valuation of the Carney property to £2 9s and sixpence. Of most interest to our researchers was a comment from the Valuation Office surveyor that Phoebe 'has now given up all the land and some of the houses that she had.' Up until this point we had believed that the Kearney family were village shoemakers. The reference to other houses hinted at a greater prosperity.

The Landed Estates Court Rentals – back another generation

The Landed Estates Court (LEC) was established in 1849 to facilitate the sale of insolvent entailed estates. Many landowners found themselves in debt at this time, as a result of a decline in the sale and rental prices of land combined with financial obligations such as annuities and mortgages that had often been set up by previous generations. The rentals themselves are effectively sales brochures prepared for prospective buyers, to show the commercial potential of bankrupt estates. As such, they include listings of tenancies and frequently maps and drawings of the properties.

Our researchers reviewed the Landed Estates Court Rentals, available at Findmypast.ie, to see whether the Minchin estate was affected. We found that in 1851 the Minchins were declared bankrupt and their entire estate, including the village of Moneygall, was sold under the Landed Estates Court. The LEC rental outlined details of a lease taken out by the Kearney family fifty years

earlier. It was a 'lease for lives' naming three family members and, importantly, how they were related. The original lease was dated 1st May 1800 and was from William Minchin to William Kearney and Joseph Kearney, in relation to two dwelling houses and two acres of lands. The lease was for the lives of William Kearney and Joseph Kearney (brother to the said William Kearney) and Joseph Kearney, son to the said William Kearney. The LEC rental of 1851 states that, of these three individuals, only one was still alive - Joseph Kearney, the son of the said lessee William Kearney.

Beyond the Nineteenth Century

The evidence found from the sources above proved to Eneclann's genealogists that more research could be done into the Kearney family. From this point, they broadened out their research to a range of records including the Church of Ireland registers for Templeharry, Dunkerrin and Shinrone; the Marriage License Bonds & testamentary records for the Diocese of Killaloe; Private Collections in the National Library of Ireland (The Lloyd Papers); eighteenth century political pamphlets in Trinity College; Barber Surgeon's Guild records; and documents in the Registry of Deeds. The research can be reviewed on the Eneclann website (www.eneclann.ie). The findings were presented to President Barack Obama on his visit to Ireland in May 2010, during which he thanked the genealogists for the work they had conducted into his Irish ancestry.

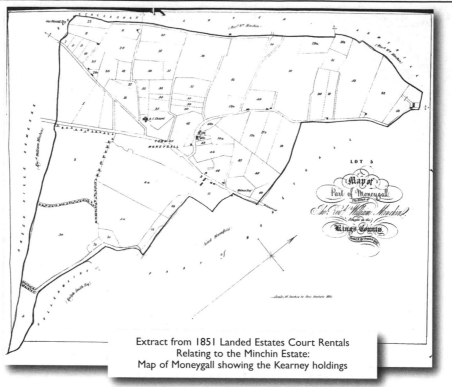

Extract from 1851 Landed Estates Court Rentals
Relating to the Minchin Estate:
Map of Moneygall showing the Kearney holdings

Conclusion

If you are setting out on your nineteenth century Irish family history research, then the work Eneclann's researchers conducted into the Obama family tree demonstrates that it is highly likely you will be able to find some information about your family. Although there are no fully extant nineteenth century Irish census returns, there are a number of other sources that you can draw on to trace your family back to the early nineteenth century. Our research has also demonstrated the importance of painstakingly and logically reviewing and cross-referencing sources: by looking at the house books as well as Griffith's Valuation we were able to discover that the Kearneys had held other properties in Moneygall. Likewise, the Landed Estates Court rentals identified that a deed had been made in 1800, which led us on to earlier deeds in the Registry of Deeds. Always you are looking for that one additional piece of evidence that may not be found elsewhere – one small detail may be all you need to open up a search.

About Eneclann

Dublin based Eneclann is the leading provider of Irish history and heritage services. Established in 1998, the award-winning company's offerings include historical and genealogical research, digitisation and digital publishing services, and archives and records management. Eneclann's customer base ranges from individuals to public institutions and private companies. Customers are located within Ireland and

across the Irish Diaspora of 80 million people. Eneclann traced President Barack Obama's Irish ancestry to the late seventeenth century and the company's research has featured in programmes such as Faces of America and Who Do You Think You Are? In May 2011 Eneclann formed findmypast.ie, a joint venture with brightsolid, the online publishing and technology group.

Sources

Online

Griffith's Valuation

This is available online at a number of websites including Findmypast Ireland.
www.findmypast.ie

Landed Estates Court Rentals

These are available online exclusively at findmypast.ie. Access is pay-per-view or subscription. www.findmypast.ie

House Books

The books have been microfilmed and are available to view at the National Archives of Ireland, Bishop Street, Dublin.

If you would like Eneclann to research your family history for you, please contact us at genealogy@eneclann.ie, or visit our website - www.eneclann.ie - for further information about our services.

137

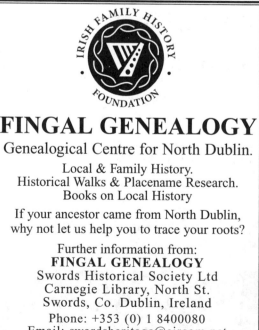

Roman Catholic Parish Registers
Mary McConnon

For the period preceding the introduction of civil registration in 1864 Roman Catholic parish registers are the main sources, and in some instances the only source, of information on Irish Catholic families. Because of their importance to family history research some brief historical note on their keeping is required.

Unlike Church of Ireland parishes where a law was passed in 1634 to keep registers no such law was made for Roman Catholic registers. This was because up until 1 January 1871 the Church of Ireland was in effect the State Church.

Within the Church itself various orders were made from the Synod of Drogheda in 1614 and later in 1670 to keep registers of baptisms and marriages. However the seventeenth century was a period of upheaval in Ireland with the Flight of the Earls in 1607 bringing to an end the power of the Gaelic Chiefs, the Ulster Plantation in 1609, the Rebellion of 1641, the Cromwellian Wars and Settlement and later the Williamite Wars followed by another plantation where lands were confiscated and given to the victors.

The defeat at the Battle of the Boyne in 1690, of the Catholic King James II by the Protestant William of Orange for the English throne, resulted in the enactment of various laws, known as the Penal Laws, against Roman Catholic in order to prevent the growth of Popery. A law passed in 1697 required all regular clergy and all clergy exercising jurisdiction to leave Ireland by the 1 May 1698. However as this was difficult to enforce further legislation was passed in 1704. This required the diocesan clergy to register with the civil authorities, to indicate the parish or parishes where they ministered, and enter into a bond with two sureties of £50 to be of good behaviour on pain of transportation. In all 1,089 registered as parish priests. According to Patrick J. Corish the law proposed 'the gradual extinction of the Catholic priesthood in Ireland, because it made no provision for successors to those who registered' (The Catholic Experience - a Historical Survey, Dublin, 1984, p.125). A further Act in 1709 provided for an oath of abjuration renouncing the Stuart claim to the throne. About forty priests took this oath and the remainder lost their status under the 1704 Act. As a result

'Lay Catholics might be summoned on oath to testify where they had last heard Mass and who had been the celebrant. There emerged a new type of 'popish discoverer', who was rewarded for turning in priests. It was not a highly regarded occupation. There was some

Going to Mass

sympathy even among Protestants for priests who had refused to take the oath.' (Ibid)

Such conditions did not allow for the general keeping of records. However by 1730 the persecution began to decline. By that time almost every diocese had a bishop and the parish structure was being formed. But some parishes were too large, some were poorly equipped, and the appointment of assistant priests was forbidden. In 1760 with the founding of the Catholic Committee efforts began to secure the repeal of the Penal Laws. By the turn of the nineteenth century their enforcement and effect had declined further although this differed from parish to parish. It was not until the Catholic Emancipation Act of 1829 that most of the remaining Penal Laws were abolished. The position in the capital city of Dublin, the centre of government and commerce, from 1745 to 1865 is summed up in a Catholic Directory:

'So late as 1745 ... Catholics were first permitted to attend public worship in the few miserable churches of the city, and scores of persons now living heard mass in a thatched chapel in the very heart of the metropolis. After the comparatively brief space of 120 years, we now find the city studded with magnificent churches, there being upwards of 40 places of Catholic worship in Dublin and the suburbs, and nearly half as many priests in the Diocese as there were in all Ireland in 1704.' (Keogh, Very Rev. Canon, Catholic Directory, Almanac and Registry of Ireland, England, and Scotland, Dublin, 1865, p.186)

While for the period 1800 to 1865 in the Diocese of Ferns in the south east of the country it states:

'The opening of this century found it with few decent chapels, many of the humble fabrics that bore the name having been burned during the rebellion, in 1798. It has now some of the most tasteful and elegant churches in the kingdom, and not alone in the leading towns, but also scattered over the rural parishes.' (ibid, p.197).

The Celebration.

These were the conditions for the saying of Mass but the celebration of baptisms, marriages and burials was also affected and were normally performed at home. It was not until well into the nineteenth century that the church was required to be used for baptisms and marriages services. Again Patrick J. Corish states:

'The 'rites of passage', traditionally celebrated in the home, made there way to the church. In 1850 the Synod of Thurles laid down that baptisms should normally take place there, and I Maynooth (1875) allowed only very few exceptions to this rule. The practice of marriage in church, with Mass and the nuptial blessing, spread more unevenly, but it too became the rule. The traditional funeral Mass in the house also drifted slowly towards the church. In 1917 the new Code of Canon Law laid down that all funeral rites must take place in the church ...' (Corish, The Catholic Experience, p.234).

Administrative Divisions.

For administrative purposes Ireland was divided into provinces or archdioceses and these were sub-divided into dioceses and further into parishes. The size of the latter varies and, unlike Church of Ireland parishes, are not exactly co-terminus with the boundaries of the civil or former medieval parish and some cross county boundaries.

Diagram 1 lists the names of the dioceses in 1865 per the Catholic Directory with the number of parishes in each and the counties covered. So what records are available, where are they and what do they contain?

Records Available

The Roman Catholic records that exist are baptisms and marriages but unlike Church of Ireland parish registers very few church burial registers were kept.

Dates

The growth in parish registers, from what is known to be extant, appears from the early nineteenth century. From the beginning of the 1820s 'it became the norm for each Catholic parish to have its own register of baptisms and marriages. Particularly in the towns and cities, a number of registers do go back well into the eighteenth century, but most begin about the year 1829 except in Ulster and the more deprived areas elsewhere.' (Ibid, p.157).

By 1865 there were 1070 parishes (see Diagram 1) but only about 31 of those parishes are known to have an extant register or registers dating pre 1750 and about half of them are in Dublin County, Dublin City and Waterford City.

However even though a register can begin at a certain date there can be parts missing or difficult to read. Also while some registers may date from the middle or late eighteenth

Kilsaran Church, County Louth
Foundation stone laid July 1814

Diocese	Total Parishes	Counties covered
Armagh	54	Almost the whole of Louth & Armagh, a greater part of Tyrone and a part of Derry
Meath	68	Meath, Westmeath, the greater part of King's County [Offaly], and a small portion of Longford and Cavan
Derry	37	Nearly the whole of Londonderry, a large portion of Tyrone and a small part of Donegal,
Clogher	38	Monaghan and Fermanagh with parts of Tyrone and Louth
Raphoe	28	Nearly the whole of Donegal
Down and Connor	45	Antrim, the greater part of Down, and the Liberties of Coleraine, in Londonderry.
Kilmore	43	Nearly all Cavan, and parts of Leitrim and Fermanagh
Ardagh	41	Nearly all Longford, and parts of King's County [Offaly], Westmeath, Roscommon, Cavan, Leitrim, Sligo
Dromore	18	Parts of the Counties of Down, Armagh and Antrim
Armagh Province	**372**	
Dublin	52	Dublin, nearly all of Wicklow, and portions of Kildare, Queen's county [Laois], Carlow and Wexford
Kildare and Leighlin	48	The entire of Carlow, and Parts of Kildare, Queen's County [Laois], King's County [Offaly], Kilkenny and Wexford
Ossory	40	Kilkenny, and portions of King's County [Offaly] and Queen's County [Laois]
Ferns	40	The entire of Wexford and part of Wicklow
Dublin Province	**180**	
Cashel & Emly	46	Most of Tipperary and part of Limerick
Cork	34	Cork, and part of Kerry
Killaloe	55	Most of Clare and parts of Tipperary, King's County [Offaly], Galway, Limerick, Queen's County [Laois]
Kerry	48	Kerry and part of Cork
Limerick	48	Most of Limerick and a small portion of Clare
Waterford & Lismore	38	Waterford and parts of Tipperary and Cork
Cloyne	45	A large portion of Cork
Ross	11	Part of Cork
Cashel Province	**325**	
Tuam	53	Portions of Galway and Mayo
Clonfert	24	Parts of Galway, Roscommon, and King's County [Offaly}
Achonry	22	Portions of Mayo and Sligo, and a small part of Roscommon
Elphin	41	Most of Roscommon, and a large portion of Sligo
Kilmacduagh & Kilfenora	18	Clare and part of Galway?
Galway	13	Part of Galway
Killala	22	Portions of Mayo and Sligo
Tuam Province	**193**	
IRELAND	**1070**	

Roman Catholic Dioceses in Ireland with the number of Parishes and Counties in each

microfilms for parishes in the six counties of Northern Ireland and for a number of those in the adjoining counties of Donegal, Cavan, Louth, Leitrim and Monaghan, are available in the self-service microfilm room of the Public Record Office of Northern Ireland, 2 Titanic Boulevard, Belfast [PRONI]. The Church of Jesus Christ of the Latter-Day Saints Family History Libraries [LDS] also hold a number of the microfilms.

From more recent years efforts have and are being made to computerize these registers and many are now available online from the date commenced to 1900. It is advisable to view on the website concerned the actual sources for each county as not all of a particular parish is indexed. The indexes are gradually being added to and proposals are to include a link to the scanned page of the original register.

The largest digital index is to be found on the website of the Irish Family History Foundation [IFHF] at www.rootsireland.ie. Part of this database relating to registers for parishes in counties Antrim and Down is also available on the website of the Ulster Historical Foundation at www.ancestryireland.com .The county indexes too are available in the IFHF heritage centres of the particular county and in some diocesan centers such as in Armagh for parishes in the dioceses concerned but access is only by a member of staff.

In the case of some parishes in the Diocese of Cork and Ross and in the Dublin Diocese the online index is to be found at www.irishgenealogy.ie For some parishes, on this website, the actual digital image of the page of the

century this may arise from a parish being formed out of an earlier parish. So if a particular baptism or marriage is not found it is always advisable to search registers of neighbouring parishes.

Where are they?

The original registers are normally held in the local parishes. However in the 1950s and early 1960s the National Library of Ireland, 2 – 3 Kildare Street, Dublin, [NLI] microfilmed most of the registers to 1880. These are available to view in the self service room in the NLI. Photocopying facilities also exist. In more recent times some registers have been filmed to 1900. Copies of the register is linked to the index entry.

Various transcriptions made by individuals on a voluntary basis for a particular surname or parish are available online and some can be found in published form in local parish histories or journals. These may related to period of years or just for particular surnames. One of the main printed ones is: *O'Casey, Albert, O'Kief Coshe Mang, Slieve Lougher and Upper Blackwater in Ireland: Historical and Genealogical Items relating to North Cork and East Kerry* (Knockagree Historical Fund, Birmingham, Alabama, 1952-68).

Dromiskin Graveyard, County Louth

What information do they contain?.

While the information may be minimal it is more than one normally finds on Church of Ireland parish registers for the same time period. Some registers can be written in Latin but most are in English although the handwriting ranges from a scribble to copperplate. There are also gaps in some and with the passage of time parts in others have become indecipherable. However today with the zoom feature on computers and microfilm machines it is possible to enlarge an image and so it may be easier to view an entry on computer or microfilm than on the actual manuscript register.

While the registers relate mainly to baptisms and marriages and to a lesser extent burials there can also be included some local information such as confirmations, local censuses, famine relief and other details not usually found in records.

Baptisms

The basic information given is date of baptism, name of child baptised (usually only one forename is given) and names of parents and sponsors to the baptism. In the case of the mother her maiden name is usually but not always provided. Some registers included address such as the townland or well known local district within the townland and in the case of urban parishes a street address, the name of the priest and sometimes the contribution made. In a small number of registers fuller information is provided such as addresses of sponsors.

Marriages

In the case of marriages the normal information is date, names of parties marrying and of witnesses to the marriage. The witness can be close relatives but sometimes neighbours. Fuller information found on some registers is an address and in a lesser number the addresses of the parents and the witnesses. In the case of the parents sometimes it is stated the name of both the father and mother and whether each are deceased although this latter information relating to both parents cannot always be relied on.

Burials

Not many parishes maintained burial or death registers pre 1900. They may only contain basic information such as a name but usually an address such as in baptism above, sometimes age at death and of most value the cemetery where the deceased was interred. These burial registers relate to the actual religious service. It should be remembered, however, that the local graveyard may not belong to the Roman Catholic parish and so burial information may be found on registers belonging to other religious denominations. Michael Leader in his article on 'Irish Parish Registers' states that

'Church of Ireland burial registers are a far better hunting-ground for Catholic entries. The first volume of St. Anne Shandon-beginning in 1778- has some forty thousand burials. Of these, I would estimate, at least three quarters are Catholics. In some parts of the book, it specifies the denomination, and you find '1808, Oct, 24, James Trant, roman, buried in a vault' (The Irish Genealogist, vol.3, no.2, (1957), pp.61-2).

This, however, will differ between parishes. Dromiskin cemetery, in County Louth, has both Protestants and Catholic burials. There was a Church of Ireland Burial register 1802-1902 for the parish which was lodged in the Public Record Office, Four Courts, Dublin but perished in 1922. The Roman Catholic burial register for the Parish of Darver which included Dromiskin for the period 1787 to 1828 is in the O'Fiaich Library in Armagh City but although in good condition is, as the writer found, not easily accessible. It was actually located among family papers of a relative although how it got there is unknown except that the family did purchase property in the townland where the priest of the time once lived. Unfortunately all were dead before the writer became aware of its existence. It is not on microfilm in the NLI. Information on it is to be found in an article by Noel Ross, 'Darver Burial Register, 1787-1828', County Louth Archaeological and Historical Society Journal, vol.XXIV, no.3 (1999), pp.435-6.

There are other non parish sources which do not come under the term 'parish registers' and so are not within the scope of this article but a brief mention is needed. Information on deaths are not only to be found in the civil deaths records from 1864 and from inscriptions from actual headstones but also from what are termed 'burial registers' which relate to the actual plot of ground and who was interred and when internment took place. In the nineteenth century the local Boards of Guardians were given powers to provide burial grounds and these functions passed to the main local authorities. A register was and possibly is still maintained for these cemeteries. Unfortunately not much effort has been made to-date to locate or make the older records available to the public and they remain an untapped source. Families still tend to bury in the same family plot so the older records may be in use.

Also a Trust could have been set up to manage and maintain a particular burial ground as in the case of the large Glasnevin Cemetery in Dublin. The records of the latter are available online at www.glasnevintrust.ie

In short obtaining some knowledge of the local parish area can be of assistance.

How to Research?

While digitization has made searching easier it is always advisable to view the original register. The database on the website www.rootsireland.ie not only includes church baptisms, marriages and burials but also civil birth, marriages and deaths and other records. In all over fourteen million records are in the index.

Searching the index is free once registered but payment is required to view a particular entry. A search by surname returns variants of that surname and the number of entries of baptisms, marriages and burials for it. But before commencing it is important to know as much information as possible about an ancestor. For example a search, in May 2011, for just the surname 'Morgan' returns 11,756 baptism, 6,435 marriage and 1.685 death entries. By clicking on each 'view'

button a breakdown is giving on a county basis but only for the first 10 entries unless a period of years is selected.

However transcriptions bring in human error as well as difficulties encountered with computer searching of Irish surnames and forenames and the website does not provide for a wildcard search. From a study, in early 2011, of the family of John Sarsfield Casey 'The Galtee Boy' and his siblings the errors found were unacceptably high. The errors ranged from 15% major ones to 25% having minor errors. For example in the case of the 13 baptism entries located:

- one son Timothy Stanislaus was listed for 1866 instead of 1886.
- a sister Ellen had a date of baptism as 22 August 1855 instead of 22 April 1855.
- on a baptism entry of a sister 'Honora' the father was listed as 'Jeremiah' instead of 'Jerry' and a sponsor was listed as 'Daniel' instead of 'Dan'.

In general, however, it is believed the error margin may be and is hopefully much less. With the implementation of future proposals to link the digital image of the page to the indexed entries these errors will lessen.

The next main database is on the website www.irishgenealogy.ie but so far only relates to parishes in County Kerry and for some in Counties Cork and Dublin including the Cities. The total number of entries for all religions can be seen in the left column of the website (Figure 2) as well as totals for each diocese and each parish within the diocese so far digitized. The parish with the largest available entries is St. Andrew's, Dublin City, with 223,993 baptism entries online. Provision is made to search by name(s) of person, parish, religion, event, time period including year, or browse the entries in each parish. It is free to search and view the

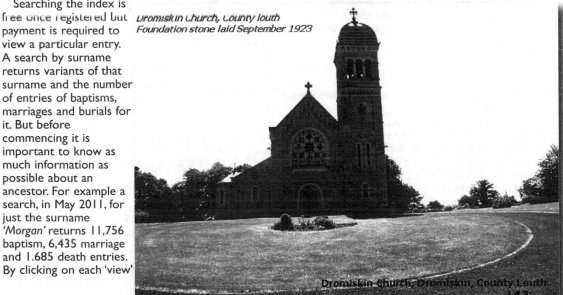

Dromiskin Church, County Louth
Foundation stone laid September 1923

Dromiskin Church, Dromiskin, County Louth

available images.

The combining of these two databases would seem appropriate considering both projects were provided directly or indirectly by public funding in both Northern Ireland and the Republic of Ireland and by other funding sources provided to help with the Peace Process between North and South. The development of research services from these database projects and the proposition that they provide local employment should also take into consideration the position of private local businesses.

Until a digital image is made available online the other main source to view the original entry is the microfilm copy of the register. For any serious researcher viewing the original entry must be stressed. It is a must for anyone involved in searching for legal purposes where civil records of births and marriages are unavailable and in the case of locating baptisms of children to specific parents it involves searching for a period of years, sometimes at least thirty, but depending on the age of the mother, from the date of the marriage.

How to search the registers on microfilm?

For those unfamiliar with microfilms I will provide a brief note. Basically microfilms are like ordinary photo negatives but in a continuous strip on a reel. Special microfilm machines are used to view the images on each microfilm.

In some cases, such as rural parishes, the registers of a couple of parishes are on the same reel but note these may not be neighbouring parishes. In larger parishes such as in cities the parish registers cover two or more reels. So having as much specific information on an ancestor is important if deciding to search the parish registers.

How to find the correct reel?

To locate the correct reel you must first find the microfilm call number. The NLI has produced *Parish Register Lists* which are available on their website at www.nli.ie/en/parish-register.aspx

The parishes in each diocese are listed alphabetically showing which registers are available with the relevant dates together with the microfilm number. In the case of PRONI, as at January 2010, an alphabetical list of parish registers of all denominations entitled *An Irish Genealogical Source A Guide To Church Records* is available online at www.proni.gov.uk/index/research_and_records_held/catalogues_guides_indexes_and_leaflets/online_guides_and_indexes.htm

It should be noted that the NLI, PRONI and the

LDS have they own system of referencing microfilms. Some published sources on Irish genealogy have also listed the various call numbers. But all of these are available within the relevant Research Room for anyone visiting the NLI & PRONI. Once the reel is located and on the microfilm machine scroll through it until the correct parish is found and then through the parish until the relevant section is found. *Enjoy the search!*

Representative Church Body Library
DR Raymond Refaussé
Librarian & archivist

Introduction

The Representative Church Body Library in Dublin is, among other things, the reference library and archives of the Church of Ireland – the Anglican/Episcopalian Church in Ireland. From the Reformation until disestablishment by the Irish Church Act of 1869 the Church of Ireland was the established church – the official church of the state – and so its records were not only the chronicles of a religious denomination but also part of the records of state. Its parishes were units of local government, its courts were the centres for matrimonial and testamentary jurisdiction, its prelates and clergy were often important officers of state, and its parish churches were, for periods, the locations of the only acts of worship which were permitted under the law.

The Church of Ireland was always a minority church but membership of the established church was critical not alone to ecclesiastical advancement but also to the attainment of office and the ownership of land. And so to the ranks of the Church of Ireland were attracted not only those who were convinced by its theology but many who out of political, social or economic expediency found it prudent to become, at least nominally, members of the established church. Thus the archives of the Church of Ireland reflect a much wider spectrum of Irish life than might otherwise be supposed. And so the Library is a place of first resort for those engaged in genealogy and family history and for those interested in local history from an ecclesiastical perspective, but is not exclusively a source for those with an Anglican background.

History & Development

The Library was founded in 1931 as a reference and lending library for the Church of Ireland but from its earliest days it was also a place of deposit for homeless church records. The archival side of the Library's work increased significantly from the 1960s with the amalgamation of parishes and dioceses and this responsibility was formalized in the 1980s with the appointment of the Church's first archivist. Today the Library manages archives from 1025 parishes, chapels and chaplaincies, 20 dioceses, 20 cathedrals, and the non-current records of the General Synod (the Church's parliament) and Representative Church Body (the Church's civil service) as well as almost 900 collections of related ecclesiastical manuscript collections.

The Library seeks to acquire a copy of all material published about or by significant members of the Church of Ireland. This of course, can never be any other than an aspiration, but the process has ensured that the Library has, *inter alia*, considerable holdings of parish, diocesan and cathedral histories; biographical studies of laity bishops and clergy; family histories; ecclesiastical directories and a wide range of ephemera about Church of Ireland people and places.

Parish Records

Parish records and, especially parish registers, are the most widely consulted sources in the Library. Although some registers have been printed and others are available on microfilm in other repositories and although, with the advent of genealogical websites, much information from registers is now available online, yet it is still the case that the information in many of the registers in the Library is not available elsewhere. Added to this, of course, is an understandable desire by researches to see the original records of their ancestors and, in some cases, a reluctance to believe that the microfilmed or digitized records have successfully captured all the information in the original. The earliest Church of Ireland parish register, that of St John the Evangelist, Dublin, dates from 1619, but few registers are extant for the years before 1650 and only a modest number begin in the second half of the 17th century.

The earliest and most substantial parish registers are, for the most part, from the old sea port towns and cities, notably Cork, Derry, Dublin, Galway, Limerick and Waterford and, with the exception of Derry and Limerick all these records have been transferred to the Library. The Library's holdings of parish registers are largely, but not exclusively, from parishes in the Republic of Ireland, and these are augmented by microfilm copies of many of the registers from parishes in Northern Ireland. The

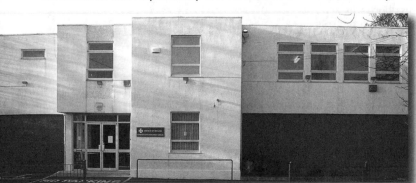

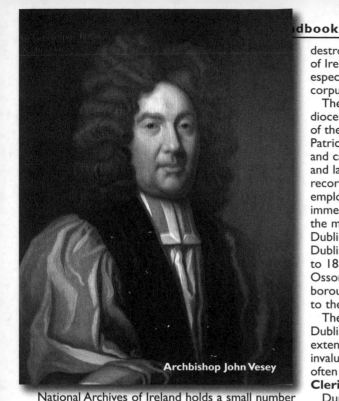

Archbishop John Vesey

National Archives of Ireland holds a small number of original registers as does the Public Record of Northern Ireland, but these custodies apart, registers may only be held by the Library or in parish custody.

Many registers were destroyed in the fire in the Public Record Office of Ireland in 1922 but rather more survives in copy and extract form than was initially supposed. Much of this is among the papers of local genealogists, historians and antiquarians while some exists in the form of transcripts made before the transfer of the original registers to the PROI but not recorded. In general the Library can advise on surviving parish registers, both in original and copy form, and on the location of registers which remain in local custody.

Parish registers, of course, provide only basic information on the Christian rites of passage – baptism, marriage and burial, and it is the records of the vestries, the committees which ran parish affairs, which can often put flesh on the bare bones of the registers. Vestry minutes, churchwardens' accounts and cess books, in particular, can provide a feast of detail on the role of individuals in local life with information on poor relief, fire fighting, policing, property values and much more. Like the parish registers, these records are richest for the cities and in some cases predate the registers, the earliest of them dating from the late 16th century.

Diocesan and Cathedral Records

Diocesan and cathedral records are a much less used source largely because most of them were

destroyed in the fire in the Public Record Office of Ireland. However, where they survive they are especially valuable as they are the only significant corpus of pre-Reformation Irish church records.

The Library holds the medieval registers of the diocese of Dublin and Ossory and the cartularies of the cathedrals of Christ Church and St Patrick's, Dublin. Because the archbishops, bishops and cathedral chapters were significant property and landowners until the late 19th century their records often contain much about tenants and employees, as well as clergy, both in their immediate locality and farther afield. For example the maps of the estates of the archbishops of Dublin contain information on landholding in Dublin, Wicklow, Westmeath and Cork from 1654 to 1850 while the records of the diocese of Ossory include records of the inhabitants of the borough of Irishtown in Kilkenny from the 14th to the 18th century.

The records of the cathedrals especially in Dublin, Kilkenny, Cork and Cloyne, and to a lesser extent in Kildare, Leighlin and Waterford are invaluable sources for their local communities and often further afield.

Clerical Succession Lists

During the first half of the 20th century Canon J.B. Leslie compiled a series of what he called biographical succession lists of Irish clergy. The sources which he used were largely destroyed in the fire in the Public Record Office of Ireland in 1922 and so his work, which he bequeathed to the Library, is the principal resource for information on Church of Ireland bishops and clergy. He produced a volume for most dioceses

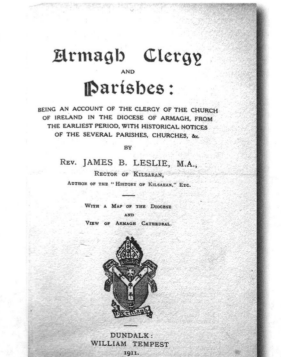

Armagh Clergy
AND
Parishes:

BEING AN ACCOUNT OF THE CLERGY OF THE CHURCH
OF IRELAND IN THE DIOCESE OF ARMAGH, FROM
THE EARLIEST PERIOD, WITH HISTORICAL NOTICES
OF THE SEVERAL PARISHES, CHURCHES, &c.

BY

REV. JAMES B. LESLIE, M.A.,
RECTOR OF KILSARAN,
AUTHOR OF THE "HISTORY OF KILSARAN," ETC.

WITH A MAP OF THE DIOCESE
AND
VIEW OF ARMAGH CATHEDRAL.

DUNDALK:
WILLIAM TEMPEST
1911.

St Patrick's Cathedral Dublin

worked as a record agent in the years before the fire. From him the Library acquired, among other items, abstracts from the 1766 Religious Census and the 1740 Lists of Protestant Householders, extracts from 17th century hearth money returns, poll tax records and subsidy rolls, and copies of 17th and 18th century episcopal visitations. H.B. Swanzy, the Dean of Down, presented his notebooks of genealogical research from chancery, exchequer and prerogative court records, first fruits returns and diocesan visitations, together with his notebooks of pedigrees of 120 Irish families and his abstracts of some 800 wills mostly relating to Ulster.

Following the death in 1960 of the genealogist, W.H. Welply, the Library acquired, by bequest, a considerable body of his research dealing mostly with Co. Cork from the 17th to the 20th century – abstracts of over 1600 wills, marriage licence bonds, deeds, chancery and exchequer bills and pedigree notebooks.

In addition to copy material the Library has become the place of deposit for records of Church of Ireland organizations and the papers of families and individuals. Records of missionary societies, youth organizations, educational bodies, orphan societies and related charities such as, for example, the Charitable Musical Society of Dublin which hosted the first performance of Handel's *Messiah*, reflect Irish life at every level of society. The correspondence of leading churchmen such as Lord John George Beresford, Archbishop of Armagh, 1822 - 1862, and Euseby Cleaver, Archbishop of Dublin, 1809 - 1819, reflect the preoccupations of those in authority while, for example, the deeds of the Hamilton family of Cos Tyrone and Londonderry and the records of the Youghal Protestant Relief Society reveal something of the lives of the laity in the 18th and 19th century.

Printed Material

As the principal point of reference for information on the Church of Ireland, the Library holds a wide range of printed material which is likely to be of interest to family and local historians. Most important are the two Church of Ireland serials – the *Church of Ireland Gazette* and the *Church of Ireland Directory*. The *Gazette* is a long running church weekly publication having begun life as the *Irish Ecclesiastical Gazette* in 1856 before changing to its present title in 1900. It is bursting with information on people, places,

and to this added a four volume index of all his work. Some of his volumes were published during his lifetime and some more recently. However, some of his work still subsists only in typescript from in the Library. The information in Leslie's lists is variable both in quality and quantity but for most clergy there will be details of family, education and career.

Miscellaneous Ecclesiastical Manuscripts

One of the principal functions of the Library following the loss of so many church records in 1922 was to gather together copies and extracts of destroyed material. Pre-eminent among the copyists of the time was Tension Groves who had

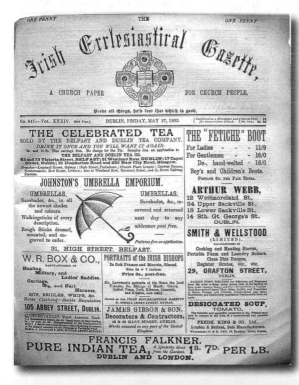

property, publications and services – the advertisements being a particularly rich source for commercial activity. The *Directory* began publication in 1862 as the *Irish Ecclesiastical Directory* and appeared every year until 1965. There was no issue in 1966 but it reappeared in 1967 as the *Church of Ireland Directory* and has been published annually since then. It is a particularly valuable source for tracking the movement of clergy and amalgamations of parishes and dioceses, while the current edition is the main source for names and addresses of clergy who may have custody of church records.

The Library has a large collection of parish, cathedral and diocesan histories, many of which appeared only as local publications with very small print runs and so are rarely to be found in the national reference collections or in the copyright libraries. The Library's catalogue of printed material is in the process of being transferred to an online catalogue and bibliographical information on much of it can already be accessed through the Library's website.

Publications

Since 1994 the Library has been publishing editions of parish registers and, so far, twelve volumes have been produced. More recently the Library, in association with Four Courts Press, has been publishing editions of older vestry records with substantial introductions and notes, and four volumes in this *'Texts and Calendars'* series have appeared. Details of the Library's publications programme is available on the Library website.

Non-Written Sources

The Library maintains databases of the Church's collections of episcopal portraits and church plate. Some of the portraits are by leading artists such as Reynolds and Orpen and so are substantial works of art. Others are more modest commissions but since many of the portraits pre-date the age of photography they are often the only representation of leading churchmen. To complement the portraits the Library is building up a photographic collection.

This is mostly of church buildings and clergy but the growing number of photographs of *'church events'* provides valuable illustrative material on the laity. The Church's extensive collection of church plate – mostly patens, chalices and flagons - are in part by the leading Dublin and provincial silversmiths and are remarkable for their beauty and rarity. However, from an historical and genealogical perspective their principal value is that they are mostly inscribed and so often have valuable information on individuals and organizations. The databases are not open to public inspection but queries regarding them will, for the most part, be dealt with by the Library staff.

Access to the Collections

The archives and manuscripts collections are, for the most part, subject to a 40 year access rule (the principal exception to this rule is that there is access to all parish registers) and in some cases collections are closed for longer periods. Otherwise collections are available to researchers in the Library's reading rooms. No appointment is necessary and most material can be produced within 15 minutes. However, it is always prudent to make contact in advance of a visit especially if travelling from a distance. General information about the Library and details of the collections are available on the Library website and all researchers should consult the website before making contact with the Library. For those who are unable to visit the Library, the Library staff may, for a fee, undertake specific searches but the Library does not offer a general research service – for the most part researchers are expected to undertake their own wok or to commission an agent to undertake it for them.

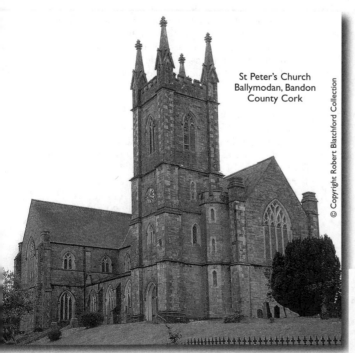

St Peter's Church Ballymodan, Bandon County Cork

© Copyright Robert Blatchford Collection

Representative Church Body Library
Braemor Park,, Churchtown, Dublin 14
T: +353 1 492 3979 F: +353 1 492 4770
E: library@ireland.anglican.org
W: www.library.ireland.anglican.org

Irish Records at The National Archives, Kew
audrey collins
tna records specialist - family history

Until 1922, all of Ireland was part of the United Kingdom. Since that date the six counties that make up Northern Ireland are still part of the UK. So most of our Irish ancestors would be classed as British, whether they liked it or not.

As a result, many useful records of their lives and activities are to be found in British sources, and the largest collection of these is held by The National Archives (TNA) at Kew, in south-west London.

The National Archives keeps records that were generated by or collected by United Kingdom government departments, and by the English legal system. Some of the records held there relate only to England, or to England and Wales, but many others cover the whole of the UK.

Most of the United Kingdom wide record series held in The National Archives cannot be split into 'English,' Irish,' 'Scottish' or 'Welsh' elements, and therefore can only be treated as a single unified collection. From a genealogical point of view the most significant example of this is the records of the armed forces and the merchant navy, where Irish men and women served alongside people from other parts of the United Kingdom and beyond.

Other records are in collections that relate specifically to Ireland, such as an extensive series known as the *Dublin Castle* records, dealing with the British administration of Ireland from the late 18th century until independence. Before that, the collection of *State Papers, Ireland 1509-1784* records the administration of first English and then British rule in Ireland. The service records of the *Royal Irish Constabulary 1816-1922* and other records kept by the Home Office form another important resource. For the 20th century there is a good deal of documentation on the dismantling of the old Dublin Castle administration, and claims for compensation for damage caused by both sides during the Troubles. There is even one early record series that appears to be Irish, but is much less useful for Irish research than it appears to be; the records of the *Irish Tontine* in series NDO 3 1773 - 1871 contain much useful information about individuals, but on inspection it turns out that only a minority of the subscribers were Irish.

The key to the holdings of The National Archives is the online Catalogue, which can be searched at www.nationalarchives.gov.uk/catalogue. There were more than 11 million catalogued items at the last count, and catalogue additions and improvements are constantly being made. However, the level of detail still varies considerably; some parts of the Catalogue can be searched by

The National Archives

the national archives

name, while others have only the briefest of descriptions. One of the best illustrations of this is in the aforementioned Irish Tontine records, where the description of NDO 3/49 reads 'Packet of sundry loose papers - more or less interesting!'

So a keyword search for a name or a place may produce some results, but these will only reveal a fraction of the potential sources of information on your Irish ancestors. To get the best research results you will need to combine Catalogue searches with guidance from other online and printed sources. The website contains a useful series of brief guides called Research Signposts, and a range of more detailed Research Guides to help you identify the records you need to consult. You will find links to dozens of Research Signposts on the page 'Looking for a person' www.nationalarchives.gov.uk /records/looking-for-person and most of them lead in turn to some of the In-depth Research Guides. These also have a page of their own where they are listed alphabetically www.nationalarchives.gov.uk /records/research-guide-listing.htm and they include a dedicated guide to Irish genealogy.

Some of the most popular and heavily used records in The National Archives have been digitised, indexed and made available online, so they can be accessed and downloaded anywhere in the world. Some of this work has been done 'in house' and the results can be found at www.nationalarchives.gov.uk /documentsonline

Only one record series within DocumentsOnline is exclusively Irish – Early Irish maps from State Papers c1558-c1610 – but most of the record sets in the military and naval categories, and some in wills and probate, include many Irish individuals.

Most of the very large digitisation projects have not been conducted in-house, but in partnership with commercial sites such as Ancestry or Find My Past. Access to these digitised images is always free on-site at The National Archives, Kew, and at some other record offices and libraries, such as Family History Centres run by the Church of Jesus Christ of Latter-Day Saints. The largest digitisation projects to date are the census for England and Wales 1841 to 1911, incoming and outgoing ships' passenger lists, and soldiers' service records from approximately 1760 to the First War. All of these are of great interest to researchers in Irish genealogy.

Census Returns

The England and Wales census may not appear to be an obvious choice, but it can be useful to establish birthplaces in Ireland for ancestors who were in England and Wales at the time of the census. Much of the time it may be of limited use, since Irish birthplaces often appear simply as 'Ireland.' This is all the information that was required from 1841 to 1901, although sometimes

a county, or even a parish, was listed. In 1911, however, the parish and county of birth was required for anyone born anywhere in the United Kingdom, including Ireland. This is great news if you have Irish born ancestors in England and Wales at that time, but if they had died before 1911, it may be worth checking for any of their siblings or other relatives who were still alive then, and who are likely to have the same birthplace.

Even if your Irish ancestor never set foot in England or Wales, it is worth remembering that the census also includes the Channel Islands and the Isle of Man as well as some returns from the Royal Navy and from merchant vessels. Additionally, the 1911 census includes for the first time a full enumeration of the army stationed abroad. Since there were always many Irishmen in the armed forces and the merchant navy, this census could be the one to provide a breakthrough for some Irish researchers.

Military Records

Before The Act of Union 1801, The British army had a separate Irish establishment with its own organisation and headquarters at Kilmainham, but the British army also drew heavily on Irish recruits. From 1801 Ireland remained a separate command, and Irish regiments kept their own identity, but the army was merged with the British army.

Estimates vary, but in the 18th, 19th and early 20th centuries it is likely that a quarter or even more of the men in British army were born in Ireland. And although many of them served in Irish regiments, they can be found in all regiments and corps throughout the army. Service records survive for many of these men, especially those who those who served long enough to earn a pension before 1913. Records for other ranks, though not for officers, may contain astonishingly detailed physical descriptions; height, chest measurement, eye colour, scars and tattoos. These are some of the most heavily used resources at The National Archives.

Unfortunately about 60% of the service records from the First World War were destroyed by enemy action during the Second World War, but the surviving ones are online and searchable by name at www.ancestry.co.uk

Where there is no service record, medal rolls and unit war diaries may provide some information about an ancestor. Service records of many men who left the army before 1913 are searchable by name at www.findmypast.co.uk

For the soldiers who do not appear in these records, for example those who died in the service, there are many other records, muster rolls, casualty lists, and description books.

Some Irishmen served in the *Royal Navy*, the *Royal Marines* and the *Royal Air Force*, and fortunately there have been no major losses from these records. Many of them can be searched and downloaded from www.nationalarchives.gov.uk /documentsonline which also includes some service records for women in the *Women's Auxiliary Army Corps*, the *Women's Royal Naval Service* and the *Women's Auxiliary Air Force* during the First World War. Those for the *Women's Auxiliary Army Corps* are particularly detailed.

After the First World War, the *Irish Sailors' and Soldiers' Land Trust* was set up to provide cottages in Ireland for ex-servicemen. Over 4000 cottages were built, up to 1932 in the Republic of Ireland, and as late as 1952 in Northern Ireland. The tenancy files are in series AP 7, and are arranged by locality, so you need to have at least an approximate address, since there are no name indexes.

For the records that are not digitised, and which have to be consulted in original format or on microfilm, there is still some good news; the Catalogue information is being improved all the time, so that some records can be searched by individual name and other keywords. Information about these can be found in the *Research Signposts and Research Guides* already mentioned.

As well as the armed forces, there are records of other services - *Coastguard, Customs and Excise* and the *Merchant Navy*. Members of the coastguard and customs and excise services were moved around the country at regular intervals, so your Irish ancestors in those services could be anywhere in the United Kingdom.

Unfortunately, few of these records are available online at the moment, although you can manually search some service records of Coastguards, as part of the Digital Microfilm project on www.nationalarchives.gov.uk /documentsonline

Digital Microfilm records are not indexed, but are basically rolls of microfilm converted into large pdf files. This means you can search through a roll of microfilm on your computer, or a terminal in The National Archives, instead of on a microfilm reader. Although this may be no quicker that searching through a film, the good news is that Digital Microfilm records are completely free to download, so you can do your searching at home. Many *Coastguards* had previously served in the *Royal Navy*, so if you have a coastguard ancestor it is worth checking the *Registers of Seaman's Services* at www.nationalarchives.gov.uk /documentsonline

Merchant Navy

If you are looking for an Irish ancestor in the merchant service you will find that research in this area is less straightforward than for men in the Royal Navy and the other armed forces. You need to bear in mind that the merchant navy was not a unified service, but a large collection of

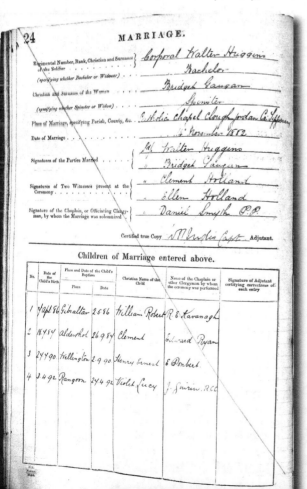

Dublin after The Easter Uprising 1916

not a unified service, but a large collection of private employers. They had to deposit various records relating to men and vessels with the Board of Trade, some of which are now held in The National Archives. As a result, there is a great deal of variation in the type, extent and survival of the records, and their current location. Other records of merchant navy ships and sailors may be found in a variety of record offices. However, The National Archives and its range of Research Guides is a good place to start. Although The National Archives holds only a small proportion of service records of merchant seamen, the good news is that they include some as recent as the mid-20th century, unlike the armed services, whose more recent personnel records are mostly retained by the Ministry of Defence. Merchant seamen's resisters of service 1918-1949 are being digitised, and will appear on www.findmypast.co.uk

Passenger Lists

Passenger lists collected by the Board of Trade from all ports in the United Kingdom to destinations outside Europe between 1890 and 1960 are online at www.findmypast.co.uk and incoming lists are on www.ancestry.co.uk The incoming series also includes a few earlier lists, back to 1878, but it was only from 1890 that all lists were required to be kept. The outgoing lists comprise a wonderful source for emigrants to Australia, New Zealand and of course to the USA and Canada, many of whom were Irish. It is worth looking at the incoming, as well as the outgoing, lists for them. Not only will you find that some people travelled back and forth, particularly across the Atlantic, but the lists will often include members of the crew, so if your Irish merchant seaman ancestor served on a passenger ship, you

might find him here.

Other Sources

Although personal records of Irish people who served in the armed forces and other United Kingdom services form a large proportion of the items of interest for Irish research, they are by no means the only ones. There are also many *Home Office* files rich in information about Ireland and the Irish, and some of these have been catalogued in detail. These include many records on crime and criminals, such as transportation registers; no matter where a crime was committed in the United Kingdom, anyone sentenced to transportation would sail from an English port, so criminals sentenced in Irish courts, under the Irish legal system, might still appear in records in England. The Home Office commissioned reports on the Irish poor, particularly during the famine years; these deal with not only with conditions in Ireland itself, but also with the many thousands of Irish people who fled to England, and how the authorities dealt with them. Sometimes they give the names of individual paupers. Home Office correspondence also covers Catholic emancipation, poor law reform and peerage claims, to name but a few, in series HO 100. These include an interesting set of records known as *'Reports of Outrages' 1836 to 1840*, weekly reports arranged by county and parish, of reported crimes. These range from petty theft, to riot and serious assault, listing the victims, and sometimes the perpetrators or suspects too. Staff records of the Royal Irish Constabulary are also part of the Home Office collection, in series HO 184, and there is a dedicated Research Guide to using this important collection. The service records are due to be digitised and indexed, and should appear

IRISH GRANTS COMMITTEE.

(THE INFORMATION GIVEN ON THIS FORM WILL BE TREATED AS CONFIDENTIAL, BUT INQUIRIES WILL IN ALL PROBABILITY BE MADE FROM THE REFERENCES GIVEN.)

1. Name (in full, and in block letters) JOHN SCANLON

2. Age   32 years

3. Address (for correspondence)   St. G. Robinson Williams
Solicitors
Sligo County Sligo

4. State here the nature of the loss in respect of which application is made, giving material dates. Detailed particulars need not be furnished at this stage.

A Ford Motor Car, my property was forcibly taken from me by marked men at 4 am. on 7th November 1921

Wills

The very first records to be digitised and published on DocumentsOnline were the Prerogative Court of Canterbury wills, which covers England and Wales. Although Ireland has always had its own completely separate system of probate, some Irish wills can be found in this series. They are mainly those left by members of Anglo-Irish landed families, or of English people who were temporarily resident in Ireland, or vice versa, such as army officers. It is therefore worth checking here for the wills of Irish people who fall into one of these categories.

Irish Nationalism

Most of the material relating to the British administration of Ireland is held in the Dublin Castle records, mainly held in record series CO 904. Many of these records deal with the rise of Irish nationalism and British attempts to deal with it.

There is a whole Research Guide devoted to the considerable amount of material on *The Easter Rising 1916*. This includes extensive records on people who were involved in the rising, especially those who were arrested and tried by court martial afterwards. When most of Ireland finally achieved home rule, a great many records were created concerning the separation of the

online in due course.

The *Irish Reproductive Loan* fund provided small loans to the industrious poor in the provinces of Munster and Connaught in the mid 19th century. Some of these records have been digitised and can be downloaded free of charge at www.movinghere.org.uk. They consist of the returns to the Clerk of the Peace for the counties of Cork, Galway, Limerick, Mayo, Roscommon and Tipperary.

Road Barricade, The Easter Uprising 1916

Name, Residence, and
Occupation of suspected
person.

O'Loughlin John
Tailor. Loughrea

Position in Organization.

Previous Information (Convictions, &c.).
and Description. 23/5/96

Height 5·7½ age 34 make very slight hair sandy. eyes grey. moustache sandy. wears Thin.

Number
of
File.

INFORMATION.

13345
5 April 1897.

O'Loughlin has taken a leading part in promoting the G.A.A. in Galway E.R. He is baronial representative on the county council. He is in sympathy with the I.N.A. movement and receives the Irish Republic from America. He is very intimate with P.J Kelly of Grangepark, M.C. Shine and Thomas Sloyan of Tuam, who are also prominent advocates of the I.N.A. He was in America from May 1880 to June 1891.

administrative functions of the two states; these include applications for passports, and questions regarding the status of Irish people resident in mainland Britain. There are also extensive records of claims for compensation for damage caused by both sides in the years leading up to independence, from all parts of Ireland. These are the records of the Irish Distress Committee, later re-named the Irish Grants Committee, comprising more than 3000 files on individual claims which can be searched by name in the Catalogue, in series CO 762.

Maps of Ireland

Finally, The National Archives holds hundreds of maps of Ireland, from the 16th century onwards. They include military maps, railway maps and some relating to property and taxation. They come in many shapes and sizes

This has been just a brief summary of some of the Irish family history resources held in The National Archives in London; further exploration would certainly reveal much more. You can find out more about records in The National Archives that might be useful to your Irish research by consulting some of the in-depth Research Guides, available for download from the website. As well as the three specifically Irish guides on Irish Genealogy, the Royal Irish Constabulary and the Easter Rising of 1916, many of the other guides on the subjects mentioned above will be helpful to you.

You can also find a detailed list of records with Irish content in Alice Prochaska's *Irish History from 1700: A Guide to Sources in the Public Record Office,* published by the British Records Association in 1986, now out of print. It is not aimed at the genealogist, and is often charmingly out of date – it refers to records being held at the old Public Record Office building in Chancery Lane, which closed in 1997. There is, understandably, no mention of The National Archives, which only came into being in 2003 as a result of the merger of the Public Record Office with the Royal Commission on Historical Manuscripts. It remains, however, the most comprehensive list of Irish material held in The National Archives, and the introduction gives a good explanation of the historical background and the origins of the records.

For the majority of records that have not been digitised or filmed, you will need to visit The National Archives at Kew in person, or have someone search the records on your behalf. You can find all the information you need about visiting at www.nationalarchives.gov.uk/visit/ including opening hours, travel directions and details of how to obtain a Reader's Ticket, which you will need to view original documents.
The National Archives, Kew, Richmond, Surrey, TW9 4DU. T: +44 (0) 20 8876 3444 W: www.nationalarchives.gov.uk/

Presbyterians in Ireland:

a guide to denominations and documentary records

William Roulston

research director - ulster historical foundation

Over many years, I have met people looking for Irish ancestors who were Presbyterians. For some there is understandable confusion at the bewildering array of manifestations of Presbyterianism in Ireland – *Seceder, Non-Subscribing, Reformed, Free,* and *Evangelical.* The aim of this article is to help those with Irish Presbyterian ancestors find out more about their forebears. It considers the different strands of Presbyterianism in Ireland, distinguishing between each of the historic Presbyterian denominations, and explores the range of records generated by these churches.

Presbyterian College, Belfast

The Presbyterian Church in Ireland

Presbyterianism emerged in Scotland in the late sixteenth century. It is characterised by worship services where reading the Bible and preaching have greatest importance and where there is a lack of emphasis on ritual and liturgy. The basic unit in the Presbyterian Church in Ireland is the congregation. In terms of church government it is democratic rather than hierarchical: every minister is considered equal, and to assist him each congregation will appoint a number of 'elders,' collectively known as the session. Church buildings have historically been known as 'meeting houses' reflecting the belief that the significance of the edifice lies not in and of itself, but rather in the group of people who have gathered there.

In the early seventeenth century, with the influx of large numbers of Scottish settlers, a number of clergymen with Presbyterian convictions arrived in Ulster from Scotland. To begin with they were accommodated within the Church of Ireland and were allowed a certain amount of freedom to practise their beliefs. However, in the 1630s there were moves to bring the Church of Ireland more closely into line with the Church of England. This resulted in the expulsion of those ministers with Presbyterian beliefs.

In 1642 an army from Scotland landed at Carrickfergus to defend Scottish settlers from attacks from Irish insurgents. Accompanying this army were a number of Presbyterian ministers acting as chaplains, and here the first Irish presbytery was founded. In the 1650s, during the Cromwellian regime, there was considerable freedom of worship and many ministers in Ulster were Scottish Presbyterians.

Following the Restoration of 1660, ministers who refused to conform to the teachings and government of the newly reinstated Church of Ireland were dismissed. Despite periods of persecution, Presbyterians began to form congregations and build their own churches from the 1660s. In 1690 an overarching ruling body known as the General Synod or Synod of Ulster was established.

For many members of the establishment, Presbyterians were regarded as more of a threat than Catholics, especially because of their numerical superiority over Anglicans in much of Ulster. Certain restrictions were placed on Presbyterians as a result of the Penal Laws passed in the Irish parliament. For example, in 1704 the 'Test Act' was extended to Ireland which required persons holding public office to produce a certificate stating that they had received communion in an Anglican church. Twenty-four Presbyterian members of the Londonderry corporation resigned rather than submit to the 'Test Act.' Even after the passing of the Toleration Act in 1719, under which Presbyterians were granted freedom of worship, there was a strong sense of estrangement from the Anglican and landed establishment, and this was a contributory factor in the large-scale emigration of Presbyterians from Ulster to America in the eighteenth century.

The distinguished historian ATQ Stewart famously observed, *'The Presbyterian is happiest when he is being a radical.'* Political radicalism was never more obvious than in the 1790s when Presbyterians were instrumental in the creation of

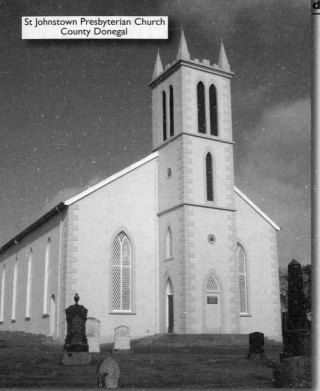

St Johnstown Presbyterian Church
County Donegal

memorials of Presbyterianism in Ireland (2 vols, Belfast 1879-80) and W. D. Killen, History of the congregations of the Presbyterian Church in Ireland (Belfast, 1886). Some of these early volumes can now be read on Google Books or Archive.org.

Most of these books look at the Church from an institutional point of view, focussing on structures of government and prominent ministers. In the twentieth century academics began to research and study Presbyterianism from different viewpoints. An academic study that considers the mental worlds of Presbyterian is The Shaping of Ulster Presbyterian Belief and Practice, 1770-1840 by Andrew Holmes (Oxford, 2006). A recent handsomely-produced volume that provides a good overview of Irish Presbyterianism is Presbyterians in Ireland: An Illustrated History by Laurence Kirkpatrick (Holywood, 2006). This volume includes photographs of virtually every Presbyterian meeting house in Ireland. Presbyterianism in Dublin is expertly covered in Dictionary of Dublin Dissent – Dublin's Protestant Dissenting Meeting Houses 1660-1920 by Steven C. Smyrl (Dublin, 2009)

Information on Congregations

An indispensable guide to the Presbyterian Church in Ireland is the History of Congregations published by the Presbyterian Historical Society in 1982. It provides brief sketches of each of the congregations, mainly focusing on the succession of ministers. It is particularly useful in determining when a particular congregation came into being. A Supplement of Additions, Emendations and Corrections with an Index was published in association with the Ulster Historical Foundation in 1996. The text of both publications can now be read online on the website of the Presbyterian Historical Society - www.presbyterianhistoryireland.com

In many of the larger towns and villages in the north of Ireland there are two or more Presbyterian congregations and the History of Congregations is particularly useful in working out their chronology and how they relate to one another. Newtownards, for example, has several Presbyterian congregations. First, Newtownards is the oldest and dates back to the seventeenth century. Second, Newtownards originally had Seceder connections, while Regent Street was established in 1834. The formation of the Greenwell Street congregation can be linked to the 1859 Revival. Strean Presbyterian Church outside the town came into existence following a disagreement in First Newtownards in 1865. It was named after its main instigator, Thomas Strean, who gave over £8,000 to build a meeting house.

the United Irishmen and were heavily involved in the revolutionary activities that led to the 1798 Rebellion. In the nineteenth century Presbyterians were active in the movement for land reform that resulted in the dismantling of the landed estate system. With the rise of Irish nationalism and the campaigns for Home Rule in the late nineteenth century, the great majority of Presbyterians became unionist in their political outlook.

Today the Presbyterian Church is the largest Protestant denomination in Northern Ireland with some 560 congregations, overwhelmingly in Northern Ireland, but with a significant number of congregations in other parts of the island, especially counties Donegal and Monaghan as well as the city of Dublin. The website of the Presbyterian Church in Ireland is www.presbyterianireland.org. This includes an extensive, though incomplete directory of congregations.

Published Works relating to the Presbyterian Church in Ireland
Histories

There is no shortage of published works on Irish Presbyterianism. In the nineteenth century several men, usually ministers in the Church, began to write detailed histories of Irish Presbyterians. Foremost among them was James Seaton Reid who wrote the magisterial History of the Presbyterian Church in Ireland, ed. W. D. Killen (3 vols, 2nd edition, Belfast, 1867). Others works include Thomas Witherow, Historical and literary

Information on Presbyterian Ministers

Biographical information on Presbyterian ministers was published as *Fasti of the Irish Presbyterian Church, 1613–1840* compiled by James McConnell and revised by his son Samuel G. McConnell (Belfast: Presbyterian Historical Society, 1951). After 1840 biographical information was published as *Fasti of the General Assembly of the Presbyterian Church in Ireland, 1840-1910*, compiled by John M. Barkley, and issued in three parts by the Presbyterian Historical Society of Ireland (1986-7). The biographical sketches are fairly succinct, but can include the name of the father and possibly mother of the minister, his own family details, where he was educated and where he served. Publications, if any, may also be noted, and perhaps something exceptional about his career.

Congregational Histories

In his book, *The Shaping of Ulster Presbyterian Belief and Practice*, the historian Dr Andrew Holmes has observed that there is a 'seemingly unique obsession of Ulster Presbyterians with writing and reading congregational histories.' To a large extent this is a reflection of the importance of the congregation within the Presbyterian system, and the way in which its identity is intertwined with its locality and the families who, often for generations, have been associated with it.

A great many congregations have their own published histories. Many of these will include appendices providing very useful information on past members of the congregation and surrounding district. For example, the appendices to John Rutherford's *Donagheady Presbyterian Churches and Parish* (1953) include the following lists of names – ratepayers in the electoral divisions of Dunalong, Ballyneaner, Dunamanagh, and Mountcastle in 1856; Donagheady wills pre-1858, the Donagheady poll book of c.1662, and hearth money rolls for Donagheady from the

1660s, as well as various other extracts from sources.

The best collection of congregational histories is in the Presbyterian Historical Society Library. There are also good collections of these histories at the Linen Hall Library and Central Library in Belfast, and in the library of the Public Record Office of Northern Ireland.

Seceders, Non-Subscribers, and Covenanters

The Secession Presbyterian Church

The Secession Church was a branch of Presbyterianism that emerged following a split in the Church of Scotland in 1712 over the issue of official patronage. Before long it had gained a foothold in Ulster and began to spread rapidly, especially in those areas where the Presbyterian Church had hitherto not been as strong. In the nineteenth century nearly all of the Secession churches were received into the Presbyterian Church in Ireland. Therefore, in the Guide to Church Records congregations that originated as Secession churches will be found listed as Presbyterian churches.

Essential reading for an understanding of the Secession Church in Ulster is David Stewart's *The Seceders in Ireland: With Annals of Their Congregations* (Belfast, 1950). Brief biographical sketches of Secession clergy appear in *Fasti of Seceder Ministers Ordained or Installed in Ireland 1716-1918*, arranged and edited by W.D. Bailie and L.S. Kirkpatrick, published by the Presbyterian Historical Society in 2005.

The Non-Subscribing Presbyterian Church

The ethos of the Non-Subscribing Presbyterian Church is *'faith guided by reason and conscience.'* The origins of this denomination go back to a dispute within the Presbyterian Church over the issue of subscription to the Westminster Confession of Faith, the statement of doctrine of the Presbyterian Church. Those who denied the necessity of subscribing to this work were known as *'New Light'* Presbyterians or *'Non-Subscribers.'* In 1725, in an attempt to deal with the situation, ministers and congregations of the *'New Light'* persuasion were placed in the Presbytery of Antrim (this did not mean that all the congregations were in County Antrim).

About 100 years later the issue of subscription again

Belfast's First (Non-Subscribing) Presbyterian Church

became a source of contention within Presbyterianism, and in 1829 a small section of the Presbyterian Church withdrew and the following year formed what was known as the Remonstrant Synod. In 1910 the General Synod of the Non-Subscribing Presbyterian Church was created following a union of the Presbytery of Antrim and the Remonstrant Synod. In 1935 this body was joined by the Synod of Munster. Today there are around 34 congregations, mainly in counties Antrim and Down.

Some of the early Non-Subscribing Presbyterian Church records, created before the split, are in fact Presbyterian records. For example, the early records of Scarva Street Presbyterian Church in Banbridge are to be found in Banbridge Non-Subscribing Presbyterian Church records. In a number of instances a Non-Subscribing Presbyterian Church will be known as the First (Old) Presbyterian Church. Rosemary Street Non-Subscribing Presbyterian Church in Belfast, for example, is generally known as First Presbyterian Church. This can give rise to confusion if there is a Presbyterian Church in a town with the designation First.

For a brief background to this denomination see *A Short History of the Non-Subscribing Presbyterian Church of Ireland* by John Campbell (Belfast: 1914). The denomination's website - www.nspresbyterian.org - includes a map showing the location of all congregations.

The Reformed Presbyterian (Covenanter) Church

The Covenanter or Reformed Presbyterian Church was composed of those who adhered most strongly to the Covenants of 1638 and 1643 and who rejected the Revolution Settlement of 1691 in Scotland. The National Covenant of 1638 was a reaction against the attempts by Charles I to bring the Scottish Church into closer conformity with the episcopal Church of England and to introduce greater ritual and a prescribed liturgy to services. It firmly established the Presbyterian form of church government in Scotland, and bound the people to uphold the principles of the Reformation. The Solemn League and Covenant of 1643 was composed on similar lines and affected England and Ireland as well as Scotland. During the reigns of Charles II (1660 – 85) and James II (1685 – 8) there was considerable persecution of

Antrim Session Book

Covenanters, and many were executed or banished. This ended with the accession of William III. In 1691 Covenanters refused to accept the Revolution Settlement as it gave the government a role in the running of the Church of Scotland. Covenanters, therefore, stood apart from mainstream Presbyterianism in Scotland.

Of the early history of the Covenanters in Ireland very little is known, save that the denomination was small and scattered. It was not until the latter part of the eighteenth century that congregations began to be organised and ministers were ordained. Very few Reformed Presbyterian records have survived from the eighteenth century. This can be partly explained by the paucity of ministers at this time; many baptisms and marriages were performed by visiting ministers from Scotland and there is little evidence of proper records being kept of these events. Congregations were divided into societies, composed of several families living within a short distance of each other. From the middle of the eighteenth century Covenanters in Ireland became much more organised with the creation of an Irish Reformed Presbytery in 1763. In 1811 a Synod of the Reformed Presbyterian Church was established. Today there are around 35 congregations.

For background information on this denomination see The Covenanters in Ireland: A History of the Reformed Presbyterian Church of Ireland by Adam Loughridge (Belfast, 1984). For information on ministers in the Reformed Presbyterian Church see Fasti of the Reformed Presbyterian Church of Ireland compiled and edited by Adam Loughridge (Belfast, 1970). An updated fasti with short historical sketches of each Reformed Presbyterian congregation was published in 2010. A recent article on researching Covenanter ancestors is 'The Origins of the Reformed Presbyterian Church of Ireland with some comments on its records' by William Roulston, published in Familia: Ulster Genealogical Review (2008), pages 86-110. The website of this denomination is www.rpc.org. This includes a map showing the location of congregations.

Documentary Records

There is little difference in the types of record generated by the three historic Presbyterian denominations, though there may be occasional differences in emphasis. Therefore, the different categories of Presbyterian records can be

Page from Belfast Funeral Register

considered together. One point I would make at this stage is that it is always worth looking at Church of Ireland registers for baptisms, marriages and burials involving Presbyterians. This is because until 1870 the Church of Ireland was the established or state church in Ireland and because of its status many people who ordinarily belonged to another denomination can turn up in the pages of its registers. Even Catholic records should not be discounted for there was much more intermarriage in Irish society than is often supposed.

Registers of Baptisms, Marriages & Burials
Baptismal Registers

Presbyterians practise infant baptism, and the registers of these baptisms form one of the most useful categories of record when looking for Irish ancestors, especially in the period prior to the introduction of civil registration of births in 1864. The basic information provided in a baptismal register is the name of the child, the name of the father and the date of baptism. The mother's name will usually be given as will a specific location. The occupation of the father and the date of birth of the child may also be provided. Although there are a number of very early Presbyterian registers of baptism, including Drumbo 1692, Killyleagh 1693, Lisburn 1692, and Portaferry 1699, in the majority of cases, baptismal records do not pre-date the nineteenth century. This may be for the very simple reason that the congregation was not established until the 1800s. Less systematic record

keeping was also a factor.

Many Presbyterian baptismal registers begin in 1819 or shortly thereafter for at the Synod of 1819 the following instructions were issued:

'That every minister of and Baptism the Synod be enjoined to register, or cause to be registered, in a book to be kept for that purpose, the names of all children baptised by him; the dates of their birth and baptism; the names of their parents, and the places of residence. This book shall be carefully preserved, and considered as the property of the congregation – to remain with them on the death, resignation, or removal of the Minister, and to be handed to his Successor, for the purpose of continuing the registry.'

Even with the ruling of 1819 some Presbyterian congregations do not have complete sets of nineteenth-century registers of baptisms. Some records were accidentally destroyed as the following extract from the baptismal register of West Church, Ballymena records:

'I preached at Churchtown on the 5th of November 1848 according to appointment by Presbytery and the list of children baptised on that day having been accidentally destroyed in my absence, I am necessitated to leave blank in the register at the same time noting its cause.'

Due to the *'negligence and disobedience of a female servant'* the records of Bready Reformed Presbyterian Church were lost in a fire in the home of the clerk of session in September 1868. Other records were destroyed deliberately. One nineteenth-century Reformed Presbyterian minister became convinced that infant baptism was contrary to Scripture and left his congregation, but not before he had destroyed many of the baptismal registers. The baptismal records of Rosemary Street Presbyterian Church, 1868 - 1941, were destroyed as a result of the *'Belfast Blitz'* during the 2nd World War.

On other occasions record-keeping was simply lax. A visitation of 1st Donagheady Presbyterian Church in County Tyrone in 1865 found that there was no baptismal register, no communicants' roll, and no session or committee minute books. In 1876 it was noted that no minutes of any committee meeting had been kept since 1871. It was not until 1878 that a baptismal register was provided. Frequently registers disappeared around the time that a minister died or moved to a new congregation.

For the most part baptismal registers will follow a fairly routine format. Occasionally, however, an entry of some interest might appear. One such entry appears in the baptismal register of Crossgar Presbyterian Church in County Londonderry. Following a record of the baptism on 4th May 1888 of David Campbell at the age of 46 the entry continues:

'This D. Campbell spent 21 years and 43 days in the Army (4 years in England, 1 in Scotland, 3 in

Limerick

Ireland, 12 years and 27 days in India) before his baptism. While in the Army he was an Episcopalian, having gone over from the Presbyterian Church like a great many others; when he got off he attended the Episcopal Church in Macosquin for some time, but he wrote on a letter asking me to baptise him which I did on sincere profession of his faith.'

Marriage Registers

One of the main grievances of Presbyterians in the early eighteenth century concerned the right of their ministers to conduct marriages. In 1737 an act of parliament was passed which, with certain caveats, permitted two Presbyterians to marry. At last in 1782 marriages performed by a Presbyterian minister were legally recognised as being *'as good in law'* as those performed by a minister of the Church of Ireland. However, it was not until the passing of another act of parliament in 1844 that Presbyterians ministers were permitted to marry a Presbyterian and a member of the Church of Ireland.

Prior to the standardisation of marriage registers from 1st April 1845, when all non-Catholic marriages were to be officially registered, these will give in their simplest form the date of the marriage and the names of the bride and groom. The residence and the name of the father of each party are occasionally provided. The names of the witnesses may also be given. At the same Synod of 1819 that exhorted ministers to keep registers of baptisms, similar directions were given for the keeping of marriage registers:

'Overtured and unanimously agreed to – That every Minister of this Synod shall keep, or cause to be kept, a regular registry of all marriages celebrated by him; stating the date of each marriage, the names of the parties, the Congregations or Parishes in which they reside, and the names of at least two of the witnesses present at the celebration of the ceremony.'

It was also agreed that every minister would be required to submit annually to his respective presbytery an accurate list of the marriages he had conducted in the previous year. These marriages would then be copied by the clerk of presbytery into a separate volume. Relatively few of these presbytery marriage books seem to have survived, or at least are in the public domain. One that does relates to the Tyrone Presbytery and covers marriages in the following congregations: Cookstown (possibly 1st), 1820-8, Loughgall, 1819-22, Tobermore, 1819-22, Vinecash, 1825-8, Carland, 1826-8, Magherafelt, 1819-28, Dungannon (possibly 1st), 1819-28, Benburb, 1827-8, Cloveneden, 1826-8, Richhill, 1826-8, Stewartstown (possibly 1st), 1820-7, Coagh, 1820-2 and Minterburn, 1819-22 (PRONI, MIC/1P/460).

From 1st April 1845, with the introduction of civil registration of non-Catholic marriages, the information on the individuals getting married includes their name, age, status, and occupation. The names and occupations of their fathers are also given. The church, the officiating minister and the witnesses to the ceremony are named. In most cases the exact age of the parties is not given, and the entry will simply read *'full age'* (i.e. over 21) or *'minor'* (i.e. under 21). If the father of one of the parties was no longer living, this may be indicated in the marriage certificate by the word *'deceased'* or by leaving the space blank, but in many cases it is not.

Burial Registers

Few Presbyterian congregations have very old burial registers. Part of the reason for this, as will be discussed presently, is the fact that not every Presbyterian meeting house has an adjoining graveyard. Those burial registers that do exist were mainly started in the late nineteenth or even the early twentieth century. Burial registers can be fairly uninformative, with the name of the deceased, the date of burial and occasionally the occupation and age at death given.

One very interesting early eighteenth-century document relating to the burial of Presbyterians survives among the records of Rosemary Street Non-Subscribing Presbyterian Church in Belfast. It is a register of the hiring of funeral gear – palls, cloaks and hats – for about 2,000 funerals which

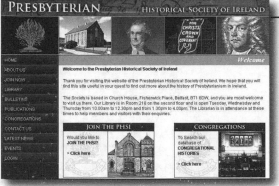

took place in Belfast between 1712 and 1736. It has been published as *Funeral register of Rosemary Street Non-Subscribing Presbyterian Church (known as the First Presbyterian Church of Belfast), 1712-36*, edited by Jean Agnew (Belfast: Ulster Historical Foundation, 1995).

Other Congregational Records

Few denominations generated as many records as the various strands of Presbyterianism with the result that a variety of other items may be found among the records kept by individual Presbyterian congregations. Some of these are discussed below.

Minutes of Session Meetings

The session was the ruling body in each congregation and was composed of the minister, designated the moderator at meetings of session, and elders in a particular congregation. One of the elders served as *'clerk of session'* and was responsible for recording the minutes of the meetings. Session records cover a range of matters, many of which relate to the internal discipline of members of the congregation for a variety of transgressions. Occasionally they may contain baptisms and marriages that are not recorded elsewhere.

Family Records and Congregational Censuses

A real boon to any researcher seeking information on the families that belonged to a particular congregation will be a congregational census. These can take different forms. At their simplest they may be a list of members of the congregation. More detailed census returns will provide the townland and will include the names of all members of the family. For example, the records of Rademon Non-Subscribing Presbyterian Church, County Down, include a census of families arranged by townland, 1836-7, with notes added at a later date indicating those who died or got married, those who left the congregation and those who had emigrated. For Carrigallen Presbyterian Church in County Leitrim there is a visitation book with details of each family by townland and dates of baptisms of children, 1837-92.

A remarkable volume is Rev. Robert Magill's family record book for the congregation of 1st Antrim (Millrow). This includes detailed information on the families that belonged to the congregation in the early nineteenth century and includes baptisms, marriages and deaths. On a number of occasions Magill even went so far as to sketch out family trees, with figure drawings of the various family members. This volume is available for inspection at the Presbyterian Historical Society Library.

Lists of Communicants

These are similar to congregational census, but they only list the names of communicant members of a particular congregation. Sometimes there may be a separate list of the names of new communicants. Occasionally lists of communicants are annotated with additional information, such as when a communicant married, emigrated or died.

Transfer Certificates

Members of one congregation who wished to transfer their congregation to another would be issued with a certificate testifying to their good standing in the church. Frequently a transfer certificate would be issued to those who were emigrating. For example, the transfer certificate given to David Carson by the Rev. Hugh Hamill of 1st Donagheady in 1784 certified that Carson *was 'born and bred of honest Protestant dissenting parents and brought up in that faith, and has lived a sober, regular life which we hope will recommend him to our brethren in America, whom he may chance to associate with.'* Carson took no chances and also sought and received a similar testimonial from a local Reformed Presbyterian Church. For a number of congregations there are lists of people who left the congregation to emigrate abroad.

Financial Records

The financial records of a congregation should not be overlooked when searching for a Presbyterian ancestor. Occasionally they will survive for a period for which registers of baptisms and marriages are absent. These records range from stipend lists (the stipend being the minister's salary), pew rent books, and account books. For 1st Lisburn Presbyterian Church there is a subscription list for the new meeting house from 1764-5.

Pew rent books can be particularly interesting documents. Formerly, the greater part of the minister's stipend was derived from pew rents, that is, from the letting of pews or seats within the meeting house for a fixed annual sum. In some congregations there were different classes of pew-sitters, reflecting a certain social stratification. For example, in Glendermott Presbyterian Church pew-sitters were divided into gentlemen, farmers, and artisans/cottiers. Some pew rent books survive from the early eighteenth century. For instance, for Rosemary Street Presbyterian Church in Belfast there are surviving pew rent books, 1726-73, 1788-96, 1816-56 and 1866-73.

ROYAL AVENUE BELFAST.

Calls to Ministers

When a congregation had settled on their choice for a new minister a *'call'* was issued to him, signed by the members. It was then up to the individual to whom the call was issued to decide whether or not he wished to accept that call. Some of these calls can incorporate fairly extensive lists of names of members of individual congregations. For example, the call issued to Thomas Clark by the Presbyterians of Ballyalbany, County Monaghan, in 1751 contains the names of over 160 individuals. It was published in S. Lyle Orr and Alex Haslett, *Historical Sketch of Ballyalbany Presbyterian Church* (1940).

Education Records

Within Presbyterianism there was a strong emphasis on education, especially on literacy and the ability to read the Bible for oneself. Many ministers conducted classes in their home or in the session room of their meeting house. Providing a Classical education, these schools were often used to prepare young men for the ministry. Few records relating to these establishments survive.

Education records that do survive among congregational records relate principally to the Sunday schools that were established in their hundreds in the early nineteenth century. For example, among the records of 2nd Portglenone Presbyterian Church, County Antrim, is a Sunday school roll book, 1821-67. The records for Antrim (Millrow) Presbyterian Church include a Sabbath School library loan book, 1870, and a Sabbath School receipt and expenditure book, 1835-62, incorporating a weekly roll of teachers and salaries, 1840-41.

Administrative Records: Minutes of Meetings of Presbytery and Synod

The Presbytery was the middle layer of government in the Presbyterian Church, above session and below Synod. It comprised the ministers and ruling elders of the congregations affiliated to the Presbytery. It dealt with matters that could not be settled at the level of session, either because there was a dispute of a nature that could not be resolved without recourse to a higher authority or because the issues related to more than one congregation. Presbytery meetings were held on a regular basis. Presbyteries were frequently reorganised. In addition, individual congregations could change presbytery if it meant that a dispute would be resolved.

The surviving minute book for the Presbytery of Strabane, covering the period 1717–40, reveals that the Presbytery dealt with a variety of matters relating to the members of the congregations within its bounds. For instance, in December 1718 John Alison came before Strabane presbytery desiring a certificate testifying to his credentials as a good Presbyterian as he was preparing to emigrate. Presbytery decided not to issue him with one until just before he was ready to leave, and then only conditional on his continued good behaviour.

The Synod of Ulster was the highest authority in the Presbyterian Church in Ulster. It met once a year, usually in June, and was composed of representatives from every congregation in each of the presbyteries. The records of the Synod of Ulster meetings for the period 1690–1820 were published in three volumes by the Presbyterian Church in 1891 (available to read online at www.archive.org). Much of the minutes deal with matters of a fairly routine nature. Occasionally, however, an item of real value will be recorded. From 1840, when the Synod of Ulster and the Secession Synod United, there are the printed minutes of the General Assembly, a set of which is in the library of the Presbyterian Historical Society.

Presbyterian Graveyards and Gravestone Inscriptions

Many, but by no means, all Presbyterian meeting houses have adjoining burial grounds. Few of the inscriptions in graveyards surrounding Presbyterian churches pre-date 1800 and in fact the practise of burying within the grounds of Presbyterian churches does not seem to have happened until the late eighteenth century. The burial ground attached to Castlereagh Presbyterian Church is unusual in having several memorials dating from the late eighteenth century. An exception to this generalisation is the graveyard at Drumbo Presbyterian Church, which includes memorials from the late seventeenth century. However, in the case of Drumbo the meeting house is unique, so far as the present writer knows, in that it stands on the site of a medieval parish church.

If looking for the burial places of Presbyterian ancestors prior to the nineteenth century, the most obvious place to check will be the old parish graveyard, probably dating from the medieval period, and which may or may not have a functioning Church of Ireland church within its bounds. Even after burial grounds began to be laid out around Presbyterian meeting houses, the practise of interment in these older graveyards continued for some families.

It was not until the second half of the nineteenth century that Presbyterians were legally entitled to open a burial ground that did not adjoin one of their own meeting houses. The background to the opening of Balmoral Cemetery in 1855 was an incident in which a Church of Ireland minister obstructed a funeral being conducted by two Presbyterian ministers. One of the ministers involved, Rev. Joseph Mackenzie, secured the ground for the cemetery, and remained its owner, though it was managed by a board of trustees. Though the cemetery was never exclusively Presbyterian, it was predominantly so and was the only burial place of its kind in nineteenth-century Ulster.

The inscriptions from many Presbyterian churchyards have been published in one form or another. The Ulster Historical Foundation has published the inscriptions from more than 50 Presbyterian churchyards in County Down as well as several more in County Antrim. A number of local historical societies have also been involved in transcribing and publishing gravestone inscriptions. Many inscriptions have been made available on the internet.

Locating Records

Over the years the Public Record Office of Northern Ireland (PRONI) has done a tremendous job in acquiring originals or copies of records kept by individual Presbyterian congregations. Most of the Presbyterian records in its custody are on microfilm. The coverage is so extensive that there are relatively few congregations whose records have not been deposited in some form in PRONI - www.proni.gov.uk The majority of these records are available on microfilm, though there are also some original documents, as well as photocopies.

The Presbyterian Historical Society, about which more will be said presently, has copies of most of the microfilms of Presbyterian registers held by PRONI and can be viewed on a microfilm reader at the Society's office in Church House, Belfast. A small number of Presbyterian records are only available at the Presbyterian Historical Society. These include some very early session books, including those of Dundonald and Aghadowey, as well as some registers of baptisms and marriages. A few pre-1900 Presbyterian registers are still in local custody.

With the advent of the internet, the indexing

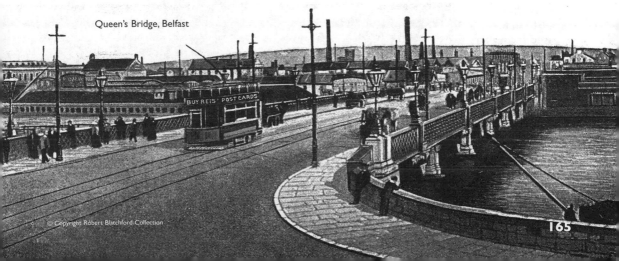

Queen's Bridge, Belfast

BUY REIS POST CARDS

© Copyright Robert Blatchford Collection

and digitisation of church records has gathered pace. Many of the centres affiliated to the Irish Family History Foundation have indexed Presbyterian registers for their respective counties and made these available online on a pay-per-view arrangement - www.rootsireland.ie - though coverage is far from complete. Local endeavour has also resulted in many registers being made available online free.

The Presbyterian Historical Society

The Presbyterian Historical Society was founded in 1906 to promote public awareness of the history of the various strands of Presbyterianism in Ireland. Once described as a *'Treasure House of Ulster's History,'* the Society's library possesses some 12,000 books and pamphlets. These are mainly concerned with ecclesiastical history and in particular Presbyterian history. The collection includes a large number of congregational histories. A set of *The Witness*, a Presbyterian newspaper, covering the period 1874-1941, is also available for consultation as are the printed minutes of the General Assembly beginning in 1840.

Manuscript material includes session minutes, baptisms and marriages from individual churches as well as some presbytery minutes. These include session accounts for Armagh Presbyterian Church for 1707-32, session minutes for Aghadowey Presbyterian Church for 1702-61 and baptisms from Cullybackey (Cunningham Memorial) Presbyterian Church covering the period 1726-1815. In addition the records of a number of now defunct congregations in the Republic of Ireland have been deposited for safekeeping in its Library. The Society also has a duplicate set of the microfilm copies of Presbyterian Church registers held by PRONI covering the vast majority of Presbyterian congregations in Ireland.

Of particular interest is the large amount of biographical data available on Presbyterian ministers. This material can be accessed through a card index, while there are also handwritten and printed *'fasti'* providing information on clergymen. A small collection of private papers of Presbyterian ministers is also available. These include some of the papers of the most

distinguished Presbyterian minister in the nineteenth century, the Reverend Henry Cooke.

The Society's library has been built up gradually over many years through donations, bequests and purchases. The Society is funded through donations and fees, together with a valuable financial contribution each year from the Incidental Fund of the General Assembly of the Presbyterian Church in Ireland. Queries on membership are welcomed and should be addressed to the Society's Librarian, Valerie Adams.

The Society now has its own website - www.presbyterianhistoryireland.com which contains information on upcoming events, membership, and other news. Members of the Society can access a digitised version of the History of Congregations, as well as past editions of the Society's annual publication, The Bulletin. A history of the Society has been published – *Times Passing: The Story of the Presbyterian Historical Society of Ireland from 1907-2007* by Dr Joe Thompson. In 2010 the Presbyterian Historical Society moved to new premises at 26 College Green, Belfast.

Conclusion

Researching Irish Presbyterian ancestors can be as fulfilling or frustrating as investigating forebears from any one of the many other denominations on this island. Among the chief frustrations is the fact that relatively few congregations have registers of baptisms and marriages prior to the 1800s. On the other hand, the large number of administrative and other records that were generated by individual congregations means that it can be possible to put real flesh on the bones of Presbyterian ancestors and so understand more about their social and religious worlds.

Glenoe Village, County Antrim

The Presbyterian Historical Society of Ireland Library and Archive
Valerie Adams

The Presbyterian Historical Society Library and Archive has been in existence since 1907 and until the autumn 2010 based at Church House in the centre of Belfast. It has now re-located to 26 College Green near to Queen's University and Union Theological College. The Society was formed to preserve books, pamphlets, archives, documents and artefacts in connection with the history of the churches of the Presbyterian Order in Ireland, and to encourage a greater awareness of the history of these churches. From the very beginning the Society has been a library, an archive and a museum.

Published Material

The extensive library of books relates to Presbyterianism in Ireland, Scotland and America and therefore reflects the close links between these three countries. Included are congregational histories (of interest to both family and local historians), biographies and autobiographies. The library also contains a very important pamphlet collection, over 500 of which date from before the mid 19th century. They cover a wide range of theological, political, social and economic issues and are indicative of an age when the production of a pamphlet was the only means of getting your message or your opinion across. A particular strength of the published material is the presence of a large number of Presbyterian magazines dating from the mid 19th century and in some cases even earlier. These are of interest not only from a theological point of view but are also a valuable source of information about churches and Presbyterian ministers.

Another very important resource held by the Society is **'The Witness'** - a Presbyterian newspaper which ran weekly from 1874 to 1941. As the original volumes had become too fragile to handle they had to be microfilmed - the films which can be consulted in the Society's library are regularly used by academics and by local and family historians. As well as details about Presbyterian churches and ministers the

The Presbyterian Historical Society Library and Archive College Green, Belfast

A typical marriage notice for 3rd July 1874 reads:

BODEL—LEGATE—July 2, at the Imperial Hotel, by special licence, by the Rev. J. D. Martin, uncle of the bride, assisted by her brothers, Rev. E. M. Legate, Ballyclare, and Rev. G. W. Legate, Dungannon, James Bodel, Esq., Katesbridge, to Helena, third daughter of Rev. G. Legate, Edengreen, Kilkinamurry, Co. Down.

newspaper is also a rich source of information on community life and events (eg reports of court cases and inquests, lists of student examination successes at Queen's University and schools, subscription lists etc) while the birth, marriages and death notices are of obvious interest to the family historian.

The published material in the Society's library also includes the minutes and reports of the General Assembly of the Presbyterian Church in Ireland from 1830 and the minutes of its predecessor, the Synod of Ulster from 1691 as well as the minutes of the Reformed Presbyterian Synod of Ireland from 1811.

Archives

The Society holds many congregational records, particularly of churches that are now closed both in Northern Ireland and in the Republic of Ireland. Complementing some unique congregational records only to be found in the Society's library are microfilm copies of the records of Presbyterian churches filmed by the Public Record Office of Northern Ireland. Among the archives held are those of missionaries, of individual Presbyterian ministers, and of Presbyteries, in addition to a large collection of individual manuscripts such as the Adair Narrative which is a 17th century account of the rise and growth of Presbyterianism in Ireland.

Compiled Resources

One of the most frequently consulted resources held by the Society is a set of index cards containing biographical information on Presbyterian ministers. Some of this 'Fasti' information has been published by the Society but there is frequently additional information on the cards not to be found in the published version. The information recorded includes dates of birth and death and often also of marriage, the name of the father and place of birth, education, and the names of the churches where the minister served and when.

The Society also holds information folders on individual churches and can include newspaper cutting, unpublished histories, photographs of ministers and churches, orders of service for ordinations and for the opening of churches, financial reports and other material.

Publications

The Society has an active publications programme. *The Society's Bulletin*, published annually, contains articles on a wide range of interesting subjects relating to Irish Presbyterianism. A series of small booklets is available on topics such as *The 1625 Six Mile Water Revival, The 1798 Rebellion*, Presbyterianism and Orangeism and Presbyterian Communion Tokens as well as biographical studies on people like the Rev Sinclair Kelburn who was involved in the 1798 Rebellion, and Francis Makemie who is regarded as the father of American Presbyterianism. A full list of the publications is available on the Society's website. The most important publication produced by the Society is the *'History of Presbyterian Congregations from 1610'* which, although now out of print, is accessible on the Society's website and has been brought right up to date.

Use of the Library

Although anyone can use the library and its resources and we do give free advice and help to enquirers we cannot provide a full genealogical research service and users are encouraged to join the Society – annual membership is £15.00, life membership is £75.00, student membership is £5.00. Becoming an Associate member gives access to the restricted part of the website that includes the *'History of Presbyterian Congregations'* and some issues of the Bulletin.

Presbyterian Historical Society of Ireland
26 College Green, Belfast BT7 1LN
T: +44 (0) 28 9072 7330 E: phsilibrarian@pcinet.org
W: www.presbyterianhistoryireland.com
Opening Hours:
Tuesday & Wednesday
 9.30.a.m. - 1.00.p.m. & 1.30.p.m. - 4.30.p.m.
Thursday 9.30.a.m. - 1.00.p.m.

Red Flag over Carrick, County Tipperary
chris paton

A common complaint about Irish family history is that the records have not survived, and it is therefore well nigh impossible to perform any meaningful research. A lot of such thought derives from the destruction of many key records during the civil war, making it at times difficult to construct the basic tree on which to hang our family stories. Yet another legacy of the civil war is the fact that many families remained silent of the ordeals that they went through during such times, with stories of great hardship, heroism. At times complete family disasters were rapidly swept under the carpet by our ancestors in an attempt to move on. Despite this veil of secrecy, it is the written record which has survived that can still reveal the truth in some of its aspects.

My wife's paternal grandfather's story would be no exception. Patrick Giles' early life contains many mysteries which have been uncovered but never satisfactorily explained, whilst other stories about him have emerged from the period of the civil war which seem almost too unbelievable to be true. Why was his birth record so difficult to find, and also those of his siblings; and was he really caught up within the creation of a workers' soviet in 1922?

Family lore had it that Patrick Giles was the son of Henry Giles and Johanna Donovan, and worked as a fitter in the Tipperary town of Carrick on Suir. He married Margaret Organ in 1906, and with her had two children, Henry and Cecilia. With Margaret's death in 1912. He married his second wife, Annie Colleton, in June 1922. Shortly after this marriage Patrick's son Henry was sent off to the United States, apparently against his will. Patrick had a further two children with Annie. Johanna, born just three months after the wedding, and Patrick (my wife's father, better known as Paddy) in 1926. Annie passed away in 1927, whilst Patrick senior had apparently died in the late 30s.

Patrick's wife Annie was a member of a well known family of bakers in Carrick on Suir, famous locally for the 'Colleton bap,' and her family story was typical of many from the time. When the First World War broke out, Irish nationalists were urged by political representatives in the country to fight for the British, in the hope of receiving a devolved parliament at the end of hostilities. Annie's brother Martin served with the British Army for many years, having initially joined a militia unit in Tipperary before transferring to the 2nd Battalion of the Connaught Rangers. On November 2nd 1914, with the war barely underway, he was killed at Ypres.

Two years later, the aftermath of the Easter Rising in Dublin had radically redefined the nationalist struggle. Martin's brother John joined the IRA and fought in the War of Independence – ironically perhaps fighting against the British this time for the same end goal as his brother.

Patrick's story was the one I wished to pursue

Carrick on Suir, County Tipperary 1925

however, and to do so I initially started my research with the aid of a book entitled 'Carrick-on-Suir Family Roots' which listed the town's inhabitants in the 1901 and 1911 censuses. This only noted the names and addresses of those residents enumerated in the censuses, but confirmed that there was only one Giles household in the whole town. Although Henry could not be found, Johanna was recorded in both censuses with several children, Patrick, Minnie, Martin, Mark and Nora. At this time there were very few resources online, and so I posted what little I had on my website, in the firm belief of making my research work as a lure in its own right.

Patrick Giles 1930

Sure enough, I was soon contacted by Waterford based Paddy Nolan, a grandson of Patrick's sister Minnie Giles. Paddy remembered Patrick from his youth, and knew that he had worked for a local creamery, part of the Condensed Milk Factory Company in Ireland, until the 1920s. With the economic depression that followed, Patrick temporarily left his children with Minnie in order to find work in England, but had returned to Ireland prior to the war in 1939. He later found employment as caretaker at the Carrick based Burke Asylum, and early each morning visited Minnie's house in William Street to light her range for her. However, by 1941, Patrick was working at the Little Sisters of the Poor convent in Waterford, where he would finally passed away in 1944.

Having obtained so much useful information from Paddy, my wife wrote to the convent to ask the staff if they had any record of her grandfather. She received a letter from the Convent saying that Patrick had died on July 6th 1944. His name was in fact recorded as Patrick Fenlon Giles, with his parents noted as Johanna Donovan and Henry Fenlon. At this point we assumed that his father's name had simply been mis-transcribed, the final Giles name having been accidentally omitted.

When transcriptions of the vital records for County Tipperary went online at the Irish Family History Foundation's RootsIreland site - www.rootsireland.ie - I searched for Patrick's birth, and those of all the other Giles children, but bizarrely could not find any of them, despite the sources information listed on the site indicating that the civil birth records from Carrick on Suir were online. With a bit of further digging I did locate a statutory death notice for a six week old Henry Giles in 1870, however, with no parents were listed, and the informant was a Honoria Donovan who was resident at Oven Lane. No civil birth record could be found for the child, but

in searching for a marriage for Johanna, I discovered that six weeks after young Henry's death, a Johanna Donovan from Oven Lane had married a Henry Fenlon of Ballyrichard Road.

On a hunch, I then searched online for the civil births of the five known Giles children, but under the surname of Fenlon instead of Giles, and suddenly they all appeared, as did two further siblings, John and Aloisia, with most born at Oven Lane. Henry 'Fenlon' himself was found to have died in September 1889 of phthisis (tuberculosis).

Suitably intrigued, I gave this information to Paddy Nolan back in Ireland, who obtained permission to view the original Roman Catholic baptismal registers in Carrick on Suir. He soon discovered a baptismal record for the young Henry Giles in 1870 – and in this record his parents were definitively noted as Johanna Donovan of Oven Lane, and Henry Giles of

Cleeve's Creamery Seizures.
Farmer who had ceased supplying milk to Messers. Cleeve's Cremery at Carrick on-Suir were prevented by creamery workers from selling butter at Carrick-on-Suir butter market. The clerical staff, numbering about 9, have left the creamery. At Birdhill, Co. Limerick, the co-operative creamery ignored an order not to take milk to Messers Cleeve's suppliers. Bridge town Co-op. Creamery acted similarly. It was stated that if necessary the farmers' sons would be called upon to act as volunteers to see that any milk going to the creamery would ot be interfered with.

Report in Irish Independent 19th May 1922

Patrick Giles
with Cecilia,
his daughter, and
son Patrick 1935

taken over forcibly, and the employees and managers who remained loyal to the owners of the creameries were expelled. Simultaneously with the taking over of the creameries, red flags were hoisted in each case over these concerns'. One of the TDs in the debate specifically stated 'There is a factory in Carrick on Suir that was taken over by the workers, and I am informed it was worked and managed in a proper manner.' (A member of the Dáil is known as a Teachta Dála, TD or Deputy.)

So what was this all about?!

Keen to learn more, I tracked down and purchased a rare copy of a text on the history of the town 'Carrick on Suir and its People' by P.C. Power, via Abe Books - www.abebooks.com The book said the company had made a small fortune during the First World War, but had refused to increase the wages of the staff at its various factories in the south of Ireland.

Following the threat of a one third pay cut, a workers committee was formed in Carrick on Suir under Michael Banks, the leader of a secretive three man strong communist cell in the town, and the secretary of the Irish Transport Workers Union. On May 12th 1922, the workers, unable to negotiate a pay settlement, had seized the premises in Carrick and declared it to be a 'soviet,' issuing a proclamation which ended with 'Long live the sovereign people' and had duly raised the Red Flag over the factory. Importantly, the book noted that all of Carrick's ninety creamery workers had taken part. In retaliation, local farmers had refused to send their milk to the creamery and bought their own separators to produce cream and butter at home instead. It was reported that on May 20th 1922, instead of the usual 12,000 to 17,500 gallons normally delivered to the factory, only 6 gallons were sent.

The book said that all of Carrick's ninety creamery workers had taken part, but was Patrick really involved? I searched the Irish Newspaper Archives collection at www.irishnewsarchive.com and in the Munster Express found no contemporary mention of Patrick's involvement. However, I did locate an obituary for him in 1944, which stated that he 'had the distinction of being one of the first group of mechanical engineers to be employed by Cleeve's Condensed Milk Factory, almost sixty years ago, and was with that firm until it closed, about 22 years ago.' This closure was therefore dated to 1922, and sure enough, following the soviet's closure, I soon established from Power's

Ballyrichard Road, and not Henry 'Fenlon.'

Within six weeks of this event it was clear that Henry had then married Johanna under the alias of 'Fenlon,' and I soon determined that the family had remained hidden under the name for the next 19 years. Following Henry's death in 1889, every subsequent family record, such as the children's marriages, referred to him as 'Henry Giles,' and each member of the 'Fenlon' family had dropped the name and taken on the Giles surname once more. Clearly Henry had been hiding both his and his family's identity from someone, though why continues to remain a secret for the moment.

But this was not the only remarkable discovery about Patrick. Knowing now that he worked for the local creamery, I searched the internet for information on the company and came across a debate transcription from the Dáil from 1924 on the Díospóireachtaí Parlaiminte (Parliamentary Debates) site at http://tinyurl.com/yzjcl45 concerning the Condensed Milk Company, owned by the Cleeves family. The motion under consideration was

'That the Dáil is of opinion that special measures should be taken by the Government to recompense the suppliers of milk to the creameries of the Condensed Milk Company of Ireland for the losses which they suffered owing to the seizure of those creameries in May, 1922, by unauthorised persons.'

The discussion centred on incidents in Tipperary, Limerick and Cork in 1922, following the taking over of several factory buildings by the workers. The report mentioned how 'they were

Street fighting - Dublin 1922

book that the entire staff of Cleeves had been dismissed and the premises closed. A few months later, twenty staff were re-employed and the premises temporarily opened again, before finally closing for good within a few short years. It seems that Patrick was indeed one of the ninety staff involved in the takeover, losing his job in the aftermath.

But what had led to the collapse of this communist soviet in Carrick? An article in the The Times, London - May 15th 1922, entitled 'Red Coup in Ireland,' provided some further context. With the communists having seized power, it reported that additional factories in Clonmel, Killmallock, Mallow and Knocklong were also falling under the Red Flag, but that whilst this was happening, an even bigger crisis was stirring further north in Dublin.

Following the British withdrawal from Ireland and the creation of the new Irish Free State, a peace committee in the Dàil was furiously trying to prevent an all out war between hardliners in the IRA who had been fighting for a fully fledged Irish Republic, and those who had been happy to accept a more limited dominion status within the British Empire via the Anglo-Irish Treaty of 1921, which had led to the country's partition. The committee failed, and on 28th June full scale civil war broke out in the south of Ireland.

By August, the hardline 'Irregulars,' were in the retreat. In Carrick on Suir, they fought against the Free State Army in a three day battle, and duly lost. Again, this was another tale involving my wife's ancestors, this time on her maternal line.

Street fighting - Dublin 1922

Damage to Four Courts Building - Dublin 1922

© Copyright Robert Blatchford Collection

the Battle of Carrick on Suir, which started on August 1st 1922, the farmhouse of Thomas Prendergast, her great grandfather, was occupied by the Free State Army, which slaughtered all of his livestock and caused so much damage to the house, later described by Thomas as a *'teetotal wreck,'* that compensation was eventually granted to the family in 1933. The damage caused by the Free State side was extensive, and somewhat bizarre. Not only had the army arrested Thomas and seized control of his farm, they had also ripped up the floorboards and a mahogany table for firewood, and had torn down curtains to make stockings (an incident provoking laughter when recalled in the courthouse looking at the compensation claim). Coincidentally, Paddy Nolan's grandfather had been the builder contracted to repair the damage.

The anti Treaty faction had several battalions in the Carrick area, one of which operated from the suburban village of Killonerry, and several of my wife's family members were in its ranks. During

In the aftermath of the battle, the Free State Army had regained control of both the town and the creamery, with Banks and other leaders duly arrested. Thomas's nephew, Michael Prendergast, an active member of the IRA, was forced to go on the run to the United States, and did not return to Ireland until 1978.

Many questions still remain unanswered however. Just two months after the Battle of Carrick on Suir and the closure of the creamery, Patrick Giles sent his 14 year old son Henry on a ship from Cork to the USA, against his will, with the young Henry on several occasions finding his way off the boat and making his way back to Carrick, before being hauled back to Cork and to a future life in Boston. Once there he would ultimately marry a Nova Scotian woman, Mary Jessie MacIsaac, and raise a family. Was Henry somehow involved in the war, or was Patrick perhaps unable to provide for him any more, having lost his job, and with a new wife and baby to care for?

As with the family name changing mysteriously from Giles to Fenlon and back again, the answers to these questions may never be revealed, but the search goes on ...

Henry Giles 1934

173

Cobh and its Place in History
Brian Parnaby

Of all the places in Ireland perhaps there is no more significant a location and contributor to the country's history, than Cóbh – originally, in Irish: an Cóbh – the word has no special meaning. The town was re-named Queenstown during a visit by Queen Victoria in 1849 but reverted to its Irish name in 1922

For hundreds of years the whole of Ireland was under the jurisdiction of the British. On occasions this rule was harsh. Especially so during the Commonwealth period of Oliver Cromwell, the 'Lord Protector.' There was mass destruction of religious artefacts such as statues, icons, vestments destroying within a few years irreplaceable works of art. The beautiful and priceless 'Book of Kells' survived and is now on display at Trinity College Library, Dublin.

Cóbh is on the south eastern corner of Ireland and is now a haven of peace and tranquillity. Its history, over the past two centuries, has been one of turmoil and has been scarred by periods of great sorrow. This historic town was founded over a thousand years ago and is situated on the shores of the largest of three islands in Cork harbour – the island known as Barry and Barrymore.

A village came into being on this site and was known as Ballyvoloon, first referred to in the mid-18th century and later renamed 'The Cove' as it overlooked the cove of the Bay. Cóbh was small with only about thirty commercial premises listed in the town in the late 18th century. One particular geographical feature was mainly responsible for the development of the town and this was the large natural deepwater harbour provided by the Cove. This served the British as a

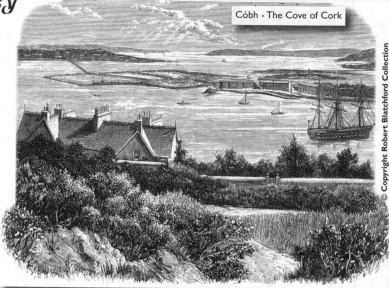

Cóbh - The Cove of Cork

© Copyright Robert Blatchford Collection

naval base, firstly during the Napoleonic wars, and later during The Great War of 1814 - 1918. One result of this was the steady growth of the town and a welcome increase in local prosperity.

However, events during the mid-19th century conspired to alter the identity of Cóbh irrevocably. That was the first of the two major Potato Famines in the land, resulting in the exodus of over two million Irish folk from their homeland, the majority never to see again the land of their birth. For many of these wretched, penniless and unfortunate people, fleeing from hunger and disease, Cóbh was their tragic last sight of their homeland. Between1848 and 1950 almost 6 million people emigrated from Ireland, 2.5 million from Cóbh alone.

A native of Ireland, Annie Moore, became the first ever emigrant to be 'processed' in Ellis Island, New York, America's reception centre for immigrants, following its opening on the 1st January 1892. She had sailed from Queenstown, with her two brothers, on the SS Nevada in December 1891. Annie travelled in steerage which was the cheapest form of sea transport and it

was an uncomfortable voyage. Statues of Annie can be found in both Cóbh and Ellis Island - symbolic of the privations suffered by countless Irish folk in their unhappy but optimistic quest for a new life.

In those less than

Ellis Island, New York

Arriving at Ellis Island, New York

assortment of crimes ranging from petty theft to murder, freeing Ireland of some overcrowding of its jails and providing much needed labour for the development of Australia.

The story of the liner *RMS Titanic* is known to most people and features in the history of Cóbh. *Titanic* was built at the Harland and Wolff shipyard in Belfast and was designed to compete with the rival Cunard Line's *Lusitania* and *Mauretania*. The ship began its maiden voyage from Southampton, bound for New York City on 10th April 1912. Captain Edward J. Smith was in command.

After crossing the English Channel, *Titanic* stopped at Cherbourg, France, to board additional passengers and stopped again the next day at Queenstown (Cóbh). Because harbour facilities at Queenstown were inadequate for a ship of *Titanic's* size it had to anchor off shore. Small boats or tenders ferried the passengers to and from the ship. When she finally set out for New York, there were 2,240 people aboard.

Queenstown was the final port of call for the liner during its fateful maiden voyage across the Atlantic to New York. One *SS Titanic* crew member, John Coffey, a 23 year old stoker, was from Cóbh but *'jumped ship'* by stowing away on one of the tenders; hiding amongst mailbags destined for Cóbh. He said later his reason for leaving the liner was because he had a foreboding about the voyage. He later signed on as on of the crew of *RMS Mauretania*. A total of 123 passengers embarked at Queenstown, the majority being in steerage (3rd class travel.) *Titanic* sailed to the mournful strains of *'Erin's Lament,'* played on the bagpipes by a passenger. The Titanic sank on 14th April 1912 after colliding with an iceberg about 100 miles south of the Grand Banks of Newfoundland.

halcyon days of the late Eighteenth and Nineteenth centuries, a period of ultra-harsh criminal punishment, transportation to foreign parts was a popular way of ridding a country, usually permanently, of unwanted felons. Cóbh was an important embarkation point for these malefactors, including females and even children. Many of the crimes were of a trivial nature. Petty theft was a common offence which resulted in transportation for a fixed term but sometimes for life if the offence was a serious one.

Records of transportations, usually to Britain's various penal colonies overseas, often in Australia, can be found in ships' logbooks of the time on a visit to Cóbh's restored Victorian Railway Station which serves as the town's principal Museum - 'The Queenstown Story.' The first convict ship to sail to Australia direct from Cóbh was the *'Queen'* in 1791 The *Queen* carried 159 prisoners sentenced for an

TITANIC DISASTER GREAT LOSS OF LIFE
EVENING NEWS

RMS Titanic

RMS Lusitania leaving New York

© Copyright Robert Blatchford Collection

Finally, to the most recent and unforgettable drama in Cóbh's history was the sinking of the *RMS Lusitania* on the 7th May 1915. The vessel was en route to Liverpool from New York. During the First World War, as Germany waged submarine warfare against Britain, after an uneventful crossing, the *Lusitania* the ship was identified about eleven miles off the Old Head of Kinsale, Ireland as it approached Queenstown. It was torpedoed by the German U-boat U-20 on 7th May 1915. Listing heavily it was difficult to launch lifeboats and the *Lusitania* sank in 300 feet of water in eighteen minutes. The ship sank killing 1,198 of the 1,959 people aboard (including the crew), leaving 761 survivors. The sinking turned public opinion in many countries against Germany, contributed to the American entry into World

War I and became an iconic symbol in military recruiting campaigns of why the war was being fought. Listing heavily it was difficult to launch lifeboats and the *Lusitania* sank in 300 feet of water. 1,198 people were drowned and the majority of bodies were never recovered. The survivors were accommodated in local Hospitals, boarding houses and private homes in Queenstown. A mass funeral of 150 victims was held three days after the tragedy and were buried in a mass grave in the old Church cemetery. Over half of these victims could not be identified.

German justification for the tragedy was that the *Lusitania* was suspected of carrying contraband in the form of munitions to aid the British War effort; though probably there was some truth in this claim it has never been proved.

It is to be hoped that the future of Cóbh will be much happier than its hitherto sad history and current events seem to confirm this as the town appears to be enoying a golden era of prosperity, with tourists flocking there from near and far, many from distant shores.

Anxious Crowds awaiting news of survivors from the RMS Luisitania outside the offices of the Cunard Steamship Company

© Copyright Robert Blatchford Collection

Terror on Easter Tuesday
chris paton

Although my mother's ancestors come from Ireland, my father's family connections to the island took a more scenic route to get there via Belgium and Scotland. Along the way they endured great hardship, and no sooner had they arrived in Belfast in the late 1930s than trouble was not far behind them.

My grandfather Charles Paton was born on 24th May 1905 in the Belgian capital of Brussels, the youngest of four children to two Scottish parents, Jessie MacFarlane from Inverness and David Hepburn Paton from Blackford. Despite a brief stay in Scotland from 1908 to 1911, the family then returned to Belgium, where my great grandfather managed a series of shoe shops for the Glasgow firm *R. & J. Dicks*. When the Germans marched into the city in August 1914 the Paton family was still present, with David having elected to stay in the country to protect his employers' interests. *'The war will be over by Christmas'* it was said, by a population not yet aware of the horrors to befall them over the next four years. Tragically the war did not end anything like as soon, and my family was to suffer greatly in the forthcoming occupation.

When an internment order was given out by the Germans in October 1914 for all British nationals aged between 18 and 45 to be arrested as *'enemy aliens,'* David was forced into hiding for sixteen months within the city. After enduring a long illness, brought about by the severe stress of his situation, he collapsed and died in April 1916. His body was tragically thrown out onto the street away from the safe house where he had been staying, in order that his hosts would not be identified by the authorities as collaborators. I have yet to discover where he was buried. This left Jessie to look after three of her children, the eldest son having managed to get back to Britain in time to sign up with the Royal Army Medical Corps, with which he served in Gallipoli.

In October of that same year my grandfather's brother John then turned 18. Now of age, he was arrested by the Germans and taken to Berlin, where he was interned for the rest of the war at the Ruhleben civilian prisoners of war camp - http://ruhleben.tripod.com - on the outskirts of the city. As inflation arose in the Belgian capital, it became increasingly difficult for Jessie to feed and look after her remaining two children. Letters held within the Foreign Office collections of the National Archives in London - www.nationalarchives.gov.uk - testify to the fact that my grandfather was *'ill with privation'* and show that my desperate great grandmother was barely able to cope. She soldiered on in her own way, fighting a mother's war, and after the hostilities had ended was finally able to make her way back to Scotland with her family.

Having survived the German occupation, my grandfather settled in Glasgow's Shettleston district and soon obtained work as a wireless salesman. In the early 1930s he met Jean Currie, the daughter of Robert Currie, a Glasgow Corporation worker from Knockloughrim parish in County Londonderry, and on 28th September 1934 the couple married. Post Office directories from Glasgow and Belfast then showed that the couple migrated over to Northern Ireland in 1936, settling at 40 Whitewell Crescent in Belfast.

As the family settled down to its new life in Ulster, the German war machine was slowly rebuilding itself under the imperial ambitions of its new Chancellor, Adolf Hitler. With the Nazis coming to power, an uneasy Britain soon realised that it would have to take the threat of a *'Third Reich'* seriously, but initially tried to appease the Germans. Chamberlain's famous piece of paper was then blown away by a wind of humiliation and the subsequent attacks on Poland, and the United Kingdom found itself at war once again in September 1939.

Charles had moved to Belfast to take up an opportunity to manage a wireless radio store for the Glasgow based Clydesdale Electrical firm, and at the start of the war he is listed in the 1939 National Register for

My Grandfather Charles Paton (right) outside his radio shop in Belfast, 1950s

My Grandmother Jean Currie Belfast 1938

My uncle Robert David Paton in Portsmouth

Northern Ireland as a branch manager residing at 40 Whitewell Crescent. This was a form of census drawn up at the start of the war for the purposes of creating a national identity scheme for wartime purposes, the details from which I was able to secure through a Freedom of Information Act enquiry made to the Public Record Office of Northern Ireland - www.proni.gov.uk - in early 2010. The Post Office directories for Belfast, as held at Belfast's Central Library - www.ni-libraries.net/libraries/belfast-central-library - further confirmed that Charles was a radio shop manager, but also showed that in 1942 the family had for some reason moved to number 42 the house next door.

In Northern Ireland, the story of the Second World War has not entered the public folk memory in the way that the sacrifices of the earlier war have, and as a child raised in the County Antrim based town of Carrickfergus I was certainly taught nothing about it at school. As far as I had known, Northern Ireland had not really experienced much of the war directly, and apart from hearing that American Rangers had been based in my home town of Carrickfergus for a

The chimney of Barn Mills in Carrickfergus, said to have been used by the Germans to navigate their way to Belfast

period, the only other tale that I remember encountering was one told to me once when I was out doing a newspaper delivery round. A conversation with one of my customers revealed that the Luftwaffe had apparently bombed Belfast during the war, using the tall chimney of the Barn Mills linen factory in Carrick as an aid to help them navigate their way along Belfast Lough towards the city. It was an interesting tale, but I never really paid much attention to it – sure the Blitz was that thing that happened in London, what would the Germans have wanted with us?!!

Of course, as I slowly worked my way through my family history research I recalled this story, and having realised by now that my family was actually residing in Belfast during the war, I decided to explore their story further. My grandparents are long dead, and I never got to meet my grandfather Charles. My father was not even born until a month after the war ended, so there was not much information that I could initially glean from either him or his siblings. The next best thing then was to do some background reading, and through eBay I had soon purchased a book by Brian Barton entitled 'The Blitz: Belfast in the War Years.' This fascinating account of Belfast's wartime experience soon confirmed that the Luftwaffe had indeed attacked the city during two separate and devastating raids, the first on Easter Tuesday 15th April 1941, and the second on 5th May. It became clear that the Northern Irish government had never considered the serious possibility of a German attack on the ports of Belfast or Londonderry, and that as a consequence, the civilian population was woefully ill prepared, with very few air raid shelters constructed. It was all very interesting, but did not seem very relevant to my particular story – until I reached page 109. Suddenly the hairs on the back of my neck were raised.

The book proclaimed the following simple statement: 'At Greencastle the raid erupted with dramatic suddenness and ferocity.' Greencastle, to the north of Belfast, is where Whitewell Crescent is situated. I then read with incredulity that the Germans had deployed parachute mines which had devastated Veryan Gardens and Vandyck Gardens, with over 130 homes destroyed or badly damaged. I grabbed a map of Belfast in my possession and soon discovered that Veryan Gardens was in fact the continuation of Whitewell Crescent, and that Vandyck Gardens was parallel to the road where my family lived. Could it be possible – had fate led my grandfather to yet another encounter with the Germans?

My eldest uncle, Robert, lives in Portsmouth in the south of England, and at the time of the raid was about two and

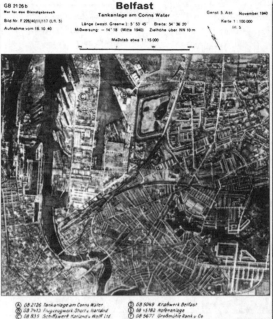

GB 21 26 b
Nur für den Dienstgebrauch

Belfast
Tankanlage am Conns Water

Genst 5. Abt.   November 1940

Bild Nr. F 228/40/II/117 (Lfl. 5)

Karte 1 : 100.000

Aufnahme vom 18. 10. 40

Länge (westl. Greenw.): 5° 53' 45"   Breite: 54° 36' 20"
Mißweisung: — 14° 18' (Mitte 1940)   Zielhöhe über NN 10 m

Inf. 5

Maßstab etwa 1 : 15.000

Ⓐ GB 2126 Tankanlage am Conns Water   Ⓓ GB 5049 Kraftwerk Belfast
Ⓑ GB 7413 Flugzeugwerk Short u. Harland   Ⓔ GB 4 5182 Hafenanlage
Ⓒ GB 835 Schiffswerft Harland u. Wolff Ltd   Ⓕ GB 5677 Großmühle Rank u Co

An aerial photograph of Belfast taken by the Luftwaffe

along the cobbled streets of Belfast towards a public shelter. Such was the panic in running down the street that my grandfather accidentally dropped Bob, who banged his head on the road as a result, and it was this that he remembered rather than German bombs blowing up all around him! After the Easter Tuesday raid, Bob also remembered how his parents took him and his baby brother Charlie out of the city every night for several weeks to sleep in a barn in the country, returning at dawn each day, a widespread practice that was known as *'ditching.'* Not long after the raid my family was able to move into number 42, next door to its former home.

With my uncle's limited recollection of the night, I posted a request on the excellent Belfast

Westbourne Street after the attack

a half years old. I immediately telephoned him to ask what he knew about it. *'Oh yes, our kid,'* he replied in a straightforward and matter of fact tone, *'our house was hit.'* What?!!

My heart nearly leapt into my mouth – I had been researching my family history for years, constantly asking questions, and not once had anybody mentioned this as being of any possible interest! I soon learned that my grandparents' house had suffered serious blast damage in the raid, although Bob's memories of the night were limited. He remembered his parents leading him and his baby brother out of the house before it was hit and

Forum website - www.belfastforum.co.uk - asking if anybody else had any memories from the event. Within a few days I received a message from a James Cassell, who not only remembered my family from Whitewell Crescent, but as an eleven year old boy had actually been inside his aunt's house at 2 Vandyck Gardens when its garden was hit by a parachute mine. The blast completely collapsed the house, but James and various members of his family survived, having been trapped inside an air pocket under a large oak table where they had sought shelter. He recalled that the night had been absolutely terrifying.

On the night of Easter Tuesday, well over 900 civilians were killed in Belfast, and 600 seriously injured. The Germans had

Salvaging possessions from damaged houses in Belfast

The Northern Whig coverage of the attack

The Northern Whig
AND BELFAST POST

BELFAST, THURSDAY, APRIL 17, 1941

200 FEARED DEAD IN NORTHERN IRELAND BLITZ

Germans Claim Attack Heavy As Any Launched On British Ports

"HUNDREDS OF BOMBERS" LEAVE BELFAST STREETS IN RUINS

Young Men Rush to Join Up

Belfast Hospital Blitzed

5 ENEMY SUPPLY SHIPS, 3 DESTROYERS ANNIHILATED
TRIPOLI CONVOY FIGHT

BELFAST TELEGRAPH, TUESDAY, APRIL 8, 1941.

ULSTER AT CLOSE QUARTERS WITH WAR
North's First Blitz: Night Of Thrills

MANY H.E. AND FIRE BOMBS DROPPED
Two A.F.S. Men Victims

A plaque on Belfast Telegraph building today recalls how the newspaper proudly published 'without interruption' during the Blitz.

One of the most famous images of the Belfast blitz – Arnott's Department Store in flames

Lower Donegall Street after the attack

mistakenly hit a heavily populated residential estate rather than their intended target, the city's harbour. They made no such mistake in May, when a second wave of bombing created a huge firestorm that utterly devastated the docks.

Many in the north have long complained of the neutrality of the Irish Free State during the Second World War, but as with many areas of life, nothing is ever quite so black and white. In Belfast's moment of crisis, the Dublin based government in fact ordered thirteen fire engines across the border to help extinguish the fires. Sean Kelly, a fireman from the south and a former republican activist, was asked later why he had done so. His response was simple: *'the people of Belfast were Irishmen too.'* Across the city, many folk from both the Protestant and Catholic communities shared air raid shelters together and

sang many hymns, as old differences were temporarily forgotten during the raids. Yet for the southern government, there was a tragic price to pay for its actions, when on 31st May 1941 a series of bombs were dropped by the Luftwaffe across Dublin, killing 23 people and injuring 145. Hitler claimed it was *'an error,'* but the popular belief was that this was a punitive raid against the Irish Free State for the breach of its neutrality.

In the north, Belfast was not the only area to be attacked, with Londonderry also seeing much damage eventually Hitler redirected his efforts towards his eastern front. Although the iconic images of history show London bearing the brunt of the Blitz attacks in England, Ireland too paid its price, both in the north and the south. The island's sufferings in the 1941 raids should equally never be forgotten.

chris paton's
essential guide to online irish resources

There is so much that you need to see but can't get to - *'the records were all destroyed in the civil war'* - and for good measure, it rains a lot in Ireland! There can be any number of excuses, but in fact researching your Irish Ancestry is getting easier by the day, as more and more material is making its way online. The following article provides a handy ready reckoner for some of the best sites to help get you started with your Irish research.

Vital records

Civil registration of births, marriages and deaths commenced in 1864 in Ireland, with the exception of non-Catholic marriages, which started earlier in 1845. Each record was indexed locally and then copies sent to the General Register Office in

Dublin, where a national register was compiled. From 1922 a separate GRO was set up in Belfast for Northern Ireland. GRO records from 1864-1958 are indexed online free at www.familysearch.org and include records for the Republic throughout this period, and for the counties of Northern Ireland up to 1922 although there are some later entries.

There are three main sites where you can then order copies of the original birth, marriage and death records. For the Republic, the General Register Office of Ireland is the cheapest

at www.groireland.ie, as you can order photocopies of original records for just €6, though you need to fax or post your application form through. To purchase records online for the south, you can do so through the Health Service Executive at www.hse.ie/eng/services/Find_a_Service/bdm/Certificates_ie/ but you will have to buy original certificates at €10 each plus €1 postage. On the plus side, this site takes credit card payments. For Northern Ireland, up to Partition the best bet is to use the GRO Ireland site, though after 1922 you will need to use the Northern Irish GRO at www.groni.gov.uk, which sadly charges the highest rate for certificates in the United Kingdom, at £14 per record, plus postage.

The Irish Family History Foundation's pay per view based Roots Ireland website at www.rootsireland.ie hosts records for most counties in Ireland, ranging from church and civil registration based records to census and other records. The offerings for each county vary so do check the sources information for each collection. Transcripts cost €5 each, but if you do a parent search for birth/baptismal records, you will find discounts are added for the more children found per family, so they can be as cheap as €2 each. If you have ancestors from Kerry, Carlow, Cork or Dublin try the alternative Irish genealogy website at www.irishgenealogy.ie as hosted by the Irish Government where you will find free transcriptions of mainly Roman Catholic and Church of Ireland records. An alternative for Northern Ireland is the Emerald Ancestors subscription based site at www.emeraldancestors.com hosting detailed indexes for many records for a basic subscription of £10 a month. Full details will cost a bit more through the purchase of additional transcripts.

Do not forget Ireland's connection to the United Kingdom, as your ancestors may well have been born in Britain. The UK version of FindmyPast - www.findmypast.co.uk - hosts birth, marriage and death indexes from 1837, as well as various British overseas indexes which include Irish entries within army chaplaincy records, consular returns etc. Digitised Scottish BMD records can be accessed at www.scotlandspeople.gov.uk, which also includes the Bishopric of the Forces Roman Catholic records for the whole of the United Kingdom.

Burials

This is a real online growth industry in Ireland just now! The Irish Genealogy Project Archives pages at www.igp-web.com include photos of many cemeteries, such as Mount Jerome in Dublin, whilst the pay per view Glasnevin Cemetery site at www.glasnevintrust.ie/genealogy lists burials from

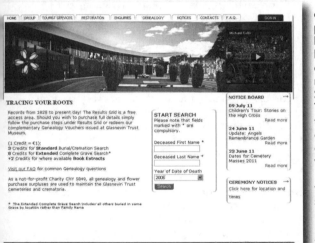

1828 to present day. The impressive Irish Graveyards - www.irishgraveyards.ie - is rapidly photographing graveyards across the island. In the north, History from Headstones - www.historyfromheadstones.com - offers a pricey way to search for Ulster based inscriptions at £4 each, but Belfast City Council's new site at www.belfastcity.gov.uk/burialrecords/search.asp offers free access to burial records for the city's three council run burial grounds, City Cemetery, Dundonald and Roselawn, with entries as far back as 1868.

Censuses

The 1901 and 1911 censuses for all of Ireland can be freely accessed at www.census.nationalarchives.ie, whilst some surviving pre-1901 census fragments have survived, with many accessible via www.censusfinder.com/ireland.htm and Roots Ireland (see above). A slightly less well known resource is the set of copies from the 1841 and 1851 censuses which were created to back up

pension applications after 1908, when those over 70 could claim a state pension for the first time. It is a bit hit and miss, but if you find an entry, the whole household may well be included in addition to the applicant. The best place to search for these is www.ireland-genealogy.com and also through Ancestry.co.uk's Irish pages.

Although most census records from 1821-1891 were destroyed, there are many census substitutes. As well as the Census Finder website, another site to check for these is that for Griffith's Valuation at www.askaboutireland.ie/griffith-valuation/index/xml which lists the rateable value of land across the island as worked out between 1847 and 1864. Heads of households only, but better than nothing!

Maps and Gazetteers

Finding out where your ancestor lived may be only half of the battle – working out where the place actually was may be a bigger challenge! To help, the Ordnance Survey of Northern Ireland at https://maps.osni.gov.uk carries both historic and current maps for the country (though you will need to register), and the modern Irish Ordnance Survey for the south is available at www.osi.ie. The principle land division in Ireland was the townland, and Historic Irish townland maps are online at www.pasthomes.com, with the locations of various townlands listed on databases at both www.seanruad.com and www.ulsterancestry.com.

Further old maps for Ulster can be found at www.ulsterancestry.com/free-ulster-maps.html, and others at www.failteromhat.com, including a map of the Irish Free State, and a road map of the island from 1877. Geograph Ireland - www.geograph.ie - is also trying to photograph every square kilometre of the island, with the results accessible via an interactive map. For Irish poor law union maps visit

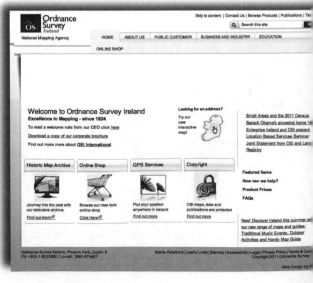

www.movinghere.org.uk/deliveryfiles/PRO/MFQ1_925/0/1.pdf.

To understand the history of a place on the island, try the *Parliamentary Gazetteer of Ireland* from 1844-45 on Google Books - http://tinyurl.com/ykrzc8h - If you need to switch between the Irish and English equivalents of place names, or are just unsure how to pronounce the name of a place, visit the Placenames Database of Ireland site at www.logainm.ie.

Archives

The Public Record Office of Northern Ireland - www.proni.gov.uk - has arguably the best online site for digitised collections, all available free. The PRONI site hosts half a million signatures to the 1912 Ulster Covenant, freeholders records, forty street directories from the north (also check www.lennonwylie.co.uk for more from 1805-1913), wills calendars entries and surviving wills from 1858-1943, a name search database with pre-1858 wills, census returns and coroners reports and more. If you are planning to visit PRONI in Belfast, two other useful sections on the site are the online guides (such as the downloadable PRONI Guide to Church Listings), and the catalogue with some one and a half million entries for items held at the archive.

With the exception of the 1901 and 1911 census site described earlier, the National Archives of Ireland site is not quite so well developed at www.nationalarchives.ie in terms of online databases, though does have some useful databases such as *Famine Relief Commission Papers* from 1845-47, an *Ireland-Australia Transportation Database* and another cataloguing records from the first Dáil from 1919-24.

The National Library of Ireland - www.nli.ie - has the impressive *Sources* catalogue from its manuscripts collections and periodicals, as well as a major photography database. The *eResources* page is particularly worthy of notes, listing items

which can be accessed within the building, such as various newspaper collections and more, and which is also hoped to be made available remotely to registered users in due course. The Family History section is also a vital area to consult at www.nli.ie/en/intro/family-history-introduction.aspx, particularly the *What We Have* section where you will find lists of Roman Catholic parish registers as held at the library in microfilm format. A list of newspapers held at the facility can also be found at www.nli.ie/en/catalogues-and-databases-printed-newspapers.aspx.

Again, don't forget the UK's National Archives site at www.nationalarchives.gov.uk, which holds various military and merchant seamen records via its Documents Online section. Plans are currently afoot to make available various Irish collections including Royal Irish Constabulary records and various items relating to the War of Independence.

Newspapers

There are many online newspaper archives site which can help with your research, such as the subscription based Irish Times - www.irishtimes.com/search - and Irish Newspaper Archives - www.irishnewsarchives.com - which holds digitised copies mainly of titles from the south.

The 19th Century British Library Newspaper Archive at http://newspapers.bl.uk/blcs contains copies of the Belfast Newsletter and The Freeman's Journal (Dublin based), and keep an eye out for FindmyPast's new project with the British Library at www.britishnewspaperarchive.co.uk, a major ten year digitisation project, which promises further offerings.

Also available for the north is Eddie Connolly's amazing newspaper intimations site at http://freepages.genealogy.rootsweb.ancestry.com/

~econnolly/, whilst free to access copies of the state based title The Belfast Gazette from 1922 can be found at www.belfast-gazette.co.uk. Although the earlier Dublin Gazette is not yet online, its replacement of *Iris Oifigiúil* partially is at www.irisoifigiuil.ie, although with an archive from 2002 only at present.

Commercial vendors

The Scottish based company Brightsolid and Dublin based Eneclann have recently set up a

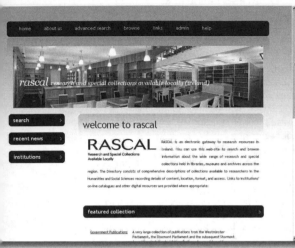

new Irish records site at www.findmypast.ie, essentially an Irish version of the British based FindmyPast.co.uk but with a completely separate set of records. Much of the material on the site has previously been made available through sites such as Irish Origins at www.irishorigins.net, but if you have used that site before and exhausted its records, don't let that deter you – as FindmyPast.ie is going to grow like the plague is in town, with various new and original datasets including land records, prison registers and more. Don't forget FindmyPast.co.uk also, particularly for military records, as digitised service records from 1760-1913 are available on the site, with British

military discharge records from Kilmainham Hospital coming in due course.

Ancestry.com is a worldwide player, with a British domain at www.ancestry.co.uk. Although there is no separate Irish domain, there is a relatively new gateway to its Irish collections at www.ancestry.co.uk/irish which splits several collections into pages for Northern Ireland and the Republic of Ireland. It is worth checking the pages for both jurisdictions, however, as some records which should be all Ireland based have curiously either been listed within one page or the other only! Ancestry also has a whole host of migration, military and other records sets in the main site itself, and will provide hours of fun in the exploration.

Other sources

There is of course a great deal more available online. To try to find more targeted resources for your particular area try the free to access 'gateway' sites such as the multilayered GENUKI - www.genuki.com; Cyndi's List - www.cyndislist.com; Fianna - www.rootsweb.ancestry.com/~fianna/county/index 1.html; Irish Ancestors - www.irishtimes.com/ancestor/browse/counties; From Ireland - www.from-ireland.net - and the Irish Genealogical Project - www.igp-web.com

For archival holdings at a local level in libraries, museums and archives, the Research and Special Collections Available Locally database, or 'RASCAL', can also help at www.rascal.ac.uk.

Scottish based family historian Chris Paton is the author of
"Tracing Your Family History on the Internet"
Pubished 2011 Pen and Sword
www.pen-and-sword.co.uk/?product_id=2974

The Irish Potato Famine
Brian Parnaby

In these days of plenty most people pay only cursory attention to the starving millions of Africa. Disregarding the upheaval of populations and subsequent horrors caused by the World Wars, it has been too easy to forget that a similar scenes to the present day tragedies in Africa were a common sight in a in the Nineteenth century. This was especially true in Ireland.

Ireland had been ruled by Britain for centuries. It was small industrially and but had large agricultural areas controlled by absentee British landlords employing 'Agents.' In the 19th Century, the majority of Ireland's people were generally poor and relied on a subsistence economy to survive.

In the early part of the 19th century, the Irish Landlords enjoyed profitable returns from their lands because prices for agricultural produce were high. Europe at the time was in a state of turmoil because of frequent hostilities involving France, Britain and Spain. Following Napoleon Bonaparte's defeat at the Battle of Waterloo in 1815, by the Duke of Wellington, competition increased when the countries of Europe, especially France, once again flourished. Prices for agricultural produce fell and recession loomed.

In desperation the Landowners and their Agents, who had originally subdivided their estates into small arable plots leased to tenants, realised that the solution to their economic problems was to dispossess the tenancy and convert the lands seized into larger grazing areas. They could then concentrate on cattle rearing as opposed to agricultural produce. The barrier to doing this was the question of what to do with the dispossessed tenants. In their heartlessness the Landlords had a simple remedy - eviction. They went about their tasks with enthusiasm, even though many of the tenants were up to date with their rent. Even their squalid huts were destroyed, thus depriving them, not only of a means to earn money, but also of roofs over their heads. The country rapidly became crowded with nomadic jobless and homeless people who wandered the land begging scraps to enable them to survive.

The 'Absentee' Landlords rarely visited their Irish properties. They gave free rein to their Agents to manage the properties as they wished, with the sole proviso that they maximised profits from their lands, paying scant regard to the welfare of their Irish tenants. Indeed, many of these peasants neither knew, nor cared to know, the identity of the person they toiled for and only knew unceasing back breaking toil.

This recession continued for years. The majority of the population were penniless and roofless whilst the minority lived in affluence. The hatred for the latter rapidly grew amongst the indigenous population and several secret societies came into being, amongst whose aims were the overthrow of the British whom they blamed for bringing their land and peoples into poverty. These societies – the Thrashers (Connaught), Ribbonmen (Munster) and Whitefoots (Queen's County) among them – began a long campaign of harassment and violence against the Landlords and succeeded in frightening them physically and harming them financially. The actions by these societies did little to alleviate the plight of the desperately poor. Many of the crimes committed by members of these secret organisations were of a trivial nature but the punishments were severe and sometimes meant transportation for life.

Life in Ireland continued like that for several years with people routinely dying of starvation and associated diseases. Despite the efforts of a number of caring British men and women to relieve the suffering and who cajoled the government into helping. However, much worse was to come.

The staple diet of the Irish people was the potato which was consumed in nearly every household especially in rural areas. Indeed, even today, the medical profession maintain that it is one of the most nutritious of foods. It has been said that one must peel a potato, boil it, peel it, then throw away the inside and eat the cooked skin which contains all the nutrients necessary for a person's daily intake. There had been warnings for some years that this

185

The Workhouse, Clifden, County Galway 1847

total dependency on the potato would have serious health and survival ramifications should the annual potato crop fail in Ireland. The warnings were ignored.

Prior to the famine years, an average worker ate between seven and fifteen pounds of potatoes every day, a colossal amount. The eating habits were, to say the least, of a basic nature. Families would boil the potatoes in a pot, drain off the water and tip the potatoes into a basket. Placing the basket on the floor between them the family would then eat their meal, dipping their potatoes into a nearby bowl of salt water or just salt. This most rudimentary method of eating was termed *'dip at the stool.'* Buttermilk or skimmed milk would complement the meal. This meal was constant regardless of whether it was breakfast, lunch or dinner, assuming of course that families observed these mealtimes, which is doubtful. A rather bizarre practice was that people would allow one thumbnail to grow very long so they could peel the potato. Knives were scarce. There must have been much goodness in this most basic of diets as Irish *'navvies'* (navigators) were in great demand in England during the Industrial Revolution, where their skills with pick and shovel were legendary during the building of England's great railway system in the 19th century.

An important reason for the popularity of the potato as the staple crop in Ireland was because a subsistence farmer could grow three times the amount of potatoes on his piece of land as he could grow grain. One acre of land devoted to potato growing could support a large family for a year. Nearly half of Ireland's people relied on the potato crop for survival.

In the summer of 1845 disaster struck! Blight affected the potato plants that year, and half of the expected annual crop was totally ruined, the remainder being only partially recoverable. Shortly after having been dug from the ground, the potatoes turned black and rotted immediately. Various explanations were given for the cause of this blight. Some of the more ridiculous reasons given were that it was the result of *'static electricity'* or caused by the smoke from railway engines. The most ridiculous of these theories must be the claim that the cause of the blight was *'mortiferous vapours'* (a word not now found in modern dictionaries but obviously indicating gangrenous or mortifying flesh) rising from underground volcanoes.

The actual cause of the potato blight was the fungus *Phytophthora infestan* which had arrived in Ireland in 1845 from Mexico (via America) in a consignment of bad tubers. It quickly spread because the organism multiplies rapidly in temperatures above 10° Centigrade and where relative humidity is above 90% - these conditions permit the exposed surface of the plant to remain wet. It rains a lot in Ireland!

The following year, 1846 was even more disastrous. Virtually all of the potato crops were ruined and was followed by the harshest winter in living memory. A third disastrous failure occurred in 1847 and the nation faced utter starvation. Reports abounded of wholesale cases of what was termed *'Famine Fever.'* Numerous cases of cholera, typhus, dysentery and scurvy occurred and the infant mortality rate soared. Bodies were hastily buried sometimes only a few inches beneath the soil surface because relatives were too physically weak to dig proper graves.

Thus began the first wave of emigrants to foreign parts, mostly to Canada, who begged, borrowed or stole the fare necessary for their escape. The emigrants travelled steerage and were often in unseaworthy vessels and in vile conditions. Naturally, because of this mass emigration to the New World, the people of

Bridget O'Donnel and her Children.
'. . . we were put out last November; we owed some rent. I was at this time lying in fever . . . they commenced knocking down the house, and had half of it knocked down when two neighbours, women, Nell Spellesley and Kate How, carried me out . . . I was carried into a cabin, and lay there for eight days, when I had the creature (the child) born dead. I lay for three weeks after that. The whole of my family got the fever, and one boy thirteen years old died with want and with hunger while we were lying sick.'
Illustrated London News, December 22, 1849

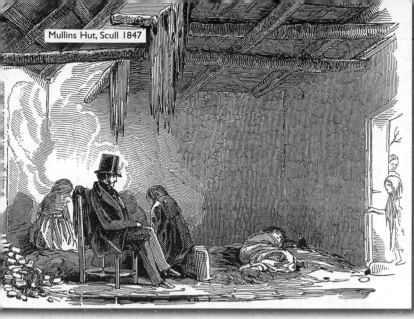
Mullins Hut, Scull 1847

instead use the funds to start an uprising. Even the supply of food through 'soup kitchens' (a common practice in deprived areas of Britain, usually financed by well meaning philanthropists) was not at first countenanced by the government. Their reasoning being the Irish would become accustomed to 'free food' and they would never become self sufficient. However by the spring of 1847 the government relented and soup kitchens were set up in Ireland.

The system of 'Workhouses' spread throughout Ireland. They had originally been introduced prior to 1840 to 'help' the poor and dispossessed. It is estimated that almost two and a half million Irish folk entered these grim institutions, of which a total of almost 10% died whilst in residence.

The famine continued through 1847, until other countries, especially the United States, began to take a strong interest in the famine in Ireland. The Religious Society of Friends – The Quakers offered to send supplies of food to feed the starving poor in Ireland.

The Government agreed to this generous offer only on the understanding that any food supplied by America would be first landed in England, transhipped to British vessels and then forwarded to Ireland. The reasoning behind this absurd and delaying tactic was allegedly to ensure that British ships could then be employed in the procedure. The American Press took full advantage of this foolish demand by questioning the motivation of the British in deliberately 'stalling' delivery of the desperately needed supplies whilst their own countrymen were starving. Shamed by this disclosure the British backed down and American ships were allowed to sail direct to Irish ports to discharge their cargoes.

During 1849, whilst Ireland was in the throes of attempting a recovery from the disastrous famine Queen Victoria made a State visit to Ireland, her ship landing at Cork (Cóbh) harbour. There was much pomp and ceremony with large displays of flags and bunting and massed bands playing. Queen Victoria though sympathetic to the recent plight of her Irish subjects was viewed as the head of a country hostile to the needs and care of its people. One man, William Kindles of Cork, endeared himself to the Irish people

those countries quickly heard of the disasters that had befallen the Irish.

Paradoxically, despite the failure in three successive years of the potato crop, other crops flourished, as did the cattle industry. Wheat and oats, beef, mutton, pork and poultry were plentiful and one would imagine that the loss of the potato crops, whilst damaging, would be offset by the plenitude of these other items. The availability of these products, absolutely necessary for survival, would have alleviated the disaster facing the Irish people; but this was not the case in respect of the poor and needy who had little or no money to purchase even the cheapest of scraps of food. There were some instances of generosity by the landlords but these were few and far between.

In 1846 the Corn Laws were repealed. These laws had stifled free trade and their repeal put an end to the protectionism that grain producing farmers had enjoyed for many years. The repeal did not relieve the famine in Ireland because the Irish were too poor to purchase grain as a substitute for the potato. Despite pleas from influential Irish sympathisers there was a refusal to supply relief in the form of money. The generally accepted reason for this refusal was the Government's view that should they supply money to the Irish to purchase food they would

Funeral - Skibbereen 1847

Copyright Robert Blatchford Collection

187

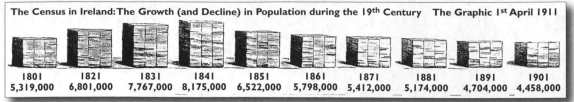

The Census in Ireland: The Growth (and Decline) in Population during the 19th Century   The Graphic 1st April 1911

1801	1821	1831	1841	1851	1861	1871	1881	1891	1901
5,319,000	6,801,000	7,767,000	8,175,000	6,522,000	5,798,000	5,412,000	5,174,000	4,704,000	4,458,000

by cutting the ropes to a flagpole where a giant Union flag had been hoisted on the Royal route, thus collapsing it. Kindles decamped to America very shortly afterwards.

Nonetheless, during the Queen's visit to this still impoverished part of her Empire, no expense was spared in lavish entertainment in the way of food and drink for the important personages attending the functions. Banquets were held, costing thousands of Pounds whilst hundreds and thousands of Victoria's subjects were still starving and where one U.S. dollar could maintain a family of six people for a whole week.

The Duke of Leinster, one of the few caring Landowners, who owned huge tracts of land 'went public' with his concerns over this profligate spending, questioning as to how and why the Government could spend such huge amounts of money at the time. There is a story that the Queen donated only a few Pounds to the famine relief but this has been denied and she is believed to have donated several thousand Pounds to the fund.

It has since been estimated that between three quarters of a million people and one and a half million people died as a direct or indirect result of the Irish Potato famine and its aftermath (many of them from 'Famine Fever') and one to two million more people emigrated to seek a better life – they could not have found a worse one elsewhere! By 1851 the population of Ireland had been reduced from its estimated peak of 8.5 million in 1845 to just over 6 million, a drop of approximately 25%. Even by the beginning of the twentieth century the country had still not made up its original highest number.

The emigrants left behind them a land denuded of a vast number of its citizens, gone forever, many of them destined never again to see the land of their birth. It is to their great credit that the majority of Irish people living in far off lands such as the United States, Canada, South Africa and Australia have never lost their love for their homeland. Irish societies proliferate throughout their new homelands and Irish songs and dances have been absorbed into the national culture of these countries.

Although the potato famine could not have been avoided and was not caused by any deliberate act or omission by the Government the subsequent inaction to provide proper relief to the population affected by the famine changed irrevocably Ireland and led to the mass emigration to all parts of the world.

Further Reading:
The Great Hunger 1845-49 Cecil Woodham-Smith Pub 1995 **ISBN:** 978-0880293853
The Famine in Ireland Mary E. Daly - Dundalgan Press (W.Tempest) Ltd 1986 ISBN: 978-0852211083
This Great Calamity: The Irish Famine 1845-52 Christine Kineal(l)y Pub 1994 ISBN: 978-0717118816
The Great Irish Famine Canon John O'Rourke - Originally published 1874 reproduced 2007 (Paperback) ISBN: 978-1426479915
Websites
John Sharp - Whitefoot from the Queen's County, Ireland http://members.pcug.org.au/~pdownes/sharp/index.htm#disturbances
Ribbonmen - http://en.wikipedia.org/wiki/Ribbonism

Pat Macnamara's Cabin Village of Clear

188 CABIN OF PAT. MACNAMARA, VILLAGE OF CLEAR,

The Famine Memorial Dublin

Irish Family History Society
Mary Beglan

The Irish Family History Society was established in 1984 and is based in Ireland with a worldwide membership. The Society is for those who are looking to trace their Irish Roots. The IFHS is a voluntary, non-profit making organisation.

The objectives of the Irish Family History Society are:

To promote the study of Irish family history and genealogy.

To promote the preservation, security and accessibility of archival material.

To advise all those interested in seeking their Irish roots.

To encourage the repatriation of information from overseas on Irish emigrants.

To collaborate with and support other societies with similar aims.

The Irish Family History Society is a member of the Council of Irish Genealogical Organisations, Federation of Local History Societies and an associate member of the Federation of Family History Societies.

The Society arranges a number of lectures and seminars throughout the year which are held at Dublin City Library & Archive, 138/144 Pearse Street, Dublin 2. The Annual General Meeting is held each April and is followed by 2 guest speakers. A full day seminar is held in early October and a morning seminar in November. Our various guest speakers cover a wide range of topics and are always very popular.

One of our objectives is to help members to do their own research through information and advice. We are pleased to help members by accessing any information we hold as well as helping them to locate the information required to further their ancestral research.

Society Website www.ifhs.ie

In 2009 the Society's new website was launched. The website provides news and information about the Society, its committee members, meetings and outings, Library Index Listings as well as Book and CD Reviews and a listing of useful Web links. The News page includes items of interest about the Society and developments in Irish Genealogy both at home and abroad. Members are encouraged to view the News Section of the Society's website on a regular basis to keep up to date with family history happenings. Members and non-members can keep up to date with details of the Society's meetings and outings as these are published online as soon as details have been finalised. Occasionally we are able to include a copy of the speaker's handout in the members' area. This is of

Irish Family History Society

The Irish Family History Society was established in 1984 and is based in Ireland with a worldwide membership.

Membership of the Society runs from 1st January to 31st December and includes a copy of the Society's annual journal *Irish Family History*. Annual subscription is €25 and can be paid by cheque or online at the Society's website via PayPal. Society publications are also available to purchase direct or online.

Our meetings are held in April, October and November at Dublin City Library & Archive, 138/144 Pearse St., Dublin 2.

The Irish Family History Society is a member of the Council of Irish Genealogical Organisations, Federation of Local History Societies and an associate member of the Federation of Family History Societies.

The Society can be contacted by:
Mail: P.O. Box 36, Naas, Co. Kildare, Ireland
E-mail: ifhs@eircom.net
Website: www.ifhs.ie

particular benefit to those members who are unable to attend our meetings. Our Members' Area includes current Members' Interests, past News Sheets, Members' Queries and Articles and much more. Access to the Members' Area is by password only, which is available to all paid up members.

Society Publications

The Society publishes an annual journal each December a copy of which is included in the annual membership. Members contribute articles for inclusion in the journal. The journal is also available for non-members to purchase. Copies of most of our past journals are available to purchase and can be purchased online via PayPal or by cheque to the Society. A list of articles in each journal can be viewed on our website. Selected past journals are available to be purchased under a *'Bundle Offer.'* To check availability please visit the Society's website www.ifhs.ie.

As well as its annual journal, the Society has also published *Table of Church of Ireland Parochial Records*. The Society is currently working on producing an updated version of this publication and expects to publish it over the next 12 months.

Membership

Membership of the Society runs from 1st January to 31st December. New members are always very welcome. Our annual subscription for all members irrespective of country of residence is €25. Payment can be made in own currency by personal cheque and rates are UK members STG £20, Australian members AUD €35, Canadian members CAD $35, New Zealand members NZD $45, USA members USD $34. Airmail is included for all overseas members. Enquiries can be posted to P. O. Box 36, Naas, Co. Kildare or by email to ifhs@eircom.net. An application form can also be downloaded from the Society's website www.ifhs.ie. Application for membership and renewal of existing membership can also be made online by Credit Card at www.ifhs.ie via Paypal. New members receive a Welcome Pack upon joining which includes copies of the previous year's News Sheet, Membership list and Members' Interest List.

Benefits of membership

Membership includes a copy of the Irish Family History journal which is published in December, the Spring and Autumn News Sheets containing up to-date Society information, members' queries, and a membership list. The Society's website also includes a Member's only area.

Activities

The Society had a very successful stand at the first "Back to Our Past" show held in the RDS, Dublin in October 2010. Here we met many of our members and welcomed new members. Over the 3 days those manning the stand gave advice to the public about finding their ancestors and what records are available to them and hopefully helped to break down some *'brick walls.'*

In July 2010 the Society was honoured to receive an invitation from President Mary McAleese to attend a Garden Party held on 8th July 2010 for various organisations which operate on a voluntary basis. Our chairman, Gerry P. Cahill, accompanied by seven committee members attended the event at Áras an Uachtaráin.

Irish Research

Interest in tracing Irish ancestors has grown a great deal over the past 5 years or so. More and more Irish records are being placed online, either for free or on a subscription basis, thereby making the records more accessible to those living in Ireland and abroad. Many are now finding that they have Irish ancestors of which they were previously unaware. The release online of the UK 1901 and 1911 censuses identified previously unknown Irish connections and this has resulted in many people from the UK visiting Ireland in an effort to trace their Irish roots. With many records worldwide now available online it is possible to sit at your computer in the comfort of your own home and follow your ancestors' roots to places using passenger lists and census records in particular.

One of the myths about Irish research is that all or most Irish records were destroyed in the Four Courts bombing of 1922. While it is true that many records of interest to genealogists were destroyed much has survived. Many important sources were destroyed including Wills and Church of Ireland records. Census records for the years 1821-1851 were also destroyed while those for 1861-1891 had earlier been destroyed on Government orders.

When starting on your Irish research take the time to go through any family papers such as old family birth or marriage certificates, any newspaper clippings and memorial cards. Also talk to older members of your family who will likely have useful information about earlier ancestors.

The 1901 and 1911 censuses are the only extant censuses available. These are available to view free online at www.census.nationalarchives.ie. Now it is possible to find ancestors in these censuses without the need to know the exact address as previously required. The census return will include details of name, age, marital status, and place of birth of each member of the household who was there on the night the census was taken. The 1911 census also asked married women how many years they had been married, how many children were born alive and how many were still living. The website also includes detailed articles about Ireland in the early 20th century for Dublin and Belfast among others.

The indexes for civil records of births, marriages and deaths are available to search at the General Register Office Research Room, Lower Abbey Street, Dublin 2. Indexes up to c1950 for Republic of Ireland and c1922 for

The Society attended to attend a Garden Party given by
President Mary McAleese held at Áras an Uachtaráin on 8th July 2010.
Left to right - Joan Sharkey, Gerry Cahill, Patricia Moorhead, Dr. Martin McAleese, Richard Flatman
President Mary McAleese, John Dyer, Bernadette Murray, John Heueston and Mary Beglan

Northern counties are available on microfilm at Latter Day Saints (LDS) libraries worldwide. Check your local LDS library for details. The indexes up to 1958 for Republic of Ireland and Northern counties up to 1922 are available to search online at www.familysearch.org.

www.irishgenealogy.ie has an extensive database available to view for free. These include Roman Catholic, Church of Ireland and Presbyterian records, many with images. See the website for details of coverage.

www.rootsireland.ie is a pay for view site which includes databases of church records and civil records for various heritage centres throughout Ireland. The initial search is free. See the website for details of coverage available.

Griffith's Valuation is a further useful source. It was carried out for tax purposes and published between 1847 and 1864 and lists those who owned or leased property. It includes details of each holding and from whom the property was leased. It is available to view for free on www.askaboutireland.ie

Griffith's Valuation is also available on the recently launched website www.FindMyPast.ie on a subscription basis. FindMyPast.ie includes many other databases such as Landed Estate Court

Rentals and Trade Directories.

The National Library www.nli.ie and National Archives www.nationalarchives.ie provide extensive information on researching Irish records. An online catalogue for the National Library is now available online.

For those with Northern Ireland Roots, the Public Records Office of Northern Ireland (PRONI) will be of particular interest. Their website www.proni.gov.uk includes a number of free online sources including Will Calendars and Street Directories.

Members of the Irish Family History Society can be helped in their Irish research by attending our many informative seminars where they will also meet like minded people and can discuss research issues with fellow members. For those unable to attend our meetings the committee will be pleased to provide assistance and advice to enable you to further your ancestral research.

© Copyright Robert Blatchford Collection

Tracing Army Ancestry at The Imperial War Museum
sarah paterson ma, diplib

Where to Find Army Service Records

The key piece of information you need to know is the unit that an individual served with (it is a sad fact that those who died during the world wars will be easier to trace than those who survived, and this information is readily obtainable from the Commonwealth War Graves Commission). The personal service record should be your starting point, but many First World War files were lost or damaged by bombing in 1940. Records are located according to an individual's date of discharge.

The Imperial War Museum only covers the period from the First World War onwards. The National Army Museum, Royal Hospital Road, Chelsea, London SW3 4HT (Tel: 020 7730 0717; W: www.national-army-museum.ac.uk) has information on military history from 1485 to date. Pre-1914 service records are held at The National Archives, Ruskin Avenue, Kew, Richmond, Surrey TW9 4DU (Tel: 020 8876 3444; Website: www.nationalarchives.gov.uk).

The National Archives (TNA), formerly Public Record Office, also holds all surviving First World War service records for officers who left the Army before 1922. These are held in record classes *WO 339* and *WO 374*, and you can now check the index to these online. Surviving First World War service records for other ranks who ceased service before 1920 are now held at TNA (unfortunately large numbers of these were destroyed by bombing in the Second World War). These can now be accessed online through the subscription based website www.ancestry.co.uk The publication *First World War Army Service Records* by William Spencer (4th Edition Pub The National Archives 2008) is essential reading for those interested in First World War records, and you can find many useful research guides on the website.

The records of any First World War soldier who saw service after the cut-off dates detailed above or who rejoined the Army, and those who served in the Second World War, are held

© Copyright Robert Blatchford Collection

an almost complete set of these from 1914 to 2007, when it ceased to be published in hard copy.

Casualty Records

The Commonwealth War Graves Commission, 2 Marlow Road, Maidenhead, Berkshire SL6 7DX (Tel: 01628 507200) has details of all service personnel who died between the dates 4 August 1914-31 August 1921 and 3 September 1939-31 December 1947. The Commonwealth War Graves Commission (CWGC) may charge a fee for postal enquiries, but the website containing their computerised database, *Debt of Honour*, can be consulted at www.cwgc.org

The new Armed Forces Memorial website has a roll of honour that allows you to search for Army personnel who died after 1948. This can be found at www.veterans-uk.info/amf2/index.php

Details of service personnel buried in 'non-World War' graves are available from the JCCC (Joint Casualty and Compassionate Centre), SPVA (Service Personnel and Veterans Agency), Innsworth House, Imjin Barracks, Innsworth, Gloucester GL3 1HW. Please mark your enquiry *'Graves Casework.'*

Sources held by the IWM include a complete set of the CWGC's memorial and cemetery registers and the 80 volume *Soldiers Died in the Great War, 1914-19*. This was originally published in 1921 by HMSO but was republished by JB Hayward in 1989. This and the less detailed *Officers Died in the Great War, 1914-19* (published in 1919) are available on a CD-ROM produced by Naval and Military Press, and also on a pay per view basis on the website www.military-genealogy.com (this can also be accessed via the family history pages at www.iwm.org.uk).

A CD-ROM for Army personnel who died in the Second World War has also been produced by Naval and Military Press, and the information is available through www.military-genealogy.com Rolls of honour for other later conflicts are also held, and in addition the IWM has a large collection of published rolls of honour for localities, schools, institutions, etc. Regimental histories and magazines often contain rolls of honour. Some rolls of honour can be found online at www.roll-of-honour.com

The soldiers' own home area should not be forgotten when researching an individual's service - there may be local war memorial records, a local account of war service may have been published, and contemporary local newspapers can prove very helpful. It is also possible that school, church or workplace records may still exist.

The United Kingdom National Inventory of

by the Ministry of Defence. These can be applied for by post from the Army Personnel Centre, Disclosures 4, MP 555, Kentigern House, 65 Brown Street, Glasgow G2 8EX. Initial contact with the Army Personnel Centre (APC) can be made by telephone (0845 600 9663) or email – please include your postal address (disc4@apc.army.mod.uk). Records will be released to proven next of kin (currently there is a £30 fee) and there is likely to be a lengthy wait for this service. You can find a copy of the application form on the Veterans UK website at: www.veterans-uk.info/service_records/service_records.html

Home Guard records are also available through the APC (although not all have survived, and they are usually brief with very little information).

The Brigade of Guards form an exception as records are held by the Regimental Headquarters Grenadier/Coldstream/Scots/Irish/Welsh Guards, Wellington Barracks, Birdcage Walk, London SW1E 6HQ. First World War officers' records are held by TNA.

The careers of Army officers can be traced using the regular official publication the *Army List*, and the Imperial War Museum (IWM) holds

War Memorials is recording details of all war memorials in the country. More information about this project can be found at www.ukniwm.org.uk

Medal Records

Campaign medals are those given to soldiers who are eligible for them because they were in a particular theatre of war within given dates. The First World War Medal Roll which provides a listing of all those who qualified for the 1914 Star, 1914/15 Star, British War Medal, Victory Medal, Territorial Force War Medal and/or the Silver War Badge is held at TNA. If a First World War record was destroyed some basic information about a soldier's service may be found in this. The index cards can now be accessed on the internet at www.nationalarchives.gov.uk/documentsonline These cards are an index to the medal rolls – these can be consulted at TNA, and may yield additional information.

You can also access these cards online at www.ancestry.co.uk – this shows both the front and back of the cards (the reverse may contain additional details).

Post First World War medal claims or enquiries can be addressed to: Ministry of Defence Medal Office, Innsworth House, Imjin Barracks, Innsworth, Gloucester GL3 1HW.

Gallantry medals are those medals awarded for an especially heroic deed or action. Records for these are held at TNA, but may not be very detailed. Notifications and citations

© Copyright Robert Blatchford Collection

(if published, which was not the case for awards such as the Military Medal and Mentions in Despatches) appeared in the official journal *London Gazette*. A complete set of this, and the all important indexes, is held at TNA. The *London Gazette Online Archive* at www.london-gazette.co.uk provides access to First and Second World War entries. The IWM has some published listings of medal awards for decorations such as the Victoria Cross and Distinguished Conduct Medal. Usually you will need to go either to the official unit war diary (held at TNA) or to a published unit history to see whether you can find out more about the action for which the decoration was awarded.

Local newspapers may also have reported medal awards. Recommendations for Honours and Awards, 1935-1990, are now available online at www.nationalarchives.gov.uk/documentsonline

Regimental Histories

The IWM has an excellent collection of regimental histories. For those unable to visit in person, *A Bibliography of Regimental Histories of the British Army* compiled by Arthur S White (London: London Stamp Exchange, 1988) provides details of published histories that may be available through your local library's inter-library loan scheme. Regimental magazines and forces newspapers should not be overlooked. *Soldier* magazine was first published in 1945, and continues to be an excellent source of information about military life. Some articles from past and present issues can be found on the website at www.soldiermagazine.co.uk

TNA has copies of the official unit war diaries – some of these for the First World War and Army of Occupation are now available online at www.nationalarchives.gov.uk/documentsonline

A useful title for locating regimental museums (although these are unlikely to hold information about individuals) is *The AMOT Guide to Military Museums in the UK* produced by the Army Museums Ogilby Trust *(Third Millennium Publishing, 2010)*. You can also find contact details at www.armymuseums.org.uk

The IWM Collections Enquiry Service can also advise on the addresses of Old Comrades Associations. The internet has made it easier to establish contact with people who may have served in the Forces, or who may be conducting research similar to your own. The Royal British Legion website at www.britishlegion.org.uk is a good place to start. The Army website at www.army.mod.uk is also useful. An excellent site for First World War Orders of Battle and Army information is www.1914-1918.net The Western Front Association at www.westernfrontassociation.com is also recommended. The Second World War is not as well covered on the internet, but one useful site is www.unithistories.com

Further Reading

More detailed information can be found in our publication *Tracing Your Family History: Army* – this is currently out of print, but copies can be viewed in the Explore History Centre. The Museum does not hold any personal service records or official documentation, but can help the enquirer as long as some basic facts are known. The Collections Division welcomes visitors by appointment and is able to provide useful reading material and advice for finding out more about those who served. Other types of material - art, documents, three-dimensional objects, film, photographs and sound recordings - may also be able to assist.

Contact
Collections Enquiry Service
Imperial War Museum
Lambeth Road, London SE1 6HZ
T: (+44) 020 7416 5342
F: (+44) 020 7416 5246
E: collections@iwm.org.uk
W: www.iwm.org.uk

Irish Family History Research at The Imperial War Museum
sarah paterson ma, diplib

An Irish visitor to the Explore History Centre at the Imperial War Museum was very surprised to hear that we would be able to help him with the history of three First World War relatives, each of whom had a typical Irish experience. The first had served at the Battle of the Somme with the Royal Munster Fusiliers as part of the British Army, the second had served with the IRA in the immediate post-war period, and the third, who had emigrated to the United States of America, had served in France with an American regiment.

One third of the regular British Army was Irish on the outbreak of the First World War. This was a huge contribution, and many of these men will have joined up in peacetime because the military provided a roof over their head, food on the table and a regular income. The Army also offered the possibility of improving their lives through promotion and education opportunities, as well as offering a chance to see the world and fulfil a young man's yearning for adventure. With the coming of the war many more Irishmen enlisted, with both patriotism and the desire for home rule being added to the economic attractions of army life. There was never conscription in Ireland (introduced elsewhere in the British Isles from 1916) and all Irishmen who enlisted in Ireland were volunteers.

Those who fell were recorded in one of the most visually attractive of the many rolls of honour produced after the conflict: *Ireland's Memorial Records, 1914 - 1918: Being the Names of Irishmen who fell in the Great European War, 1914-1918*. This eight-volume work was compiled by the *Committee of the Irish National War Memorial*, under the direction of the Earl of Ypres, and published in very limited numbers in 1923. One hundred copies were printed

'for distribution through the principal libraries of the country.' of the eight-volume set were printed. The printing; decoration and binding of the volumes was carried out by Irish artists and workers of the highest reputation and efficiency.

There are eight different page border designs by the artist Harry Clarke, best known for his work in stained glass. These repay close examination since they are filled with intricately worked cap badges, medals, and silhouettes, many taken from iconic photographs of the conflict. Over 49,000 names are listed – men serving with Irish regiments, or those in other units, including commonwealth forces, who had Irish connections. It is not totally comprehensive – these rolls of honour seldom are – and gathering the names together must have been hampered by the political situation that had developed since the end of the First World War.

The actual details recorded vary from record to record. Name, Rank, Regiment and Regimental Number, and in most cases Place of Birth/County are recorded. In many cases Place of Death is also recorded.

Over 30,986 declared Ireland as their country of birth. For 741 individuals just Ireland was listed. 11,299 were from the six counties of Northern Ireland while 18,946 came from the remaining twenty-six counties. 7,405 had no place of birth recorded. The remaining 11,000 plus had Places of Birth spread throughout Britain, continental Europe, the United States of America, Canada and the rest of the World. These men and women considered themselves to be Irish, of Irish Heritage or fought with an Irish Regiment.

Many of the Irish infantry regiments disbanded in 1922 – The Connaught Rangers, The Royal Dublin

A page from Ireland's Memorial Records 1914 - 1918 showing the entry for John (Jack) Kipling son of Rudyard Kipling - Author & Poet

IRELAND'S MEMORIAL RECORDS 1914-1918

KINSLEY, MICHAEL. Reg. No. 5572. Rank, Corporal, Royal Munster Fusiliers, 2nd Batt.; killed in action, France, May 9, 1915; born Fothera, Co. Clare.

KINSLEY, PERCY. Reg. No. 7223. Rank, Private, Royal Irish Regiment, 2nd Batt.; killed in action, France, September 3, 1916; born High Barnet, Middlesex.

KIPLING, JOHN. Rank, Lieutenant, Irish Guards; killed in action, September 27, 1915.

KIRBY, JOHN. Reg. No. 22751. Rank, Corporal, King's Liverpool Regiment, 13th Batt.; killed in action, France, May 3, 1917; born Listowel, Ireland.

KIRBY, JOHN. Reg. No. WR/313219. Rank, Sapper, Royal Engineers (Inland Water Transport); died, home, August 6, 1918; born Cork.

KIRBY, MICHAEL. Reg. No. 6382. Rank, Private, Royal Irish Regiment, 2nd Batt.; died of wounds, France, January 22, 1915; born Trinity Without, Waterford.

Useful Websites

www.findmypast.ie/search-records/Military-and-rebellion

www.findmypast.ie/content/irelands-memorial-record-world-war-1-1914-1918

www.findmypast.co.uk/irelands-memorial-records-search-start.action?product=IMR

Further Reading

Ireland's Memorial Records: World War 1 1914-1918 - CD-Rom ENEC011 Pub:
Eneclann Ltd, Unit 1 Trinity College Enterprise Centre, Pearse Street, Dublin 2
(www.eneclann.ie/acatalog/ENEC011.html) ISBN: 1 905118 01 5

Fusiliers, The Royal Irish Regiment, The Leinster Regiment and The Royal Munster Fusiliers - and although the Imperial War Museum has always been able to provide regimental histories, photographs and some personal letters and diaries, we have felt the lack of regimental museums and other places to which people can be referred. It has been wonderful to see the interest in the Great War that has been reawakening in Ireland over the last decade – the publications that are pouring out, the stamp commemorating the 90th anniversary of the Battle of the Somme in 2006, and the regimental associations that are now flourishing.

Relating to our visitor's second strand of interest, although the Imperial War Museum does not have an extensive collection of material on the Irish Republican Army, there is certainly some. There will also be collections relating to the British Army stationed in Ireland – and anybody wanting to look at IRA actions in the early 1920s would presumably be interested in looking at what the forces they were campaigning against were doing.

Finally, the Imperial War Museum is able to help with regard to Irish émigrés who may have ended up in the American Army – or that of Commonwealth countries such as Australia, Canada or New Zealand. We have an extensive collection of regimental histories from all of these countries which can be consulted by making an appointment to visit our Research Room. This is open Monday-Friday between 10.00.a.m. and 5.00.p.m. We also have the drop in Explore History Centre open every day of the week, where you can look at basic reference works, watch selected film footage and listen to interviews with veterans, as well as consult our catalogues and view selected websites.

Ireland has an immensely rich and varied history, which will make genealogical research interesting. The First World War played a huge part in the history of the country, and whatever your political stance, all those who served were individuals who deserve to be remembered.

Although the Imperial War Museum does not have personal service records or official documentation, we do have a wealth of material that can help you find out about what their unit did, and provide information about what the experience was like – at home and overseas, in both peace and war.

Contact

Collections Enquiry Service, Imperial War Museum, Lambeth Road, London SE1 6HZ

T: 020 7416 5346 E: collections@iwm.org.uk W: www.iwm.org.uk

michael o'leary v.c.
Robert Blatchford

Michael John O'Leary VC (29th September 1890 – 2nd August 1961) was an Irish recipient of the Victoria Cross,

Michael O'Leary was born on 29th September1890, one of four children of Daniel and Margaret O'Leary, who owned a farm at Inchigeela, near Macroom in County Cork, Ireland. Daniel O'Leary was a fervent Irish nationalist and keen sportsman who participated in competitive weightlifting and football.

At the age of 16 and unwilling to continue to work on his parent's land, Michael O'Leary joined the Royal Navy, serving at the shore establishment *HMS Vivid, Devonport* for several years until rheumatism in his knees forced his departure from the service. Within a few months of returning home, O'Leary had again tired of the farm and joined the Irish Guards regiment of the British Army.

O'Leary served three years with the Irish Guards and left in August 1913 joining the *Royal North West Mounted Police* in Saskatchewan, Canada.

At the outbreak of the First World War O'Leary returned to Ireland and rejoined the Irish Guards on 22nd October 1914 and on 23rd November he was posted to his regiment in France. During December 1914, O'Leary saw heavy fighting with the Irish Guards and was Mentioned in Despatches.

He was promoted Lance Corporal on 5th January 1915. Three weeks later, on 30th January, the Irish Guards were ordered to prepare for an attack on German positions near Cuinchy on the La Bassée Canal, a response to a successful German operation in the area five days before. On the morning of 1st February 1915 the Germans attacked first and seized a stretch of canal embankment on the western end of the 2nd Brigade line from a company of Coldstream Guards. The area was known as *The Hollow*. It was tactically important because it defended a culvert that passed underneath a railway embankment.

Held originally in reserve 4 Company Irish Guards were tasked with joining the Coldstream Guards in retaking the position at 04:00 hours.

The attack was met with heavy machine gun fire and most of the assault party, including all of the Irish Guards officers, were killed or wounded.

To replace these officers, Second Lieutenant Innes of 1 Company was ordered forward to group the survivors together and withdraw. They formed up at a barricade on the edge of the *Hollow*. Innes regrouped the survivors and after a heavy bombardment from supporting artillery, with his own company providing covering fire, assisted the Coldstream Guards in a second attack on the German positions at 10:15.

Weighed down with entrenching equipment, the attacking Coldstream Guardsmen slowed and began to suffer heavy casualties. Innes too came under heavy fire from a German barricade to their front equipped with a machine gun.

Michael O'Leary had been serving as Innes's orderly, and had joined him in the operations earlier in the morning and again in the second attack.

O'Leary charged past the rest of the assault party and closed with the first German barricade at the top of the railway embankment. He fired

MICHAEL O'LEARY AT HOME
Characteristic photograph of the gallant Irish Guardsman taken near his home in Co. Cork when he was in the Old Country on leave.

Daniel & Mrs O'Leary
Father and Mother of
Michael O' Leary

Michael O' Leary's Home ar Macroom

Images © Copyright Robert Blatchford Collection

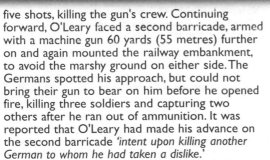

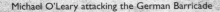
Michael O'Leary attacking the German Barricade

five shots, killing the gun's crew. Continuing forward, O'Leary faced a second barricade, armed with a machine gun 60 yards (55 metres) further on and again mounted the railway embankment, to avoid the marshy ground on either side. The Germans spotted his approach, but could not bring their gun to bear on him before he opened fire, killing three soldiers and capturing two others after he ran out of ammunition. It was reported that O'Leary had made his advance on the second barricade *'intent upon killing another German to whom he had taken a dislike.'*

Having disabled both guns and enabled the recapture of the British position, O'Leary returned to his unit with his prisoners, apparently *'as cool as if he had been for a walk in the park.'*

For his actions, O'Leary received a battlefield promotion to Sergeant on 4th February and was recommended for the Victoria Cross, which was gazetted on the 16th February 1915:

O'Leary returned to Britain to receive his medal from King George V at Buckingham Palace on 22nd June 1915

O'Leary retired from the British Army in 1921 with the rank of Lieutenant. He served in the British army again during the Second World War. At his final demobilization from the military in 1945, O'Leary was an Army Major in command of a prisoner of war camp. Following the Second World War he lived and worked as a building contractor in London until his death in 1961.

No. 3556 **Lance-Corporal Michael O'Leary**, 1st Battalion, Irish Guards

For conspicuous bravery at Cuinchy on the 1st February, 1915. When forming one of the storming party which advanced against the enemy's barricades he rushed to the front and himself killed five Germans who were holding the first barricade, after which he attacked a second barricade, about 60 yards further on, on which he captured, after killing three of the enemy and making prisoners of two more. Lance-Corporal O'Leary thus practically captured the enemy's position by himself and prevented the attacking party from being fired upon.

The London Gazette - 16th February 1915

THE GUARDS·BEGGARS BUSH··IRISH REPUBLICAN·ARMY·FEBRUARY· 4ᵀᴴ 1922·
- THE MEN WHO FOUGHT FOR THE FREEDOM OF IRELAND -

óglaigh na héireann
the irish defence forces military archives

The mission of the Military Archives is to acquire, preserve and make available to the public the documentary heritage of the Defence Forces and the Department of Defence. Apart from serving the evidential, legal and heritage needs of the Defence Forces and the Department of Defence, Military Archives can provide public services to a broad spectrum of interests, from family history queries to academic research, to material for television and radio documentaries. Some services that may be of interest to your particular needs include:
• Advisory service in relations to family history and genealogy
• Facilities for academic and scholarly research
• Research assistance to the media, cultural institutions, local history groups and academic societies

The Military Archives is the place of deposit for the archives of the Defence Forces, the Department of Defence and the Army Pensions Board, under the terms of the National Archives Act, 1986. Archives are records with a special significance, records that are deemed to be of enduring value, for a variety of reasons.

The Military Archives holds a significant volume of material that constitutes an extremely important part of the record for Ireland's history in the 20ᵗʰ century. The reading room at Military Archives has eight seats. The reading room is open from 10.00.a.m. to 4.00.p.m Tuesday to Thursday (inclusive) and **access is by prior appointment only**. The Duty Archivist can be contacted by phone Monday – Friday 900.a.m. – 4.00.p.m

The Military Archives will continue to add content to our web pages over the coming months. Please keep an eye on www.militaryarchives.ie for up to date visitor information, news features and details of online collections.
Our most accessed collections include;
• Bureau of Military History (1913 - 1921 period)
• Civil War Operations and Intelligence Reports Collection (February 1922 – February 1927)
• Civil War Prisoners Collection (1922 – 1925)
• Civil War Captured Documents (1922 – 1925)

• Defence Forces Annual & General Reports (1940 – 1957)
• German Submarine U260 Collection (1940 – 1945)
• Liaison and Evacuation Papers (1921-1922)
• Emergency Defence Plans (1939-1946)
• Crashes and Forced Landings (1939-1946)
• Army Census returns (11/12 November 1922)
• Department of Defence files (includes early Ministry of Defence files dated 1922 and annual file release material)
• Maps, Plans and Drawings (including 19ᵗʰ century barrack maps and plans)
• Collins Papers (includes papers of General Michael Collins when Director of Organisation and Director of Intelligence during 1919-1921 period)
• Publications including An tÓglach, An Cosantoir and special in-house commemorative publications relating to Eucharistic Congress, the Emergency Period and Ireland's contribution to United Nations.
• Military Intelligence G2 Collection (1939 – 1946)
• Unit histories from Irish contingents that have served in UN Forces overseas since 1958.

Contact:
The Irish Defence Forces Military Archives can be contacted as follows:
Officer in Charge, Military Archives
Cathal Brugha Barracks, Rathmines, Dublin 6
T: + 00 353 1 8046457 W: www.militaryarchives.ie

The Defence Forces Cap Badge

The Badge design (common to all Corps and Services and all orders of dress) is derived from the badge of the Irish Volunteers and was designed by Professor Eoin MacNeill, Chairman of the National Executive of the Irish Volunteers.

This badge was originally adopted by the Irish Volunteers in October 1914 as the official badge of the organisation. The Centrepiece is formed of the letters 'FF'. These letters signify 'Fianna Fáil.' The word 'Fianna' is the name of the ancient military organisation (circa 3ʳᵈ Century A.D.) forming what then corresponded to the standing Army of the country. The word 'Fáil' means 'Destiny.'

One of the ancient names of Ireland was 'Inishfáil' (the Isle of Destiny) and 'Fianna Fáil' thus signifies the 'Fianna (or Army) of Ireland.' The two letters are surrounded by a representation of an ancient warriors sword belt and a circle of flames which represent the 'Sunburst' - the traditional battle symbol of the Fianna.

The words 'Óglaigh na h-Éireann' inscribed around the sword belt mean 'Soldiers of Ireland.' No particular significance is attached to the representation of the star which was included to balance the design.

The Irish Genealogical Services Directory

archives, record offices & repositories

national

An tSeirbhís um Chlárú Sibhialta - The General Register Office Convent Road , Roscommon, Co Roscommon T: +353 9 0663 2900 E: gro.groireland.ie W: www.groireland.ie

Church of Ireland Representative Church Body - Library Representative Church Body Library, Braemor Park, Churchtown, Dublin 14, T: +353 1 492 3979 E: library@ireland.anglican.org W: www.library@ireland.anglican.org/

Commonwealth War Graves Commission 2 Marlow Road, Maidenhead, Berkshire SL6 7DX T: 01628 634221 E: casualty.enq@cwgc.org W: www.cwgc.org

Garda Historical Society - www.policehistory.com 8 Aisling Close, Ballincollig, County Cork T: +353 86 806 0385 E: pressoffice@garda.ie W: www.policehistory.com

Garda Siochana Museum & Archives The Records Tower, Dublin, 2 T: +353 1 6719 597 E: j_herlihy@esatclear.ie W: www.esatclear.ie/~garda/museum.html

General Register Office of Northern Ireland Oxford House, 49 - 55 Chichester Street, Belfast, BT1 4HL T: (028) 90 252000 E: gro.nisra@dfpni.gov.uk W: www.nidirect.gov.uk

Grand Lodge of Freemasons of Ireland Freemasons' Hall, 17 Molesworth Street, Dublin 2 T: + 353 01 6761337 E: office@freemason.ie W: www.irish-freemasons.org/

Irish World Heritage Centre 51 Dungannon Road, Coalisland, BT71 4HP T: 028 877 46055 E: info@irish-world.com W: www.irish-world.com/

Irish World Heritage Centre 51 Dungannon Road, Coalisland, BT71 4HP T: 028 877 46055 E: info@irish-world.com W: www.irish-world.com/

National Archives of Ireland Bishop Street, Dublin 8, T: +353 1 407 2300 E: mail@nationalarchives.ie W: www..nationalarchives.ie

Office of the Chief Herald of Ireland Kildare Street, Dublin 2, County Dublin T: +353 1 603 0200 E: herald@nli.ie W: www.nli.ie

Óglaigh na hÉireann - The Defence Forces Military Archives Officer in Charge - Military Archives, Cathal Brugha Barracks, Rathmines, Dublin, Dublin 6 T: + 353 1 8046457 E: info@military.ie W: www.military.ie/info-centre/military-archives

Presbyterian Historical Society of Ireland 26 College Green, Belfast, BT7 ILN T: 028 9072 7330 E: phsilibrarian@pcinet.org W: www.presbyterianhistoryireland.com

Public Record Office of Northern Ireland 66 Balmoral Avenue, Belfast, BT9 6NY T: 028 9025 5905 E: Ann.McVeigh@dcalni.gov.uk W: www.proni.gov.uk

Registry of Deeds Henrietta Street, Dublin 1, T: +353 1 8716533 E: declan.ward@prai.ie W: www.landregistry.ie

Religious Society of Friends (Quakers) in Ireland Quaker House, Stocking Lane, Dublin, 16 T: +353 1 4998003 F: +353 1 4998005 E: office@quakers-in-ireland.ie W: www quakers.ie

The National Archives Kew, Richmond, Surrey TW9 4DU T: 020 8876 3444 E: Online contact Form W: www.nationalarchives.gov.uk/

Valuation Office Irish Life Centre, Lower abbey Street, Dublin 1, T: +353 1 817 1000 E: info@valoff.ie W: www.valoff.ie

Imperial War Museum Lambeth Road, London, SE1 6HZ T: 020 7416 5342 E: collections@iwm.org.uk W: www.iwm.org.uk

National Army Museum Royal Hospital Road, Chelsea, London, SW3 4HT T: 020 7730 0717 E: info@nam.ac.uk W: www.nam.ac.uk

Probate Principal Registry of the Family Division First Avenue House, 42 - 49 High Holborn, London, WC1V 6NP T: (020) 7947 6939 W: www.courtservice.gov.uk

Probate Service Probate Sub Registry, 1st Floor, Castle Chambers, Clifford Street, York, YO1 9RG T: 01904 666777 W: www.courtservice.gov.uk

Royal Air Force Museum Grahame Park Way, Hendon, London, NW9 5LL T: (020) 8200 1763 E: london@rafmuseum.org W: www.rafmuseum.org.uk

Royal Marines Museum Eastney, Southsea, Hampshire PO4 9PX T: (023) 9281 9385 Exts 224 E: info@royalmarinesmuseum.co.uk W: www.royalmarinesmuseum.co.uk

The Australian Irish Heritage Association PO Box1583 , Subiaco , 6904 T: (08) 9345 3530 E: aiha@irishheritage.net

U.K. National Inventory of War Memorials Imperial War Museum, Lambeth Road, London, SE1 6HZ T: 020 7207 9863/9851 E: memorials@iwm.org.uk W: www.ukniwm.org.uk

regional

Belfast
Belfast Central Library Belfast Ulster Irish Studies, Royal Avenue, Belfast, BT1 1EA T: (028) 9024 3233 E: sheila.mcclean@librariesni.org.uk W: www.librariesni.org.uk

Belfast Family History & Cultural Heritage Centre 64 Wellington Place, Belfast, BT1 6GE T: (028) 9023 5392 E: office@iwhc.com

County Antrim
Belfast Central Library Belfast Ulster Irish Studies, Royal Avenue, Belfast, BT1 1EA T: (028) 9024 3233 E: sheila.mcclean@librariesni.org.uk W: www.librariesni.org.uk

County Armagh
Armagh Public Library 43 Abbey Street, Armagh, County Armagh BT61 1DY T: 028 37 523 142 E: admin@armaghpubliclibrary.co.uk W: www.armaghrobinsonlibrary.org

County Carlow
Carlow County Library Tullow Street, Carlow, County Carlow T: +353 0 59 917 0094 E: library@carlowcoco.ie

County Cavan
Cavan County Library & Archives Farnham Centre, Farnham Street, Cavan, County Cavan T: +3530 49 437 8500 E: library@cavancoco.ie archives@cavancoco.ie

County Clare
Clare County Archives Clare County Council - Áras Contae an Chláir, New Road, Ennis, Co Clare T: +353 65 684 6414 E: archivesrecords@clarecoco.ie W: www.clarelibrary.ie/eolas/archives/archives_index.htm

Clare Heritage & Genealogical Centre Church Street, Corofin, County Clare T: + 353 65 683 7955 E: clareheritage@eircom.net W: www.clareroots.com

County Cork
Cork City & County Archives The Seamus Murphy Building, 33a Great William O'Brien Street, Blackpool, Cork City, County Cork T: + 353 (0) 21 450 5876 E: archivist@corkcity.ie W: www.corkarchives.ie

Cork City Ancestral project c/o Cork County Library, Carrigrohane Road, , Cork, County Cork T: +353 21 428 5648 E: corkancestry@corkcoco.ie

Mallow Heritage Centre 27-28 Bank Place, Mallow, County Cork T: +353 22 50302 E: mallowheritagecentre@gmail.com W: www.rootsireland.ie/

Skibbereen Heritage Centre Old Gas Works Building, Upper Bridge Street, Skibbereen, County Cork T: +353 28 40900 E: skibbheritage1@gmail.com W: www.skibbheritage.com

County Donegal
Donegal Ancestry Centre The Quay, Ramleton, County Donegal T: +353 74 915 1266 E: info@donegalancestry.com W: www.donegalancestry.com

Donegal County Archives Cultural Services, 3 Rivers Centre, Lifford, County Donegal T: + 00353 74 72490 E: archivist@donegalcoco.ie W: www.donegal.ie

Donegal Local Studies Centre Central Library & Arts Centre, Oliver Plunkett Road, Letterkenny, County Donegal T: 00353 74 24950 E: Portal@donegalcoco.ie W: www.donegal.ie/library

County Down
Banbridge Genealogy Services Tourist Information Centre, F E McWilliam Gallery & Studio, 200 Newry Road, Banbridge, County Down BT32 3NB T: +44 (0)28 4062 3322 F: +44 (0)28 4062 5933 E: info@banbridgegenealogy.com W: www.banbridgegenealogy.com/

Belfast Central Library - see Belfast

County Dublin
Dun Laoghaire Heritage & Genealogy Centre Craft Courtyard, Marlay Park, Rathfarnham, County Dublin T: +353 1 204 7264 E: cmalone@dlrcoco.ie W: www.dlrcoco.ie/library/lhistory.htm

Fingal Genealogy / North Dublin - Swords Historical Society Ltd Carnegie Library, North Street, Swords, County Dublin T: +353 1 8400080 E: swordsheritage@eircom.net : fingalgenealogy@gmail.com W: www.rootsireland.ie

Dublin
Dublin City Archives Dublin City Library & Archive, 138 - 144 Pearse Street, Dublin, 2 T: + 353 1 674 4800 E: cityarchives@dublincity.ie

County Kildare
Kildare Heritage & Genealogy Riverbank, Main Street, Newbridge, County Kildare T: +353 45 448350 E: kildaregenealogy@iol.ie W: http://kildare.rootsireland.ie

County Limerick
Limerick City Archives Limerick City Council, Merchant's Quay, Limerick, County Limerick T: +353 61 407293 E: archives@limerickcity.ie W: www.limerickcity.ie/

Limerick Genealogy Lissanalta House, Dooradoyle Road, Limerick, County Limerick T: +353 61 496 542 E: research@limerickgenealogy.com W: www.limerickgenealogy.com

Limerick Studies Lissanalta House, Dooradoyle Road, Limerick, T: +353 61 496 526 E: limerickstudies@limerickcoco.ie W: www.limerickcoco.ie

County Londonderry
Derry City Council Heritage & Museum Service Archive & Genealogical Service. The Harbour Museum is closing for refurbishment in December 2011, Harbour Square, Derry, County Londonderry BT48 6AF T: 028 7137 7331 (Harbour Museum) Contact details during 2012: Archive & Genealogical Service, Tower Museum, Union Hall Place, Derry, County Londonderry BT48 6LU The archives of Derry City Council are an invaluable source of information for the history of both the City and the Council from the early 17th century to the present day. E: genealogy@derrycity.gov.uk W: www.derry.rootsireland.ie

County Longford
Longford Genealogy 17 Dublin Street, Longford, County Longford T: +353 43 334 1235 E: longroot@iol.ie

County Louth
Louth County Archive Service Old Gaol, Ardee Road, Dundalk, Co Louth T: + 353 (0)42 933 9387 E: archive@louthcoco.ie W: www.louthnewryarchives.ie www.louthcoco.ie
Louth County Library Roden Place, Dundalk, County Louth T: +353 42 935 3190 E: libraryhelpdesk@louthcoco.ie W: www.louthcoco.ie
Louth County Reference Library Roden Place, Dundalk, County Louth T: +353 42 933 5457 E: referencelibary@louthcoco.ie

County Mayo
Local Record Offices The Registration Office, New Antrim Street, Castlebar, County Mayo T: + 353 964 3024
Mayo North Family History Research Centre Enniscoe, Castlehill, Ballina, County Mayo T: + 353 96 31809 E: normayo@iol.ie W: www.mayo.irish-roots.net
South Mayo Family Research Centre Main Street, Ballinrobe, County Mayo T: +353 94 954 1214 F: +353 94 954 1103 E: soumayo@iol.ie W: http://mayo.irishroots.net/

County Meath
Meath Heritage Centre Town Hall, Castle Street, Trim, County Meath T: +353 46 943 6633 E: meathhc@iol.ie

County Offaly
Irish Midlands Ancestry Bury Quay, Tullamore, County Offaly T: +353 506 21421 E: info@irishmidlandsancestry.com W: www.irishmidlandsancestry.com

County Roscommon
Roscommon Heritage & Genealogical Centre Church Street, Strokestown, County Roscommon T: +353 71 963 3380 E: info@roscommonroots.com W: www.roscommonroots.com

County Sligo
County Sligo Heritage & Genealogy Society Aras Reddan, Temple Street, Sligo, County Sligo T: +353 71 914 3728 E: heritagesligo@eircom.net

County Tipperary
Tipperary Excel Heritage Co. Ltd Mitchell Street, Tipperary Town, County Tipperary T: + 353 62380520 E: manager@tipperary-excel.com W: www.tipperary-excel.com
Tipperary Family History Research Mitchell Street, Tipperary Town, County Tipperary T: + 353 62 80555 E: research@tfhr.org W: www.tfhr.org
Tipperary North Genealogy Centre The Governor's House, Kickham Street, Nenagh, County Tipperary T: +353 673 3850 E: tipperarynorthgenealogy@eircom.net W: www.tipperarynorth.ie/genealogy www.rootsireland.ie www.facebook.com/GenealogyinNorthTipperary

Tipperary South - Bru Boru Cultural Centre Rock of Cashel, Cashel, County Tipperary T: +353 62 61122 E: eolas@bruboru.ie

County Waterford
Waterford Archives & Local Records St Joseph's Hospital, Dungarvan, County Waterford T: 058-42199 E: dungarvanlibrary@waterfordcoco.ie
Waterford Heritage Services St Patrick's Church, Jenkin's Lane, Waterford, County Waterford T: +353 51 876 123 E: mnoc@iol.ie

County Westmeath
Athlone - Westmeath County Library - Local Studies Athlone Civic offices, Church Avenue, Athlone, County Westmeath T: +353 90 644 2157 E: athlib@westmeathcoco.ie W: www.westmeathcoco.i
Dun na Si Heritage Centre Knockdomney, Moate, County Westmeath T: +353 90 648 1183 E: dunnasimoate@eircom.net
Mullingar - Westmeath County Library - Local Studies County Buildings, Mount Street, Mullingar, County Westmeath T: +353 44 933 2161 E: mgarlib@westmeathcoco.ie

County Wicklow
Wicklow Family History Centre Wicklow County Archives, County Buildings, Station Road, Wicklow, County Wicklow T: +353 404 20126 E: wfh@eircom.net W: www.wicklow.ie/familyhistorycentre

Military
Óglaigh na hÉireann - The Defence Forces Military Archives Officer in Charge - Military Archives, Cathal Brugha Barracks, Rathmines, Dublin, Dublin 6 T: + 353 1 8046457 E: info@military.ie W: www.military.ie/info-centre/military-archives

Police
Garda Historical Society - www.policehistory.com 8 Aisling Close, Ballincollig, County Cork T: +353 86 806 0385 E: pressoffice@garda.ie W: www.policehistory.com
Garda Siochana Museum & Archives The Records Tower, Dublin, 2 T: +353 1 6719 597 E: j_herlihy@esatclear.ie W: www.esatclear.ie/~garda/museum.html

county genealogy centres

Belfast
Ulster Historical Foundation 49 Malone Road, Belfast, BT9 6RY T: 028 9066 1988 F: 028 9066 1977 E: enquiry@uhf.org.uk W: www.ancestryireland.com

County Antrim
Ulster Historical Foundation 49 Malone Road, Belfast, BT9 6RY T: 028 9066 1988 F: 028 9066 1977 E: enquiry@uhf.org.uk W: www.ancestryireland.com

County Armagh
Armagh Ancestry 40 English Street, Armagh, County Armagh BT61 7BA T: 028 3752 1800 E: researcher@armagh.gov.uk W: www.armagh.co.uk

County Carlow - No Service

County Cavan
Cavan Genealogy Johnston Central Library, Farnham Street, Cavan, County Cavan T: +353 49 436 1094 E: cavangenealogy@eircom.net

County Clare
Clare Heritage & Genealogical Centre Church Street, Corofin, County Clare T: + 353 65 683 7955 E: clareheritage@eircom.net W: www.clareroots.com

County Cork
Cork City Ancestral project c/o Cork County Library, Carrigrohane Road, Cork, County Cork T: +353 21 428 5648 E: corkancestry@corkcoco.ie
Mallow Heritage Centre 27-28 Bank Place, Mallow, County Cork T: +353 22 50302 E: mallowheritagecentre@gmail.com W: www.rootsireland.ie/
Skibbereen Heritage Centre Old Gas Works Building, Upper Bridge Street, Skibbereen, Co Cork T: +353 28 40900 E: skibbheritage1@gmail.com W: www.skibbheritage.com

County Donegal
Donegal Ancestry Centre The Quay, Ramleton, County Donegal T: +353 74 915 1266 E: info@donegalancestry.com W: www.donegalancestry.com

County Down
Ulster Historical Foundation 49 Malone Road, Belfast, BT9 6RY T: 028 9066 1988 F: 028 9066 1977 E: enquiry@uhf.org.uk W: www.ancestryireland.com

County Dublin
Dublin North
Fingal Genealogy / North Dublin - Swords Historical Society Ltd Carnegie Library, North Street, Swords, County Dublin T: +353 1 8400080 E: swordsheritage@eircom.net fingalgenealogy@gmail.com W: www.rootsireland.ie
Dublin South
Dun Laoghaire Heritage & Genealogy Centre Craft Courtyard, Marlay Park, Rathfarnham, County Dublin T: +353 1 204 7264 E: cmalone@dlrcoco.ie W: www.dlrcoco.ie/library/lhistory.htm

County Fermanagh
Irish World Heritage Centre 51 Dungannon Road, Coalisland, BT71 4HP T: 028 877 46055 E: info@irish-world.com W: www.irish-world.com/

County Galway
East Galway Family History Society Company Ltd Woodford Heritage Centre, Woodford, Loughrea, County Galway T: +353 90 974 9309 F: +353 90 974 9546 E: galwayroots@eircom.net galwayroots@gmail.com W: www.galwaysroots.com www.rootsireland.ie
Galway Family History Society (West) Ltd St. Joseph's Community Centre, Ashe Road, Shantalla, County Galway T: +353 (0)91 860464 F: +353 (0)91 860432 E: galwaywestroots@eircom.net W: www.rootsireland.ie

County Kerry - No Service

County Kildare
Kildare Heritage & Genealogy Riverbank, Main Street, Newbridge, County Kildare T: +353 45 448350 E: kildaregenealogy@iol.ie W: http://kildare.rootsireland.ie

County Kilkenny
Rothe House Family History Rothe House, Kilkenny, County Kilkenny T: +353 56 7722893 E: kilkennyfamilyhistory@rothehouse.com W: www.rothehouse.com

County Leitrim
Leitrim Genealogy Centre Main Street, Ballinamore, Co Leitrim T: +353 71 964 4012 E: leitrimgenealogy@eircom.net W: www.leitrimroots.com

County Limerick
Limerick Genealogy Lissanalta House, Dooradoyle Road, Limerick, Co Limerick T: +353 61 496 542 E: research@limerickgenealogy.com W: www.limerickgenealogy.com

County Londonderry
Derry Genealogy Centre Harbour Museum, Harbour Square, Londonderry BT48 6AF T: 028 7137 7331 E: genealogy@derrycity.gov.uk W: www.derry.rootsireland.ie

County Longford
Longford Genealogy 17 Dublin Street, Longford, Co Longford T: +353 43 334 1235 E: longroot@iol.ie

County Louth
Louth County Library Roden Place, Dundalk, County Louth T: +353 42 935 3190 E: libraryhelpdesk@louthcoco.ie W: www.louthcoco.ie

County Mayo
Mayo North Family History Research Centre Enniscoe, Castlehill, Ballina, County Mayo T: + 353 96 31809 E: normayo@iol.ie W: www.mayo.irish-roots.net
South Mayo Family Research Centre Main Street, Ballinrobe, County Mayo T: +353 94 954 1214 F: +353 94 954 1103 E: soumayo@iol.ie W: http://mayo.irishroots.net/

County Meath
Meath Heritage Centre Town Hall, Castle Street, Trim, County Meath T: +353 46 943 6633 E: meathhc@iol.ie

County Monaghan
Monaghan Genealogy 6 Tully, Monaghan, County Monaghan T: +353 4 783 469
E: theomcmahon@eircom.net
Over 14,000 new records covering Kilmore & Drumsnat Catholic Marriages; Monaghan Catholic Parish marriages; Clontibret Parish Catholic marriages, Aghabog Catholic Marriages, Ematris Catholic marriages, Muckno (Castleblayney) Catholic marriages; Tullycorbet (Ballybay) Catholic marriages; Drumully (Currin) Catholic marriages are available on the County Monaghan Genealogy website. Additional baptismal records for Monaghan parish and Aghabog are nearing completion. Over 8,000 Clones COI baptismal records will also be available

County Offaly
Irish Midlands Ancestry Bury Quay, Tullamore, County Offaly T: +353 506 21421
E: info@irishmidlandsancestry.com
W: www.irishmidlandsancestry.com

County Roscommon
Roscommon Heritage & Genealogical Centre Church Street, Strokestown, County Roscommon
T: +353 71 963 3380 E: info@roscommonroots.com
W: www.roscommonroots.com

County Sligo
County Sligo Heritage & Genealogy Society Aras Reddan, Temple Street, Sligo, County Sligo
T: +353 71 914 3728 E: heritagesligo@eircom.net

County Tipperary
Tipperary North Genealogy Centre The Governor's House, Kickham Street, Nenagh, County Tipperary T: +353 673 3850
E: tipperarynorthgenealogy@eircom.net
W: www.tipperarynorth.ie/genealogy www.rootsireland.ie
W: www.facebook.com/GenealogyinNorthTipperary

Tipperary South - Bru Boru Cultural Centre Rock of Cashel, Cashel, County Tipperary
T: +353 62 61122 E: eolas@bruboru.ie

County Tyrone
Centre for Migration Studies Ulster American Folk Park, Mellon Road, Castletown, Omagh, County Tyrone BT78 5QY T: 028 82 256315
E: cms@librariesni.org.uk W: www.qub.ac.uk/cms
Irish World Heritage Centre 51 Dungannon Road, Coalisland, BT71 4HP T: 028 877 46055 E: info@irish-world.com W: www.irish-world.com/

County Waterford
Waterford Heritage Services St Patrick's Church, Jenkin's Lane, Waterford, County Waterford
T: +353 51 876 123 E: mnoc@iol.ie

County Westmeath
Dun na Si Heritage Centre Knockdomney, Moate, County Westmeath T: +353 90 648 1183
E: dunnasimoate@eircom.net

County Wexford - E: info@ifhf.ie

County Wicklow
Wicklow Family History Centre Wicklow County Archives, County Buildings, Station Road, Wicklow, County Wicklow T: +353 404 20126
E: wfh@eircom.net
W: www.wicklow.ie/familyhistorycentre

Bridge Street & Gardiner Street
Ballina, County Mayo

Libraries

National

Centre for Migration Studies Ulster American Folk Park, Mellon Road, Castletown, Omagh, County Tyrone BT78 5QY T: 028 82 256315 E: cms@librariesni.org.uk W: www.qub.ac.uk/cms

Linen Hall Library 17 Donegall Square North, Belfast, BT1 5GB T: 028 9032 1707 E: info@linenhall.com W: www.discovernorthernireland.com/The-Linen-Hall-Library-Belfast-P3057

National Library of Ireland Kildare Street, Dublin, 2 T: +353 1 6030 200 E: info@nli.ie W: www.nli.ie

Religious Society of Friends (Quakers) in Ireland Quaker House, Stocking Lane, Dublin, 16 T: +353 1 4998003 F: +353 1 4998005 E: office@quakers-in-ireland.ie W: www quakers.ie

Regional

Belfast

Belfast Central Library Belfast Ulster Irish Studies, Royal Avenue, Belfast, BT1 1EA T: (028) 9024 3233 E: sheila.mcclean@librariesni.org.uk W: www.librariesni.org.uk

Derry

Derry Central Library 35 Foyle Street, Derry, BT48 6AL T: 028 7127 2300 E: derrycentrallibrary@librariesni.org.uk

Dublin

Dublin City Library & Archive 138 - 144 Pearse Street, Dublin, 2 T: + 353 1 674 4999 E: dublinstudies@dublincity.ie cityarchives@dublincity.ie W: www.dublincitypubliclibraries.ie (Heritage & History) www.dublincitypubliclibraries.com www.dublinheritage.ie

County Antrim

NEELB Local Studies Service Ballymena Central Library, 5 Pat's Brae, Ballymena, County Antrim BT43 5AX T: (028) 2563 3960 E: localstudies.neelb@ni-libraries.net W: www.neelb.org.uk

North Eastern Library Board & Local Studies Area Reference Library, Demesne Avenue, Ballymena, Antrim BT43 7BG T: (028) 25 6641212 E: yvonne_hirst@hotmail.com W: www.neelb.org.uk

South Antrim

South Eastern Library Board & Local Studies Library HQ, Windmill Hill, Ballynahinch, County Down BT24 8DH T: (028) 9756 6400 E: ballynahinchlibrary@librariesni.org.uk

County Armagh

Armagh Public Library 43 Abbey Street, Armagh, County Armagh BT61 1DY T: 028 37 523 142 E: admin@armaghpubliclibrary.co.uk W: www.armaghrobinsonlibrary.org

County Carlow

Carlow County Library Tullow Street, Carlow, County Carlow T: +353 0 59 917 0094 E: library@carlowcoco.ie

County Cavan

Cavan County Library & Archives Farnham Centre, Farnham Street, Cavan, County Cavan T: +3530 49 437 8500 E: library@cavancoco.ie archives@cavancoco.ie

County Clare

Clare County Library The Manse, Harmony Row, Ennis, County Clare T: +353 65 684 6271 E: mailbox@clarelibrary.ie W: www.clarelibrary.ie

County Cork

Cork City Library 57 - 61 Grand Parade, Cork, County Cork T: +353 21 492 4900 E: libraries@corkcity.ie W: www.corkcitylibraries.ie/

Cork County Library and Arts Service County Libary Building, Carrigrohane Road, Cork, Co Cork T: +353 21 454 6499 E: corkcountylibrary@corkcoco.ie W: www.corkcoco.ie/library http://twitter.com/corkcolibrary

Mallow Heritage Centre 27-28 Bank Place, Mallow, County Cork T: +353 22 50302 E: mallowheritagecentre@gmail.com W: www.rootsireland.ie/

County Donegal

Donegal Central Library Oliver Plunkett Road, Letterkenny, County Donegal T: +353 74 912 4950 E: central@donegallibrary.ie

Donegal Local Studies Centre Central Library & Arts Centre, Oliver Plunkett Road, Letterkenny, County Donegal T: 00353 74 24950 E: Portal@donegalcoco.ie W: www.donegal.ie/library

County Down

South Eastern Library Board & Local Studies Library HQ, Windmill Hill, Ballynahinch, County Down BT24 8DH T: (028) 9756 6400 E: ballynahinchlibrary@librariesni.org.uk

County Dublin

Ballyfermot Public Library Ballyfermot Road, Dublin, 10 T: +353 1 626 9324 E: ballyfermotlibrary@dublincity.ie W: www.dublincity.ie

Dun Laoghaire Library Lower George's Street, Dun Laoghaire, County Dublin T: 2801147 E: localhistory@dlrcoco.ie W: www.dlrcoco.ie/library/lhistory.htm

Fingal Local Studies & Archives Clonmel House, Forster Way, Swords, County Dublin T: +353 1 870 4495 E: local.studies@fingalcoco.ie

County Fermanagh

Enniskillen Library Irish and Local Studies, Halls Lane, Enniskillen, County Fermanagh BT74 7DR T: 028 6632 2886 E: enniskillenlibrary@librariesni.org.uk

Enniskillen Library Halls Lane, Enniskillen, County Fermanagh T74 7DR T: 028 6632 2886 E: enniskillenlibrary@librariesni.org.uk

County Galway

Galway County library Island House, Cathedral Square, Galway, County Galway T: +353 91 562 471 E: info@galwaylibrary.ie W: www.galwaylibrary.ie

County Kerry

Kerry County Library Genealogical Centre
Cathedral Walk, Killarney, County Kerry T: +353 64
359 946 E: culture@kerrycoco.ie
Kerry Library Moyderwell, Tralee, County Kerry T:
+353 66 712 1200 E: info@kerrylibrary.ie
localhistory@kerrylibrary.ie
archivist@kerrylibrary.ie W: www.kerrylibrary.ie

County Kildare

Kidare Library & Arts Centre Kildare
Collections & Research Services, Riverbank Arts
Centre, Main Street, Newbridge, County Kildare T:
+353 45 448351/448352 E: localhistory@kildarecoco.ie
W: www.kildare.ie/library
Kildare County Library Newbridge, County
Kildare T: 045-431109 E: Kildarelib@kildarecoco.ie
W: www.kildare.ie/countycouncil/
Kildare Heritage & Genealogy Riverbank, Main
Street, Newbridge, County Kildare T: +353 45
448350 E: kildaregenealogy@iol.ie W:
http://kildare.rootsireland.ie

County Kilkenny

Kilkenny County Library John Green's House,
John's Green, Kilkenny, County Kilkenny T: +353 56
779 4160 E: info@kilkennylibrary.ie

County Laois

Laois County Library J.F.L. Avenue, Portlaoise,
County Laois T: +353 57 867 4315 E:
laoislibrary@laoiscoco.ie

County Leitrim

Leitrim County Library Main Street, Ballinamore,
County Leitrim T: +353 71 964 5582 E:
leitrimlibrary@leitrimcoco.ie

County Limerick

Limerick City Archives Limerick City Council,
Merchant's Quay, Limerick, County Limerick T: +353
61 407293 E: archives@limerickcity.ie W:
www.limerickcity.ie/
Limerick County library Lissanalta House,
Dooradoyle Road, Limericl, County Limerick T:
+353 61 496 526 E: libinfo@limerickcoco.ie
Longford County library Town Centre, Longford,
County Longford T: +353 43 334 1124 E:
library@longfordcoco.ie

County Londonderry

Central and Reference Library 35 Foyle Street,
Londonderry, County Londonderry BT24 6AL T:
(028) 71272300 E:
derrycentrallibrary@librariesni.org.uk
Irish Room Coleraine County Hall, Castlerock
Road, Ballymena, County Londonderry BT1 3HP T:
028 705 1026 E:
educationlibraryservice@librariesni.org.uk W:
www.neelb.org.uk
Irish Room Coleraine County Hall, Castlerock
Road, Ballymena, County Londonderry BT1 3HP T:
028 705 1026 E:
educationlibraryservice@librariesni.org.uk W:
www.neelb.org.uk

County Louth

Louth County Library Roden Place, Dundalk,
County Louth T: +353 42 935 3190 E:
libraryhelpdesk@louthcoco.ie W: www.louthcoco.ie
Louth County Reference Library Roden Place,
Dundalk, County Louth T: +353 42 933 5457 E:
referencelibary@louthcoco.ie

County Mayo

Central Library John Moore Road, Castlebar,
County Mayo T: + 353 94 9047936 E:
plmccart@mayococo.ie W: www.mayococo.ie
Mayo County Library John Moore Road,
Castlebar, County Mayo T: +353 94 9047921 E:
librarymayo@mayococo.ie W: www.mayolibrary.ie

County Meath

Meath County Library Railway Street, Navan,
County Meath T: +353 46 902 1134 E:
localstudies@meathcoco.ie W: www.meath.ie/library

County Offaly

Offaly County Library O'Connor Square,
Tullamore, County Offaly T: +353 57 934 6832
E: libraryhq@offalycoco.ie

County Roscommon

Roscommon County Library Abbey Street,
Roscommon, County Roscommon T: +353 90 663
7275 E: roslib@roscommoncoco.ie

County Sligo

Sligo County Library Stephen Street, Sligo,
County Sligo T: +353 71 9111 1850 E:
sligolib@sligococo.ie W: www.sligococo.ie/
Sligo Reference & Local Studies Library
Westward Town Centre, Bridge Street, Sligo, County
Sligo T: +353 71 911 1858 E: sligolib@sligococo.ie
W: www.sligolibrary.ie

County Tipperary

**Tipperary County Libary Local Studies
Department** Castle Avenue, Thurles, County
Tipperary T: +353 504 21555 E:
studies@tipplibs.iol.ie W: www.iol.ie/~TIPPLIBS
Tipperary Studies Source Library, Cathedral
Street, Thurles, County Tipperary T: +353 504 292
78 E: studies@tipperarylibraries.ie

County Tyrone

Omagh Library 1 Spillars Place, Omagh, County
Tyrone BT78 1HL T: 028 8224 4821 E:
omaghlibrary@librariesni.org.uk W:
www.librariesni.org.uk

County Waterford

Waterford County Library Dungarvan Central
Library, Davitt's Quay, Dungarvan, County Waterford
T: +353 58 412 31 E:
dungarvanlibrary@waterfordcoco.ie W:
www.waterfordcoco.ie/

County Westmeath

**Athlone - Westmeath County Library - Local
Studies** Athlone Civic offices, Church Avenue,
Athlone, County Westmeath T: +353 90 644 2157 E:
athlib@westmeathcoco.ie W: www.westmeathcoco.i

Mullingar - Westmeath County Library - Local Studies County Buildings, Mount Street, Mullingar, County Westmeath T: +353 44 933 2161 E: mgarlib@westmeathcoco.ie

County Wexford
Enniscorthy Branch Library Lymington Road, Enniscorthy, County Wexford T: +353 53 923 6055 E: enniscorthylib@wexfordcoco.ie W: www.wexford.ie/library
New Ross Branch Library Barrack Lane, New Ross, County Wexford T: +353 51 21877 E: newrosslib@wexfordcoco.ie W: www.wexford.ie/

Wexford Library McCauley's Car Park, Off Redmond Square, Wexford, County Wexford T: +353 53 912 1637 E: wexfordlib@wexfordcoco.ie W: www.wexford.ie/

County Wicklow
Wicklow County Library Boghall Road, Bray, County Wicklow T: +353 1 286 6566 E: library@wicklowcoco.ie W: www.wicklow.ie

Couny Monaghan
Monaghan County Library 98 Avenue, Clones, Couny Monaghan T: +353 47 74712 or +353 47 74713 E: clennon@monaghancoco.ie

National
The National Museum of Ireland The National Museum of Ireland - Archaeology, Kildare Street, Dublin 2 next door to Leinster House (Government Buildings).
The National Museum of Ireland - Decorative Arts & History, Collins Barracks, Dublin 7
The National Museum of Ireland - Natural History, Merrion Street, Dublin 2
The National Museum of Ireland - Natural History is centrally located on Merrion Street, Dublin 2, next door to the National Gallery.
The National Museum of Ireland - Country Life, Turlough Park, Castlebar, Co. Mayo
The National Museum of Ireland – Country Life has modern exhibition galleries in the magnificent grounds of Turlough Park House with its magnificent gardens and lake. T: +353 1 6777444 W: www.museum.ie
Opening Times: (All four museums)
Tuesday to Saturday 10.00.a.m – 5.00.p.m.; Sunday 2.00.p.m. – 5.00.p.m. Closed Mondays (including Bank Holidays), Christmas Day and Good Friday Admission is free to all four museums.
Garda Slochana Museum & Archives The Records Tower, Dublin, 2 T: 1353 1 6719 597 E: j_herlihy@esatclear.ie W: www.esatclear.ie/~garda/museum.html
Police Museum - Police Service of Northern Ireland Brooklyn, 65 Knock Road, Belfast BT5 6LE T: 0845 600 8000 Ext: 22499 E: museum@psni.police.uk W: www.psni.police.uk/index/about-us/police_museum.htm
The Police Museum holds microfilm copies of the Royal Irish Constabulary service records 1822-1922, the originals of which are held at the Public Record Office at Kew in London

Regional
Belfast
Royal Ulster Rifles Regimental Museum 5 Waring Street, Belfast, BT1 2EW T: (028) 9023 2086 E: rurmuseum@yahoo.co.uk W: www.armymuseums.org.uk/museums/0000000121-Royal-Ulster-Rifles-Museum.htm
http://news.bbc.co.uk/1/hi/northern_ireland/8175481.stm
Ulster Museum Botanic Gardens Botanic Gardens, Stranmillis Road, Belfast, BT9 5AB T: (028) 9038125 E: info@nmni.com W: www.nmni.com/

museums

County Antrim
Ballymoney Museum Ballymoney Town Hall, 1 Townhead Street, Ballymoney, Co Antrim BT53 6BE T: 028 2766 0230 E: museum@ballymoney.gov.uk W: www.ballymoneyancestry.com
Friends of the Ulster Museum 12 Malone Road, Belfast, County Antrim BT9 5BN T: (028) 90681606 E: info@nmni.com
Irish Linen Centre & Lisburn Museum Market Square, Lisburn, County Antrim BT28 1AG T: 028 9266 3377 E: irishlinencentre@lisburn.gov.uk W: www.lisburncity.gov.uk
NI Museums Council 66 Donegall Pass, Belfast, County Antrim BT7 1BU T: (028) 90550215 E: info@nmni.com W: www.nimc.co.uk
The Braid
Ballymena Town Hall Museum & Arts Centre, 1 - 29 Bridge Street, Ballymena, County Antrim BT43 5EJ T: 028 2565 7161 F: 028 2563 5941 E: braid.enquiries@ballymena.gov.uk
The Museum Of The Royal Irish Regiment Royal Irish Fusiliers Museum, Sovereign's House, The Mall, Armagh, County Armagh BT61 9DL T: (028) 3752 2911 E: fusiliersmuseum@yahoo.co.uk W: http://www.army.mod.uk/infantry/regiments/royalirish
Ulster American Folk Park Project Team Belfast 1 The Mount Albert Bridge Rd, Belfast, County Antrim BT5 4NA T: (028) 90452250 E: info@nmni.com
Ulster Aviation Society Langford Lodge Airfield 97, Largy Rd, Crumlin, County Antrim BT29 4RT T: (028) 9445 4444 E: ernie@airni.freeserve.co.uk W: www.ulsteraviationsociety.org/

County Armagh
Armagh County Museum The Mall East, Armagh, County Armagh BT61 9BE T: (028) 37523070 E: info@nics.gov.uk W: www.nmni.com/acm
Royal Irish Fusiliers Museum Sovereign's House, Mall East, Armagh, BT61 9DL T: (028) 3752 2911 E: fusiliersmuseum@yahoo.co.uk W: www.armymuseums.org.uk/museums/0000000103-Royal-Irish-Fusiliers-Regimental-Museum.htm

County Down
Down County Museum The Mall, Downpatrick, County Down BT30 6AH T: (028) 44615218 E: madeleine.mcallister@downdc.gov.uk W: www.downcountymuseum.com

Downpatrick Railway Museum Railway Station, Market St, Downpatrick, County Down BT30 6LZ T: (028) 44615779 E: downtrains@yahoo.co.uk W: www.downrail.co.uk/
The Ferguson Linen Centre 54 Scarva Road, Banbridge, County Down BT32 3QD T: 028 4062 3491 E: info@fergusonsirishlinen.com W: www.fergusonsirishlinen.com
The Somme Heritage Centre 233 Bangor Road, Newtownards, County Down BT23 7PH T: 028 9182 3202 E: enquiry.shc@hotmail.co.uk W: www.irishsoldier.org
Ulster Folk and Transport Museum Cultra, Holywood, County Down BT18 0EU T: 028 9042 8428 E: info@nmni.com W: www.nmni.com/uftm

County Dublin
Dublin Civic Museum 58 South William Street, Dublin, 2 T: +353 679 4260 E: customerservices@dublincity.ie W: www.dublincity.ie/RecreationandCulture/MuseumsGalleriesandTheatres/Pages/Museums.aspx

County Fermanagh
Fermanagh County Museum Enniskillen Castle Castle Barracks, Enniskillen, Co Fermanagh BT74 7HL T: 028 66 32 5000 E: castle@fermanagh.gov.uk W: www.enniskillencastle.co.uk
Roslea Heritage Centre Monaghan Road, Rosslea, Enniskillen, County Fermanagh BT92 7DF T: 028 6775 1750 E: clairybums@o2.co.uk W: www.claires-rosleaancestry.co.uk/
Royal Inniskilling Fusiliers Regimental Museum The Castle, Enniskillen, County Fermanagh BT74 7HL T: (028) 66323142 E: info@inniskillingsmuseum.com W: www.inniskillingsmuseum.com

County Londonderry
Foyle Valley Railway Museum Foyle Rd, Londonderry, County Londonderry BT48 6SQ T: (028) 71265234 E: museums@derrycity.gov.uk W: www.derrycity.gov.uk/museums

Garvagh Museum 142a Main St, Garvagh, County Londonderry BT51 5AE T: (028) 2955 7924 E: info@garvaghmuseum.com W: www.garvaghmuseum.com
Londonderry Harbour Museum Harbour Square, Londonderry, County Londonderry BT48 6AF T: 028 7137 7331 E: museums@derrycity.gov.uk W: www.derrycity.gov.uk

County Tyrone
The Ulster History Park Cullion, Lislap, County Tyrone BT79 7SU T: (028) 8164 8188 E: mail@sperrincottages.com W: www.omagh.gov.uk/historypark.htm
Ulster American Folk Park Centre for Migration Studies, Mellon Rd, Castletown, Omagh, County Tyrone BT78 5QY T: (028) 8225 6315 E: info@nmni.com W: www.nmni.com

Other Museums
Imperial War Museum Lambeth Road, London, SE1 6HZ T: 020 7416 5342 E: collections@iwm.org.uk W: www.iwm.org.uk
Irish Jewish Museum 3 - 4 Walworth Road, South Circular Road, Dublin, 8 T: +353 857 067 357 E: museum@jewishireland.org W: www.jewishireland.org/
Irish World Heritage Centre & Irish Diaspora Museum 10 Queens Road, Cheetham Hill, Manchester, M8 8UF T: 0161 205 4007 E: office@iwhc.com W: www.iwhc.com
London Irish Rifles Regimental Museum Connaught House, Flodden Road,, Camberwell, London, SE5 9LL   T: 020 7820 4040 E: nwilkinson@googlemail.com W: www.londonirishrifles.com
Sussex Combined Services Museum (Royal Sussex Regiment and Queen's Royal Irish Hussars) Redoubt Fortress, Royal Parade, Eastbourne, Sussex BN22 7AQ T: 01323 410300 E: redoubtmuseum@eastbourne.gov.uk W: www.eastbournemuseums.co.uk

Bandon
County Cork

registration records for births, marriages & deaths

The General Register Office
(Oifig An Ard-Chláraitheora)
Government Offices,, Convent Road, Roscommon
T: +353 (0) 90 663 2900 W: www.groireland.ie/
Email certificate application (must be sent with
appropriate downloadable form)
The General Register Office also maintains a
family history research facility at 3rd Floor, Block
7, Irish Life Centre, Lower Abbey Street, Dublin
This is the central repository for all records
relating to life events (Births, Deaths, Marriages,
Legal Domestic Adoptions, Stillbirths) in the Irish
State. The General Register Office (Oifig An Ard-
Chláraitheora) maintains a genealogical/family
history research facility at 3rd Floor, Block 7, Irish
Life Centre, Lower Abbey Street, Dublin I.
The Research facility is open Monday to Friday,
(excluding public holidays) from 9.30 a.m. to 4.30
p.m. for the purpose of searching indexes to birth,
death and marriage records and for obtaining
photocopies of records identified from the
indexes.
The indexes in relation to the following records
of life events are available for inspection at the
Research Facility:
1. Births registered in the island of Ireland
between 1st January, 1864 and 31st December,
1921 inclusive, and in Ireland (excluding the six
north-eastern counties of Derry, Antrim, Down,
Armagh, Fermanagh and Tyrone known as
Northern Ireland) from 1922 onwards.
2. Deaths registered in the island of Ireland
between 1st January, 1864 and 31st December,
1921 inclusive and in Ireland (excluding
Northern Ireland) from 1922 onwards.
3. Non-Roman Catholic Marriages registered in
the island of Ireland between 1st April, 1845 and
31st December, 1863 inclusive.
4. Marriages registered in the island of Ireland
between 1st January, 1864 and 31st December,
1921 inclusive and in Ireland (excluding
Northern Ireland) from 1922 onwards.
5. Legal Domestic Adoptions registered in
Ireland from 10th July, 1953 onwards.

Searches & Fees
Two types of searches may be undertaken at
the Research Facility's Reading Room:
a specific search covering a maximum of 5 years
Fee: €2.00
a general search covering any number of years
Fee: €20.00 per day
A photocopy of an entry in the records (where
the search has been carried out and the entry
identified) can be purchased for €4.00.
Photocopies which cannot be provided
immediately on request can be posted to
applicants or may be collected by them at a
later date. All search fees are payable in
advance.

The General Register Office (GRO)
(Oifig An Ard-Chláraitheora)
Government Offices, Convent Road, Roscommon,
County Roscommon, Ireland. It is the central
repository for all records relating to life events
(Births, Deaths, Marriages, Legal Domestic
Adoptions, Stillbirths) in the State. In addition to
the records maintained at the genealogical/family
history research facility, indexes to following
registers of life events are maintained solely at
GRO:
• Births at Sea of children, one of whose parents
was born on the island of Ireland between 1st
January, 1864 and 31st December, 1921. Births at
Sea of Children, one of whose parents was born
in Ireland after 1921.
• Deaths at Sea of persons born on the island of
Ireland between 1st January, 1864 and
31stDecember, 1921 and of persons born in
Ireland after 1921.
• Births of children of Irish parents, certified by
British Consuls abroad, between 1st January,
1864 and 31st December, 1921.
• Deaths of Irish-born persons, certified by
British Consuls abroad, between 1st January,
1864 and 31st December, 1921.
• Marriages celebrated in Dublin by the late Rev.
J F G Schulze, Minister of the German
Protestant Church , Poolbeg Street , Dublin ,
from 1806 to 1837 inclusive.
• Births, Deaths & Marriages registered under
The (Army) Act, 1879.
• Births & Deaths registered under The Defence
(Amendment) (No. 2) Act, 1960.
• Certain births and deaths occurring outside
the State (under The Births, Deaths and
Marriages Registration Act, 1972, Sec. 4).
• Certain Lourdes Marriages (under the
Marriages Act, 1972, Sec.2).
• Stillbirths registered in Ireland from 1st January
1995 (certified copies available to parents only).
• Deaths of Irish officers and enlisted persons
killed in action or who died while serving
abroad in The Great War (WWI) 1914 - 1919.
• Death returns relating to the South African
War (1899 – 1902) in so far as they relate to
Irish subjects.

Northern Ireland
**General Register Office of Northern
Ireland**, Oxford House, 49 - 55 Chichester
Street, Belfast, BT1 4HL T: (028) 90 252000 E:
gro.nisra@dfpni.gov.uk W: www.groni.gov.uk

Scotland
General Register Office for Scotland New Register House, Edinburgh, EH1 3YT T: 0131 314 4300 (Family History) E: enquiries@scotlandspeoplehub.gov.uk records@gro-scotland.gsi.gov.uk W: www.gro-scotland.gov.uk www.scotlandpeople.gov.uk

England & Wales
The General Register Office Room E201, Trafalgar Road, Birkdale, Southport, PR8 2HH T: 0845 603 7788 W: www.direct.gov.uk/gro

Isle of Man
Civil Registry Registries Building, Deemster's Walk, Bucks Road, Douglas IM1 3AR T: 01624 687039 E: civil@registry.gov.im W: www.gov.im/registries/general/civilregistry/birth.xml

Channel Islands
Guernsey
HM Greffier Royal Court House, St Peter Port, Guernsey GY1 2PB T: 01481 725277 W: www.gov.gg/ccm/portal/
Jersey
Judicial Greffe Morier House, Halkett Place, St Helier, Jersey JE1 1DD T: 01534-502300 E: jgreffe@super.net.uk W: www.gov.je/
Jersey 10 Royal Square, St Helier, Jersey JE2 4WA T: 01534 502335

family history societies

National
**Cumann Geinealais na hÉireann :
Genealogical Society of Ireland** Archive: An Daonchartlann, Carlisle Pier, Dún Laoghaire Harbour, Co. Dublin, Ireland, Secretary: 11 Desmond Avenue, Dún Laoghaire, Co Dublin T: + 353 1 284 2711 E: eolas@familyhistory.ie W: www.familyhistory.ie
FamilySearch - (Genealogical Society of Utah) 185 Penns Lane, Sutton Coldfield, West Midlands B76 1JU T: 0121 384 9921 E: withingtonk@familysearch.org W: www.familysearch.org
Huguenot Society of Great Britain & Ireland - Irish Section Echo Hall, Spa, County Down BT24 8PT E: secretary@huguenotsociety.org.uk W: http://huguenotsociety.org.uk/
The Huguenot Society of Great Britain & Ireland PO Box 3067, Warlingham, CR6 0AN T: 020 7679 5199 E: secretary@huguenotsociety.org.uk W: www.huguenotsociety.org.uk
Irish Ancestry Group Clayton House, 59 Piccadilly, Manchester, M1 2AQ T: 0161 236 9750 E: office@mlfhs.org.uk W: www.mlfhs.org.uk
Irish Family History Forum PO Box 67, Plainview, New York 11803-0067 E: Web Form W: www.ifhf.org
Irish Family History Foundation c/o Riverbank, Newbridge, County Kildare T: 00 353 45 448 350 E: enquiries@rootsireland.ie W: www.rootsireland.ie
Irish Family History Society PO Box 36, Naas, Co Kildare E: ifhs@eircom.net W: www.ifhs.ie
Irish Genealogical Society International 1185 Concord Street North, Suite 218, South St Paul, Minnesota 55075 E: Membership@IrishGenealogical.org W: www.irishgenealogical.org/
Irish Genealogical Research Society 18 Stratford Avenue, Rainham, Gillingham, Kent ME8 0EP E: info@igrsoc.org W: www.igrsoc.org
Irish Heritage Association PO Box 1583, Subiaco, 6904 T: 028 90455325 E: aiha@irishheritage.net W: www.irishheritage.net/

Irish Jewish Genealogical Society (A Division of the Irish Jewish Museum) Jasonia Centre., 76 Dame Street, Dublin, 2 T: +353 1 677 3808 E: srosenblatt@irishjewishroots.com W: For Baltic research Len Yodaiken - shoshly@kfar-hanassi.org.il
Jewish Irish Group - ShalomIreland@yahoogroups.com For **Lithuanian research:** http://litvaksig.org/
Irish Jewish Community W: www.jewishireland.org/genealogy
Irish Palatine Association Old Railway Buildings, Rathkeale, County Limerick T: +353 (0)69 63511 E: info@irishpalatines.org W: www.irishpalatines.org
Irish Genealogical Research Society 18 Stratford Avenue, Rainham, Gillingham, Kent ME8 0EP E: info@igrsoc.org W: www.igrsoc.org
North of Ireland Family History Society Graduate School of Education, Queen's University of Belfast, 69 University Street, Belfast, BT7 1HL E: web@nifhs.org W: www.nifhs.org
Society of Genealogists Enterprises Ltd 14 Charterhouse Buildings, Goswell Road, London, EC1M 7BA T: 020 7251 8799 E: genealogy@sog.org.uk W: www.sog.org.uk
The Clans of Ireland - Finte na hÉireann 3 Cherry Park, Quinsboro Road, Newcastle, County Galway Ireland T: +353 91 524 811 E: info@clansofireland.ie W: www.clansofireland.ie
Ulster Historical Foundation 49 Malone Road, Belfast, BT9 6RY T: 028 9066 1988 F: 028 9066 1977 E: enquiry@uhf.org.uk W: www.ancestryireland.com

Regional
Belfast
Belfast Family & Community History 39 Rugby Road, Belfast, BT7 1PT W: www.belfasthistory.com
County Armagh
Armagh Ancestry 40 English Street, Armagh, County Armagh BT61 7BA T: 028 3752 1800 E: researcher@armagh.gov.uk W: www.armagh.co.uk
County Cavan
Cavan Genealogy Johnston Central Library, Farnham Street, Cavan, County Cavan T: +353 49 436 1094 E: cavangenealogy@eircom.net

County Cork

Bandon Genealogy Group Kilbrogan House, Kilbrogan Hill, Bandon, County Cork T: 00 353 23 88 44935 E: bandon.genealogy@gmail.com W: www.kilbrogan.com www.bandon-genealogy.com

Cork Genealogical Society 22 Elm Drive, Shamrock Lawn, Douglas, County Cork T: 086 8198359 E: enquiries@corkgenealogicalsociety.com info@corkgenealogicalsociety.com W: www.corkgenealogicalsociety.com

County Dublin

**Cumann Geinealais na hÉireann :
Genealogical Society of Ireland** Archive: An Daonchartlann, Carlisle Pier, Dún Laoghaire Harbour, Co. Dublin, Ireland, Secretary: 11 Desmond Avenue, Dún Laoghaire, Co Dublin T: 353 1 284 2711 E: eolas@familyhistory.ie W: www.familyhistory.ie

County Galway

East Galway Family History Society Company Ltd Woodford Heritage Centre, Woodford, Loughrea, Co Galway T: +353 90 974 9309 F: +353 90 974 9546 E: galwayroots@eircom.net galwayroots@gmail.com W: www.galwaysroots.com www.rootsireland.ie

Galway Family History Society (West) Ltd St. Joseph's Community Centre, Ashe Road, Shantalla, County Galway T: +353 (0)91 860464 F: +353 (0)91 860432 E: galwaywestroots@eircom.net W: www.rootsireland.ie

County Kikenny

Rothe House Family History Rothe House, Kilkenny, County Kilkenny T: +353 56 7722893 E: kilkennyfamilyhistory@rothehouse.com W: www.rothehouse.com

County Wexford

County Wexford Heritage and Genealogy Society County Wexford Heritage and Genealogy Society, Yola Farmstead, Folk Park, Tagoat, Rosslare, Co Wexford T: +353 53 9132610 E: wexgen@eircom.net W: http://homepage.eircom.net/~yolawexford/contactyola.htm

Wexford Family History Society 24 Parklands, Wexford, Co Wexford T: +353 53 22973 E: murphyh@tinet.ie

County Wicklow

Wicklow County Genealogical Society 55 Seafield, Wicklow Town, Co Wicklow E: info@cigo.ie

Dublin

Ballinteer Family History Society 29 The View, Woodpark, Ballinteer, Dundrum, Dublin 16 T: +353 1 298 8082 E: ryanct@eircom.net

Council of Irish Genealogical Organisations 31a All Saints Road, Raheny, Dublin 5, T: +353 1 406 3542 E: info@cigo.ie W: www.cigo.ie/

Flannery Clan / Clann Fhlannabhra 81 Woodford Drive, Clondalkin, Dublin, 22 E: oflannery@eircom.net W: www.flanneryclan.ie

Raheny Heritage Society 101 Collins Park, Donnycarney, Dublin 9, Dublin T: + 353 8 6160 5099 E: bjwray@eircom.net

One Name Studies

Guild of One Name Studies Box G, 14 Charterhouse Buildings, Goswell Road, London, EC1M 7BA T: 0800 011 2182 : E: guild@one-name.org W: www.one-name.org

Clan Davidson Association 58 Chandos Avenue, Whetstone, London, N20 9DX T: +44 2084 452 787 E: contactus@clandavidson.org.uk W: www.clandavidson.org.uk/

Overseas

The Australian Irish Heritage Association PO Box1583 , Subiaco , 6904 T: (08) 9345 3530 E: aiha@irishheritage.net

The Irish Ancestral Research Association Department W, 2120 Commonwealth Avenue, Auburndale, Massachusetts 02466-1909 E: president@tiara.ie W: www.tiara.ie

Local History Societies

Archives & Records Association (UK & Ireland) Prioryfield House, 20 Canon Street, Taunton, Somerset TA1 1SW T: 01823 327030 E: ara@archives.org.uk W: www.archives.org.uk

British Association for Local History PO Box 6549, Somersal Herbert, Ashbourne, Derbyshire DE6 5WH T: 01283 585947 E: mail@balh.co.uk W: www.balh.co.uk

Federation of Local History Societies - Ireland Winter's Hill, Kinsale, County Cork E: historyfed@eircom.net W: http://homepage.eircom.net/~localhist/index.html

Federation for Ulster Local Studies 18 Ardmore Avenue, Downpatrick , County Down BT30 6JU T: +44(0)28 4461 2986 E: info@fuls.org.uk W: www.fuls.org

Hugenot Society of Great Britain & Ireland Hugenot Library University College, Gower Street, London, WC1E 6BT T: 020 7679 5199 E: secretary@huguenotsociety.org.uk W: www.hugenotsociety.org.uk

Hugenot Society - Irish Section Echo Hall, Spa, County Down BT24 8PT E: secretary@huguenotsociety.org.uk W: http://huguenotsociety.org.uk/

Irish Georgian Society 74 Merrion Square, Dublin, 2 T: +353 1 676 7053 E: Emmeline.henderson@igs.ie W: www.igs.ie

Presbyterian Historical Society of Ireland 26 College Green, Belfast, BT7 1LN T: 028 9072 7330 E: phsilibrarian@pcinet.org W: www.presbyterianhistoryireland.com

Wesley Historical Society Methodist Study Centre, Edgehill College, 9 Lennoxvale, Belfast, BT9 5BY T: 028 9068 6936 E: libr@edgehillcollege.org W: www.edgehillcollege.org/library

Regional

County Carlow

Carlow Historical & Archaeological Society 38 Kennedy Street, Carlow, County Carlow E: info@carlowhistorical.com W: www.carlowhistorical.com

County Cork
Bandon Genealogy Group Kilbrogan House, Kilbrogan Hill, Bandon, County Cork T: 00 353 23 88 44935 E: bandon.genealogy@gmail.com W: www.kilbrogan.com www.bandon-genealogy.com

County Dublin
Ballyfermot Heritage Group c/o Ballyfermot Library, Ballyfermot Road, Dublin, 10 E: heritagegroup@ballyfermot.ie W: www.ballyfermot.ie/heritage
Raheny Heritage Society 101 Collins Park, Donnycarney, Dublin 9, Dublin T: + 353 8 6160 5099 E: bjwray@eircom.net

County Londonderry
Roe Valley Historical Society 36 Drumachose Park, Limavady, County Londonderry BT49 0NZ E: r.w-guthrie@tiscali.co.uk

County Mayo
Mayo North Family History Research Centre Enniscoe, Castlehill, Ballina, County Mayo T: + 353 96 31809 E: normayo@iol.ie W: www.mayo.irish-roots.net
South Mayo Family Research Centre Main Street, Ballinrobe, County Mayo T: +353 94 954 1214 F: +353 94 954 1103 E: soumayo@iol.ie W: http://mayo.irishroots.net/

County Offaly
Offaly Historical & Archaeological Society Offaly Research & Exhibition Centre, Bury Quay, Tullamore, County Offaly T: + 353 5 062 1421 W: www.offalyhistory.com/

County Tyrone
Centre for Migration Studies Ulster American Folk Park, Mellon Road, Castletown, Omagh, County Tyrone BT78 5QY T: 028 82 256315 E: cms@librariesni.org.uk W: www.qub.ac.uk/cms

County Wexford
Wexford Historical Society c/o Melford House, Ballyhealy, Kilmore, County Wexford E: chair@wexfordhistoricalsociety.com W: www.wexfordhistoricalsociety.com

Police
Garda Historical Society - www.policehistory.com 8 Aisling Close, Ballincollig, County Cork T: +353 86 806 0385 E: pressoffice@garda.ie W: www.policehistory.com

cemeteries & crematoria

County Antrim
Ballymena Cemetery Cushendall Rd, Ballymena, County Antrim BT43 6QE T: 01266 656026 E: council.reception@ballymena.gov.uk
Ballymoney Cemetery 44 Knock Rd, Ballymoney, County Antrim BT53 6LX T: 012656 66364 E: info@ballymoney.gov.uk
Blaris New Cemetery 25 Blaris Rd, Lisburn, County Antrim BT27 5RA T: 01846 607143 E: council@downdc.gov.uk
Carnmoney Cemetery 10 Prince Charles Way, Newtownabbey, County Antrim BT36 7LG T: 01232 832428 E: gmcburney@newtownabbey.gov.uk
City Cemetery 511 Falls Rd, Belfast, Co Antrim BT12 6DE T: 028 9032 3112 E: generalenquiries@belfastcity.gov.uk W: www.belfastcity.gov.uk/citycemetery
Greenland Cemetery Upper Cairncastle Road, Larne, County Antrim BT40 2EG T: 01574 272543 E: admin@larne.gov.uk
Milltown Cemetery Office 546 Falls Rd, Belfast, County Antrim BT12 6EQ T: 01232 613972 E: cemeteries@antrim.gov.uk

County Armagh
Kernan Cemetery Kernan Hill Rd, Portadown, Craigavon, County Armagh BT63 5YB T: 028 38339059 E: info@armagh.gov.uk
Lurgan Cemetery 57 Tandragee Rd, Lurgan, Craigavon, Co Armagh BT66 8TL T: 028 38342853 E: Info@armagh.gov.uk

County Down
Ballyvestry Cemetery 6 Edgewater Millisle, Millisle, Donaghadee, County Down BT21 0EF T: 01247 882657 E: council@downdc.gov.uk
Banbridge Public Cemetery Newry Rd, Banbridge, County Down BT32 3NB T: 018206 62623 E: council@downdc.gov.uk
Bangor Cemetery 62 Newtownards Rd, Bangor, County Down BT20 4DN T: 028 91271909 E: council@downdc.gov.uk
City of Belfast Crematorium 129 Ballgowan Road, Crossacreevy, Belfast, County Down BT5 7TZ T: 028 9044 8342 E: crematorium@belfastcity.gov.uk W: www.belfastcity.gov.uk/crematorium
Clandeboye Cemetery 300 Old Belfast Rd, Bangor, County Down BT19 1RH T: 028 91853246 E: council@downdc.gov.uk W: www.downdc.gov.uk
Comber Cemetery 31 Newtownards Rd, Comber, Newtownards, County Down BT23 5AZ T: 01247 872529 E: council@downdc.gov.uk W: www.downdc.gov.uk
Struell Cemetery, Old Course Rd, Downpatrick, County Down BT30 8AQ T: 01396 613086 E: council@downdc.gov.uk W: www.downdc.gov.uk
Down District Council - Lough Inch Cemetery Lough Inch Cemetery, Riverside Rd, Ballynahinch, County Down BT24 8JB T: 01238 562987 E: council@downdc.gov.uk W: www.downdc.gov.uk
Kirkistown Cemetery Main Rd, Portavogie, Newtownards, County Down BT22 1EL T: 012477 71773 E: council@downdc.gov.uk

Movilla Cemetary Movilla Rd, Newtownards, County Down BT23 8EY T: 01247 812276 E: council@downdc.gov.uk
Redburn Cemetery Old Holywood Rd, Holywood, County Down BT18 9QH T: 01232 425547 E: council@downdc.gov.uk
Roselawn Cemetery 127 Ballygowan Rd, Crossnacreevy, Belfast, County Down BT5 7TZ T: 01232 448288 E: generalenquiries@belfastcity.gov.uk
Whitechurch Cemetary 19 Dunover Rd, Newtownards, County Down BT22 2LE T: 012477 58659 E: council@downdc.gov.uk

Dublin & County Dublin
Glasnevin Trust, Finglas Road Dublin 11 T: + 353 (0) 1 8826500, E: info@glasnevintrust.ie W: www.glasnevintrust.ie
Dardistown Cemetery, Collinstown Cross, Old Airport Road, Cloghran, Co. Dublin T: + 353 (0) 1 8424677 F: + 353 (0) 1 8424294 E: dardistowncemetery@glasnevintrust.ie
Glasnevin Cemetery & Crematorium, Finglas Road, Dublin 11 T: + 353 (0) 1 882 6500 F: + 353 (0) 1 830 1594 E: info@glasnevintrust.ie
Goldenbridge Cemetery, St. Vincents Street, Inchicore, Dublin 8 T: + 353 (0) 1 8301133 F: + 353 (0) 1 8301594 E: info@glasnevintrust.ie
Newlands Cemetery & Crematorium, Ballymount Road, Dublin 24 T: + 353 (0) 1 4592288 F: + 353 (0) 1 4592423 E: newlandscemetery@glasnevintrust.ie
Palmerstown Cemetery, Kennelsfort Road, Palmerstown Dublin 20 T: + 353 (0) 1 4592288 F: + 353 (0) 1 4592423 F: palmerstowncemetery@glasnevintrust.ie
Dublin City Archives Dublin City Library & Archive, 138 - 144 Pearse Street, Dublin, 2 T: + 353 1 674 4800 E: cityarchives@dublincity.ie The archives hold the *Registers of Mount Jerome Cemetery, Dublin 1836 - 1972; Registers of Deansgrange Cemetery, Dublin 1865 - 1972;* The archives also hold a copy of *Memorials of the Dead* which is a series of volumes which list gravestone inscriptions in cemeteries in Dublin, Wicklow and Wexford. They are not published but are available in bound typescripts.

Dublin City Council is responsible for the following cemeteries. St. Canice's Cemetery, Killester Cemetery, Raheny Cemetery, Clontarf Cemetery, Bluebell Cemetery, Donnybrook Cemetery, Merrion Cemetery.

County Londonderry
Altnagelvin Cemetery Church Brae, Altnagelvin, Londonderry, County Londonderry BT47 3QG T: 01504 343351 E: willie.burke@derrycity.gov.uk
City Cemetery Lone Moor Road, Londonderry, County Londonderry BT48 9LA T: 028 7136 2615 E: info@derrycity.gov.uk W: www.derrycity.gov.uk

County Tyrone
Cookstown Cemetery Westland Rd, Cookstown, County Tyrone BT80 8BX T: 028 8676 6087 E: info@cookstown.gov.uk W: www.cookstown.gov.uk
Greenhill Cemetery Mountjoy Road, Omagh, County Tyrone BT79 7BL T: 028 8224 4918 E: info@omagh.gov.uk W: www.omagh.gov.uk/

Interment.net is a publisher of cemetery transcriptions with online FREE listings and many of the transcriptions are of cemeteries that no longer exist. Cemeteries listed include the Counties of Antrim, Armagh, Carlow, Cavan, Clare, Cork, Derry (Londonderry), Donegal, Down, Dublin, Fermanagh, Galway, Kerry, Kildare, Kilkenny, Laois, Leitrim, Limerick, Longford, Louth, Mayo, Meath, Monaghan, Offaly, Roscommon, Sligo, Tipperary, Tyrone, Waterford, Westmeath, Wexford, Wicklow

DeceasedOnline.com is the a central database of statutory burial and cremation registers for the UK and Republic of Ireland. In the past in order to search cemetery records it was necessary to contact one of nearly 3,250 burial authorities and crematoria. Each holding their own registers, mostly as old fragile books. DeceasedOnline.com are making it possible for burial and cremation authorities around the country to convert their register records, maps and photographs into digital form and bring them together into a central searchable collection.

It is a growing database, holding records mainly from the 1850s onwards which can provide invaluable information for researching family trees, and can reveal previously unknown family links from other interments recorded in the same grave.

The aim is to build a substantial database of tens of millions of burial and cremation records. Data is continually being added from all over the UK and Ireland.

professional genealogists & researchers

The Association of Professional Genealogists in Ireland (MAPGI), which was founded in 1986, acts as a regulating body to maintain high standards amongst its members and to protect the interests of clients. Members are drawn from every part of Ireland and represent a wide variety of interests and expertise. **E: info@apgi.ie W: www.apgi.ie**
Members are fully involved in lecturing and publishing and areat the forefront of genealogical developments in Ireland.

Society of Genealogists Northern Ireland (SGNI) 280 Castlereagh Road, Belfast , BT5 6AD
E: secretary@sgni.net W: www.sgni.net
The Society of Genealogists Northern Ireland (SGNI) is a professional association comprising genealogists based in the six counties of Northern Ireland (Antrim, Armagh, Down, Fermanagh, Londonderry (Derry) and Tyrone).
Members adhere to a Code of Practice and aim to promote genealogy at all levels and to provide a high quality of genealogical research. SGNI's website is www.sgni.net and the Secretary can be contacted at secretary@sgni.net To commission research contact Members direct.

Aiden Feerick MAPGI 17 Brooklawn Avenue, Blackrock, County Dublin E:
aidenfeerick@gmail.com W: www.ancestor.ie
Ancestor Network Limited MAPGI 63 Fosterbrook, Stillorgan Road, Booterstown, County Dublin T: +353 (0)1 219 5799
E: john.hamrock@ancestor.ie W: www.ancestor.ie
Brendan O'Donoghue MAPGI 47 Kerrymount Rise, Foxrock, Dublin, 18 T: +353 1 289 4462
E: brendan@researchireland.com
W: www.researchireland.com
Carmel Gilbride MAPGI 49 Fitzwilliam Square, Dublin , 4 E: carmel@itsyourhistory.ie
W: www.itsyouririshhistory.com
David McElroy MAPGI IGS Ltd, 94 University Avenue, Belfast, BT17 1GY T: 028 9066 7274 F: 028 9066 1277 E: research@igslimited.com W: www.igslimited.com
Deirdre Bryan - Bradan Research Services MAPGI 91 Beech House, Sussex Road, Dublin, 4 T: + 353 86 047 7609 E: info@bradanresearch.com W: www.bradanresearch.com

Eileen O Duill M.A., C.G. MAPGI 47 Delwood Road, Castleknock, Dublin, 15 T: + 353 1 821 7272
E: info@heirsireland.com W: www.heirsireland.com
Eneclann - Irish Research MAPGI Unit 1 Trinity College Enterprise Centre, Pearse Street, Dublin 2, T: +353 1 671 0338 E: rachel.murphy@eneclann.ie
brian.donovan@eneclann.ie W: www.eneclann.ie
Fiona Fitzsimons MAPGI Eneclann Ltd, Unit 18 Trinity College Enterprise Centre, Pearse Street, Dublin, 2 T: + 353 1 671 0338 F: + 353 1 671 0281
E: info@eneclann.ie W: Member of Association of Professional Genealogists in Ireland
Gillian Weir Scully - Gillian's Genealogy Service MAPGI Tivoli Mews, 7 Tivoli Terrace South, Dun Laoghaire, County Dublin
T: + 353 1663 6668 E: help@gilliansgenealogy.ie
W: www.gilliansgenealogy.ie
Helen Kelly 30 Harlech Street, Closkeagh, Dublin, 14 T: + 353 1 278 4040 E: helen@helenkelly.com W: www.helenkelly.com
Hilda McGauley MSc MAPGI - Records Ireland 13 The Glade, Woodfarm Acres, Palmerstown, Dublin 20 T: 0353 1 626 0189 E: roots@recordsireland.ie W: www.recordsireland.ie
John Hamrock MAPGI 63 Fosterbrook, Stillorgan Road, Booterstown, County Dublin T: +353 (0)1 219 5799 E: john.hamrock@ancestor.ie
W: www.ancestor.ie
Joan Sharkey MAPGI 68 Raheny Park, Raheny, Dublin, 5 T: + 353 1 831 4729 E: joan.sharkey@gmail.com W: Member of Association of Professional Genealogists in Ireland
Justin Horman Martin MAPGI 9 Forfield Gardens, Rathmines, Dublin, 6 T: + 353 1 492 2617 E: justinhmartin@timeline.ie W: www.timeline.ie
Maire MacConghail BA FIGRS MAPGI 14 Ascaill Ghairbhile, Rath Garbh, Baile Atha Cliath, 6 T: + 353 1 497 4621 E: mhicongl@indigo.ie
MC Research MAPGI Seabank, Castlebellingham, Dundalk, County Louth T: +353 42 937 2046
E: mcres@iol.ie W: www.mc-research.com
O D Cresswell 54 Rosscoole Park, Belfast, BT14 8JX E: ulsterfamilies@btinternet.com **(SGNI)**
Pamela Bradley - Research Ireland MAPI Blue Rock, Killough, Kilmacanogue, County Wicklow T: + 353 1 286 9645 E: pamelabradley52@gmail.com

---

Professional Genealogists and Researchers

This list of researchers - private individuals and organisations - have indicated their willingness to carry out family history and other research on a professional, fee-paying basis.

The Editors and Publishers of **The Irish Family & Local History Handbook** do not sponsor nor do they endorse the individuals or organisations listed here. We make every effort to verify all information published.

The professional genealogists listed are expected to provide a high standard of service to our readers. If there is a failure to provide such a service the Editor and Publishers reserve the right to refuse to accept the inclusion of their details in future issues or reprints.

We cannot accept responsibilty for research arrangements, payments or results or for any errors or omissions or for any losses however they may arise.

The Editors and Publishers cannot be held responsible for the errors, omissions or non performance by these individuals or organisations and where their performance falls below an acceptable level readers are asked to notify the Editors and Publishers in writing.

Peter Kenny - Irish Family Ancestry MAPGI
Sligo, E: info@irishfamilyancestry.com
W: www.irishfamilyancestry.com
Robert C Davison - Enquireland MAPGI
Ballynester House, 1a Cardy Road, Greyabbey,
Newtownards, County Down BT22 2LS T: 028 4278
8386 F: 028 4278 8986 E: enquireland@tiscali.co.uk
Rosaleen Underwood MAPGI 15 Whitechurch
Drive, Ballyboden, Dublin, 5
E: underwor.rmc@gmail.com
Steven C fferay-Smyrl FIGRS MAPGI 6
Brighton Road, Rathgar, Dublin, 6 T: + 353 1 406
3542 E: steven@masseyandking.com
Sylvia Cresswell 54 Rosscoole Park, Belfast, BT14
8JX E: ulsterfamilies@btinternet.com (**SGNI**)
Timeline Research Ltd - Nicola Morris
MAPGI 146 Tritonville Road, Sandymount, Dublin, 4
T: +353 87 632 5673 E: research@timeline.ie
W: www.timeline.ie
Ulster Ancestors - Heather Flanders 280
Castlereagh Road, Belfast BT5 6AD
E: heather.flanders@ntlworld.com
W: www.ballynagarrick.net/ulsterancestors (**SGNI**)
Ulster Ancestree - Janet Abernethy 23 Larch
Hill, Craigavad, Holywood, County Down BT18 0JN
E: janet@ulsterancestree.com
W: www.ulsterancestree.com (**SGNI**)
William Noel Jenkins MAPGI Dublin, 18
T: + 353 129 597 15 E: wnoel@eircom.net
W: www.family-tree-research.com

Belfast
Family Ulster - Brian Watson B.Sc. (Hons) 24
Moyne Park, Belfast, BT5 7QT T: 028 90798551
E: info@familyulster.com W: www.familyulster.com
(**SGNI**)
County Cork
Margaret Jordan MAPGI 27 The Cloisters,
Ballincollig, County Cork E: m.jordan246@gmail.com
County Down
Brookhill Ancestry - Kathleen McClure B.Sc.
(Hons) 20 Croft Park, Holywood, County Down
BT18 0PF E: kmcc953041@aol.com (**SGNI**)
Specialises in tracing living relatives
County Kerry
Gregory Kiara MAPGI 47 Highfield Grove,
Cathersless, Tralee, County Kerry
E: gregoryk@eircom.net
County Kildare
Henry McDowell FIGRS MAPGI Celbridge
Lodge, Celbridge, County Kildare T: + 353 628 8347
County Wicklow
Paul Gorry FSG FIGRS MAPGI 84 Ardglass,
Baltinglass, County Wicklow E: gorry@indigo.ie
W: www.apgi.ie/members-gorry.html

Please mention
The Irish Family and Local History Handbook
when contacting any of the listed Professional
Genealogists and Researchers

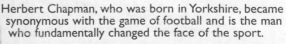

About the Editors & Publishers

Robert Blatchford LL.B (Hons)

is a law graduate of The University of Hull, England. He is a member of The Society of Genealogists as well as Cleveland, The City of York, Devon, Dyfed, Glamorgan, Somerset & Dorset & Gwent Family History Societies. He is a former Chairman of The City of York FHS and former Vice Chairman of the North East Group of Family History Societies. He has undertaken research in England, Wales, Scotland, Belgium and France as well as in Ireland, Australia and the United States. He has edited and published all of the issues of *The Family and Local History Handbook*. A Data CD was published containing issues 1 - 10 of the Handbook in pdf format when they became *Out of Print*. A *new* Data DVD has now been published containing issues 1 - 13 of the Handbook in pdf format. He has also published *Herbert Chapman on Football* - a facsimile.

Elizabeth Blatchford

has been involved in genealogy and family history for over 25 years. She is a member of several family and local history societies. Elizabeth has been involved with this publication since its inception and has assisted with the editing of several editions. Since taking early retirement from Local Governement Elizabeth is fully involved in the editing of *The Family and Local History Handbook*. She has an Training and Consultancy business in Health & Social Care and is fully involved with her four grandchildren and her new kitten, Alfie!

Production Information

© Images Courtesy of Apple

For the technically minded, all design, layout and preparation is done in house on Apple Macintosh computers, 27 inch and 20 inch Intel iMacs, a MacBook, and an iPad. Software used includes using Quark Xpress 9, Adobe Photoshop CS4 and Adobe Acrobat 9 Pro. The *Handbook* is produced electronically.

The electronic files are sent to the printers and are printed directly to paper. The first time the files are seen in book form is when the *Handbook* is delivered from the printers.

Index to Advertisers

Index to Articles

~~~~~~~~~~

The Irish Family & Local History Handbook

ISBN 978 0 9552399 5 3

Published by
Robert Blatchford Publishing Ltd
33 Nursery Road, Nether Poppleton YORK, YO26 6NN U.K.
T: 01904 332638 E: sales@genealogical.co.uk W: www.genealogical.co.uk

The Genealogical Services Directory
Volume 1 Published March 1997 ISBN 0 9530297 0 0 ISSN 1368-9150
Volume 2 Published January 1998 ISBN 0 9530297 1 9 ISSN 1368-9150
Volume 3 Published January 1999 ISBN 0 9530297 2 7 ISSN 1368-9150
Volume 4 Published January 2000 ISBN 0 9530297 3 5 ISSN 1368-9150

The Family & Local History Handbook
Volume 5 Published January 2001 ISBN 0 9530297 4 3 ISSN 1745-3887
Volume 6 Published February 2002 ISBN 0 9530297 5 1 ISSN 1745-3887
Volume 7 Published February 2003 ISBN 0 9530297 6 X ISSN 1745-3887
Volume 8 Published March 2004 ISBN 0 9530297 7 8 ISSN 1745-3887
Volume 9 Published March 2005 ISBN 0 9530297 8 6 ISSN 1745-3887
Volume 10 Published September 2006 ISBN 978 0 9530297 9 2 ISSN 1745-3887
Volume 11 Published May 2008 ISBN 978 0 9552399 1 5 ISSN 1745-3887
Volumes 1 - 10 Omnibus CD Published March 2009 ISBN 978 0 9552399 2 2 ISSN 1745-3887
Volume 12 Published November 2009 ISBN 978 0 9552399 3 9 ISSN 1745-3887
Volume 13 Published May 2011 ISBN 978 0 9552399 4 6 ISSN 1745-3887

The Irish Family & Local History Handbook
Published February 2012 ISBN 978 0 9552399 5 3

Printed by Charlesworth Press, Flanshaw Way, Flanshaw Lane, Wakefield WF2 9LP UK
T: +44 (0) 1924 204 830 E: info @charlesworth.com W: www.charlesworth.com

take a closer look inside...

Search for your Irish roots online using a database of the largest collection of parish records and other sources on the island of Ireland. Or commission one of our county genealogy centres to research your Irish family history.

www.rootsireland.ie